DEAN KOONTZ:
A Writer's Biography

ALSO BY KATHERINE RAMSLAND

Prism of the Night: A Biography of Anne Rice

The Vampire Companion: The Official Guide to Anne Rice's
The Vampire Chronicles

The Witches' Companion: The Official Guide to Anne Rice's
Lives of the Mayfair Witches

The Anne Rice Reader

The Roquelaure Reader: A Companion to Anne Rice's Erotica

The Art of Learning

Engaging the Immediate: Applying Kierkegaard's
Indirect Communication to Psychotherapy

Quesadillas

DEAN KOONTZ:
A Writer's Biography

BY KATHERINE RAMSLAND

HarperPrism

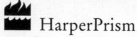

HarperPrism
A Division of HarperCollins*Publishers*
10 East 53rd Street, New York, N.Y. 10022-5299

HarperCollins®, 🔥 ®, and HarperPrism® are trademarks of HarperCollins*Publishers* Inc.

HarperPrism books may be purchased for educational, business, or sales promotional use. For information, please write: Special Markets Department, HarperCollins*Publishers*, 10 East 53rd Street, New York, N.Y. 10022-5299.

Printed in the United States of America

First printing: November 1997

Designed by Colleen Davie

Library of Congress Cataloging-in-Publication Data

Ramsland, Katherine M., 1953–
    Dean Koontz : a writer's biography / by Katherine Ramsland.
        p.   cm.
    Includes bibliographical references and index.
    ISBN 0-06-105271-X
    1. Koontz, Dean R. (Dean Ray) , 1945—   --Biography.
    2. Authors.
    American--20th century--Biography.   I. Title.
    PS3561.O55Z87   1997
    813'.54--dc21   97-30839
    [B]   CIP

Visit HarperPrism on the World Wide Web at
http://www.harpercollins.com

97 98 99 00 ❖ 10 9 8 7 6 5 4 3 2 1

In memory of my dearest friend, Corey,
who wanted me to write this book, but who died two
hours before I could tell him that I was going to,

and

For Deanna Justine Woodall and Mark Thomas Spivey,
who were there, always, when I needed them,
and for Jim Kerr,
who inadvertently launched my writing career.

TABLE OF CONTENTS

INTRODUCTION

A FEW YEARS AGO, WHEN I HAD FINISHED WRITING A BIOGRAPHY of Anne Rice, I pondered other possibilities. The first name that came to mind was Dean Koontz. I knew that he'd had a rough childhood with an alcoholic father, and I'd read some of his dark suspense. I thought he might have an interesting story. Yet I hesitated to contact him, because friends had told me he was quite private and *very* busy.

So I went on to write other books. Then one day in April 1994, I saw Dean at a breakfast that Ballantine Books was giving for authors at the American Booksellers Association convention. I thought, why not? I introduced myself. He knew my work with Rice, so I asked rather bluntly, "How about a biography of you?"

That's not the proper way to do it, of course. I should have done some research first, should have been prepared, but he was standing right there. So I jumped in.

To my surprise, he was open to the idea—if I thought I could get an editor interested in such a project. Well, there were thousands of editors at that conference, many within a few feet of us. I knew that wouldn't be any problem. I returned within five minutes with an assurance that there was interest, and that began the intense association that resulted in this book.

Before I had even written a proposal, Dean sent me copies of all of his books. This was the first of his generous gestures, which were to continue throughout the course of this project— and one of many that I was to hear about along the way. I also learned a lot about the business of writing, and Dean and his friends all have such a great sense of fun that I thoroughly enjoyed every interview.

I was especially pleased with how willing Dean was to explore his childhood terrain. Our interviews could go on for hours, whether over the phone or face-to-face. No matter how personal the questions, he never told me to go mind my own business. (Well, this *is* my business, but even so, I didn't really expect him to answer *every* question.)

In the end, I had so much material that I could not possibly use it all, so I had to pick and choose according to a central theme that had gradually formed as I became familiar with his work: toxic intimacy between people closely related to each other and the dread of contamination, resisted through loving human bonds. I saw this in nearly every book, and it became quite clear that Dean had put his personal fears into motion in many different ways, formed from a childhood spent with an unpredictable, sociopathic father.

Now, before anyone accuses me of doing a Freudian analysis on an anti-Freudian writer, let me explain my basic approach. There are people who see the word "subconscious" or hear "childhood issues" and automatically think, "that's Freud." But that reaction is an oversimplification. A great many psychological theories utilize these notions, but in ways quite different from what Freud proposed. In fact, my approach mixes Jung's theories and existentialism with recent work in psychoneurology. With all of that, I write psychobiography with a philosophical twist. In other words, I think the subconscious has a strong bodily component, but I leave room for a bit of conceptual finesse. I do believe that, despite the strong influence on us of many factors, we have a certain amount of free will, which means that we have some responsibility in what we become. The following account, in the most simple terms, is the way I understand it.

First, the technical part:

All systems that make up who we are—emotional, physical, mental—are organized around information. Each part processes information in its own way, and any given piece of information can be transformed through neural messengers from one system into another. Emotional stress, for example, can translate into the body as illness, and physical illness can adversely affect one's moods. That's common knowledge, but there is a much stronger relationship between mind and body than many people realize. According to research, emotional patterns from long-term exposure to various situations are absorbed by the body, and these become encoded at a cellular level. They are stored as body memories. What we learn—and the strength of any given memory—is contingent on our psychophysiological state at the time. Certain things can heighten emotional response, and those memories get more readily stored, often remaining imprinted for years. If we are in a state of fear, for example, hormones are released that influence our memory of that situation, and we will recall the experience more vividly than, say, something we had for breakfast two weeks ago.

In addition to emotional encoding, another factor comes into play. Our systems tend toward homeostasis—toward keeping our inner world constant. When an emotional scenario becomes physically imprinted, we tend to bring into our lives whatever will recreate that scenario, even if we find it painful. Someone who grows up attuned to the low energy level of a quiet family may have difficulty adjusting to the chaos of a spouse's boisterous family. Or a person with many siblings may have trouble living alone later in life. Each "knows" within his body the energy level that has become part of his personal rhythms, and body memories seek to retain the status quo.

This is not to fall back on yet another form of cause-and-effect psychology. There is no one-to-one correlation between a set of circumstances and future behavior. Children from the same family may develop quite different ways of processing and storing this information, and some may be more aware than others of how to resist certain patterns. Yet it becomes clear from the patterns displayed in any person's life just what his or her form of encoding might be. I have seen a woman who did not have osteoporosis nevertheless develop the stooped posture of her mother, who did. I have seen a man who grew up in a family that suppressed emotion have difficulty caring for his wife or children. Modeling and the household arena have a strong impact on our emotio-physical identities. Yet those patterns can be brought to awareness, and changed.

Thus, there is nothing inherently Freudian when discussing subconscious factors. I believe that the subconscious can have a profound influence on who we are and what we do, but I also believe that no one is trapped by that. We can transcend such influences and initiate change that will make us into people quite different from what might be predicted from childhood factors. I think Dean Koontz exhibits this transformation. The repeated patterns in his novels of his understanding of evil show great consistency, but the way he has chosen to live in awareness of what his father was, with the determination to be something different, presents a person for whom psychological fate may have diminished force. This book therefore is a "eurography" rather than a "pathography," in that it maps the life of a person who has become psychologically healthy.

The term "psychobiography" means that I read through the novels and stories looking for things that confirmed or illuminated aspects of Dean's life. Often I learned things about him from the books that deepened my understanding of life experiences about which he had already told me; sometimes the books inspired me to ask questions I had not thought of during our interviews. Since there is an organic relationship between life and art, a writer's experience and his work will each inform the other. There is a theory that the serious works of an author are always about the same theme, and that seems to hold true. Writers keep trying over and over to make sense of the world through whatever most concerns them. Since the kinds of life experiences that might preoccupy a writer are usually complicated and unfinished, it makes sense to look for repeated psychological patterns in the work.

I should make it clear that this is *not* an "authorized" biography as such, because Dean did not seek me out to write it or tell me what I should write; he neither guided nor endorsed my analysis of his work or my interpretation of its meaning. The word "authorized" on the biography of a living person can also imply that the subject has no intention of writing an autobiography; but Dean does, indeed, have that intention. He was a highly cooperative subject, however, helping me with sources and fact-checking.

I spoke with people from every period of his life, but when I could not reach or persuade someone to talk with me, I relied on Dean's memory of important events. I read all of the novels, stories, poems, and articles that he has written. I also used reviews, interviews, newspaper and magazine accounts, and my own experience of the places where Dean has lived. I talked with fans and kept up with an Internet chat line to form a sense of what his readers feel about his work. Where I needed more scholarly material, such as information about adult children of alcoholics or about schizophrenia, I frequently relied on several different types of sources. A complete bibliography is listed in the back.

All quotes, unless otherwise specified, are from interviews that I personally conducted.

Admittedly there were times when I ran into dead ends,

often due to the fact that some people have devised false documents and attributed them to Dean. There are letters in circulation among some collectors that purport to be his, but the facts contradict the information contained in those letters. Collectors should know that even from his earliest years as a writer, Dean used letterhead; any letter not on the stationery of that period is fraudulent. Material that was added to his early nonfiction books by Aware Press also supported a myth that he participated in things that he did not. Some collectors attribute to him pen names that were not his, such as Shane Stevens—who is a real person—or works by authors such as John Hill, whose real name happens to match one of Dean's pseudonyms. Even Dean's wife, Gerda, has been subject to rumors. She was supposedly married to another bestselling writer before Dean, though they have been together since high school!

I have checked everything in these pages with Dean and Gerda. Wherever one person's memory is different from what Dean recalls and the difference seemed significant, I have supplied both accounts—with the idea that no one's memory is one hundred percent reliable and perceptions may differ. Overall, however, this is the story of Dean Koontz, told in a way that feels authentic to him, without it being exclusively his perspective. The interpretation of the books is entirely mine.

A final note to readers: There are "spoilers" within, as they say on the Internet, remarks about the novels that give away pertinent information. This is because whenever I read biographies of other writers, I dislike the assumption that I'm familiar with all of that person's work. With that experience in mind, I included basic plots for all of the novels, and for some, I revealed the ending if it seemed germane to the point that I wished to make. Anyone who has not read a certain novel, and wishes to do so, should skip over the paragraphs that summarize plots, and perhaps even my analysis. Except for the more ambitious novels in recent years, lack of familiarity with the plot of early books will not hinder anyone's ability to read this biography. It should be noted that plot summaries can give the wrong impression that a book is simplistic—particularly with science fiction. No one should substitute my summaries for the fuller experience of reading any given novel.

ACKNOWLEDGMENTS

EVERY BIOGRAPHY IS A TEAM EFFORT. MANY PEOPLE CONTRIBUTE to its success, not the least of which may be the subject himself. Foremost, of course, I would like to thank Dean Koontz for extending himself so generously, and for making certain that I got things right. After him, I wish to thank Gerda Koontz for her assistance and for tolerating my numerous intrusions.

Among my resources were Dean and Gerda's friends and family, business associates, fans, supporters, and colleagues. Then there were my own friends, who sent things, offered encouragement, or alerted me to important resources. Everyone was generous with his or her time and some were unbelievably hospitable. Just listing names fails to convey the quality of the moments I spent with these people, but in the interests of space, my eternal thanks to Susan Allison, Jean Hastings Ardell, Kimberly Barker, Marcella Barkman, George Beahm, Paul Beers, Greg Benford, Fay Bitting, Vera (Houck) Blackburn, James Blaylock, John Bodnar, Linda Borland, David Bradley, Don Brautigam, Helen (Morgart) Carberry, Anthony Ceddia, Richard Chizmar, Doug Clegg, Michael Collings, Angelo Costanza, Matthew Costello, Stacy Creamer, Norma (Ickes) Cuppett, Dorothy DeGrange, Terry DiDomenico, Tom Doyle, Nancy Eckard, Harlan Ellison, Elizabeth Engstrom, Jack Faust, O. Richard Forsythe, Ned Frear, Harold Gleason, Ed Gorman, Robert Gottlieb, Martin Greenberg, Linda Farner Holtry, Corey Hudson and the Canine Companions for Independence, Tim Hely Hutchinson, Gary Ickes, Larry Johnson, Donna Johnston, Ming Johnston, Don Jones, Pat Karlan, Jonathan Kellerman, Dana Kennedy, Louise Kinzey, Joe and Karen Lansdale, Richard Laymon, Bentley Little, Nancy Logue, John Maclay, Farhad Mann, Robert R. McCammon, Don McQuinn, Jane Miller, Henry Morrison, Bill Munster, Michael Naidus, Yvonne Navarro, George Newill, Maxine O'Callaghan, Ruth Osborne, Phil Parks, Lee Pieterse, Tim Powers, Barry Price, Harold Recard, Michael Sauers, Jim Seels, Dave Silva, Robert Silverberg,

Joe Stefko, Jeff Stevenson, Bob Tanner, Grant Thiessen, Lisa Tuttle, Robert Weinberg, Pelli Wheaton, Stan Wiater, David Williams, Alan Williams, Mary Jeanne (Heit) Wilt, F. Paul Wilson, Chris Zavisa, and Gail and Al Zimmerman.

I also want to express appreciation for the readers on the Dean Koontz chat list who kept letting me know how eager they were to see this book. It was a pleasure to be among them, particularly those for whom Dean's novels have had a profound impact. Special thanks to Gareth.

One of the most enthusiastic supporters was Lori Perkins, my agent, who had been urging me for years to approach Dean and who was thrilled that it all worked out.

My editor, John Silbersack, was especially patient and encouraging, and had a good sense of perspective—a must for anyone immersed inside someone else's life story. He kept my head above water, so to speak. I also wish to thank his assistant, Noelle La Corbiniere, for her patience and persistence in maintaining the flow.

"It is dangerous to prove to a man too plainly how nearly he is on a level with the brutes without showing him his greatness; it is also dangerous to show him his greatness too clearly apart from his vileness. It is still more dangerous to leave him in ignorance of both. But it is of great advantage to show him both."

—PASCAL

"Words are like a thin surface over deep water."

—WITTGENSTEIN

"We see so little of anything at which we look, that we are usually satisfied with simple surfaces, perhaps because the deeper view is often terrifying in its complexity."

—DEAN KOONTZ, *TWILIGHT EYES*

PROLOGUE

ALTHOUGH MOST OF HIS PROFESSORS DISMISSED GENRE FICTION, Dean Koontz continued to read science fiction, fantasy, and suspense throughout his college years. As a boy, he had found in these stories an escape from unpleasant reality, and he now wanted to write such tales himself.

Since his freshman year, he had sat in classes listening to educated people telling him about the merits of the classics and the Great Ideas of the Western world; he also heard their opinions that the types of writing he liked were shallow and uninspired. Yet it still seemed to him that the force of fiction lay in telling a good story. That's what *he* liked. No matter what his professors claimed, he felt that the style and subject should not matter. Science fiction and suspense were as good as anything else. Therefore, when it came time for him to commit his own words to paper for a short story class, he ignored pressure to imitate the literary styles that his professors used as models, and chose instead to just tell a good story. He knew what felt right. His tale, "The Kittens," was about a girl who repays her father's cruelty in a particularly shocking way. He finished it and turned it in.

He then showed "The Kittens" to the advisor for the college's literary magazine. She saw merit in his work, and submitted the story to *The Atlantic Monthly*'s contest for college students. Since this was a prestigious contest with a lot of competition no one had high expectations. Yet a few months later, to everyone's surprise, Dean's story won a top prize. It also won respect from his teachers. That same year, he sold it to a literary magazine and earned, with his own voice, his first professional money.

He had successfully followed his instincts, against the advice of those who claimed to know better, and had proven standard wisdom to be only a perspective—one that could be mistaken.

It would not be the last time.

ONE

The Early Years

1

THEY CALLED HIM THEIR MIRACLE CHILD. WHEN FLORENCE and Ray Koontz had a baby boy, Dean Ray Koontz, on Monday, July 9, 1945, they greeted his healthy arrival with great joy. Ray was thirty-five and Florence twenty-nine, which was late in those days for a first child. They had been married for over a decade. Although they were barely surviving on the meager sums that Ray earned in his erratic periods of employment, they had tried for a long time to start a family. They had been told that they might never be parents, but finally they had succeeded.

The Koontzes joined the rest of the country in anticipation of better times. Hitler's suicide that year on April 30 had preceded Germany's surrender to the Allies. Truman, blunt and practical, had replaced the more elegant Roosevelt as president, and the rationing of gas, at fifteen cents per gallon, came to an end. With Hitler and Mussolini both dead, Japan was soon to surrender, albeit not before atomic bombs on August 6 and 9 decimated Hiroshima and Nagasaki.

Wartime production had ended the Great Depression and its haunting deprivations, and inspired visions of a better life. The culture stood on the brink of a flourishing consumerism, made possible by a burgeoning middle class and a government determined to create an image of prosperity. Life expectancy for men was sixty-three years. The average new car cost around $1,000, average annual wages were $2,400, a new house averaged $4,600, and a loaf of bread cost nine cents.

That same year, Jackie Robinson became the first black baseball player, and *The Lost Weekend* won the Academy Award for best picture. John Steinbeck published *Cannery Row* and Norman Mailer's first novel was *The Naked and the Dead*. New inventions included microwave ovens, Tupperware, frozen meals, the three-fold sofa bed, and streptomycin. An ideology of benign nationalism formed, even as the government performed clandestine plutonium experiments on unwitting subjects. Naïve optimism had its shadow side, and Dean Koontz's generation would grow up attuned to both.

In the postwar mid-forties, the economy recovered more slowly in some places than others. Dean's father had been a miner in Jerome, Pennsylvania, and then had taught shoe repair to inmates in a prison near Huntingdon. Eventually he and Florence moved to Everett, Pennsylvania, where Ray opened a shoe repair shop. The talk was that Everett would become an exit from the Pennsylvania Turnpike, the principal route between Philadelphia and Pittsburgh. With its gas stations, restaurants, and motels, that meant much-needed jobs for this farm community. There were few opportunities to earn a living one hundred miles west of Harrisburg, the state capital, and the same distance east of Pittsburgh. Turnpike business could mean financial salvation for many young families.

In 1946, Florence and Ray lived in a small upstairs apartment across from the G.C. Murphy store in Everett. Their neighbors were Bob and Marcella Barkman. Marcella would sometimes watch the baby and she remembers Florence as a devoted mother. "She was very thin and frail, but that didn't deter her from keeping a very clean apartment and a well-kept child," she says. "On a sunny morning, she would take the baby carriage down a steep flight of stairs and come back for the baby. That had to be quite a chore because carriages were very awkward in those days." The Koontzes, she says, kept to themselves, except when Ray later came to sell them insurance. "They were quiet people. Mrs. Koontz told me they wouldn't be able to have more children and I was under the impression she'd had a hysterectomy. I'm sure Dean was very precious to them."

Eventually it was Bedford, a few miles west, that earned the dubious honor of getting the turnpike business, so Ray and Florence moved there. Bedford was special to Florence. She had visited this well-kept town, with its colonial homes and perfect lawns, during her summers growing up. Her father had built a small vacation home there and had run a grocery business. Two of her sisters lived there with their husbands.

Bedford, with a population of just over three thousand when Dean was born, has an eclectic history. At the foot of the

Alleghenies in western Pennsylvania, where peaks soar to over three thousand feet, Bedford had become the county seat. A branch of the Juniata River flowed through the fertile valley. The town was first settled in 1751 as a trading post called Raystown. Eight years later, Fort Raystown became Fort Bedford to honor an English duke. The area soon attracted traders and settlers, many of whom were then massacred by Indians. George Washington camped here with six thousand troops, and decades later as president put down the infamous Whiskey Rebellion. By 1766, citizens had designed a grid of streets named for members of William Penn's family. The residents, mostly Scotch-Irish or German, worked hard to establish the state's first steel works. They built a courthouse and jail, then schools and churches. Then came a surprising discovery.

In 1796, a worker bathing a sore limb in the nearby springs and a fisherman taking a drink both experienced the water's medicinal qualities. Magnesia, sulfur, and other minerals in the water showed wondrous results with arthritis and liver ailments. A local physician set up a health resort, and his enterprise grew into a grand hotel and spa. Eventually the Bedford Springs Resort Hotel attracted eminent visitors like President James Buchanan, who christened it his summer White House. In 1853, he was at this hotel when he received the first message from Queen Victoria in London on the Atlantic cable (which parted after only three days and was not fixed for thirteen years). Several other presidents visited the small town at various times, as did Daniel Webster, Henry Clay, Alexander Hamilton, and Aaron Burr. Even John Brown stopped here on his way to Harper's Ferry. The town had much to be proud of. It mirrored America's eagerness to mine opportunity, but it also harbored some of the same social biases that would throw the country into chaos by the 1960s.[1]

2

There were many families named Koontz in the Bedford area, although none was closely related to Dean's. His mother was from Pittsburgh and his father from Huntingdon County, to the northeast. "I was always told that the name Koontz is

Dutch or German-Dutch," he explains, "but there was no ethnic tradition in our family that makes this clear. We had no
sense of a family past and no one talked about it. My mother's
maiden name, Logue, was probably German."

Florence and Ray had lived in several small towns in rural
Pennsylvania before settling in Bedford. They had met in
Pittsburgh, where Florence had been raised with her brother,
George, and three sisters — Virginia, Kate, and Betty. They
also had a stepsister, Thelma. Florence was five-foot-two,
pretty and slim, with a round face, brown hair, and dark
brown eyes. Her sisters called her Dodie, but others referred
to her as Molly. Her manner was soft-spoken and gentle, her
sense of fun girlish, and though she suffered from chronic ill
health, she had a store of nervous energy. In high school, Florence had shown real talent with music. She could pick up
almost any instrument and, with little practice, learn to play it.
Teachers had urged her to pursue a musical career, but inexplicably, she had put those dreams aside. "I never saw my mother
play a musical instrument," Dean recalls. "I never heard her
sing around the house. She just didn't do that sort of thing."
That she had once had such a predilection mystifies him, but in
those years of the Great Depression, women often sacrificed
their dreams to have security and a family.

Dean's cousin, Jane Miller, who was nine when Dean was
born and who grew up in the same town, remembers his
mother's concern with keeping things neat: "Every hair had to
be in place. That's the way she was. She was also an immacu-
late housekeeper. Everything had to be scrubbed to perfection."
Jane describes Florence as the diplomat in a family where one
sibling seemed always to be squabbling with another. "She was
the peacemaker. She could talk to everyone. And she was generous. She'd have given you the last thing she had if you needed
it. And honest beyond anyone's thinking. One day she went
into a phone booth and there lay some change. She put it into
her pocketbook and wouldn't spend it, even though she needed
it, because she was afraid someone would come looking for that
money. She knew what it was like not to have very much. But
she loved life. She never complained."

Florence never hesitated to extend herself to someone in
need. Once she helped a young woman remain in college by

giving her what money she could. For a period of time, she drove a neighbor to the doctor every day, thirty miles each way, and she always listened to people's problems. She liked to help. Townspeople remember her as friendly and reliable. Nancy Eckard recalls that when she first moved to town in 1962, Florence made her feel that she belonged there and she was quite grateful. "She always gave me a big hug and she always laughed. If she was feeling down, you wouldn't know it because she'd always have a smile and something nice to say."

Dean's father, Ray, was blond, about five-foot-six, with a long, narrow face, hawkish nose, pale brown eyes, and a medium but solid build. He usually made a good first impression, although some people thought him slick. When he met Florence, he liked what he saw and asked her to marry him. These were the Depression years, just before World War II. Florence was just out of high school and had a domineering mother who never failed to browbeat those within her reach. Florence's siblings were in constant conflict. In the midst of all this, marriage seemed a desirable option. Ray was six years older, with an air of someone who had been around. He claimed to be an inventor with good ideas who would soon become wealthy and keep her in style. Given her circumstances, it was easy for Florence to believe him.

As the country recovered from a brutal recession, the entrepreneurial spirit that Ray Koontz projected was highly encouraged. People with innovative ideas that catered to the middle class were finding a market. It seemed that anyone with a good plan and solid financial backing could make it big. Ray absorbed this optimism from the culture at large. Prone to ego-enhancing delusions, he made getting rich from his own designs his ultimate goal.

Whether Florence truly believed him or just wanted to escape her home, she defied her family's opposition and married him. It was not long before she discovered that Ray was a dreamer, short on attention and long on problems, who failed to realize his limitations. Florence never discussed her feelings about Ray with her son, so Dean was not certain why they had married. As he observed many anxious years of hardship and stress, he had reason to believe that if romantic love had ever motivated his mother, it had died early.

Dean himself was to become the main focus for Florence. After watching her sisters marry and start their families, she was eager to be a mother. Before Dean was born, she had suffered four miscarriages and had delivered a stillborn son, so Dean's birth had been especially significant. Although Florence had little money to buy him things, she doted on him in every other way.

As an only child, Dean had both advantages and disadvantages. There were no other children to play with or to help him bear the burden of parental expectations, which meant loneliness and a heavy sense of responsibility. Yet he did not have to share family resources. Being an only child probably helped set his path to success. According to child development studies, most children without siblings develop language skills more rapidly. Being the center of adult attention, they often have a high IQ and a more mature perception and ability to tolerate pressure. Organized, conscientious, persistent, and reliable, they are likely to achieve their goals. Even as they strive for perfection, however, they feel insecure, which inspires a repetitive need to prove themselves. Many of these traits were certainly true of Dean, and the aspirations, doubts, and tolerance for solitude that he developed as an only child were to serve him well as a writer.

3

Dean's first home in Bedford was a three-room apartment on the ground floor of a plain, white frame, two-story building on West Pitt Street. Nearby were several small bars. Behind the building was the Raystown Branch of the Juniata River and in front was a busy street that accessed a main highway. Florence had to be diligent about watching her toddler on this stretch of road. (It was nearly half a mile to Juliana Street at the center of town.)

Although the apartment had a sizable kitchen, there were no built-in appliances. It had only a sink, some counter space, and an icebox. Because appliances were expensive, Florence used a galvanized washtub for laundry and baths. She cooked meals on a hotplate and, like most other young families, hoped one day to own a house. Ray's earnings were meager and he had difficulty keeping a job, but with assistance from Florence's father, Florence believed that they just might manage it within a few years. In the meantime, she had to make do.

Dean's earliest memory at that apartment is of a summer day when he was three years old. His parents were sitting with friends on a grassy area in front of the building. Dean went around back to play on the riverbank. As he stood looking into the flowing water, a snake coiled nearby and struck at him. It missed and went sailing through the air, startling him. "I went running like hell, absolutely terrified," he recalls. Breathlessly he described the incident to the adults, but they only laughed at his cute manner. "Everybody made fun of me. Nobody believed that anything had really happened. I think that's when I began to distrust adults."

It was during this time, while Dean was a toddler, that a local football team adopted him as their mascot. These teams, formed in several local towns, were made up of high school graduates and returning veterans. Bedford's was known as the Blue Devils. Although the league lasted only a few years, hundreds of people showed up for the games.[2] Jack Faust, one of the Blue Devils, recalls that Ray Koontz came often with his young son. The team even gave Dean his own uniform. Photos from this period show him in this outfit.

Ray could not have been more pleased. It confirmed his aspirations for Dean. Although he claimed to enjoy being a father, he had difficulty feeling good about himself. Thus, he placed his ambition squarely on the shoulders of his son. He bragged that Dean would become the big, powerful man *he* wanted to be. "When I was a little kid," Dean remembers, "my father would tell people that I was going to grow up to be a football star. Even when it became obvious at the age of twelve that I was not going to be huge and weigh two hundred forty pounds, he'd tell everybody, 'He's going to be six-foot-two and he's going to play for the Steelers, and if he doesn't, he's no son of mine.'"

In a way, Ray's prophecy did play itself out in Dean's adult life, but not as he had hoped. One day Dean would have cause to question whether he really was Ray's son.

As a child, Dean had a vague awareness that all was not right in the household. Although his father sweet-talked Florence in front of others, his moods in private were often erratic. Despite how little money they had, Ray often came home drunk. Sometimes he disappeared on fishing trips for days at a time. Other times he would stay home and create havoc. At that age, Dean knew only that his father's behavior made his mother unhappy, so he tried to keep her in good spirits.

"I was a pretty good kid," he says. "The things I did that got me in trouble were usually stupid, not mean."

The worst incident he can remember was with a playmate, Nancy Logue, the daughter of the people who owned the apartment building where he lived (no relation to his mother). They were friends of his parents and lived half a block away. Dean and Nancy were both around four when he got into the worst trouble of his young life. "She and I were playing together in her father's garage, where he had all these cans of paint," Dean remembers, "and we wanted to see what would happen when we mixed different colors." As they were about to open the cans, Nancy's mother called her. She had to leave, but told Dean she would be back soon and urged him to stay.

"So they went away," he continues, "and I kept working on this paint can with this screwdriver. Finally, somewhere in my dim little kid mind, I realized there might be a mess, so I took the can into their kitchen to open it in the sink. When the lid popped, red paint splattered all over the sink. I desperately tried to clean it up and made an even greater mess. Then I panicked and started to cry. I left the house and went running home."

His mother was entertaining Louise Kinzey from nearby Schellsburg when she saw Dean coming down the street, spattered in red. She was sure it was blood. In terror for his life, she ran to him. Dean blurted out what he had done and then knew he was in trouble. "When she discovered the red stuff was paint," he says, "and that I had made a mess at someone else's house, she was horrified." Florence dragged him into the house and heated water for the washtub. Then she pulled off his pants, threw him over her knees, and spanked him. She wanted to wallop him good, but Louise urged her to go easy. The boy had meant no harm.

"That's the only spanking I ever got that I can remember," says Dean. "I'm sure my mother never hurt me, but I loved her so much that earning her displeasure was punishment enough. You just never wanted her to look at you and think, 'Oh, how could you do that?' It was too awful."

4

On top of troubles with her marriage—and perhaps because of them—Florence struggled with serious health problems. Dean's cousin Jane remembers that Florence always had some kind of ailment. "She got phlebitis all the time," Jane says. "She would have to keep her legs elevated."

The worst problem was her high blood pressure, which made her perspire profusely. "Her blood pressure was only partially controllable," Dean states, "and she would break into these sweats. This sounds unbelievable, but she would sit at the kitchen table and go very pale. Her heart would accelerate into the two hundred range. She would be in a desperate state, with sweat pouring. She'd take a washcloth and blot her face and arms and wring it out in this basin. She'd fill the basin with sweat, two or three inches deep, until the trouble passed. I remember it clearly because it's so traumatic to see your mother suffering like that."

Dean was only four when Florence was rushed to the hospital in Pittsburgh one winter for the first of several treatments. The doctors there decided on experimental surgery to reduce her blood pressure. Unsure what would happen, they cut nerves along the spinal chord in hope of relieving the stress, but the only effect was to further debilitate her. She nearly died and had to be hospitalized for ten weeks.

Ray was unable to care for his son, and since no relatives could take Dean in for that long, Florence's good friend Louise Kinzey volunteered.

"She's very nurturing," says Dorothy de Grange about her Aunt Louise. "Her door was always open to anyone and everyone. She took care of people."

Louise lived only a few miles to the west and Florence had often taken Dean there for a visit. Louise liked Dean—had once saved him from that serious spanking—and she and her husband, Bird, were happy to help. Their grown daughter, Pat, was on her own and Tom, their son, was leaving for the army. There was plenty of room for a little boy.

"They were two of the kindest souls you'd ever hope to know," Dean recalls.[3]

So Ray, whose primary concern was how he would get his own needs met while his wife was away—including making a pass at a sister-in-law—dropped Dean off at the Kinzey home and left. No one realized it at the time, but this was to be one of Dean's earliest transformative encounters—someone who would have a significant impact on the direction his life would take. Dean found himself with a warm, stable, and loving couple who paid him a lot of attention.

"He was a sweet little boy," Louise remembers. "We just fell in love with him." She even devised an affectionate moniker: "We nicknamed him Butch." (Much to Dean's chagrin, his cousins adopted the nickname for most of his childhood.)

The Kinzeys lived in a white weatherboard house with a wondrous wraparound porch. Although it was too cold to use the backyard swing, Dean recalls how the ceaseless snow that winter left delightful drifts that "seemed as high as the Empire State Building." Inside, knickknacks, glass figurines, and interesting clocks decorated the orderly house. The smell of furniture polish and home cooking, the sound of laughter, and the constant warm embraces gave Dean the feeling that he was home—in a better home. He felt secure there. "I found stability."

Dean stayed in the bedroom that Pat Kinzey had vacated. It was a dormer room with a sloping ceiling, which seemed quite magical to him. The bed, dresser, and table were painted gray, and a reading lamp was hooked over the bedframe. Louise came in every night to tuck him in.

She believed that children should eat something before bed, so she served her own favorite dessert. "I got lots of cherry ice cream sodas," Dean remembers. As he sat in bed eating his treat, Louise introduced him to the children's classics that she had read years earlier to Pat and Tom. "He loved being read to," she recalls.

"I think that's where I started getting this love of books," Dean says. He associated the magical tales with warmth, security, and loving attention, or, as he puts it, with "salvation." Louise always kissed him good-night and he went off to sleep with exciting plots and characters fresh in his mind.

During those ten weeks, Ray stayed away. "I never saw his father from the time he dropped Dean off to the time he picked him up," Louise states. But Dean did not miss him. He helped feed the hunting dogs that Bird raised and, to his heart's content, looked through comics from Tom Kinzey's collection. He discovered Donald Duck, Scrooge McDuck, Mutt and Jeff, Nancy and Sluggo, and Felix the Cat. Although his parents would never approve of wasting time and money on comic books, Dean probably benefited. Children who read comics get early practice using their imagination. They learn to fill in the missing action between frames, attribute different dialogue sounds to diverse characters, anticipate plot, generalize from characters to their own concerns, and synthesize story lines. With comics, the mind is compelled to pay attention rather than conditioned, as with many television programs, to be passively entertained.[4]

Louise kept Dean fully supplied. As she baked cookies and made him delicious healthy meals, she watched him with a mother's caring eye. "I felt as if I had done something for him," she says. It may be that the character Mercy Ealing, the image of grace in the form of a cookie-baking rancher's wife in Dean's novel *Sole Survivor*, has something of Louise Kinzey in her.

Finally, when Florence was out of the hospital, Ray arrived to retrieve his son. Dean wanted to see his mother, but he did not want to leave the Kinzeys. "He cried when he left," says Louise. Yet he took with him a deep love for stories that could be read and savored during good times and bad, that could take him into a more exciting world. "I remember that time as being magical and wonderful," Dean affirms.

Since Florence still needed time to recover, she took her son for two months to the home of her sister Virginia, who lived in Bedford. Aunt Ginny had two daughters, Jane and Shirley, who were several years older than Dean. "I slept in Janie's room," he explains, "and my mother slept in another room while Aunt Ginny took care of her. She took a long time to recover."

Jane can remember how excruciating the experience was

for Florence. "She was in so much pain, she couldn't stand the sheets on her back."

"Even after the surgery," says Dean, "my mother continued to have these attacks. Her back thereafter carried enormous scars. My mother was an indomitable kind of person, but she was frequently ill and I think that's one reason she stayed with my father. Maybe she wondered, if anything happened to her, what would happen to me?"

5

Dean never knew his father's parents because they had died before he was born, but his maternal grandparents were part of his life. His grandfather, John Logue, was a large, good-hearted man who fancied himself a carpenter. As a younger man, he had built a vacation home with a garage just off U.S. 220 in the outskirts of Bedford, and had taken his family there during the summers. While Dean was growing up, three of John Logue's daughters lived in town with their families, so he moved into this little house.

Dean liked his grandfather's humor, but remembers his grandmother as more of a "dragon lady." She frightened him. Apparently she bothered his grandfather as well, for at a time when divorce was rare, John Logue obtained a legal separation and lived apart from her.

"She was a holy terror," Dean says. "She'd come right at you like a giant bird. Nothing ever satisfied her. She did not show affection. She was stern, domineering, and glowering. I never saw my grandmother laugh."

His cousin Jane affirms this: "She looked real sweet, but she wasn't. She was not a nice person. Whatever she wanted, she expected you to do it. She was very firm."

"All I remember of her," says Dean, "is that I never liked to be with her because it was like being put through the third degree. Even when I was a little kid, if she was in the room alone with me, she'd just start lecturing me or hectoring me. She was a very threatening figure."

It makes some sense that, after living with such a mother, Florence might marry a man with Ray's problems. People unaware of covert psychological traps can inadvertently attract someone just like the very parent they desire to escape, especially if they marry before they have much self-awareness. It is not what they want, but it is the energy pattern with which they are familiar. At a young age, Florence had learned to adapt to a demanding, self-centered person. With the additional negative charge of sibling conflicts, she was bound to be subconsciously attuned to anyone who might recreate patterns of tension and chaos. Although Ray had seemed to Florence to promise a way out, he ended up reproducing the feeling of being home: her attempt to escape had led right back in. This is the classic pattern of unresolved, self-perpetuating need that prepared Florence to become the enabling partner of an aggressive alcoholic. Her mother had made a strong subconscious impression, but Florence might have been happier with a man like her father. That he was nearby was a source of relief and consolation.

Dean enjoyed his Grandfather Logue's company, watching him putter around, and listening to his stories as they sat together on the porch. Unfortunately this relationship was short-lived. When Dean was eight, his grandfather had a stroke. After a brief hospitalization, he died.

Grandmother Logue lasted a while longer, living with her daughter Betty in Lancaster, Pennsylvania, and then with Virginia in Bedford.

6

Before he died, Dean's grandfather invited Florence to move into his summer house, while he moved into a smaller house that he had rebuilt next door. It was a step backward for her. She had to move in because she and Ray could no longer afford the rent on their apartment. The house was situated on the other side of town, along a gravel lane known then as Spring Street. It faced the expansive state fairgrounds, which were surrounded by woods, with mountains as a backdrop. Between the front of the house and the busy highway was a gas station and a restaurant shaped like a giant coffeepot. Not far away was a neighborhood known as Tiday Town, the most depressed economic area in Bedford. This was the "wrong" side of the tracks, a fact that Dean was to realize only later when he went to school. All he knew at the age of five was that his mother was happy to have her own home, and that there was more fun to have here than in the cramped apartment.

In his earliest years here, Dean learned the joys of even the harshest winters. He was awed after a snowfall by the open white fields, front and back. "On the fairgrounds there was all this snowy wilderness and even behind our house was open land. I used to love being out in the snow." Even when he moved to California as an adult, fond memories of snow infused his novels. "I'm always writing snow scenes," he says. And the fairgrounds in summer, with its weeklong car races and carnivals, were to play a significant role as he grew up.

Perched on the side of a hill, the small two-story frame house had clapboard siding and a tarpaper roof. Upstairs were two bedrooms, while downstairs a kitchen and living room occupied the main level. From her meager resources, Florence bought inexpensive furniture and hung framed photos and prints to make the place homey. The bathroom was an outhouse, while water for drinking, bathing, and cooking came from a kitchen hand pump. In one corner of the kitchen was the cellar door, where Florence hung calendars from the bank. Down those stairs, a crudely dug out basement housed a kerosene water heater and a coal-burning furnace, which was prone to dangerous flue fires. On the assumption that hot air rises, a single register on the main floor was supposed to warm all the rooms.

The house was not quite to standards. The roof leaked and the furnace failed to heat much of anything but the chimney. Up in his confining second-floor room at the back of the house, Dean learned every year just how cold a Pennsylvania winter could get. "God bless him," says Dean of his grandfather, "but he wasn't much of a builder."

Dean depicted this house vividly in his 1995 novel, *Strange Highways*, the title story of a collection by the same name. It is the childhood home of Joey Shannon, who reluctantly returns to it only after his parents have died. As Joey walks around inside, he reexperiences the place: "He carried his suitcase to the second floor. A short, narrow hallway with badly worn gray-and-yellow flecked linoleum led from the head of the stairs to the bathroom at the back [in real life, installed years later]. Beyond the single door at the right was his parents' room. . . . The single door on the left side of the hall led to his old bedroom. . . . The house was so small, humble, narrow, plain . . . "[5] The only fictional addition to this house is the bedroom in the basement for PJ, Joey's brother, who grew up to become a psychopathic killer.

By the age of ten, Dean had the responsibility of keeping the kerosene heater going strong, and each week he walked to the nearby gas station to purchase five gallons of fuel. Eventually his chores extended to filling the glass kerosene jug that hung upside down over a wick ring, making sure the jug dripped properly so he could light the wick. "I was certain I would set the house on fire," he says. Sometimes it took him as long as ten minutes to work up the courage to perform this daunting task.

The basement disturbed him, and it would one day become associated with his father in one of Dean's most frightening nightmares. There was just something about it that made him anxious. It is no wonder that in *Strange Highways*, Dean uses this crude cellar as a metaphor of forces that influenced the older brother's demented character. Shannon had slept near the furnace all during childhood and his personality was seemingly shaped by something from hell.

Even worse at times was the outhouse in back, which served as the only toilet for five years before indoor plumbing was finally installed. Between winter's ice and summer's spiders, Dean learned to hate the ordeal. In the house, he bathed in the galvanized washtub, set up in the basement and filled from a hose attached to the water heater.

Despite these problems, Florence kept her new home spotless. Everything had its place and she tolerated no mess. Dean came to associate order and cleanliness with a highly moral personality, and many of his principled characters would possess his mother's sense of tidiness. (Roy Borden's mother in *The Voice of the Night* is an exception; in her this trait signals her emotional sterility.) The Koontz family lived a mile from Aunt Ginny and only two houses from Aunt Kate, which made

Florence happy. She visited her sisters often and depended on
them when things got rough.

7

And from time to time, things did get rough. Although Ray's
smooth manner and golden tongue had once won her heart,
Florence had learned the exhausting reality of living with a
mentally unstable alcoholic. Sometimes Ray was sweet to her,
but other times he seemed to resent her existence. He often
blamed her for not making things better for him, although it
was only her resourcefulness that stood between him and living on the streets. On the surface, things seemed tolerable to
others—just the problems that the average family had—but
her sisters suspected that the situation was darker than Florence would admit. Ray was known for the fights he provoked
in bars, so there was reason to believe he might be violent at
home. Seeing Ray's drunken flares of temper, they asked Florence if he ever beat her, but she always denied it. He might
throw chairs or raise his hand to strike her, she said, but he did
not hit her. Virginia, at least, was skeptical.

As years went by, Ray drank to excess and had an increasingly difficult time holding down a job. He would get himself
into trouble or confront the boss and get fired. He wanted to
go into business for himself, so he opened a shoe repair shop
and bragged around town that he would put the town's other
cobbler, Ross Cerra, out of business. In fact, it was the other
way around, although Jane Miller remembers that Ray was
quite skillful. "If he would have stayed with that," she claims,
"he might have succeeded, but his head was full of scatter-
brained ideas. He didn't do anything for very long." Ray also
tried an army-navy store for several months, but soon gave up
on that.

Other times, he talked acquaintances into investing in some
ill-fated project. He worked best in sales because he was gre-
garious, persuasive, and in his good moods, a lot of fun. He
visited people around town, particularly in the bars, and set
about seducing them. As he bought rounds of drinks, he
described grand schemes of what he would soon achieve.

Since there were many stories of people successfully launching such ventures—the Holiday Inn franchises, Levittown's modular homes—and since Ray seemed so confident, even visionary, people were easily suckered. Yet his personal problems only worsened.

Ray liked to gamble. Often what little money he managed to make was lost on cards or racetrack bets before he could bring it home. He might lose his entire salary in one game, yet still expect his wife to put food on the table. From an early age, Dean recalls their constant arguments over money. Finally Florence issued an ultimatum: Either Ray contribute a minimum of fifty dollars every week to the household or he had to leave. Ray resisted, but when she stood her ground, he complied. It seemed to Dean that his mother provided an anchor that his father desperately needed, despite how much Ray fought it. The rounds of anger and threats were endless, but Florence remained firm. Even so, she always tried to keep Dean out of the way.

"On some level my mother must have thought that sending me to my room when all this raging was going on downstairs hid most of it from me," Dean believes. "She must have thought that I just didn't understand the full awfulness of the situation. Or she might have thought that in spite of all this, I loved my father. We all supposedly loved our parents, no matter what they did to us. Not to love them was incomprehensible."

So Dean remained in his room and worried. Sometimes he stared at the doorknob, waiting to see it turn, expecting his father to come in and grab him. He plotted elaborate ways to escape, or read comics to keep his mind off what was happening downstairs. In the summer, he sometimes went out his window onto the roof of the back porch, jumped to the ground, and ran to the property's edge. Even then, he could still hear them arguing.

Ray's drinking eventually worsened into frightening but predictable behavior. "When the car started coming up the hill," Dean recalls, "you could tell he'd been drinking because he'd be driving too fast and—boom—Mom would get me upstairs and into my room with the door closed. Then I would hear them arguing downstairs. Once in a while I was present, and my mother would use the fact that I was there to control my father's outbursts. 'Look what your son is seeing you do,' she would say to him. 'Do you want your son to see you doing this?' He'd be in this shaking state of rage and he'd look at me. A couple of times he came at me, but she interposed herself."

Other times, Ray changed his tactics. He would try to get Dean to side with him by offering him a dime or quarter, which infuriated Florence. "I remember her saying, 'You can't buy your son!' Then she'd pull me away from him. The actual physical violence never got bad with me, but the threats were continuous. When you're a kid you think, well, some night he's going to go over the top. I'd see him threatening my mother and I'd think he might do something extreme." The suspense of what could happen was unrelenting.

"I often think about this relationship," says Dean. "My father had big hands and he would push my mother up against the wall and stand with his fist over her. I think on some level, he was afraid of her. I don't know why, because she was small, but she would glare at him so intensely and get this set to her jaw. I don't know whether he hit her, because I was sent to my room so many times, but he never hit her in front of me. There were bruises, but she would explain them away with, 'Oh, I fell down,' or 'I bumped into something.'"

As Dean got older, he became more aware of the frighten-ing quality of some of his father's moods, such as Ray's restless depression. "It had a wildness about it. He'd get in a brooding state and he'd go on about how there's no one to turn to in this world and nobody cares. He would never say he was going to kill us, but he'd say we'd all be better off if we weren't here. He'd say things like, 'There's no future for this family anyway,' and you knew what he meant."

This kind of brooding made an impression on Dean. In one of his Gothic novels, he later wrote, "The person who is mad . . . might not look upon death with the same viewpoint as the sane. The madman . . . might very well see death as a new beginning, a chance to start over."[6] A psychiatrist would one day tell Dean that he was fortunate to have escaped.

"Those were the times, I think, when my mother was most afraid of him," he says, "but even then she would say to him, 'You're talking nonsense.' She'd get combative. I used to be afraid sometimes. She was not argumentative by nature. She was actually quite a gentle person, and as a kid it scared me when my father got in these moods and my mother would argue with him. Instead of being conciliatory, she would stand her ground. Yet I look back on it now and think it might have been a very smart thing to do. Trying to gentle him down, trying to commiserate with him, might have actually made things worse. She might have had some native sense of good psychology when she ridiculed these moods."

His mother's way of dealing with Ray's latent mental illness turned up decades later in Dean's novel *Cold Fire*, in the scene where Jim Ironheart begs Holly Thorne to be more conciliatory with a seemingly maniacal alien being. Holly refuses, insisting on firmness as the best way to treat instability.

"That was how she always handled my father," says Dean of his mother. "Sometimes, when he was not getting the 'poor Ray' consolation that he was looking for, he would storm out of the house. As a consequence, my mother's handling of his moods had the beneficial effect of causing him to leave in his worst moments."

Between spells of "reptilian coldness" and forced joviality, Ray went through religious phases as well, feeling noble but misunderstood, and seeming to think that obeisance to God would put things in order. "He'd go through these sporadic religious periods during which he would quote from the Bible. That was always when he was at his worst. He never went to church, but when things got bad he'd start reading the Bible and he'd force me to read it."

At any moment, Ray might burst into tears. Or he might sit without speaking, giving Dean the feeling of a crouched predator, "full of slyness and patience and grim need."[7] Dean thought that Ray even took secret delight in the degree of chaos he created around him. The long-term dread, the sleepless hours, the concern for his mother left Dean exhausted and depressed. "Life with him was sometimes a quiet hell, sometimes a shrieking Bedlam."[8] Dean craved some semblance of stability, even the stability of a foul mood prolonged. At least it would have been more predictable.

Florence was clearly distressed. "I saw her cry at times," says Dean. "It was usually when he was supposed to come home for something and didn't show. For instance, relatives would be visiting and everybody was getting together somewhere. He wouldn't show up to drive us there and it was humiliating for her. The family knew what the problem was. Then he'd come home late and I'd hear these fights and he'd slam out, and maybe not come home the next day. I'd hear her crying then, but she tried to do it in private."

Nevertheless, Florence was committed to this marriage, for better or for worse. She had made a bad choice, but she was determined to make the best of it. There were still many good things to be had in life. She had a child to look after and for that she was grateful. Having Dean around mitigated the tension.

8

In the early fifties, no one called it codependence. Alcoholism was not even viewed as a disease. It was a sin, a weakness of the will, a personal failing that embarrassed the family and was kept private. Partners of alcoholics often fell into patterns of unintentionally enabling their spouses to keep on some destructive path. They learned to block the pain and adapt to the abuse. To hide their fear and anger, they put on a public face. Often they became compulsive, for instance developing an obsession with neatness, as a way to retain some feeling of control. They also experienced stress reactions, such as migraines or high blood pressure, because they spent so much energy denying how bad things really were. They lost sight of their own needs. To many of them, the family unit was sacred. Often they feared being abandoned, or blamed themselves for the situation. It would be decades before anyone could show these people a way out.

The children of such self-destructive partnerships also suffered, and often developed a pervasive sense of insecurity. Forced into collusion and unsure what might happen, they learned to mistrust others and even to mistrust themselves. They carried the family shame and felt different from other children. They lived secret lives. Their own needs got shortchanged as family resources supported the alcoholic. They, too, developed a powerful need to keep control of their lives.

For a son with an alcoholic father, it was difficult to grow into the apparently toxic space of manhood. That was not the parent with whom he wished to identify, and his aversion forced him to seek alternative role models, act out, or remain stunted in a childish identity. Dean and Florence both bore the consequences of Ray's abuse, but Dean found ways to avoid falling victim to it.

Ray's drinking got so bad that he would often disappear for several days without notifying his wife. Although Dean liked this because there was peace in the house, Florence would get the inevitable call from a local bar to come and pick up her inebriated husband. Since Ray had the car, she had to walk. "Usually it was midnight or one in the morning, when a bar was closing," Dean recalls. "They would say something like, 'He's here and he's unconscious on the floor.' My mother would get me up, and we would have to walk to wherever this bar was. It might be a mile, it might be two or three. So we'd go load him into the car and drive him home."

Back at the house, Florence supported Ray. "He would lean on her and stumble and fall, and she would get him up and get him inside," Dean remembers. It was classic codependence — rescuing Ray ensured that his behavior would continue. No matter what she might say or how angry she got, Florence showed her husband that he could count on her support. She would always bring him home. Even after Dean got his driver's license in high school, he and his mother were still rescuing Ray. They would go together to get him, and Dean would drive his mother's car home.

"I think some part of my mother always believed that things might straighten out," Dean muses, "that somehow she would bring him around. Of course, that never happened and never could happen because whatever was wrong with my father was probably genetic. There was no way that he was going to change."

It would be more than four decades before Dean would hear an official diagnosis of borderline schizophrenia, but Ray was a classic example. That particular diagnosis is not used today, but in the past, it referred to a person whose behavior resembled schizophrenia across many traits, but who was not fully psychotic. This condition is now more commonly called "schizotypal personality disorder" and, like schizophrenia, is an organic disease.

According to standard psychiatric manuals, such people display a pervasive pattern of peculiar ideas, behaviors, and appearances. They may believe that their own whims will make something happen; they may have bizarre preoccupations, and be suspicious or paranoid. They fear not being accepted. When unconditional approval is withheld, they attack those from whom they need affirmation. They seem to know instinctively how to hurt the other person.

Often they over- or underreact to a situation and may exhibit excessive anxiety. Chaos frightens them, though they generate it, and they may look to religious dogmatism for gaining control, or make vague threats about ending it all. Generally they are highly excitable, with shifting and unpredictable moods. Concerned about their health, they suffer bouts of hypochondria or fear that they may be dying. They experience difficulties with family relationships, financial planning, and holding a job, and they blame others for their problems, but they function well enough to avoid being locked up. Their thinking is rigid and simplistic. Above all, they want the world to be ordered in a certain way, and feel extreme frustration — even despair—when it does not support their vision. At best, they interpret the world through some imaginative metaphor that has only the barest connection to reality.

Before the biological and genetic components of this illness were understood, society viewed the disorder as a character flaw—something to be feared. Like alcoholics, such people were considered immoral or weak. This is the type of person from which many fictional psychopaths are drawn, and Dean's villains, not surprisingly, often fit this pattern. The one who most closely resembles what he saw in his father shows up in his 1983 novel, *Phantoms*. Fletcher Kale, who murders his family, is not fully a psychopath or a sociopath, but when triggered in just the right way, has the potential for violence. He has vitality and "more than his share of shallow charm." He has no opinions on issues of substance, his religious phases are misfortune-inspired, he's impulsive and unreliable, cheats on his wife, lies, exaggerates, overspends, and "knows he's going to be rich one day but [he] has no specific plan for acquiring that wealth." He worries only about his own needs. He's one of those kinds of people who are "not burdened by remorse, morality, love, or empathy. Often they led lives of acceptable destruction."[9] Although most criminal types will protect friends and family, a sociopath has no such allegiances. Anyone who gets in the way is a potential victim.

In the case of Ray Koontz, who exhibited all of these traits, antisocial elements were strongly present in the form of violating commitments to those around him who did not support his perspective. He also attacked in others those traits in himself that he despised, such as weakness, insecurity, and lack of manliness. Sometimes he was compliant, at other times demanding. He often viewed people as intruders, or blamed them for things he did not like. Their concerns meant nothing to him. The way Dean saw it, Ray only went through the motions of having feelings. He was of some peculiar alien breed. If he hurt someone, he felt no remorse.

Forever searching for his niche, Ray was certain that one of his ideas would make him rich; but restless, irresponsible, and unfocused, he met only short-lived success at best. To his mind, he simply had not been given a chance; it had nothing to do with his inability to concentrate or to hold his temper. Oversensitive and irritable at home, he reached for friends to build safety around himself, but usually ended up hurt and distrustful from some minor slight. As a result, he became deceitful and cunning. Acceptance to him meant total devotion. All or nothing. Any little event had the power to trigger a crisis, which sent him out to the bars.

To make matters worse, he instigated lawsuits against anyone who seemed to have offended or hampered him. He thought it would one day make him rich. Over the years, he totaled half a dozen cars and sued the other driver each time. Every fender-bender had to be handled by a lawyer, even though they were often Ray's fault. He had little luck with this pursuit, but once, when Dean was in grade school, Ray hit a truck and broke his back. He sued the company and won a settlement of sixteen thousand dollars, despite the open beer cans littering his car. Getting money from this accident only reinforced his belief that lawsuits were effective, so he continued to use them.

There is good indication that Ray's illness had a predominantly genetic source, exacerbated by stressful situational factors. He was from a troubled family. Although his father, who had died relatively young, had owned a successful restaurant and a shoe repair shop, the family was plagued by other problems. Ray's mother apparently had died quite young and his father had married Mabel, Ray's stepmother. Over the years, several family members exhibited signs of instability.

One brother, Faye, committed suicide in his late thirties. Dean was around three or four at the time. Ray also had four half brothers, one of whom was a musician who, in his late fifties, also committed suicide. He had been part of the Big Band era and had succeeded so well that he refused to wear the same white shirt twice. "He peaked early and then had difficulty holding a job," says Dean. "His life was like my father's in many ways—one degree of chaos or another—and he seemed to have difficulty functioning. I think his wife divorced him and it wasn't long afterward that he killed himself. Like my father, he might have needed that stable person to rely upon."

Another of Ray's brothers, Danny, had died as a teenager. Mabel had become a Christian Scientist and when Danny was stricken with appendicitis, he did not get the medical care he needed. After he died, Mabel switched her faith.

9

Perhaps as a result of his drinking or his mental problems, Ray grew increasingly distant. Although relatives remember him being happy when Dean was young, Ray eventually withdrew from his family. He preferred bars or fishing holes to being at home.

His few attempts to take Dean fishing served only to widen the gap. On such trips, Ray always had a buddy or two along and plenty to drink. Since they liked fishing at night, it meant camping out. The whole experience seemed gruesome to Dean, who was six at the time. "That was a big deal, to take me fishing," he says. "I hated fishing. It was so boring. You just sit with the pole. I didn't want to bait the hook, so he ridiculed me. And when I didn't want to sleep on the ground, he and his friends made fun of me. Then we went home and he said to my mother, 'I'm never taking him again. He's a sissy.'"

Dean wrote about this experience in *The Voice of the Night*. Fourteen-year-old Colin has to go on a fishing trip with his father, who is divorced from his mother. He dislikes the bloody brutality of the men who revel in the gore of a gutted shark, and the experience leaves him shaken and nauseated. His father disapproves, insisting that Colin is trying to embarrass him—and he nearly disowns the boy. Colin does not share his father's love of the sport, and the realization that they are so different leaves him feeling vulnerable.

A year later, Florence encouraged Ray to try one more time to invite Dean along. "I guess she thought it was a good thing that fathers and sons do something together," he muses, "so he took me fishing again. I didn't really want to go and it was the same story all over again, and that was the end of that."

Following this inability to engage his son in the one activity that he loved, Ray withdrew. Dean was not the son he wanted and he made little effort to be involved with Dean's life. If Dean was in a play at school, he ignored it, as he did with Dean's birthday. Even at Christmas, when the bars were closed, he usually just slept in, leaving Dean to open his gifts with his mother. When Ray did get up, he started drinking. "The worst thing I can remember about Christmas day," says Dean, "is that he'd make eggnog, and that was just a cover for all the whiskey he'd put in." As father and son, they just did not get along.

10

Yet there were normal aspects to Dean's childhood. The fifties image of the ideal family included a dog, so along came a black and white mongrel pup named Tiny. Dean loved this compan- ion, but as the dog grew increasingly less tiny, he became diffi- cult to control. He liked to dig, and he was energetic and untrained, so he had to be chained in the yard. One day as Dean played with him, Tiny exuberantly wrapped his chain around Dean's neck and trapped him on the ground. It nearly asphyxiated him. His mother rescued him just in time and insisted Tiny had to go. Dean was heartbroken.

A few years later, they tried a two-year-old terrier mix named Lucky, who had a nervous stomach and regurgitated at every opportunity. She eventually became ill, which meant vet bills that strained the family budget, so Florence had her put to sleep. There were no further experiments with having a family pet.

Another typical childhood experience was church. Florence took Dean to the Saint John's Reformed United Church of Christ on a regular basis, although Ray refused to accompany them. "I was impressed with the minister there," says Dean, "Reverend Harry Carolus. He initiated all kinds of programs for kids. So every Sunday I would get dressed up in my one set of good clothes and go to Sunday school and church." In junior high, Dean took a confirmation class and joined the Church, although his future interest in religion was to take a very different turn.

In Dean's 1974 novel, *After the Last Race*, one character, Annie, describes her home life in the way that Dean's might have been in the days of fifties ideologies: "I was raised in a home that was about as traditional, conservative, all-American, live-by-the-rules as you could find. I grew up thinking the world was fair, that God was good, and that you could always trust the government."[10] As a boy, Dean believed in the benevolence of authority and was raised to respect it.

This was the influence of his mother and those members of his extended family who compensated for Ray's poor fathering. Although some thought Dean would grow up to be just like his father, others nurtured him.

One of the most important figures of Dean's childhood was his uncle Ray Mock, who was married to his mother's sister Kate. At five-foot-seven, he was a stocky man with a pleasing round face, a brushcut, and a receding hairline. He had served in World War II, and when Dean was a boy, worked as a truck mechanic. Until Dean was thirteen, Uncle Ray and Aunt Kate lived two houses away and had a son, Jim, who was nearly four years older than Dean.

Looking back, Dean thought that Kate seemed to suffer from a bipolar disorder, which sometimes made things difficult. "Aunt Kate could be real sweet," he recalls, "and the next time you saw her, she was just like my grandmother, a real dragon lady. She was so erratic. I don't think my Uncle Ray had a whole lot of pleasure going home." When Aunt Kate was in her darker moods, Uncle Ray seemed like the classic hen-pecked husband. He hung his head and did what she asked.

As a result of their mutual misfortunes in marriage, Uncle Ray grew close to Dean's mother, and he treated Dean as his own son. "I think there was a thin line always being walked there," says Dean, "because Uncle Ray paid more attention to me than my father did."

Uncle Ray was fun-loving. For Dean's entertainment, he devised games, such as sneaky ways to get a beer when Kate was not looking. Once when all the relatives came together for the annual fair, they decided to have a seance. Uncle Ray put a shuffleboard puck on his knee under the table to provide the spooky knocking sound that everyone expected. Dean loved these pranks.

"Ray Mock was the kind of person who drew everyone," says Nancy Eckard, who became his daughter-in-law. "He did things for Dean that Dean would have wanted from his father. Ray loved kids. He had a following. He handed out candy to every kid in the neighborhood."

Uncle Ray provided for Dean the kinds of adventures fathers give to their sons, especially as his own son Jim became a teenager. One thing he liked to do was brew peach brandy. Late in the summer, he would pick Dean up and take him around to neighbors to collect discarded peach peelings. "He knew everybody who had peach trees and who canned them or made peach jelly," says Dean, "and he'd arrange to get all their peelings. Then we'd take them back and put them in these big drums and add some yeast and sugar and put the lid on. We'd be in this oddly lighted basement, brewing this stuff together, and there was a hushed quality about it, because Kate really wouldn't want him to make it. It had this sort of mystical aura. But when the fermentation process started, you had to be careful because the brew could build so much pressure that the cap exploded off the drum. I can remember comic moments when I'd be going down into the cellar and I'd hear this *BOOM* and I'd see peach peelings all over the ceiling. It was great fun.

"I think in some ways, Uncle Ray knew that I had no father and he tried to make sure there was a male in the family with whom I could do a little bonding; I wouldn't have thought of it in those terms, but if I was around and he had an errand, he'd come by and see if I'd want to go with him. I always would. We'd talk for hours about stuff that was going on. Sometimes he'd stop at this one bar and have a draft and I'd get a Coke. It always made me feel like I was grown up, and no matter where we went, everybody liked to see him."

Ray Mock proved to be a positive figure in Dean's life. "I think he had an impact on me. I'm sentimental and so was he. We both cry easily. I'd like to think there's a good deal of him in me." Dean later dedicated his 1997 novel, *Sole Survivor*, to this man. To some degree, Uncle Ray also influenced the character of Joe Carpenter's father in that novel and of Marty Stillwater in *Mr. Murder*. "When I have a male character who is good-hearted and good with kids, I would say there are elements of my Uncle Ray in him," Dean affirms. "Marty Stillwater is probably the ultimate example of a male character who is tough in everything but when it really comes down to it, he's soft-hearted, and that aspect is definitely from my Uncle Ray. He was a funny guy, absolutely one of the most sweet-tempered people you'd ever meet in your life."

Nancy Eckard adds a significant observation: "Flo and Ray were so much alike in the way they treated people, in their kindness, their humor, and their upbeat personalities. My husband Jim made the comment more than once that his dad should have married Aunt Dodie."

11

Dean also spent a lot of time with his mother, talking and playing card games. When they could afford a television set, they watched that together. Before Dean's grandfather died, the three of them often sat on rocking chairs on the porch, just passing the time in lazy conversation. Or Florence would take Dean over to Ginny's or Kate's. "I spent a lot of time sitting in the kitchen, the only kid present, listening to adults talk. I used to love that. It could be why I like writing dialogue."

His mother also took him visiting. When she could get the car for a Sunday outing, they might drive all the way to Pittsburgh to visit Uncle George, or to Lancaster to see Aunt Betty's family. Eventually Florence got a cheap used car of her own, and these trips increased in frequency. Her old Studebaker wheezed and rattled but never broke down. About once a month when the weather was good, they would get in and drive.

Dean loved his mother's company. "I can remember being in that car when I was seven or eight. When we were on the road, there was no danger that my father would show up. We were free. Maybe this is where my love of the highway comes from. I can get in the car and drive for eight, ten, twelve hours, and love every minute of it. I just love being on the road and seeing new places."

Without realizing the connection, Dean included this feeling of safety as part of Chyna Shepherd's character in his 1996 novel, *Intensity*. "Chyna says the only peace she had was on the road, going to and from somewhere," Dean notes. "As long as I was in the car, there was no chance of my father being around and we were safe."

One of Dean's favorite places to go was Jerome, where his parents once had lived. It was an hour or so west of Bedford. His mother had friends there named Helen and Steve Harmon. Steve had been a coal miner, but as a young man had come down with rheumatoid arthritis that crippled him. Yet he did not let his handicap depress him. Dean found him delightful to be around, and he and his wife and two daughters seemed straight out of those fifties television shows that featured perfect families. Although Ray claimed that Steve Harmon was actually *his* best friend, Florence could rarely get him to give up fishing to join them for a visit. He went once or twice and never went back. Dean did not mind; he liked having Stevie's full attention.

"When I first knew Stevie," he recalls, "he hobbled with a cane, but you never heard him complain, never a peep, although he must have been in terrible pain most of the time. He was a very gentle person, always in good humor, despite suffering. He was a very appealing person in his basic manners, the kind of person you like as a kid. In a strange way, he always reminded me of Uncle Ray. They were both gentle and both had a good sense of humor. They never strained to be liked—but everyone *did* like them. They had a good handle on life and had a fairly humble sense of themselves. They actually had a little bit of a physical resemblance, too." Stevie, as much as Uncle Ray, influenced the way Dean developed the character of Joe Carpenter's good-natured, long-suffering father in *Sole Survivor*.

"I was so impressed with Stevie. In later years, he wore leg braces and had a torturous time getting around, but he just would not give up." Dean watched this heroic response to a difficult situation and wondered how he himself would act in such circumstances. It inspired him that Stevie and his wife remained cheerful and warm. "They were very solid people, and for me to see him always keep his good humor and never get angry or blame anybody for it—in that sense, he was a model for me, a model of a survivor. Of not letting life get you down no matter what happens. That's a gift to everyone around you. I think probably there's a lot of Stevie in Regina in *Hideaway*. Regina has this leg brace and a deformed leg and hand, but she's a totally positive person. She was a character I just adored writing about. She has Stevie's indomitable spirit and his good heart. She has her conversations with God all the time, and it would never occur to her to move away from faith just because she's got these afflictions."

Some of Stevie also went into the character of Joel Tuck in *Twilight Eyes*. Despite Tuck's alarming physical handicaps, he retains a sense of dignity and compassion that defies expectation.

Florence Koontz, Stevie Harmon, and Ray Mock together had a decidedly significant influence on Dean. In them, he saw people who did not feel victimized just because things were not going well. Life went on and one made the best of it. Love and caring went a long way toward making difficult situations tolerable. Being close to his mother and to the people she befriended provided Dean with important resources for defying the prophecy of those who believed that he would grow up to be just like his father. From people who modeled a positive outlook, he absorbed the attitudes he would need to make his own way. Even as a young boy, he was developing a strength of character that would stand him in good stead.

[1]Ned Frear, *Bedford County: A Brief History* (Bedford, PA: Frear Publications, 1985).

[2]According to Ned Frear, publisher of the *Bedford Gazette*.

[3]Martin Greenberg, Ed Gorman, and Bill Munster, *The Dean Koontz Companion* (New York: Berkley, 1994), p. 21.

[4]Gianni Rodari, *The Grammar of Fantasy*, translated by Jack Zipes (New York: Teachers and Writers Collaborative, 1973), 1996.

[5]Dean Koontz, *Strange Highways*, in *Strange Highways* (New York: Warner Books, 1995), p. 5.

[6]Dean Koontz writing as Deanna Dwyer, *Legacy of Terror* (New York: Lancer, 1972), p. 88.

[7]Dean Koontz, "Beautiful Death" in *Beautiful Death*, edited by David Robinson (New York: Penguin Studio, 1996).

[8]Ibid.

[9]Dean R. Koontz, *Phantoms* (New York: G.P. Putnam's Sons, Berkley edition, 1983), pp. 60–61.

[10]Dean R. Koontz, *After the Last Race* (New York: Atheneum, 1974), p. 42.

TWO

New Discoveries

1

IT WAS THE AGE OF ABUNDANCE; IT WAS THE AGE OF INFECTION.
Thirteen million homes were built across the country and personal income rose, but a polio epidemic, the fear of radioactive
fallout, and a rash of films about space aliens all attested to a
broad cultural anxiety. Despite national optimism, people
feared invasion. The peace following World War II seemed
fragile. Germany was finished, but a new enemy loomed:
Soviet Russia. Their aggression in Eastern Europe raised suspicions about designs on America and the Cold War began.

A rising birthrate and an emphasis on family fostered blind
patriotism. The images of what a true American family should
be were channeled into every home that could afford a television. Kids saw other kids who behaved themselves (Timmy on
Lassie) or got into a manageable amount of trouble (Beaver on
Leave it to Beaver). From *Dick and Jane* reading primers, boys
had a clear idea of how to be responsible young men, and girls
understood their future domestic goals. In such families, no
need went unmet, no problem unresolved, and togetherness
was unrelenting. Minorities and others different from the
norm were ignored.

Early in this decade, the ideal of a fulfilled mother guiding
the nuclear family reached its zenith. The fifties "baby boom"
seemed a guarantee against recession, and people were urged
to keep it up. Even small towns like Bedford had to find ways
to fund education for the increasing population.

There was no kindergarten in Bedford, so Dean started
school in the first grade. He took a bus to North Bedford Elementary, a typical fifties style, single-level brick building situated on a main road that ran between the heart of town and
turnpike operations two miles away. Dot Duncan, who works
at the *Bedford Gazette*, was in his class and remembers that in

grade school Dean wanted to be a monster on the playground: "Just any kind of monster. He was always into monsters." Dean, who was shy at that age, does not remember having this preoccupation.

His first grade teacher, Vera (Houck) Blackburn, recalls that he was well behaved and a good student. "He was quiet and shy," she states. "I think he had a rough life. I don't remember him being creative, but he was young." Ms. Blackburn apparently made a strong impression on Dean, for in 1989, he autographed a book for her with an inscription that said, "I was always in love with my first grade teacher."

Eventually he learned to read. "There were no books around the house," Dean remembers, "but some kids in the neighborhood had comic books. That's the first thing I could really remember reading. It wasn't until I was around nine or ten that I realized there was a library where I could take books out."

Having already met characters like Bugs Bunny and Donald Duck, he eventually discovered comic renditions of the classics, such as Jack London's *Call of the Wild* and Robert Louis Stevenson's *Treasure Island*. He also read about superheroes.

One of the earliest books Dean read was *The Wind in the Willows*. "That book had the most influence on me and I still read it every three or four years," he says. All of the characters in the story are animals: Mole, Ratty, Toad, and Mr. Badger. Although each has his own habits and customs, they tolerate one another's differences and celebrate a devoted friendship that transcends dissimilarities. The aura of the story is one of adventure, discovery, security, and guardianship. Much of it happens in the warmth of a cozy hearth. Dean had no friends his age, little sense of protection, and an imagination that resonated to a good story, so the community of friends presented in these pages held a charismatic allure.

"I loved the humor and the sense of camaraderie among all these animals," he explains. "It was this fully realized separate world, I think, that so completely appealed to me, as well as the sense of community spirit."

Years later in *Dragonfly*, Dean's 1975 novel of international intrigue, this children's story was the sourcebook for codes that

were passed from "The Committee" to a triggerman whose task
it was to wipe out millions of people in communist China.

2

Despite the apparent sense of calm, there was an undercurrent
of fear among adults that affected children at a subtle level. At
the close of World War II, the United States kept a monopoly
on nuclear weapons for only four years. In 1949, Russia
exploded their own A-bomb, which sent American scientists
scurrying to perfect the more powerful hydrogen bomb. The
government feared that the Soviets intended to take over the
world, so as the Defense Department devised sophisticated
military operations, the CIA began covert activities to control
Third World countries. At the same time, Senator McCarthy
and his sensation-hungry entourage led a national witch-hunt
for suspected communists. These Cold War tactics would
influence many writers in later years, Dean among them.
Much of his suspicion of government officials would derive
from covert activities that would explode into the open in
decades to come.

Everyone feared a first nuclear strike, and talk of World
War III, particularly in the wake of the Korean takeover by
communist forces, made human annihilation seem imminent.
Teachers drilled schoolchildren in what to do in the event of a
nuclear attack, while radio and television stations played frequent warnings with a high-pitched tone, explaining, "This has
been a test. In the event of a real emergency . . ."

Dean remembers the tension. As a child just going to
school, he feared that the Russians would surely target his
hometown for a nuclear blast. He thought he might escape by
hiding in the coal bin in the basement of his ramshackle house.

"I can remember the drills about what to do," he says.
"We'd all move out in the hall and sit with our backs against
the wall and our heads cradled. I had lots of dreams about
nuclear war. Of course, when you're a kid, it's this two-edged
thing: It's terrifying and it's kind of interesting. The destruction of the world! So I had dreams where the Russians would
attack and that we'd have to run away and live in caves in the

mountains above the fairgrounds. Actually it was pretty ridiculous to be worried that we would sustain a direct nuclear hit, but I was much older before I realized that there were not a lot of wicked Soviet generals saying, 'Yeah, we gotta take out that malt shop in Bedford.'"

Simultaneous with the fear of foreign attack was a growing public awareness of the possibility of extraterrestrials approaching Earth. In the summer of 1947, when Dean was two, Kenneth Arnold, a forest service employee, had reported nine flying objects traveling at a fantastic speed near Mount Rainier. During the same period, many Scandinavians claimed to witness cigar-shaped flying objects. More reports turned up, including the rumor of a UFO crash near the Roswell air force base in New Mexico. The air force adopted an official stand that "flying saucers" were not real, drawing charges of conspiracy and cover-up. By the early fifties, people reported being contacted and even abducted by short, human-like creatures that emerged from alien aircraft.

In 1952, reporters revealed that the air force had placed its pilots on alert to shoot down any "flying saucers" that refused to land. Only three months before, *Life* magazine had featured accounts of UFOs that defied explanation. By November, cult leader George Adamski claimed to have met a Nordic-looking "human being" from Venus who revealed that many Venusians lived on Earth in disguise. His books became bestsellers.

Novelists and screenwriters were clearly influenced. Science fiction movies reeled forth, one after another, on the dangers of postwar disasters, from giant monsters produced by nuclear fallout to aliens in disguise who meant us only harm. Such films as *Invasion of the Body Snatchers* and *Invaders from Mars* captured the pervasive suspicion that even the people closest to you could harm you: The source of your demise was within arm's length, and possibly already within you.

Dean knew this feeling intimately. As he watched these films, he sometimes wondered how real they might be. In *Invaders from Mars*, starring William Menzies and Helena Carter, a young boy Dean's age witnesses a flying saucer landing in his backyard and disappearing into the sand. His father investigates, and returns staring vacantly and acting strangely. The boy knows that something has happened to his father, but since the man looks the same as he always did on the outside, no one believes the boy's story. That makes them all vulnerable to invasion. It turns out that the aliens are taking people on board their ship and surgically altering them, with no one the wiser.

"That one was scary," Dean says. "You think, oh my God, my parents could be aliens." The movie resonated with him because of the alien-like behavior of his father.

Some characters in Dean's future novels would experience this same unsettling fear. Fourteen-year-old Colin Jacobs, in *The Voice of the Night*, spots the monstrous potential in the mother of his demented friend, Roy. It was Mrs. Borden's abominable treatment of her son, Colin believes, that turned Roy into a killer. "[Colin] thought she was far more terrifying than any of the monsters he'd feared through his childhood . . . doubly dangerous because she was so well disguised."[1]

Dean was an avid fan of these films. Whenever he heard that a new one was coming to the town's only theater, he would dig into his meager savings to see it. "I always had an affinity for science fiction and horror movies. Radiation accident movies like *Them* were big then. Almost anything in that genre, I had to see."

Dean was one of many young people to cut his teeth on the images of the Japanese monsters Gorgo and Godzilla, huge irradiated ants in desert caves near bomb testing sites, and malformed alien invaders. The impression for kids everywhere was that adults felt impotent to protect them, and that their world was largely vulnerable. Numerous images converged to become part of their shared cultural heritage.

Dean also loved horror. Monster films from the thirties such as *Dracula* and *Frankenstein* were still going strong, scaring kids of all ages. Dean was particularly affected by Boris Karloff's Frankenstein monster, and he had recurring nightmares about being pursued by this ungainly, manmade image of uncontrolled chaos:

"Until after the first couple of years I was married, I had a dream about being pursued by that Karloffian figure. In the dream, I would be in bed sleeping and I'd wake up just as someone was trying to open the door. Then the Frankenstein monster would burst into the room. There were no exits, and

I'd try to keep furniture between him and me. By the time I was an adult, I realized that this dream was about my father."[2]

Most of the time, however, Dean's room was a sanctuary, "the eye of the hurricane, where the storm could not touch him, where it could even be forgotten for a while."[3] While his parents argued downstairs, his room healed him and "made him feel that in some mystical way, he was part of something far, far more important and *better* than everyday life."[4] It was a refuge and a stage—a laboratory where he could act out his fantasies. He did not have the monster models that he later describes some of his boy characters having, but he had comic books and the science fiction and horror novels that characters like Colin Jacobs and Joey Harper read. Since his parents disapproved, he often read with a flashlight under the covers. Whenever the world seemed harsh, Dean retreated here to escape to other worlds, where boys could be heroes, and all heroes were cunning, strong, and confident. Perversely, even monsters were survivors, and sometimes even transcendent.

3

When Dean was around eight, he began to write his own stories. Bored with the simplistic books that taught him to "look and see," he filled tablets of paper with exotic tales influenced by watching television and reading comics. He remembers that they had robots and monsters in them, like the stories that young Joey writes in *The Funhouse*. He also illustrated them with cartoonish drawings. Then he put the pages together with staples and black electrician's tape, and peddled them to relatives for a nickel or dime. His mother bought a few, as did his aunts and his Uncle Ray.

At first they thought his entrepreneurial spirit was cute. Then he produced more books and became persistent. People who once had donated to the cause were now annoyed, so Dean's mother put a stop to it.

"One day I was told in no uncertain terms," says Dean, "that I wasn't to try to sell these to relatives and neighbors anymore."

When he was around eleven, he entered a contest

sponsored by one of the Sunday supplements in the Johnstown *Tribune-Democrat*. He wrote an essay on "What it Means
to Be an American," and won a twenty-five dollar gift certificate and a wristwatch. "In no time at all, the watch just
exploded off my wrist," Dean recalls. "It blew to pieces." The
gift certificate, however, was welcome to a boy with only a
sporadic income from birthday money or the occasional
allowance.

One person who recalls his creative talent is Helen (Morgart) Carberry, his fourth grade teacher. There were about
forty-five students in Dean's class, but she claims to remember
them all. "Dean sat in the first row, the last seat," she said. "He
was a very intelligent child. He studied and worked hard for
the grades he got and he was one of the top five in my class.
We stressed English and writing, and he loved to write." Since
she required that her students present something in front of
the class, Dean learned early what it was like to have an audience. Although he does not remember being this bold, his
teacher insists that while other students sang songs or showed
their classmates some interesting item, Dean preferred to read
something he had written. "His stories were quite good and
the other children liked to listen to him," said Ms. Carberry. "I
remember one of the stories was about a black cat with green
eyes. It was quite long and had an intricate plot and a surprise
ending."

4

It was around age ten that Dean discovered the library. He
was soon reading as much science fiction as he could find, just
as Colin Jacobs in *The Voice of the Night* could hardly wait for
the next book by one of his favorite authors. "I found all this
great stuff as a teenager," says Dean, "and I read it all the way
through college. I don't think I read much else." He also collected *Famous Monsters of Filmland* magazines, the first issue of
which hit the stands in February 1958, when Dean was
twelve.

He started with the various juvenile series. Aimed at
teenage boys, there were dozens of series that featured inter-

planetary exploration, time travel, and far-future scenarios. Heroes were always male, and sometimes were brainy boys who could use their wits to expedite the action. Often they were alienated from their peers or had dormant powers that set them apart. There was great emphasis on stories that involved psionic powers such as ESP, an emphasis which remained constant through the sixties.

Robert Heinlein's juveniles were quite successful. He was one of the authors who helped to shape the "Golden Age" of science fiction with his folksy and inventive yarns about solipsism, time paradoxes, and alien life forms. His heroes were competent men of intellect and action. Like many science fiction books at the time, the greatest value was placed on problem-solving aptitude, a facet of this genre that became part of Dean's evolving world view. No matter what type of story he would write in the future, he honored rational ways to solve dilemmas and triumph over evil.

"Heinlein may be the writer that I can remember most clearly as a kid," says Dean. "I was in high school before I discovered that he had written adult books. That was a function of living in a town with no bookstore. The only books were on a paperback rack in Turner News."

Throughout his adolescence, he also read Ray Bradbury and Theodore Sturgeon, both of whom had a strong influence on his imagination. Bradbury's work was inspired by the films of traveling-show veteran Tod Browning, and he made dark carnival images central to his work, with references to freaks, shapeless things in bottles, and black Ferris wheels. One of Bradbury's most famous books, *Something Wicked This Way Comes*, features a strange carnival called Cooger and Dark's Pandemonium Shadow Show that rolls into a small town. Two boys, Jim and Will, become aware of its hidden evils, so Mr. Dark entices the more vulnerable Jim into participating. Only Will's commitment to him saves him. "I identified with Bradbury's book," says Dean. "Those two boys would go out on their porch roofs and talk. They were always getting out of the house in ways their parents didn't know, and I identified with that. There's a certain magical feeling about getting in and out without your parents knowing."

Sturgeon was the pen name of Edward Hamilton Waldo.

He, too, was a central figure in the Golden Age of science fiction and he was sympathetic toward tortured adolescents. He often wrote about children with paranormal powers who struggled against repressive orders, met others like themselves, and formed the foundation of a new world.

One of his novels, *The Dreaming Jewels*, became a favorite for Dean. It is about a boy who escapes his adoptive family and joins the carnival to feel safe among the freaks. One of the carnies is the Maneater, who controls jewels that can be used for either harm or good. The boy, who discovers he was made by the jewels, defeats the evil.

Another novel, *Some of Your Blood*, gave Dean a firsthand look at a sociopathic mind. It was an epistolary novel about a blood-drinking borderline psychotic who, Dean felt, bore startling similarities to his father. His mother had never said that his father was different or dangerous, yet here was an author that he loved telling him otherwise. He began to think about his father in a new light. "It was the first time I had realized there was something wrong with him. It was a great revelation to me."

5

The town of Bedford was based on Midwestern values, infused with a rising drive toward material status. People tried to live as well as they could, and they desired an orderly, well-kept community. "Teachers and doctors were respected," says Tom Doyle, who taught high school history in Bedford. "Churches were filled and children behaved respectfully. The town was always clean."

Dean was painfully aware that he was not part of any "in group." He lived on the edge of town rather than up on Juliana Heights, where pristine homes with well-kept lawns defined an elite merchant community. Sometimes he walked up this hill to look out at the town, but knew he was not part of the Bedford gentility. "Bedford was the kind of town that made someone like me feel like an outsider," he says. "I didn't have what most of the people who lived there had."

As a smallish kid who did not quite fit in, he became a

prime target for practical jokes, and one of these resulted in Dean's first taste of fame. "I was out playing at night in the big field behind the house," he recalls, "and I was grabbed and terrorized by someone making monster noises. I turned around and got pushed down this hill, and right at the bottom, this thing was on fire in a hole in the ground." According to a published report in the *Bedford Gazette*, Dean "narrowly missed getting hit by a small meteorite near his home." A picture features him showing the rock, "three times the size of an egg," to a friend. Dean claimed that he carried it around in his pocket so he would not lose it, although "he has been asked to part with it long enough for scientists at Penn State to subject it to spectroscopic analysis." Dean then went around telling everyone about this amazing event, and some townspeople recall that he showed them the hole where it purportedly had landed.

Dean does not remember these scientists or what, if anything, they discovered. By the time all the interest died down, he was convinced that perhaps it had not been a meteorite after all. "I think my cousin Jim played a joke on me," he admits. "He liked to tease me, but I took it all very seriously as a kid."

He also became a target for bullies. "There were certain kids who mocked you if you were not among their group. When I was in seventh and eighth grades, I was terrorized by a couple of bullies on the school bus. At first I resolved the problem by walking home every evening. I handled it by avoidance until I was old enough to realize that even if they were bigger than I was, being willing to strike back could put an end to it pretty quickly. I think most kids arrive at that moment of revelation, where they say, 'To hell with this. I may get beaten up but I'm going to hurt somebody back in the process.' Bullies hate that and they'll beat you twice as hard, but they'll be more reluctant to come at you the next time."

His change in perspective carried through years later into his work. Characters in his novels learn this same lesson, most notably Colin Jacobs in *The Voice of the Night*. When his friend Roy, who is physically stronger, turns on him, he initially runs, but then fights back. He convinces Roy to come to an abandoned house and tricks him into confessing his deadly intentions. Then, with all the courage he can muster, Colin pulls a gun and stands up to Roy, who cowers in fear.

In *Shadowfires*, Dean offers the same wisdom. A man faced with following orders, or standing up against a sadistic superior, realizes the bully is the real coward. "He might shoot you in the back or sneak up on you and slit your throat . . . but in a face-to-face confrontation, he would chicken out if the stakes got high enough."[5]

6

For much of Dean's childhood, his father changed from one job to another, never staying with anything more than a few months. As Dean looks back, he estimates that Ray held some forty jobs in the space of thirty-four years, and that for part of that time, he was unemployed. When Dean was about eight or nine, Ray started to sell premiums for Washington National Insurance and managed to keep this job for a couple of years. "It was the longest job he ever held," says Dean. Even so, Ray still had troubles. He continued to get into fights, and nearly had a run-in with the law.

"There was scuttlebutt," reports Dean's cousin Jane, "that Ray spent the insurance premiums on himself."

"I'd never heard that," says Dean, "but there was a situation where he punched someone at the company. The nature of that was always very mysterious, but thinking back, I remember that there was some fear he might go to jail. It could well have been over the premiums. Washington National didn't push the issue, so he didn't go to jail, and there was great relief at home."

Despite Ray's temper, he could be quite engaging. "I always thought he was easygoing," says Jane. "If he and Aunt Dodie got into an argument, he'd smile and say, 'Now Molly.' I never saw him the way Dean describes him, but in those days you didn't show your problems to kids. He could have put on one face for the public and another at home."

"Sometimes I can't begin to understand how people couldn't see through him," Dean now remarks. "My father, like a lot of sociopathic people, could be enormously charming, but I could see through every lie and nonsense story. He seemed almost childishly transparent. I could see his motivation and how he was trying to manipulate me, but it was clear that a lot of people couldn't. There are people who take some-one at face value and seem unable to see the kind of deception that my father could project."

Despite the times of fear and uncertainty, Dean experi-enced the atmosphere of an enthusiastically creative mind. His father fancied himself an inventor and an entrepreneur. It mat-tered little if one invention failed to pay off. There would always be another idea. He managed to persuade people time and again to back him. Unfortunately for Dean and his mother, Ray's repeated failures were often at their expense. For example, when Dean was ten, Ray invented a camping stove—an idea before its time. He worked on it sporadically for almost a decade.

"He created it from sheets of aluminum that collapsed and went into a little plastic pack," Dean recalls. "It was about a foot square. It was a clever device but impractical. You could stick it in your backpack and take a pack of charcoal to toast frankfurters, but to use it more than once, you had to carry a lot of charcoal. The beauty was that it was small and easy to carry, but that also meant you couldn't do much with it."

There seemed no end to Ray's inventions. "The ideas came," Dean explains, "he proceeded with them, and then they receded. He would get financial backers and the thing would collapse, so he'd forget about it for a few years, but then he'd return to it. He'd never let go. There was this novelty thing he invented that he would drag out periodically when I was a kid. It was a plastic dog with a little dog dish, and you pressed its snout into a waxy substance in the dish. The dog had coiled springs in its legs, and by forcing the head down, you created this kinetic energy. As soon as the snout broke loose from the stuff in the dish, the dog would do a total three hundred sixty degree flip and land on its feet." Ray believed he could per-suade companies or tourist places like Atlantic City to buy this invention and imprint it with their logos. He was sure he could sell millions. He had a plastic model made and managed to produce a few to sell, but no one had the vision to take it fur-ther.

Another scheme that Ray devised required Dean's assis-tance. "He got this steam-cleaning thing," says Dean. "He could use it to clean anything made of metal, but he used it mostly for car and truck engines. It was like a rolling boiler. I worked on this one summer with him and this boiler would always be over-pressurizing and the pressure-release valve wouldn't always kick off quite right. It would start screaming and I'd have to run and turn it off. I was always sure the thing was going to blow up before I could get to it and that I would be killed by all the flying shrapnel. It did blow up at the end of the summer and that was the end of that. Fortunately it didn't kill anyone."

7

Since the fairgrounds were across the street from Dean's house, he could look out to that expanse of land and watch the weedy lot each August blossom into an extravaganza of amusement rides, stock car races, games, and food joints. At night, fireworks lit up the entire sky in a spectacle of color.

As the carnival trucks rolled in, Dean eagerly watched the preparations and dreamed about becoming part of the crew. The carnies unloaded tents, booths, and colorful metal frames for rides like the merry-go-round and Ferris wheel. As they started up their motors to test the rides, the smell of grease wafted through the summer air. Dean longed to go down and mingle with them, to listen to their slang, and merge into a community that seemed exotic and romantic. These people were footloose and free; they could go wherever they wanted.

Once the show was up and rolling, Dean found ways to get in. "I couldn't afford to pay," he says, "but the fairgrounds were surrounded by forest and it was easy to sneak through the fence. If you got caught, all they did was take you to the entrance and throw you out."

The carnival was set up like a street fair, with games, "grab joints," and arcades toward the front, while the "Back End" consisted mostly of rides and shows. Sometimes concessions would be placed down the middle, with rides to the sides.

Each day that the carnival was in town, Dean walked the Midway. He might look at farm animals and crafts, but his favorite place was among all the lights. As he listened to the calliope and smelled cotton candy, popcorn, and corn dogs, he wandered from one game of chance to another to watch the barkers hawk their wares. This one had darts and that one invited him to spin a wheel. Over there was a Haunted House and here were games of manly skill, such as the High Striker. The surging press of people filled the air with excitement, and Dean heard the unrestrained yelling and shrieking from rides like the Tilt-A-Whirl. He always saved money to go on these rides, but for him, that was only part of the spectacle: "A carnival isn't just about the rides," he insists. "You could walk around for hours and spend only fifty cents. Just walking the Midway, looking at all this amazing exotic stuff—that was the carnival!"

While he was young, these carnivals were relatively small. The Dell and Travers Shows ran, according to their slogan, "The finest Midway for family entertainment." Then came the James E. Strates Traveling Show, one of the largest in the country. They owned their own train and brought exotic sideshows to give people a glimpse of things rarely seen.

Dean's favorite sideshow was the Ten-in-One, the collection of human oddities, such as the Fat Man or Fat Lady, the Alligator Man, and the Bearded Lady. One of his more memorable characters, Joel Tuck in *Twilight Eyes*, is a man with a third eye whose personality was inspired by a real three-eyed man that Dean actually saw. He felt a strange kinship with these people who did not belong to "normal America." For years afterward, he would think of this association whenever he felt like an outsider. Dean was not so much repulsed as drawn to them and he tried to imagine what they must be feeling. He later wrote about people considered by the average gawker as not quite human, and many of his science fiction stories feature "muties"—deformed, shunned beings. The settings for both *The Funhouse* and *Twilight Eyes* came directly from these childhood experiences.

8

As Dean read stories of the fantastic, he came across allegedly true tales of strange phenomena. Around the age of twelve, he became engrossed with legends of bizarre disappearances around the world.

"I've always been interested in that kind of stuff," he admits. "There were books on it that purported to be real. Probably some stories were real and some were made up, but to me as a kid, they were all real and they were terrific. So I got fascinated with people just suddenly disappearing."

His favorite books of this type, such as *Stranger than Science*, were written by Frank Edwards. What Dean learned would later influence his 1983 novel, *Phantoms*. He was amazed to read about the missing colony of early settlers at Roanoke, Virginia, and the 1939 disappearance of thousands of Chinese soldiers. He thrilled to the stories of airplanes that vanished from radar, with no evidence of a crash and no word ever heard again from passengers or crew. On the Great Lakes, not far away, numerous ships had disappeared—sometimes allegedly before the eyes of startled witnesses—and then reappeared years later, or were never heard from again. He was especially enthralled with the accounts of the *Mary Celeste* and her mysteriously missing crew. Even better, whole civilizations, like the Maya and the Anasazi, seemed to have been whisked off the face of the earth. The possibility of the existence of other dimensions was exciting to a boy who dreamed of somehow escaping his own situation.

"I'm sure that was probably why I liked those stories," he admits. "I might have thought, 'Gee, maybe aliens will come and take me up. I'll be on another world where everything is nice.'"

As he read, he created scenarios that offered him a sense of control over the chaos in which he lived. The fantasies and "true" stories of other dimensions provided more than mere entertainment. They fueled his imagination with possibility. He did not have to be limited to what his five senses told him. He did not have to live only in Bedford. He could travel to any world that he devised and populate it in any manner he chose. These stories helped him transcend loneliness and feel happy, safe, and inventive.

9

Throughout his youth and into high school, Dean had little to do with his father. Often Ray was just not around or not sober, but when he was, Dean tried to avoid him. For a while, he had his Uncle Ray nearby. Since Ray was a hunter, Dean was often cajoled into helping to dress deer carcasses—an activity he would gladly have skipped. "As a bonding experience, skiing weekends and camping trips . . . pale compared to standing in a drafty basement in your skivvies with your uncle and your cousin, everyone spattered with blood and bits of deer fat . . ."[6]

One Thanksgiving when Dean was around eleven, Ray decided to show him how to kill a turkey. "That was the first time I discovered that when a turkey's head is chopped off, the turkey still runs around," Dean states. "It's gross and horrifying beyond belief. Uncle Ray held it down and chopped its head off, and the thing just suddenly kicked and leaped up and went dashing around in circles before it flopped over. This is pretty horrifying stuff when you're eleven, but at the same time, it struck me as hilarious. He'd push the bird into a drum of boiling water to saturate the feathers, and it was my job to pluck them. Given how squeamish I was about things, it amazed me that I would do this, but Uncle Ray was so funny. It was like a Laurel and Hardy movie. He'd lose control of the bird and he'd chase it all over the place and fall over things. Whether he just did that to make me laugh, I don't know."

Although Dean did not like the idea of hunting any better than fishing, he once went with Uncle Ray and his cousin Jim during small game season. "I had an air gun," Dean recalls, "and you could possibly get a squirrel or a rabbit with it, but I was not a real hunter. I didn't hit anything and they started joking that I was purposely missing animals."

Dean liked to fantasize that Uncle Ray Mock was really his father. He thought he looked a lot like his cousin, Jim, and he was certain Uncle Ray's attention to him was special. He imagined Uncle Ray and his mother together rather than married to their respective spouses. One day, he overheard a conversation that made him wonder.

Uncle Ray had come in to talk about some distressing thing that Kate had done. Florence sent Dean on an errand, but he lingered. Uncle Ray was in such an agitated state, it had to be something important. Then he heard Uncle Ray ask his mother, "How did it happen, Molly? How did we both marry the wrong person?"

Florence hushed him. "Don't talk about that," she insisted. "It's too late now. It's been too late for a long time."

"But it should have been me and you."

Florence laughed a little bitterly. "Don't talk that way," she urged him. "Someone might hear. Anyway, it just makes everything worse."

Dean withdrew, feeling stunned. What did it mean? He was never to know, but many years later, it made him speculate about the possibilities.

The Christmas that Dean was twelve, Uncle Ray gave him a special gift. Since Dean's father had a habit of sleeping in on Christmas morning, the family had shifted its gift-opening ritual to Christmas Eve so everyone could share in it together. "I remember that my Uncle Ray was so excited this Christmas Eve," Dean says, "and when I opened his gift to me, I was floored. It was a new bike, my very first bike. When he saw my delight, he cried. It was the nicest gift I got that year—that *decade*. I was aware then that there was some tension that night because my father was insanely jealous. It was obviously an extravagant gift."

Dean kept the maroon bike all through high school, and it allowed him a greater sense of freedom and escape. "That bike was my best friend."

It also allowed him to see his Uncle Ray when Ray and Kate eventually moved across town. "They lived close until I was about thirteen, and then they built this house that was far enough away that I couldn't go over there easily."

Much as he missed his uncle, he was glad to have some respite from Aunt Kate. "On my mother's side, there was endless bickering among brothers and sisters," he explains. "Often it was about my grandmother, who engineered these kinds of things. She thrived on setting people against each other, and when I was a kid, there was a lot of that in the family. My Aunt Kate had her good side, but she did not feel content if everybody else was content, so she would cause bickering."

For a long time, Dean's Aunt Virginia was Kate's target, and she pulled Dean into it: "When my Grandmother Logue needed to live with someone, she first moved in with my Aunt Betty, but after a few years, this caused tremendous strain on Betty's marriage. Then Aunt Ginny and Uncle Henry took her in, but they were young and liked to go out. Aunt Kate would get furious that they weren't staying home, so she would sit in her car and watch their house. Once in a while, she picked me up to keep her company. We'd sit outside their house, up the street, and watch to see where they went, and then follow them. Aunt Kate would keep this little record so she could prove they weren't treating Grandmother Logue properly. It was pretty bizarre."

What Dean did not realize was how closely his Aunt Kate watched him. "Kate cared a lot about Dean," says Nancy Eckard, who married Dean's cousin Jim and who was privy to Kate's confidences. "She watched her sister [Florence] lose so many babies. Kate was funny about showing her feelings and she came across as being pushy. She was a hard person to deal with, but when Flo was worried about Dean, Kate was worried right along with her."

10

Dean's family rarely went on vacations, but when Ray won his settlement from the accident with the truck, he decided to use money left over from installing their first bathroom to go on a fishing trip to Florida. That had always been his dream. They already knew someone there, Florence's stepsister Thelma, so they made plans. Aunt Kate protested that it was too far and would cost too much, but Ray had made up his mind.

He drove all the way without stopping overnight, since a motel would diminish the funds. "We left at four in the morning and drove for however long it took to drive over fifteen hundred miles," says Dean. "The idea was that if you had to pay for a hotel coming and going, you couldn't spend much time there." They arrived at the Matecumbe Key, south of Key Largo, checking in to an isolated motel. Each day, Ray went behind the motel to fish on the beach, while Dean and his mother swam in the ocean. On the third day there, Dean saw a stingray swim past him and up the beach, where it stung a man standing in the water. He had to be taken to the hospital. "Seeing that," says Dean, "I didn't go back in the water."

During the week, a dog at the motel bit Dean. Florence applied first aid and took him to the nearest doctor, who dressed the wound. Florence watched her son carefully over the last few days there and during the long trip back, but by the time they reached home, he was running a high fever and was delirious. Afraid he had rabies, Florence took him immediately to the hospital for a series of shots. The dog, however, tested negative and Dean recovered.

The following year, they went to Hollywood, Florida, situated between Fort Lauderdale and North Miami Beach. Florence insisted on a motel with a swimming pool this time, so that Dean could learn to swim. They took a room at Playland Motel and Dean was in heaven. Each day for most of the week, his father crossed the highway to go to the fishing beach, while Dean and his mother swam in the pool. "My mother would throw a handful of pennies into the pool, so I'd put on my goggles and dive for them. It didn't take much to entertain me, but it was great fun."

The only time Dean felt anxious was when his father would forgo fishing to join him in the water. Even looking at photographs nearly four decades later of the two of them in the pool evokes a negative visceral reaction. Dean remembers the dark undercurrent of their "horseplay." "My father would get into the pool only to come after me. He'd pretend that he was playing, but he did some mean things. His only reason to get in was to frighten me. He'd horse around, and then he'd grab me and force me under the water. He'd do it at unexpected times. He'd say, 'I'm going out to fish,' and instead of fishing, he'd come to the pool. I had to play along, but it was pretty terrifying when he held me under. It was mean play, like the way someone will tickle you until you're sick. It got to the point that when I'd see him come from fishing, I'd leave the pool."

Dean and his mother also spent time with her stepsister while Ray was fishing. Dean especially loved Pete, Thelma's cocker spaniel. He ran around the yard with the dog, delighting in Pete's rambunctious play. Just in the sheer joy of romping around, he realized how much a dog like this could make life better.

Then in 1959, the same month Dean turned fourteen, his parents decided to return to Florida, to the Playland Motel. The vacation week proved uneventful, but the return trip was a nightmare. Florence was driving their station wagon at night through the Carolinas when she hit a car that was stopped dead in the road, its lights off. "She saw it at the last minute," Dean recalls. "We were traveling at a high speed and she hit the back end and our car rolled. I remember waking up as I hit the floor with all the suitcases flying from the back of the station wagon onto the seats. My father was sleeping and he hit the dashboard and got a cut over his eye."

Dean's parents ended up in the hospital for several days, while some local people took care of Dean. He was unhurt, but he understood the repercussions. The car was totaled. "It was this catastrophic thing because we couldn't afford a loss like this. My mother had four or five teeth knocked out, and always after, my father had a dent in his skull." Dean called his Uncle Ray, who drove down to help them.

It turned out that the people in the car—two men and a woman—had been drunk, naked, and engaging in sex, but they had no idea that they had stopped in the middle of the road. "After we hit them, they started their car and drove a couple of miles up the road and stopped again. That's where the police found them. My parents were hoping to get some sort of settlement, but they were from out of state and got nothing. That was the last time we went to Florida."

11

Even into Dean's teenage years, Ray's behavior filled the house with tension. "It wasn't just that you knew he was in the house," says Dean. "You could feel him. Even if he was downstairs and you were upstairs and he was in a stable mood, everything felt different. I could wake up in bed and tell if he was in the house, without any clue other than the way the house felt."

When he was fourteen, Dean accidentally discovered part of the source of his mother's unhappiness. It shed a new light on his father's frequent absences.

"I was involved in a play at school and there was practice afterward. It was winter, on a Friday, and my mother didn't want me walking home in the dark, so my dad had to pick me up and bring me home. First he stopped someplace and went in to get something, while I stayed in the car. I knew he always had Dentyne because it covered the liquor smell on his breath, so I opened the glove compartment and rooted through stuff. Then I saw this letter. It was in a flowery envelope that smelled of perfume, and—I hate to say this—I snooped. I guess the thing was so exotic looking and to some extent I suspect I knew what it was. So I took out the envelope and read the letter and discovered it was a love letter to my father from a woman. She was asking for money and saying he knew how tough her life was and it would help if he could just give her a little more than he's given her before. I wasn't shocked, but I put it back in the glove compartment.

"My dad came back and got in the car and I never said anything to him. He went somewhere else, stopped and went in, and I sat there thinking that my mother might find this letter. I took it from the glove compartment and put it in my pocket. When I got home, I cut it into little pieces and threw it in the waste can. I think this was the first time I realized that this was part of my dad's life. He never said anything to me, but at some point he must have gone to get that letter and found it wasn't there. I often wonder what he thought and whether he wondered if my mother had found it.

"After that, I started looking at things in a different way, especially the times he was away. I had always assumed he was just out drinking. Then I discovered this and I was able to see why certain odd things had happened in my parents' relationships with other people. Several relationships fell apart and I began to think the reason was that my father had made a pass at the wife of the other couple. I remember my mother being embarrassed in one case and I had never understood why she was so angry at my father. I had assumed that he'd been drunk and had made a fool of himself, but then I began to wonder if it wasn't this other thing."

Years later, Dean's Aunt Virginia confirmed that his father had been a philanderer—naming names. "And I knew some of these women," Dean recalls. "I had seen my father with them at functions we'd go to, like when he worked for an insurance agency. I think one of these women either worked there or came with someone who worked there and they would spend a lot of time with us. And these women weren't ten percent as attractive as my mother. I think to some extent, my father was a victim to his illness, but I also think he could have made choices—he wasn't utterly compelled to do these things."

Dean began to realize the full extent of his mother's misery and he resolved to do what he could to be a comfort to her. Yet he had his own problems. He was about to enter high school and he still did not have real friends, nor did he take much pleasure in school work. Within the next few years, however, he was to meet several people who would make a big difference in his life.

[1]Dean Koontz writing as Brian Coffey, *The Voice of the Night* (New York: Doubleday, 1980), p. 307.

[2]Patrick Mott, "Scared Silly," *Los Angeles Times* (October 28, 1989), N1.

[3]*The Voice of the Night*, p. 274.

[4]Ibid., p. 274.

[5]Dean Koontz writing as Leigh Nichols, *Shadowfires* (New York: Berkley, 1990), p. 227.

[6]Martin Greenberg, Ed Gorman, and Bill Munster, *The Dean Koontz Companion* (New York: Berkley, 1994), p. 4.

THREE

Significant Encounters

1

DURING THE YEARS THAT DEAN WAS IN HIGH SCHOOL, HE experienced many things for the first time: a best friend, a girlfriend, a job, and the feeling that he might have a talent that could provide a real sense of direction.

Bedford High School served most of the small towns in the county, so there were nearly two thousand students. Dean's class had around one hundred and forty. He was a class clown, but not a dedicated student, unless some subject caught his attention. He continued to read science fiction and to teach himself with great fervor about subjects that interested him, yet remained relatively unaware of events in the culture at large that would one day have a significant impact.

The political climate was heating up. Kennedy's Bay of Pigs fiasco in 1961, during Dean's sophomore year, exposed the CIA's clandestine little universe. Then there was the "situation" in Vietnam that became a hot potato for both political parties, since neither wanted to be considered soft on the Reds. That same year, Germany constructed the Berlin Wall, the United States launched its first manned space flight, and whites in Birmingham brutalized the black "freedom riders." Two books were published that, years later, would catch Dean's interest: Joseph Heller's *Catch-22* and Robert Heinlein's *Stranger in a Strange Land*.

The following year, the United States established a military council in South Vietnam and television brought the conflict into homes across America. The Soviet Union tried to send arms to communist Cuba and Kennedy's answering blockade threatened to start a nuclear war. America held its collective breath as the confrontation escalated, but the Reds ultimately backed down. For the moment, the Cold War remained tepid.

Things boiled up on the spiritual front, however, as the second Vatican Council met in Rome to consider "updating" the Catholic Church. Ken Kesey wrote *One Flew Over the Cuckoo's Nest*, and Marilyn Monroe ended her conflicted life with an overdose of sleeping pills. Around the country, angry black voices demanded to be heard.

People in Bedford discussed these changes, but their town was fairly isolated. David Bradley, a black man who grew up there and who later become a writer and one of Dean's editors, remembers the sense of oppression. "There was a strict class consciousness," he states. "There were lines that were not to be crossed. You had Republican and Democrat, Catholic and Protestant, black and white, an upper class and a lower class. It was not an equal opportunity kind of place. There was a coffee shop in town that would not serve you if you were black, and if you had black people living next door, you were not in the right part of town."

The civil rights movement had minimal impact on Dean at that time. He knew that blacks had trouble with prejudice and poverty, but little was said in his own home. "I suppose there was a degree of prejudice in my family, but no one really talked about it. I think I was actually in college before I understood that there were people who had negative attitudes about other people just based on their race. But in our little town, I didn't see much racial diversity and the black families there seemed relatively prominent, especially compared to mine. There were probably no more than five to ten black families, and the kids in one family were sports stars. Everyone adored them. So I didn't grow up with any sense of racial tension."

2

Ray Koontz still had his problems with keeping a job, so Florence worked part-time in the local G.C. Murphy five-and-dime in order to have steady, if meager, income. She bought her own car and worked hard to pay off their five thousand dollar mortgage, but Ray would sometimes forge her signature on another mortgage to finance his debts. This devious practice found its way into Dean's 1974 novel, *After the Last Race*. He invented a character, Ely Grimes, a salesman who continually loses money at the track, but who endlessly envisions a big killing. He takes out a five thousand dollar mortgage on his home (which his wife had paid off), because he is dying of cancer and he has a "sure-fire" way to win money for her. (As if in retribution, Dean ensures that this man's wife actually gets the money, but not because Ely has been a successful gambler.)

Dean could see that his mother was under terrible stress from her unhappy marriage. In high school, he took a job stocking groceries to help save for college, but there was little he could do for his mother's situation. They were all trapped together in an escalating codependence that would reverberate in Dean's life for many years to come.

Ray continued to cajole people into investing in his inventions. Another that Dean remembers was a tent-like structure meant as a sun shield for small fishing boats. "The idea was that you'd take this tent with you," he explains, "and if it got too hot, you could put it up while you were in the boat. More than once, as my father tried to attach it to the boat, he fell right into the water. And since it was made of canvas, it grew very hot inside. He was sure this one was going to be very big, but it didn't sell."

When Dean was around seventeen, Ray came up with a rather expensive and bizarre idea. He was working again as an insurance salesman, but he hoped to quit once he got enough investors. This time, he was absolutely certain he had a winner: an electric jump rope machine.

"It was the first electric exercise machine that anyone had ever manufactured. That was the selling point. It consisted of a big, blocky pine console, like an old-fashioned television, that stood about three and a half feet high and three feet wide, and it housed a big motor. On one side was a hole with a little hook and when you pulled on the hook, a rope came out of the hole. You pulled out as much as you needed to attach to an eye fastened to the wall. Then you turned on the machine and it turned the rope."

According to Ray, this invention was going to become the biggest thing anyone had ever seen, but Dean was puzzled.

"Dad," he said, "this doesn't make any sense. People who jump rope want to exercise their upper bodies as much as their legs. They want to turn the rope themselves."

Ray hated to be challenged. "This damn machine," he insisted, "is for people who don't want to exercise too damn much!"

Dean did not know how to respond. Under other circumstances, his father's creative oddities might have been amusing, but he knew his mother struggled to make ends meet and these gizmos drained the available funds. "It's not funny when your mother has to work to put food on the table and your father doesn't bring home more than fifty dollars a week, and he's always running up debts."

Nevertheless, other people apparently saw the potential. "He got people to put up money and they produced it," Dean says. "They never sold any, but at some point, I think they had eighty or ninety of them built and had a warehouse where they kept them. And the machine was not cheap. It was really expensive."

Dean wondered out loud just who would buy it when they could pay a dollar for a regular jump rope.

Ray blew up at him. "You people don't believe in me! You don't have vision. These other people believe in me, they're putting up money, we're going to make these machines, and we're going to be rich!"

When Dean continued to press him on its practicality, Ray finally thought of an answer that should satisfy his son. "This," he said, "is the only exercise machine that blind people can use."

"Blind people?" Dean asked. "How can a blind person use this?"

"Besides having the machine turn the rope," Ray pointed out, "when the rope reaches the top of its arc, the machine rings a bell, so a blind person knows when the rope is coming down." This was self-evident to him. What more was there to say?

For Ray, the mere idea of forming a company and having stock made him a success. "Even though the company had nothing," says Dean, "and you had to pay the attorney's fees, you had stock and something to manufacture. That was enough for him. He'd get people to put money in it and I'm sure he filched some of it to spend on girlfriends and gambling, but he never brought it home. And when one of these things failed, that was not the end of it. You heard about these inventions forever. There was always some reason why it had gone wrong and he was always hustling to get new people involved to start it up again. There were six or eight of these things going on at once and it would drive us crazy. You knew that none of what he predicted was ever going to happen, but it was his dream. He was always going to get rich."

Not everything Ray envisioned involved an invention. In the early sixties, he decided to manage a country singer. "My father put together a consortium to sponsor this guy named Smiling Jack. The guy was in his fifties. My father had probably seen him playing in a bar. He started chatting him up—my father was always good about chatting people up—and he presented himself as this big important person. My father claimed that Smiling Jack was a big success, that he'd sold more records than Bing Crosby, but his career just hadn't gone as well as it should have, so my father was going to manage it. Now, what that meant was, he was going to put together a bunch of people who would put up money for recording sessions and advertising. But when I met the guy, I wanted to go wash after shaking hands with him. He seemed real oily. You knew exactly the kind of person you were dealing with, but of course, my father didn't. My father could never see deception in other people because he was so deceptive himself."

Never one to accept his father's word, Dean challenged him: "If Smiling Jack has sold more records than Bing Crosby, why does he need money?"

"Well," said Ray, "he's fallen on some hard times."

"But why hasn't anyone ever heard of him?"

Ray flew into a rage. His face reddened as he yelled that his son just did not understand. Then he stalked off. The people who believed him were the ones who counted.

Dean was mystified that other people were not asking the same questions. Instead, they seemed just to accept whatever Ray claimed, and he managed to get the backers he needed. "I knew someone who actually put twenty thousand dollars into Smiling Jack," Dean says.

The Smiling Jack craze lasted a year. Ray got recordings made and landed some gigs in local bars, but eventually the steam ran out, people lost money, and Ray moved on to his

next project. That people were hurt by this debacle seemed not
to bother him.

"Periodically people came after him to get money back,"
Dean acknowledges, "but there was never any money to get
back. We were poor; we never knew if we were going to have
a roof over our heads the next day. Even when my father was
making acceptable money, he never held on to it for any length
of time. So there would be lawsuit threats, but the attorneys
would finally tell their clients that they were just throwing
money away because even if they won, there was nothing to
take."

Another problem was that Ray got into many car accidents,
often caused by his drinking. "Over the years, he had totaled I
don't know how many cars," Dean states. "He was always
drunk and he always would get off without any fines. He was
ticketed once or twice for drunk driving, but generally when
he was stopped, even if there'd been an accident, he'd talk his
way out of it. There were even instances where cops would call
up my mother and say, 'We've stopped Ray down here. He
shouldn't be driving. Can you come down here and drive this
car? I don't want to have to give him a ticket, but I can't put
him back on the road.' He would always be able to charm them
into that."

3

As family life continued to be stressful, Dean became a more
avid fan of horror and science fiction. He continued to read
Bradbury and Heinlein, but as he began paying more attention
to language, he became fascinated with other writers as well.
"I liked H. P. Lovecraft because of the way he overwhelmed
you with language. Bradbury, too, had this incredible language
in some of his books and it was much more refined and controlled than Lovecraft. There was a whole string of writers
that I liked for that reason."

Dean bought paperbacks from the local pharmacy, which
he later described in *Cold Fire*, his 1991 novel about a man
named Jim Ironheart who came from a similar town. Jim
shows the pharmacy to Holly Thorne and admits that, even as

a kid, he had loved books and could not get enough of them. The pharmacist describes Jim's passion — and he could as well have been describing Dean: "Used to spend his allowance buying most every science fiction or spook-'em paperback that came in the door."[1]

Another similarity was that Jim had developed a passion for reading Edgar Allan Poe and had memorized all the macabre pieces of his poetry. Dean, too, read Poe. He also read Bram Stoker's *Dracula*, Jack London's adventure stories, and Mark Twain's tales of Tom Sawyer and Huck Finn.

When Dean was fifteen, he encountered the writings of Richard Matheson. He was reading a science fiction anthology when he discovered Matheson's debut story from a decade earlier, "Born of Man and Woman." About a mutant child kept locked in a basement, it was one of the earliest representations of psychological realism in the field. As a way to draw sympathy, the story was told from the perspective of the child, yet all the while it was building toward the startling realization that the child had been locked in the basement for good reason.

Dean was in awe of Matheson's ability to elicit the chills he felt. He had always hoped one day to be a writer, but that night he wanted, specifically, to *be* Richard Matheson. He wanted to make readers feel the way he felt in that moment. He thought that the unusual voice in which the story was told was unbelievably effective. Over three decades later, he would write a Foreword to a reissue of Matheson's *Hell House* explaining the unique power of his writing and pointing out how impressed he had been with the way this writer had recast ancient myths into modern form to make them strikingly relevant.

4

Besides reading, Dean loved music, particularly rock 'n' roll. He managed to save up enough money from odd jobs — hawking souvenirs during special events or gathering coins below the fairground bandstand — to buy a small record player and some records. Inspired, he tried his hand at several instruments. "I played the drums for a while, and the trumpet. I also tried the guitar." He quickly discovered, however, that he had not inherited his mother's musical talent. "I could never play any of them well and I felt that even with a lot of practice, I'd never be first-rate, so I didn't want to do it. That's a character flaw, I assume. I wanted all or nothing."

Dean joined the chorus in high school and it soon became his primary activity, partly because he had a best friend now who was also involved. "I met Larry Johnson in high school," he recalls. "Larry's dad was the town banker whose public persona was very sober, but Larry was exactly the opposite. He was outgoing and always looking for something to laugh about. That appealed to me. He saved my sanity as a kid."

They had homeroom and several classes together throughout high school, so they saw each other fairly frequently.

"The class of '63," Larry explains, "was the first class that had accelerated programs for math and English and other subjects. There were twenty or thirty kids in certain classes for three or four years. Dean and I were among that group. We took Latin, which both of us regretted, and French, which was also not our strong suit."

One of their favorite teachers was the chorus director, Arch Stewart. He enjoyed his students and got them involved in school plays and musicals. "We didn't have anything quite like that until he was there," says Dean. "One year we did an elaborate production of *Oklahoma*, which was a lot of fun. Larry had a good singing voice and he played Jud, the bad guy. I had a minor role, just a few lines and part of a song. I was basically the chorus treasurer." Yet it would be in this role that he would have his first contact with one of the most significant people he was ever to meet.

Other than a brief stint in a band in college, that was the extent of Dean's musical directions.

5

Dean admired Larry and envied his normal, happy family. For special events, Larry told him, they went to Ed's Steak House near the turnpike, which seemed to Dean to be *the* place to go—it was where rich people went. He wondered if he'd ever get to eat in such a fine restaurant.

Dean often went after school to Larry's house rather than risk having Larry encounter his father. "When I did go to his house," Larry recalls, "it was rare that his father was there. I really never saw Dean's father, so I didn't realize what Dean was going through. He didn't talk to me about it. He was kind of funny that way. He was private. He never bragged and never complained. I knew his dad wasn't much in favor with a lot of people in town. He was strange. He was in and out of a million little businesses, but my father never had anything to say about him, and that was a negative to me."

Larry did go over to sneak into the fairgrounds with Dean, and he liked Dean's mother. "She was very sweet. I don't remember ever seeing her in a bad mood. She was a spectacular housekeeper and the house was always well cared for."

At Larry's they often played in the adjacent cemetery, or passed hours inside playing monopoly or pretending to be disc jockeys on the radio. "We'd sit and laugh for hours," Larry remarks. "We laughed at ourselves all the time." Although Larry read Westerns and had no interest in science fiction, they shared a passion for *Mad* magazine. "We'd go around putting Alfred E. Newman faces on everything," Larry laughs.

Eventually another boy, Steve Shriner, joined them, and their small group established camaraderie in a shared sense of humor, particularly in practical jokes.

"Dean loved to fool people," says Larry. "He'd dream up pranks, but they rarely worked in actuality. One night he and two friends were outside my house making all kinds of racket to make me think aliens had landed. My dad thought it was the furnace and he got up to check it. Everyone in the house woke up except me."

One day, Dean and Larry decided to announce a school event that would never materialize. "That one worked well," Larry remembers. "We got on the radio with that." Because of chorus, they were familiar with the backstage area, where they had discovered a way to get into the school after hours. To parody all the programs established to encourage school spirit, they made hundreds of posters featuring a bear-like creature announcing "Grep Day" on the upcoming Friday. They hung these posters all over the school. "Bring a Grep to school," they urged. "Be a school booster." Some students attempted to observe it with strange hairstyles or by carrying teddy bears to school that day, but people were confused as to what they were actually supposed to do. Then Dean and Larry broke into the school the following Sunday night and hung more posters reprimanding students for failing to show the proper spirit: "You missed Grep Day. Where were you?" or "*That* is how you celebrate the Grep?"

On Monday, the administration wised up and attempted to root out the perpetrators. "They called in the class officers, the chorus officers, the band officers, some of the clubs, and just all kinds of people," says Larry. "It was so interesting to watch everyone trying to figure it out." Larry and Dean remained silent and no one ever figured out who had done it.

Another prank was to "borrow" a six-foot-high, ten-foot-long masonite "For Sale" sign from Arch Stewart's property out by the Elks Club, carry it across town without being seen, and hoist it onto the roof of the high school. They managed to get it in place, though while they were tying it, a police car cruised by and shone a light over the building. They froze, but the car continued on. The next day when the principal, Mr. Townsend, saw the sign, he laughed and kept laughing even as he climbed up to take it down. "I never saw him laugh so hard," Larry claims.

They also figured out how to skip out of the last period at school by signing fake excuses so they could go to the Dairy Dell and indulge in cherry Cokes. One day, Mr. Townsend came in, greeted them, and left without realizing that they should have been in school at that hour. They looked at each other in relief. They had gotten away with yet another misdeed.

6

As part of the college-bound track, Dean took subjects that would prepare him. One of his teachers, Winona Garbrick, taught the advanced English course. A former WAC, she had a stern military manner, but she also knew her subject. Concerned that students from a small town might not get noticed by colleges, she had taken it upon herself to find out what they needed in order to impress admissions committees.

"Kids feared her because she was so gruff," Dean remarks, "and she could certainly take your head off. She would be really sharp with us, but only when it was deserved or when she thought we weren't working up to our potential. But then as we got older and had her for a second year, most of us came to love her and just thought she was wonderful. She did care about us. She was a good teacher."

One of Miss Garbrick's course assignments was a class newsletter, to which Dean contributed several pieces, including cartoons. He ended up as the editor. "I even made up a crossword puzzle," he says. "The clues were embarrassing traits of teachers and the answers were their names."

One day, Miss Garbrick brought a tape recorder to class. It was a large, bulky machine, but very exotic to the students. Dean decided to use it for some of his own creative endeavors. "We had a radio station in Bedford," Dean explains. "KFBD was a little five-thousand-watt station that played rock 'n' roll part of the day and country music the other part. I did a series of things on the recorder that purported to be shows on KFBD. I would pretend to be a disc jockey. I'd tell jokes related to songs, or interview people and do both voices. I also did funny commercials, which were a hit in the class. I was willing to risk humor at the teachers' expense. I had these Big Band records that some well-meaning relative had given me, and one of the songs I really liked was "Big Wind Blew in from Winnetka." I taped this song, but sang over it and changed the words to "Big Wind Blew in from Winona." Of course, the kids loved the teacher being mocked, and she had a good sense of humor. She'd get kind of red-faced, but she'd laugh."

He got along well with Tom Doyle, who taught history at the school and who was his homeroom and driver's education teacher. "Dean wasn't outgoing unless you spent some time with him," Doyle recalls. In homeroom, Doyle would read verses from the Bible and have the kids recite the Pledge of Allegiance each day. He had students read out loud, and went out of his way to make holidays special for those who did not have much. He also took them to see historical places in town, such as the building that had once been part of the Underground Railroad. Years later, after Dean got published, he sent this man each of his books.

As Dean began to think about college, he decided it would be best for him to major in history. That was his easiest subject. Miss Garbrick heard about this from the principal's office, and one day in the hall, she shouted at Dean that she wanted to speak to him. "Every other kid in the hall scattered because they thought I was in deep trouble," says Dean. "She marched up to me and said she'd heard I was going to major in history. She was really steamed." To her mind, what he should do with his life was quite clear.

"She told me that I wanted to study history only because I was lazy," Dean continues. "Then she said I should major in English because I had writing talent and that was going to be harder to develop. That had a profound effect. She impressed me so much that I changed my mind."

Later he dedicated *Prison of Ice*, subsequently reissued as *Icebound*, to Winona Garbrick in appreciation; his editor on that book was also one of her former students, David Bradley. Dean kept her informed throughout his career about what he was writing until she died. She was happy to know he was succeeding as a writer, but she never quite approved of the kinds of novels he wrote. Even so, his meeting with her in the hall proved to be pivotal.

7

At that age, Dean was painfully shy. He went out with a few girls, but no relationships had materialized for him. In part, he was hampered by not having a car and being unsure when he could use his mother's, but he also did not pick up clues that girls liked him and wanted him to ask them out. He was friendly with some of the girls in his class and they tossed him hints, but he did not realize they might truly be interested in him.

"The first time I went out on a date," he remembers, "my mother had to drive us because I was fifteen. The girl's name was Jamie Fries and we went bowling. Not long thereafter, her parents moved out of town and she transferred to another school—I hope not because I had dated her. I also dated a girl named Alice Whisker for a while, but I didn't date anybody for an extended period of time."

During his senior year, Dean was with his friend Larry when he spotted a thin and pretty young woman with dark hair standing on a street corner.

"Who's that?" he asked.

"Gerda Cerra," Larry said. "Ross Cerra's daughter. You know, the shoemaker?"

Dean knew of the man. He was a first-generation Italian immigrant who lived at 127 South Bedford Street. Dean's father had once bragged that his own shoe shop would put Ross Cerra out of business.

As Dean watched Gerda, he was struck. He had to ask her out. He knew he would have trouble approaching her, but there was no turning back. She was beautiful!

He soon learned that she was a junior, and very busy. She was the president of her class and actively involved in her church.

"She was probably the smartest kid in that high school," says David Bradley, a few grades behind her. "She had a lot of talent. You worshipped her from afar."

"She was a good student and very personable," remembers classmate Norma Cuppett. "I don't know of anyone who disliked her. She was a hard worker and very ambitious."

Mary Jeanne (Heit) Wilt went all the way through school with Gerda. "She was quiet and shy," she recalls. "That was the way she was raised. You would walk into their home and it was very quiet and religious. She had a nice personality and a dry sense of humor."

The one drawback, some people warned Dean, was that she was Catholic. In a town that small and conservative, there would be prejudices.

Dean was not deterred. He had a plan.

"The school chorus was putting on *Oklahoma* and I was the treasurer, so I had to have a meeting with the class presidents because they were involved in ticket sales." He talked to Gerda twice, briefly. She did not show any interest, but at least now she knew who he was. He could say something personal the next time he saw her.

"I noticed her in the hall going to or from a class, so I stopped her and asked her out to a movie. She said, 'Oh, I can't, I've got to work at the dry cleaner that night.'

"I was a shy kid and I did not approach girls and ask for dates easily, so I went away all clammy. The rejection was so terrible. And once rejected I never asked again. I never, ever asked again, not even if the girl said, 'Oh, I'd love to, why don't you ask me another time?' A rejection meant that was the end of it."

Even so, two weeks later, Dean worked up his courage again. "I stopped Gerda in the hall and asked her out again and she said, 'Oh, I can't. I've got to work at the movie theater.' So I thought, 'Huh? It was the dry cleaner last week, lady! You know, you should keep your story straight.' But somehow or other, I went back and asked her out a *third* time and that time she said, 'I can't. I've got to baby-sit.'

"So by this point I feel like I'm bleeding from the nose. I waited probably a month and I got it into my head that, okay, she's class president. Her class dance is coming. She has to go to her class dance. She can't make up some story about working."

Dean waited until it was close to the event, but far enough away where Gerda would probably not yet have a date. He approached her and asked if he could take her to her class dance.

Gerda brushed him off with, "Oh, I can't. I'm busy that night."

"You can't be," said Dean. "You're the president and you have to go to the dance."

"I'll be there," she responded, "but the first part of the evening, I have to take my turn selling tickets at the door. Then I have to sell refreshments, and the last third of the evening, I have to run the record player. Afterward, I have to clean up the gym."

Thinking quickly, Dean said, "I'll do all those things with you. Why don't we just make that the date?"

Gerda shrugged. "Okay," she said.

Thus, Dean had his first date with the girl who had caught his eye. He was elated.

At the dance, as Dean helped Gerda with preparations, the

record player, and cleanup, he cracked jokes and made her laugh so hard that her stomach hurt the next day. They both felt good about each other.

"Dean had a sense of humor unlike anyone I'd ever known," Gerda said. "I really enjoyed him and I liked the fact that we both liked to read."

What Dean later wrote of Gerda was this: "She was intelligent, creative, warm, sexy, had darting, dark eyes that took everything in."[2] At the end of the evening, he gave her a chaste kiss good-night. He was in love.

As he got to know her, Dean discovered that Gerda did indeed have all those jobs. Not only was she involved at school and church, but she worked at the dry cleaners and the movie theater to help with expenses at home. Her father, Ross Cerra, was an Old World Italian who had immigrated as a teenager, and Gerda was his eldest daughter. She had two older brothers, Ross and Vito, and a younger sister, Donna. As the oldest girl in the family, she was expected to work and pay some of her own way. Her mother, Dorothy, had died of leukemia when Gerda was thirteen, and she had acquired a stepmother, Angie, by the time she was sixteen.

Gerda sewed her own clothes or put aside money to buy the few she did not make. She could embroider, cook, and knit, but never felt much kinship with other girls. She and her best friend, Sheila Rawlings, were more like tomboys. Gerda was stronger, more determined, and more focused than other girls she knew. She had never liked playing with dolls or discussing fashion. Yet those other girls respected her.

"She was real smart," said Mary Jeanne Wilt. "When the school was having its seventy-fifth anniversary, she's the one who noticed and then organized events for it. We even had a parade."

Even her teachers respected her. "Gerda was from a real good family," says Tom Doyle. "She was quiet and very serious."

Gerda's father, however, was not keen on this budding romance. He warned her that Dean was Ray Koontz's son, and Ray Koontz was unreliable. "He told me not to trust the things that Dean said," she remembers. Yet she felt differently. Dean seemed to her to be quite sincere and responsible.

All in all, Dean had found a person with whom he felt comfortable. She laughed at his jokes and knew the difficulty of being from a home where tensions and hardship were part of growing up. Gerda's strength of character would serve Dean not only as a model for female characters in his future novels, but for males as well. "I see more of me in his male characters," Gerda says. She considers herself a realist who relies on reason and logic to make sense of the world, and she does not tolerate nonsense or poor treatment from thoughtless people.

When Gerda had time, she and Dean began to see each other. Within a few weeks, by the third or fourth date, Dean was ready to pop the question: Would she wear his high school class ring? He had never before asked this of any girl, but it felt right. He wanted to go steady with this dark-haired, intelligent beauty.

Toward the end of the evening, when they were standing at her back door, Dean took off his ring and offered it to Gerda. She looked at it, accepted it, and then said in her matter-of-fact way, "Okay, for a week."

Dean was thrilled, even with this qualified commitment. It was a big step toward a real relationship. She was *his* girl now, at least for the next seven days.

Gerda's indecision stemmed from having had a long-term relationship that had gone sour. "I didn't want to get attached again," she explains, "so I was hesitant about accepting Dean's ring."

Yet Mary Jeanne Wilt remembers that Gerda was quite excited about it. "Dean was good for her because she was so quiet," she remarks. "He was studious, but he was a character. He brought out a lot of her personality."

They soon became a couple.

"At the end of the week," Dean says, "I asked whether she was going to give the ring back and she said, 'I think I'll keep it if that's okay.'"

Their relationship developed in a similar fashion to that of the two young adolescents in Dean's 1980 novel, *The Voice of the Night*. Colin, a shy, insecure teenage boy, meets Heather, a girl his age who suffers from low self-esteem, although he cannot fathom why. They team up to fight off a psychotic bully who threatens to kill Colin, and Heather proves her mettle by staying with the plan even when it becomes increasingly dangerous for her. She is committed to Colin, and the impression by the end of the book is that their friendship is solid and could lead to something more.

So Dean and Gerda went steady. Everyone who knew them expected they would eventually get married. Dean's mother approved. "My mother really liked Gerda. She's quiet and very considerate of other people and I think my mother saw in her some of herself. She liked her industriousness. They had the same inner strength. I think Gerda is tougher-minded than my mother. And she has a much greater sense of humor than my mother did. Gerda has an extremely dry wit. One of the things that has helped us is that we both share a sense of the absurd, and there's a lot in life we don't take too seriously."

Since Bedford was such a small town, their dates consisted of school dances, bowling, movies, and just driving around talking and listening to music on the radio. Sometimes they drove to Altoona and Johnstown to visit Gerda's extended family, and Dean was impressed with their liveliness and warmth. "Every house we went to we'd be offered something to eat," he says. "First thing when you walked in the door, bang, there would be a plate of cookies here, cakes there. Her Uncle Pete made homemade wine so he'd go down to the cellar and get some. Their strong ethnic tradition was very exotic to me." He also enjoyed the fact that they were a large family, but they did not bicker the way his own did.

8

In the spring of 1963, Dean graduated from high school. His father had to be cajoled into attending the ceremony. "I remember the giant argument my mother had with him about going," says Dean, "and he finally went, but he made a big issue about it."

Dean did not care. He was getting away. He had already decided, based on finances, that he would attend the state teachers college in Shippensburg, Pennsylvania, just over an hour away. He had worked for the past two years in a part-time position at the Acme grocery store and would continue to work over the summer. Gerda had one more year of high school and then, should they decide to stay together, they could make real plans. What Dean knew as he graduated was that, from that day forward, his life would be different.

[1]Dean R. Koontz, *Cold Fire* (New York: Putnam, 1991), p. 328.
[2]Dean R. Koontz, *Soft Come the Dragons* (New York: Ace, 1970), p. 5.

FOUR

Setting Directions

1

SHIPPENSBURG UNIVERSITY, LOCATED AN HOUR WEST OF HAR-risburg in the Cumberland Valley of south-central Pennsylvania, was founded in 1871. It was approved as a teachers college in 1926. When Dean went to school there, it was known as Shippensburg State College. At that time, the campus covered one hundred acres; it has since doubled in size. The emphasis was on teaching and quality interaction between teachers and students, with the idea of developing a community in which the student is central. When Dean attended, there were around three thousand students.

To enroll in the English program, with secondary certification for teaching, meant that Dean would take basic courses in composition, psychology, grammar, and teaching methods. Then he would learn about such writers as Shakespeare, Hawthorne, Melville, and Dickens. By the time he was a senior, he would be studying specific literary genres and literary criticism. Along the way, he would learn various teaching philosophies and techniques.

Dean chose Shippensburg in part because it was inexpensive. He had worked part of the summer at Acme and part in another grocery story called Lowry's. At school, he briefly washed dishes in the dining room to continue to help pay expenses.

The other consideration was that Shippensburg was close enough to Bedford for him to go home weekends—as long as his father came to pick him up—to see Gerda and his mother. He had a car, but the school did not allow cars on campus for freshmen.

As Dean went off to college, Gerda thought they might drift apart, but it was not long before he asked her to marry him. It had taken some time, but he had finally put together enough money to buy a ring and pop the question. "It surprised me," she says, but she accepted.

Dean's mother was a little worried by the proposal. "She was in shock," Dean admits. "She assumed it was going to be a 'necessary wedding.' I think it took her a couple of months to believe that we didn't *have* to get married, and then I think she was happy."

It was difficult for them to see each other regularly because Dean had to rely on someone else driving him. They kept in touch by writing daily letters. "We had a huge collection of letters," Dean remembers, "and most of them were funny because not that much would happen to us in a day, so we'd make up stuff." By his second year, he had brought back his black and white '52 Buick. "I think that car had only cost a couple hundred dollars, but it worked."

2

During his first two quarters, he resided in a dorm built in 1870 known as Old Main. His roommate was Harry Recard, a history major. "Dean and I got along very well from the first," Harry states. "We have a similar sense of humor, which is a little weird. You had to be quick-witted to pick up on it. We could cut someone off without them ever knowing it. We'd have a hell of a laugh and they'd be wondering what was going on. Dean was shy, but sure of himself. We went through Orientation together, but he would not participate in hazing activities. He was that sure of himself."

"You could be thrown out of college if you got too many demerits for violating hazing rules," Dean explains. "The first week was Hell Week and you had to do all kinds of things, but they overplayed it. They made us all stand in the gym one day during a very hot September, and there was no air-conditioning. We had to run in place with our little beanies on and then stand shoulder to shoulder with all that body heat. People started passing out and some of them got very ill. Whoever was running the hazing left them on the floor. It quickly reached the point at which I refused to do any more, and I started piling up demerits. I saw no educational value or character building in any of it. It was pretty stupid stuff. It was like turning over the university to the most witless elements."

What really annoyed him was that students were not allowed to go home for the first month. He had a girlfriend whom he wanted to see, so he defied the rules and went home three of the four weekends. "Of course, I'd get in trouble," he admits, "but because they overplayed their hand, hazing was drastically reduced in scope after that year."

The dorm room Dean shared with Harry was long and narrow. "It was very small," Harry remembers. "You walked in and the closet was on your immediate left, which made it offset in the room. There was a bunk bed behind that, longways, and there were two desks that were lengthwise in the room. You could barely get up out of bed and walk straight out the door." Dean had the top bunk and Harry, who was larger, took the bottom.

Harry immediately got Dean involved in playing pinochle, which grew into tournaments involving other boys on the floor. Generally they played in someone else's room, using the top of a trunk. "We played a lot of pinochle," Harry admits.

"In my first year there," Dean recalls, "I was just a get-by kind of student. My major desire was to become the best pinochle player there ever was, and I'd never even heard of pinochle until I went to college. Harry and I were killer partners. We were tough to beat. We had these tournaments that would start at five o'clock in the afternoon, and everyone would go down to the student cafeteria, called the Raider Room, to get sandwiches and Cokes. We'd bring dinner back to the room and these games would go all night."

Linda Farner Holtry met Dean during that time in the student lounge. She was a "townie," but she liked to hang around on campus. She knew Dean from their educational psychology course, where they would pass notes. She liked him, but thought he was shy. "He always seemed to be by himself," she says. "He wasn't a joiner, but I remember that he played a lot of cards."

3

In 1963, the civil rights movement became more pronounced and Martin Luther King was arrested in Alabama. Over two hundred thousand freedom fighters demonstrated in Washington, D.C. Then in November, Lee Harvey Oswald shot and killed President Kennedy in Dallas, Texas. Most people over a certain age can recall exactly where they were and what they were doing when they heard the news.

"The word came through just as my father was picking me up for the holiday break," Dean relates. "I had returned back from my last class and was scrambling to go pack. I walked in the room and Harry was sitting there. He was just shaking his head and in kind of a weird state, and I asked, 'What's wrong?' He said, 'Kennedy's been shot.'"

Dean was stunned. As he was riding home in the car, he turned up the radio and heard the announcement that Kennedy was dead. "It had a profound impact on all of us who were old enough to react to it emotionally and intellectually. It was a fundamental event—especially if you were in your teens or early twenties—that shattered forever the idea that there is any such thing as stability. It introduced to you the notion that everything can change and it can change very suddenly. Since then, I've always been aware of how easily a stable society can turn into something else."

4

His first year at school, Dean experimented with various activities, such as playing in a band. "I knocked around on drums, and several people who played instruments got together and we actually became a little group and played a couple of things—but not for any money to speak of. We had aspirations—which evaporated quickly—of doing something more."

He also knew some people on the college radio crew. "I was involved with that," he says, "but not on a long-term basis. I've always found radio sort of fascinating. I think I'm a frustrated performer."

Since childhood he had loved to draw and he continued to dabble in artistic ventures. "I had this idea that I might someday become an artist, an illustrator, and when I was in college, I did some drawings and actually sold a few pieces. People paid about fifteen dollars for them. But at some point, I realized that while I had some talent in that direction, I would never be able to develop it the way I would have liked. I did some watercolors, too, and I liked to work with pastels. I was still drawing until my junior or senior year in college, but once I realized that I would never be first-rate, I lost interest. I had a friend at Shippensburg, Jeff Steele, who *was* a terrific artist, and if I couldn't be as good as he was—then forget it."

There would come a time when Dean would be famous enough to contribute his quirky drawings to raise money for charity.

"I also wrote a lot of bad poetry in college. That form of writing fascinates me because of the condensation of the language. My interest in verse comes out of reading Poe. I enjoyed his insistent rhythms. Poetry has played a tremendous role in shaping the kind of writer I am. I like extremely vigorous poetry, like Yeats and T. S. Eliot. I also read Emily Dickinson because of the enormous condensation of emotion in her language. She wrote very short pieces and some of them carry tremendous punch."

Dean showed his mother some of what he had written. "I can't remember any response," he says. "When she realized I was drawn toward being a writer, she possibly saw it as one of these crazy kind of dreams that people on my father's side of the family have but which they never pursue in any meaningful way. I think it scared her, so she didn't encourage it. She had no comment, as if she was almost afraid to think about it."

For a brief period, he joined the Newman Club, which was for students of the Roman Catholic faith. According to the 1964 yearbook, they devoted themselves "to wholesome activities." Dean had decided to explore the religion in which Gerda had been raised.

"I became a Catholic after I met Gerda, but not because of her," he clarifies. "It wasn't to marry her. She didn't require that. College is a time in your life when you're searching for things. From dating Gerda, I had seen these large families in the Italian community that all seemed interknit, while my own family had been sort of shattered. On my father's side, people just didn't even relate, and on my mother's side, there was always some conflict."

He had been impressed with the positive effect that attending

Mass seemed to have on their family life. "I didn't see any husband who drank to excess. They all liked their wine, but I didn't see any of these uncles who were drunk or who didn't work to support their families. Generally people got along with each other and there was all this stability. I hadn't had much of that in my own life. So on my own, without telling Gerda, I found a class at the Catholic Church in Shippensburg for instruction.

"Now, in those days the Mass was in Latin. I fell in love with the beauty of it all, and also I began to see why it provides a certain structure that's good for people. I finally became Catholic, and that was before I really knew that we were going to marry."

Dean began to read Catholic philosophers. "During my Catholic conversion, I read Saint Augustine quite a lot. He fascinated me because he was the first person I came across who brought intellectualism to writing about religion. It's that aspect of Catholicism that I've found most redeeming. Many years later, I liked to read Malcolm Muggeridge for some of the same pleasures, and I also read G. K. Chesterton. I had found his Father Brown series first and got interested in his mind."

The religious thinker who most impressed him was the thirteenth-century Catholic philosopher Saint Thomas Aquinas, who harmonized faith and reason. Known for his philosophy of intellectualism, and influenced by Aristotle and Augustine, Thomas Aquinas represented the high point of medieval Scholasticism in his *Summa Theologica*. According to him, God's revelation is fundamentally rational and is revealed to some degree in all creation. All truth stems from God's personality, and divine revelation never contradicts logic. Although Dean was to change some of his attitudes toward God and the Church, these ideas would remain fundamental to him.

The Catholic idea of free will was also appealing to Dean. He liked to view decision-making as an exercise of the spiritual faculty, and he particularly embraced the notion of choice and responsibility. Even when a person seemed to be acting under subconscious influences, choice was exercised somewhere in the process. Thus, no one was really off the hook for his actions. No one had a good excuse for not acting morally—not even his father.

5

As soon as possible that first year, Dean found a room to rent off campus. "I wasn't made for institutional living," he admits. "I hated the dorms." He went to a gray two-story colonial house almost a mile from campus where Fay and Albert Bitting rented a room to male college students. Fay Bitting approved of Dean at once.

"Dean was special," she recalls. "He came in and inquired about a room, and there was something about how he presented himself that I liked. He had nice manners and a sense of humor, so I showed him the house. And after he moved in, he always paused to talk a little. He didn't just rush out the door."

The second-floor room that she showed Dean had two single beds, one for him and one for a roommate. It was painted blue, with white curtains framing three large colonial windows. She also supplied a bureau and a desk for each, and fresh towels. The bathroom was down the hall and they had a small kitchenette to use, as well as a room in which to sit and read.

"I had a roommate who was different from me," Dean says. "He had something like eleven pairs of shoes and forty-eight ties. He knew exactly what to wear with everything, and college for him meant getting into the right fraternity. He was a dedicated frat man." Eventually the roommate moved out and Dean had the room to himself. Whenever he wrote stories, he asked Mrs. Bitting to read them and tell him what she thought. "Give it your best," she would encourage him. "It'll grow by leaps and bounds."

Dean stayed at the Bitting's house for the rest of his time at Shippensburg. Years afterward, he kept in touch with his former landlady and sent her a signed copy of every one of his books. When she saw him again after he had become successful, she was pleased that he had not changed much from the boy she had known. "He was so down to earth," she says.

6

At the end of Dean's first year, he was nearly kicked out of school. He had one more final to take in math—a course in which he was doing only average work. "I wasn't feeling good the day before and the next morning when I woke up I couldn't move. I literally couldn't even lift my arms. I gradually began to be able to move, but I couldn't stand up. I was running a fever, but I managed to crawl to the phone. It was a Friday and my father was supposed to be picking me up, so I called to see if he was really going to come because once in a while he would forget. I missed the final and when my father came around three o'clock, I was barely able to get into the car. When I got home I was in such bad shape, I couldn't even hold down water. I was severely dehydrated. My mother took me to the hospital and the doctors hooked me up intravenously. I was there for sixteen days with an exceptionally severe case of mononucleosis."

Gerda and Florence visited him, but for the first few days, he did not even realize where he was. His fever was high and he had to be closely watched. He finally recovered, but he was too weak for the remainder of the summer to try to find a job.

Then Shippensburg sent a notice that Dean had missed his final, had not reported his departure, and therefore should not return. Although his mother called to explain what had happened, the dean of student personnel was adamant that he was not allowed to leave campus without the proper notification. When Dean returned to school to plead his case, he was informed that his grades were poor and he had failed to follow procedure, so there seemed little point in readmitting him.

"I had to write letters to my various teachers," he remembers, "asking if they would step forward on my behalf. The only one who did was the math teacher whose exam I had missed. He wrote a letter saying that I shouldn't have been kicked out and that I might have gotten a C. With that, they let me back in—provisionally."

Little did they know that they would one day award him an honorary doctorate!

7

As Dean progressed in his major, he took three creative writing courses, in which he was expected to produce samples of his own work. "A creative writing teacher can be of significant value to a student during the early stages of his growth," he later stated in a book on writing.[1] However, he disagreed with them that the process was communal, and ever afterward he distrusted the idea of writing groups. "I've always advised young writers who get together in these groups not to do it," he explains, "because what you have to sell is your unique view of the world, your voice, and what writers generally criticize about another writer is his or her style."

During the early sixties, college English departments emphasized realism and naturalism. Professors elevated mainstream writing as relevant, timeless, and meaningful. Critical praise showed a retrospective tendency, looking to past works for artistic merit. As Dean learned about the writers whom his professors wanted him to emulate, he continued to read science fiction, fantasy, and some mysteries. Many of his teachers viewed such genres with disdain, however. That was not the place from which ideas of substance derived, they insisted, and they encouraged students to model their work on the fiction of authors of established "greatness." Dean listened to this, read these authors, watched his classmates write to please the professors, and then went off in his own directions. To write simply for the grade struck him as cynical. Instinctively he knew that the best path was to follow his heart and write what he liked to read.

Reactions to his stories were often condescending. "Everything was scorned except what was considered 'literary fiction,' and when I would turn in a writing sample it would be in one of these genres that they dismissed." Most of his teachers urged him to aspire toward what they considered higher standards, but he resisted the pressure. In some ways, college was a good training ground for similar struggles in the years to come.

Dean made friends with other of his English professors. He especially liked those who were passionate about their subjects, and skillful in communicating that passion. O. Richard Forsythe, who was director of English Education and Communication Arts, was one. His books include *Games Teens Play with Adolescent Literature* and *Practical Remedies for English Teachers in Distress*. He taught Early American Literature, World

Literature, Literary Criticism, and basic composition courses. He remembers having Dean in his course on Teaching English in Secondary Schools.

"I remember the major project that he did," Forsythe states. "It was a three-week summer course. Students had to have a unit plan for what they would teach and Dean's was on science fiction. It was very well done and I commended him on it."

Richard would throw parties and invite students to his home. "I let them call me by my first name," he says, "and the kids appreciated that. Dean came in to my office and we had some very lengthy discussions. I remember that he was atheistic in college. He used to be incredibly cynical, although I never saw him as a radical. I shied away from having these discussions too often because sometimes when people are cynical, you have to let them be cynical. He had a friend, Paul, and they used to come over. We would all get smashed. Dean saw teachers as human beings. I think the impact I had on him was about the rapport we achieved. I was a teacher and he was going to become one. That put us on equal levels."

John Bodnar, another professor, also became a good friend. Dean, as a junior, took Bodnar's American Novel course, which included *The Deerslayer*; *Moby Dick*; *Sister Carrie*; *Look Homeward, Angel*; *Maggie, A Girl of the Streets*; *The Old Man and the Sea*; and *The Catcher in the Rye*.

"I spent more time on *Look Homeward, Angel*," Bodnar explains, "because I was crazy about the work and the language. It's sheer poesy. Those opening symbols: 'A stone, a leaf, a door . . .' You open a *door* into life, and then there's the uncertainty of your life as if it were a *leaf* driven by the wind. And then a *stone*, which is about developing a good solid sense of principles to guide you through life. I emphasized symbolism, character development, and morality (good versus evil); for example, in *Moby Dick*, I stressed the numerous levels of meaning. 'Look at the white whale in *Moby Dick* as God,' I might say, 'and look how each chapter refers to the Bible.' Shippensburg is a fundamentalist area and we professors had to be careful of what we said; but I wanted them to think, even if literary devices and philosophical theories upset them."

His style was to walk up and down between the rows of seats and make eye contact to elicit answers from the class.

"Dean was attentive," he recalls. "He sat in the fourth seat from the front, in the third row from the main aisle. If I looked at him questioningly, he responded with insight, but succinctly. He never missed a class and he earned an A for the course."

During those days, most of literary criticism was influenced by Freudian theory. Freud, the originator of psychoanalysis, postulated the existence of three basic forces that govern a person's actions: the id (the unconscious instinctual drive), the ego (the executive structure of the psyche that connects with the real world), and the superego (the moral conscience). He maintained that the primary motivating factor in behavior is the sexual instinct, or libido, and that most neurotic behaviors derive from repressed sexual drives. He also categorized the psychotic behaviors. Although his theories were controversial, they filtered beyond psychology into other disciplines, notably literary theory.

"Freudianism and determinism were the bases for critical analysis of many works in the sixties," says Bodnar.

Between his English courses and a few psychology courses, Dean received substantial exposure. "I was totally swept up in Freud," he admits. "His ideas made a very deep impression, and when I found something that intrigued me like that, I did outside reading. That's why so many of my early books are saturated with it, but my attitude has evolved since that time."

At first, Dean set his sights on a teaching career, with writing as a sideline. His stint at student teaching was at the eighth grade level, but he had a problem with the woman who was his supervisor. She disliked him because of the length of his hair — which, in fact, was relatively short for the time — and for his sense of humor. "She put me through hell. She said I was ill prepared, I should never teach, and I should be taken out of this program." There were other teachers at the school, however, who sided with him and assured him that her reports would not count for much. Dean eventually got his certification.

8

Back in 1962, the U.S. Military Council had been established in Vietnam. By the time Dean was a sophomore two years later, the war had escalated and the U.S. was sending more aid. Johnson had been elected president following Kennedy's assassination, and even as the Beatles burst upon the scene, there were dark undercurrents about what the U.S. was doing in southeast Asia. Student demonstrations began against U.S. bombing in Vietnam and many young men protested and even dodged the draft. Dean was not among them.

"While I was in college, I was deferred," he explains, "but it was at the height of the Vietnam War, and as I was nearing graduation, I had to go for a physical."

To his surprise, the doctors showed great interest in his feet. Three different doctors had a look at them. His feet were narrow and on each foot he had two oddly shaped toes.

"Don't you have a foot problem?" they asked. "Pain when you walk any distance?"

"No," Dean responded.

Then he filled out a psychological test and was called in to talk to a doctor later in the day. He was nervous, wondering if he was going to be sent overseas. The doctor beckoned him into a private room and Dean saw his file on the man's desk.

The doctor looked at him and asked, "Have you had problems through your life with discipline?"

Dean thought it was a weird question. He had no juvenile record and he had always been a shy, quiet kid. He shook his head and answered, "No."

The man continued to look at him for several long seconds and then asked, "If you were given orders, do you think you would find it easy to follow them?"

Having no idea what the right answer might be, Dean simply said, "I wouldn't have any problem."

"In school," the man went on, "do you have problems doing assignments? Do you turn things in on time?"

"I'm about to graduate from college," said Dean. "If I didn't, I wouldn't be graduating."

Dean's interrogator gave him a long stare and said, "I don't think it would be good for either you or the army if you were drafted. What do you think?"

Dean had no idea what to say. He sat there thinking that whatever answer he gave would land him in Vietnam. He simply said, "I don't know."

The doctor nodded and told him, "That's all."

Dean left the office. When he got his classification, he was not A-1, which meant he was not prime material for the army. He thought it had something to do with his feet, but he was never sure. "I guess they thought, 'Foot problem, won't fit in an army boot,' or whatever. I never got called to serve, but if I'd have been drafted, I would have gone. It didn't seem like you really had a choice. I'd say I was against the war, but I didn't participate in protests. I wasn't a radical about it."

9

As young men in the sixties began to grow their hair longer to express defiance and individualism, Dean kept his relatively short. "I was looking for a teaching job. In those days, you had to have a teacher image. You wore a suit and tie to school."

He also shunned the use of drugs such as LSD that were becoming a fad among college students. "Drugs always terrified me," he explains. "The example of my father with alcohol was daunting. I could look around at the kids who were doing drugs and it was very obvious where this life was going to end up, so that never had any appeal to me. I liked the music of the time, which was rebellious, but most of the people I hung around with were not hugely political. We were at a small Pennsylvania teachers college. We were in the middle of Amish country."

He did participate in one radical act that he recalls. "There was a sit-in at the president's office. We were protesting women's dorm hours. It was no big political protest. During the week, women had to be back in their dorms at nine-thirty and on weekends they could stay out until eleven-thirty. I didn't even date anyone there, but this was this big protest.

"So we all went in and we thought we were going to shut down the university, but unfortunately we picked a time when the president was about to go to South America on a vacation. He was leaving that afternoon, so he couldn't have cared less whether we sat in his office or not. When the whole group showed up—it was probably thirty or forty people sitting in the outer office—he sent out soft drinks and coffee, and asked if everyone was comfortable. You could hardly be rebellious when you were being sent soft drinks and coffee."

Politics aside, Dean's primary interest was writing.

10

As Dean studied the great writers, he had ambitions of his own. To test the waters, he sent a short novel that he had written to the Scott Meredith Agency, which evaluated manuscripts for a fee. He got back a critique. "Even in college," he says, "I was smart enough to realize that they didn't even read what I'd sent them. This was based on the fact that the advice sent was in ignorance of some of the story line." Never again would he pay a fee, but as it turned out, this agency was the first to represent him as a professional.

In his junior year, Dean surprised some of his English teachers. To a nationwide college writing competition sponsored by *The Atlantic Monthly*, one of his writing teachers, Mabel Lindner, submitted an essay he had written and a dark suspense story called "The Kittens." Although he had written the story for a composition course, he had shown it to her, but he was unaware that she had then entered it in this contest.

"The Kittens" is about a girl named Marnie whose father had drowned a litter of kittens and assured her that God had taken them to live with him. He is a religious man who reads Bible passages and teaches Sunday School, so she trusts him. Still, she cannot understand why God had chosen her kittens. Subsequently her mother gives birth to twins, and soon thereafter Marnie's cat has another litter. More vigilant this time, Marnie sees her father drown the kittens. Her entire world changes. She decides to strike back at God and his agent of destruction—her father—by drowning the newborn twins.

Marnie feels violated. The two beings that were supposed to protect her had instead deceived and betrayed her. This was the first of Dean's stories to explore this theme and to give the child a fighting chance. It was more than just a story; he knew those feelings of vulnerability. As the story's creator, he felt the power of striking back against a paternal religion that expected blind obedience, no matter what the cost.

No one from Shippensburg had ever received notice from this contest after years of trying, so Mabel Lindner did not expect any response. When Dean's story won one of the five fiction prizes, therefore, *and* when he received additional recognition for the essay, the faculty members were impressed.

His success caused a stir in the English department when two different professors wanted to take credit. "When Dean wrote this story," says Richard Forsythe, "he did it in one professor's class. Then he had a creative writing class, and Mabel Lindner recognized it as good, but the other teacher wanted the credit. Dean came to me and said, 'What am I going to do?' I don't remember what I did, but somehow I solved the problem."

"It was unbelievable," says Dean. "When this flared up, I was stuck. I had both of them in a class and this battle erupted. I was trapped in the middle. I had a grade coming from one teacher and I had Mabel Lindner—whom I liked—rightly saying she was the one who saw the value in the story."

While they argued, Dean submitted the story to *Readers and Writers*, a magazine devoted to short stories, film critique, and art, with no taboos regarding subject or style. This publication's target audience was made up of students and faculty at colleges around the country. Dean's letter to them described the story as "an agglomeration of observed fact and imagined fantasy." They accepted "The Kittens" for their May issue and paid him his first professional money: fifty dollars. For someone who had grown up with so little, this proved a real windfall.

Mabel Lindner acted as advisor to the college literary journal, *The Reflector*, and the year that Dean won the contest, he joined the editorial staff. He enjoyed working with Lindner, but she had her moments. "There was always about her this air of gentility and grace," Dean remembers, "but she was also a tough and emotionally demanding woman."

The Reflector was published each of the three terms that made up the school year. For two issues, Dean was the short story editor, and during his tenure, the paper won high honors from the Columbia University Scholastic Press Association in their annual survey of college newspapers.

In the Winter 1965–66 issue, Dean published his prizewinning "The Kittens" (later he dropped "The" from the title), "Of Childhood," and "This Fence." Only a year before, a girl named Judy Elliott had published a story in *The Reflector* called "The Kittens," which was about a girl who believes a drowned litter of kittens will go to heaven. It was only a page long. Dean was not the short story editor at the time and it is unclear whether he saw this story before he wrote his own; he does not believe that he did. Yet even if that may have happened, it is not unusual for writers to subconsciously process material over which they have briefly glanced and come out with an original twist on a similar theme. The only items on which the two stories converge are the names of the protagonists—Marcy and Marnie—and the fact that they are concerned about what happens to dead kittens. Dean's story is much longer, far more descriptive, and more menacing. He brings to bear on the subject matter his own anger at a religion exploited for the purpose of deceit and a father who has no concern for the feelings of others.

His other two stories are poetic in tone. His poignant "Of Childhood" is a page-long essay on the idea that pleasant memories outweigh the unpleasantness in a child's life. The key to this lies in the child's awareness of the senses. "It is the only time in a man's life," he writes, "when he feels and is a part of nature." This foreshadows his heavy reliance on nature for metaphors in later works. The third story, "This Fence," is about boys in Florida watching a rocket blast off and dreaming of a powerful future. To them the rocket "was the mind of a young boy made concrete." Yet a fence keeps them from the wonders of space—they can only dream.

The next issue of *The Reflector* was a poetry issue that included four poems by Dean. "Sam, the Adventurous, Exciting, Well-Traveled Man," imitating e.e. cummings, dispenses with capitalization in its portrayal of a man who has nothing but the mundanity of beers and leers in his sorry life. "Something About This City" attempts to portray Paris, while "Hey, Good Christian" attacks religious hypocrisy. The last poem, "It," shows conscience to be an unrelenting force:

> *It calls out to you through the thick of your walls,*
> *through the plaster and maple and long, narrow halls.*

It screams and it whines till your ears cry in pain
  from tortured, high-pitched constant refrain.
It sniffs and it growls at your strong, locked door,
  sniffs at the keyhole and hard at the floor.
It wants in, it needs in; there's much it must do.
  You fight it, you hate it; and you're scared, too.
Not a monster, my friend,
  that will do you in —
    simply your conscience.

When "The Kittens" appeared in *The Reflector*, other students stopped Dean in the hall to comment on it. It was the first positive feedback he received for his writing, and he liked it.

11

Although Dean took summer courses to accelerate his progress, he was still able to work for the latter part of the summer during his sophomore and junior years. He took a job as a park ranger at Shawnee State Park, not far from Bedford.

"I was officially called a forest ranger," he explains, "but I was no forest ranger. I was a kid wearing a forest ranger outfit, but my duties were clerical. It was a campground and I held down the front desk. If anybody came in for camping, I'd issue them a ticket and take their money. Some weeks I worked days, and some weeks I came in at ten at night and worked until six. Mostly I sat at a desk and read novels. I got terrific pay because I was a state employee."

It was not all peaceful, however. Once he had to race a kid to the emergency room in Bedford, many miles distant. Another time, he was the victim of a holdup, and for this he got his picture in the paper.

On the last day of July in 1966, around ten-thirty at night, Dean was in the camping office. Two men came to the door, and the one who stepped inside was armed with a revolver. Dean had seen him the day before, trying to get a camping permit. He had curly blond hair, acne scars, and was wearing a black jacket with a map of Korea on the back; the other man was taller and had dark hair. The blond ordered Dean to stay seated as he rifled through the park receipts for the day. He also ordered Dean to give him whatever money he had. The robbers left with over two hundred dollars, including five from Dean. He ran to the door and watched them ride north on a motorcycle. Then he called the state police, who ordered roadblocks, but the culprits escaped. Dean later told a reporter that the gun that was trained on him had "looked like a cannon."[2]

Soon thereafter, Dean returned to school for his last semester. Before long, he would be married and working at his first professional job.

[1]Dean R. Koontz, *How to Write Best-selling Fiction*, (Cincinnati, OH: Writer's Digest Books, 1981), p. 4.

[2]*Bedford Gazette* (Bedford, PA, August 2, 1966).

FIVE

Starting Out

1

AS SEPTEMBER BROUGHT IN A NEW SCHOOL YEAR, DEAN MOVED into Fay Bitting's home again for his last few months. Although he was officially part of the class of 1967, he had taken summer courses so that he could finish his classes before Christmas in 1966. He and Gerda had set a date in October to get married, just before his final exams. This semester would be spent on job interviews.

As short story editor again on *The Reflector*, he contributed more material than ever. This time he published nine of his poems and two short stories. One was about the ways in which various people interpret the fall of a statue of the Virgin Mary in Agna Scalientes in Mexico. The other was science fiction. Its theme was population control and destinies decided by androids. Several of the poems expressed antiwar sentiments and anger at religious hypocrisy.

The last issue of *The Reflector* in which he was published was in the spring of 1967, after he was already gone. It was a poem called "Where No One Fell," depicting a paradise made of the most delectable foods imaginable, such as cherries and chocolate.

> *Feel the wind of Cherry Mountain*
> *Taste the sugar of Chocolate Sea*
> *Hear the music of Harmony Forest*
> *See the girl - so pretty is she...*
> *...Hold her close and hold her well*
> *Enjoy a land where no one fell.*

2

As Dean and Gerda planned their wedding, Dean ran into a family conflict. He had known it was building, but he had not foreseen how nasty it might get.

Sometime earlier, Aunt Kate had asked him to come over because she needed to tell him something important. To his surprise, she insisted that his mother did not really like Gerda and that if they planned to get married, Florence would put a stop to it.

Dean knew it was not true, but when he related this odd event to his mother, she dismissed it with, "Well, you know your Aunt Kate."

After that, every once in a while, Kate took him aside to tell him that Florence was saying negative things about Gerda. When Dean ignored her, she became surly.

As the wedding date approached, Dean and Gerda prepared the announcements. They sent one to Aunt Kate and Uncle Ray.

"I got summoned over to their house," Dean recalls, "and Aunt Kate said that she had told us before anyone else about [her son] Jim getting married, and she was unhappy that we didn't have the courtesy to tell her about my wedding, that she just received an invitation like everybody else. Of course, she'd known for years that Gerda and I were going to get married. I'm sure she knew the time and date, but still she said she would not come to the wedding. She turned it into this big feud and my Uncle Ray got caught in the middle."

Dean was unhappy that Uncle Ray would not be there to witness this joyous event, but he had seen how long these feuds could last. There was nothing he could do.

For the past two years, Gerda had begrudgingly lived at home to save money and had worked at the First National Bank in Bedford. The plan was that after they were married, Dean would move into her small bedroom in her parents' home for a month or two so they could save money. Gerda had been reluctant to do this because she wanted to leave home, but eventually she gave in. At least they would be together.

Then, shortly before their wedding, Dean came home from Shippensburg for a weekend. He spoke with his mother about his plans, that he and Gerda would have a short honeymoon before he took his final exams. At the end of the weekend, as he was about to leave, his mother came out to the car. Dean kissed her good-bye and was about to get in when Florence asked, "What would you think of me if I divorced your father? Would you think I'm a terrible person?"

Dean was stunned. He stared at her a moment and then managed to say, "No, I wouldn't. The only thing I have to say is why in the hell didn't you divorce him twenty years ago?"

Florence was shocked by his response.

"Are you going to do it?" he pressed.

But now she was reticent. "I don't want to talk about it."

"Why not?"

"I can't believe what you just said."

"I just asked you why you didn't do it twenty years ago."

Florence turned away and would not say another word. Dean asked her again if she intended to divorce his father, but she refused to address it. "Later," was all she would say. "Maybe later." Dean had to return to school with his question unanswered.

"And she never raised the issue again," he says. "I couldn't get her to talk about it. All I ever could figure out from that conversation was that on some level, my mother thought that I had been oblivious to certain things. How she could think that, when I had been there through it all, is a mystery to me."

It may have been that, faced with her son's imminent departure and the idea of being alone with Ray for the rest of her life, she finally had confronted the terrible truth about her future.

3

The wedding day approached. Relatives arrived and friends gathered, although Dean's longtime friend Larry was out of town. There was little money, but Gerda had bought, rather than made, her wedding gown. Her stepmother Angie helped her prepare.

On October 15 at Saint Thomas Catholic Church in Bedford, Dean and Gerda were married. This church was renowned for its elaborately carved wooden altar, which was enhanced that day by white gladiola and red carnations. White carnations also adorned the side altar.

"My mother had a little trouble with it being a Catholic ceremony at first," says Dean, "but it was not a serious issue with her."

Gerda wore an Alfred Angelo original of white satin with long, pointed sleeves and a butterfly train. The bodice was embroidered with swirls of seed pearls. Three satin roses anchored a veil, and Gerda carried a cascade of white fugi mums and red roses.

"Gerda was very tiny in her lacy dress," recalls Mary Jeanne Wilt, a bridesmaid. "She was beautiful."

Gerda's younger sister Donna was maid of honor, wearing an empire-waisted gown of red velvet. She carried white fugi mums with bronze centers. The bridesmaids were Gerda's friends, Barbara Webber and Mary Jeanne. Their empire-waisted gowns were bronze velvet and they carried bouquets of bronze fugi mums. All three attendants wore headpieces made of a velvet rose. Both mothers wore green suits.

Dean had rented a tuxedo. Paul Perencevic from school was his best man. Ushers were also college friends, Andy Wickstrom and Robert Wilson. His first roommate, Harry Recard, was in attendance, along with about sixty other people.

Father Edward F. McConnell officiated. He did not really know Dean, and during rehearsal had repeatedly called him "Dan." Dean and Gerda had thought he was trying to make it very clear that Dean did not belong to his church. Gerda corrected him quite sternly on several occasions, and during the actual ceremony, he got it right.

Dean's mother had felt sure that Aunt Kate was still determined that she and Uncle Ray would not come, but they showed up after all. Dean greeted them afterward.

"I hugged them," he says, "and my Uncle Ray was crying, of course, but Aunt Kate was in one of her glowering states. I said that I was so happy they had come and hoped to see them at the reception. Kate said, 'I've come to the wedding but by God if I'll go to the reception.' And she stormed off."

The reception took place at the American Legion Hall.

Gerda's Italian family loved weddings and made it a fun time. Dean's father got thoroughly drunk.

"Gerda did not toss her bouquet," says Mary Jeanne. "After the reception, they went back to their house to change and she put her bouquet on her mother's grave."

They had bought a used blue Ford Galaxy together while Dean was still in college, and they packed it up for a weekend away.

"We drove down to Williamsburg, Virginia, and stayed overnight," says Dean. "We just had a few nights before I had to take finals." Both of them thoroughly enjoyed this restored colonial town, although they were novices at taking a vacation. "We didn't even know how to check in to a hotel," Gerda remembers. "We had to learn." Even so, it was fun just to be alone together.

Afterward, Dean finished his courses and went immediately to his first teaching job.

4

In 1967, seven hundred thousand people marched in New York to support the war in Vietnam, while fifty thousand demonstrated against it in Washington. Martin Luther King, freed from prison, led an antiwar march in New York. Hippies in San Francisco's Haight-Ashbury responded to Timothy Leary's invitation to "tune in, turn on, and drop out." They proclaimed the Summer of Love, while blacks rioted in Detroit, Newark, and Cleveland. China exploded its first A-bomb, *Rosemary's Baby* was the year's sensational film, and Twiggy made an impact on the fashion world, with her skinny legs and doll-like eyes. Stanford biochemists produced synthetic DNA.

It was during this time that Dean took a teaching job in the former coal-mining town of Saxton, Pennsylvania, tutoring students in English in the Tussey Mountain School District. The mines were played out and the town relied on one of the early nuclear research plants for employment. Dean had gone on job interviews over to Chambersburg and as far north as Wilkes-Barre, Pennsylvania, but had ended up taking over a position in Title III of the Appalachian Poverty Program for a teacher who was in the hospital. It was administered by local school districts, and Dean was assigned to Saxton, which was not far from Bedford.

The job affirmed his idealistic bent. College students everywhere were devoting themselves to the environment, the Peace Corps, and the civil rights movement. Middle-class students identified with the oppressed and wanted to reject the self-centered materialism of their parents. They believed that the world would only improve with their involvement, and even as they protested the thirty billion dollars per year that the government was spending to send young men to war, they spread doctrines of peace and cooperation. Over two hundred anti-war demonstrations disrupted college campuses, and young people insisted on freedom and respect to be who they wanted, love whomever they desired, and do whatever they pleased. A job working with a poverty program was one in which to take some pride, although it could be more challenging than a regular teaching position.

"This is the one I wanted to do," Dean states. "It had the most appeal to me and sounded the most interesting and exciting. I was idealistic and thought I would have more impact on the kids."

The program was introduced as part of President Johnson's Great Society agenda. Teachers in the school district were to identify the most gifted children from poverty-stricken families—those kids who would benefit from one-on-one attention not readily available in larger classes. However, when asked to select students to leave their classrooms, some teachers were inclined simply to get rid of those that caused the most trouble.

When Dean first met some of the other teachers, one man said, "I think it really takes guts to do what you're doing." Others made similar comments. Unsure what to make of that, he dismissed it. Then he found out what they were talking about.

Dean thought he was walking into a situation where he could do something important, but what he found was a room full of kids who had little going for them. It did not take long to discover that the man he had replaced in this program had in fact been run off the road by these same students and beaten so badly that he had been hospitalized. Dean was not at all sure what might be in store for him.

"When I taught that group of troubled kids, none of them had any discipline. I assumed I was going to get the crap beat out of me just like the guy before me, but I set requirements for behavior. I was fair. I was not arbitrary. There were standards and you met them. There was never a problem—which told me that these 'worst case' kids really wanted to be shown a way to behave. They would test your limits, but they wouldn't go too far.

"I realized early that many of these kids had been in trouble at one time or another—some more seriously than others—and all of them were discipline problems, which is why their teachers had pushed them onto me. Those teachers didn't choose the kids who might have been able to benefit from extra tutoring, and with a number of these kids, there wasn't a lot going on upstairs. That didn't make them bad kids. Some were definitely bad, but a few were just fine once you were willing to address them one-on-one. When they knew you actually cared about them, they opened up."

One boy in particular became Dean's protector. His name was Glenn and he was seventeen, tall, and strong, but he was only in eighth grade. His parents would not allow him to leave school because they wanted the welfare check they received for him as long as he was there. "Glenn was smart," Dean says. "I had real rapport with him, but he just didn't think that learning was worthwhile. The future to him just meant get out of high school, get some menial job, or go on the dole. He had no aspirations, and it seemed almost impossible to get him to see his potential." Some of the other kids, however, seemed to show potential, though few would go on to benefit from higher education.

Dean commuted an hour back and forth between Saxton and Bedford. He lived in the Cerra's home while Gerda continued to work at the bank, but after living there for two weeks, they reconsidered. All they had was a used Ford, a couple of hundred dollars, and their clothes, but they decided to see if there were any houses in Saxton for rent. They wanted to be on their own.

"We desperately wanted out," says Dean. "We looked at

six or seven places and only one had an indoor bathroom. That settled it; it didn't matter that we couldn't afford it. I'd spent six years of childhood without indoor plumbing and I wasn't going back to that. So we rented this seven-room house. I think it was fifty or sixty dollars a month—a week's take-home pay—and we really had to scrape to pull that together. We had a budget of a hundred and fifty dollars to furnish the place."

It was a modest two-story frame house on a corner not far from the fire station, but it was home.

Along with many of the other women in Saxton, Gerda found a job in a shoe factory near Altoona. Since it was located on the other side of a mountain, a factory-owned bus picked them all up at five each morning. Other women on the bus did not socialize with Gerda, so she made few friends, which made the ride over the mountain rather cold and lonely. Then she sat for eight hours every day on a hard wooden chair, working as a bartack which meant cutting out and forming squares to sew into shoes where the strap going over the instep met the body of the shoe. All day long, after a difficult bus ride, she sewed the same pattern over and over. Then she went home to cook dinner on a simple hotplate.

This was in the Pennsylvania mountains in the dead of winter. She would walk through snow and cold to the bus to face hard stares and earn scant wages at a tedious job to pay rent on a tiny house, while Dean taught for pay that was just as bad.

Yet they were happy. "We were on our own," says Gerda. "We could do whatever we wanted."

"I don't think either one of us really felt like we were suffering," Dean agrees, "or that this was a hardship. We were so happy to be on our own and with each other that it was an endless adventure."

5

While he was teaching and grading papers, Dean continued to write and send out stories. When he received personal notes from a rejecting editor who offered advice, he felt encouraged.

He sent a story, "Soft Come the Dragons," to one of these kind editors, along with a note explaining that he had a Druid friend who was going to cast a spell on the entire staff of the magazine to make them buy his work. Not long afterward, he received a note from Ed Ferman, editor of *The Magazine of Science Fiction and Fantasy*, that said, "I had thought Druid spells were long ago impotent, but . . ." and with it was a check for one hundred twenty dollars for the story. Dean was elated. In the same year that Twiggy, Rosemary, and Vietnam dominated the news, Dean had made his first sale in science fiction.

Ed Ferman was an important contact. He had taken over the editorship of *The Magazine of Fantasy and Science Fiction* in 1966 and it prospered under his guidance. He also edited anthologies, so Dean's acceptance gave him a shot at being invited into some.

"My life has never been the same," Dean claims. That same year, Ferman also bought "To Behold the Sun."

"Soft Come the Dragons" tackled the theme of how myth and science are each bereft without the other; myth fails to advance us beyond superstition, but enriches us spiritually, whereas science alone makes us somewhat sterile as human beings. A secondary theme in this story is racial insecurity and the way that most human beings react to strangers. It may take contact with truly alien life-forms, Dean asserts, to free us of our tendency to hate others unlike ourselves. Interestingly, one character asks another why he writes. His response: "To detail Truth."

In the second story, "To Behold the Sun," a man prepares to fly with a crew toward the sun to study its energy for use in space travel. It is a gruesome tale about the paralysis that results from an intense desire for the very thing that one most fears. When Dean first submitted this story, Ferman returned it with a note that indicated it needed more scientific grounding. He included two paragraphs that he had requested from Isaac Asimov, who offered them for Dean's use. Dean was astonished, but he went to work. He managed to slip in Asimov's rationalizations without disruption, and sold the revised story forthwith. Two years later, when Dean met Asimov at a fan convention in Philadelphia, he jokingly offered him a share of the proceeds—about a quarter—for his contribution. Asimov smiled and said, "If you don't mind, I'd rather kiss your wife," whereupon he took Gerda in his arms and kissed her.

Both stories were reprinted in a collection three years later called *Soft Come the Dragons*, and the first story was included in other anthologies, such as *The Liberated Future* and *Dragon Tales*. From his first publication, Dean elected to use his middle initial, R., for his authorship.

He also tried his hand at short novels. "The first few novels I wrote didn't sell, so I put them aside," he admits. "I didn't keep revising them. I went on to something else."

6

In their limited free time, Dean and Gerda set about furnishing their little house. Gerda sold her wedding dress for sixty dollars so she could buy a sewing machine. (Some people she knew were upset by this and warned her of dire consequences.) They needed curtains and she was practical. She knew she would never again need the wedding dress.

"Everywhere we lived, we've made it our home," says Dean, "so we repainted this place and haunted garage sales and auctions. We bought an old sofa for five dollars in one of these country auctions. To fix it up, I learned how to use an upholstery gun and Gerda sewed slipcovers. We also bought a used sleeper sofa to use as a bed, and when we folded this thing out, it was the size of a king-size bed, but it was very low to the floor."

In the attic, they found some old doors in storage. They asked the landlord if they could have one. He liked the fact that they were painting his house, so he told them they could. They brought one downstairs and transformed it into a dining room table. "It was paneled," says Dean, "so we covered it with a sheet of masonite and put a latticework trim around the edge. We painted it black and brown and put short legs on it to make a Japanese dining table. We had everyone in the family saving plastic breadbags for which Gerda sewed pillow covers. We shredded the plastic bags and stuffed the pillow covers and made pillows to sit on the floor and eat Japanese-style."

They also put up bamboo blinds and Gerda sewed curtains

to hang along the sides of the windows. They kept the blinds closed most of the time. They had two used kitchen chairs to sit on and Dean built some bookcases — "the worst constructed bookcases in the history of the Western world" — for their small collection.

"We had taken an Oriental theme throughout the house," Dean explains, "and it worked. We were just in heaven."

The house had no oven or stove, so Gerda cooked on a hot-plate. "It was really amazing what she could do," Dean relates. "She'd put a Corningware dish on it and cook everything in that. She'd make stuffed pork chops, cakes, everything but pies on that hotplate, and we ate very well."

When they were ready to have guests, they invited Dean's parents for Sunday dinner. "When my mother came for the first time, she cried all the way through the meal," Dean laughs. "'You're eating on the *floor*,' she'd say. 'This is terrible.'"

He wanted to show them how they had fixed up the bed-room, so he invited them to tour the house. "I guess they hadn't stopped to think how we were sleeping, but we couldn't afford to go out and buy a bed. When my mother saw the old sofabed, she started crying even more because we were sleep-ing on the floor."

He could not make her understand that they *wanted* to live that way.

7

As Dean went to school each day, he discovered that the posi-tion involved more than just teaching. "I was expected to know the background on these kids and do counseling."

Some of what Dean saw around him for those few months would inspire one of his most popular stories, *Twilight Eyes*. One of the protagonists, Rya, comes from a town similar to Saxton. "That was sort of based on what I saw with some of these kids," he acknowledges. "There was one girl who was fourteen and had a reputation around school that she was 'beyond easy.' I heard other teachers joking about her. There were eleven kids in her family and her parents had children to get welfare payments. The father hired out some of the girls for prostitution. There was some truck traffic up through those mountains, so this man would set up an air mattress at a rest-area picnic table and offer his daughters on that. I found out that everybody knew and nobody cared; I think it was at that point that I knew I had to get out of this job."

Dean became disillusioned with these social welfare programs. What sounded good on paper became corrupted in the hands of greedy politicians and bureaucrats.

"The system didn't really care about these kids. Most of the money that was supposed to be targeted toward books and educational materials was funneled into building a gymnasium. To get a few dollars for books, I had to fight for weeks. If you cared or believed you could make a change, you were seen as an odd duck. I was convinced that someone somewhere was pocketing the money."

He perceived how government programs fed attitudes of entitlement among these people. They seemed to think that the government owed them something because they were poor, and getting funds for such things as child welfare took away initiative and inspired some people to find ways to cheat the system. "By the end of the year," says Dean, "I realized these kids would never be helped by this system."

Dean discovered that his protector, Glenn, came from a large family. He lived in abominable conditions. "I saw where his family lived," Dean recalls. "It was a shack that could comfortably accommodate three people, but there were all these kids. I remember asking Glenn where he slept and he told me, 'On the porch'—even during the winter. You start looking at that and you think: As long as they're in the orbit of parents who have this incredibly screwed-up worldview and no ambition, they won't make it. These kids would have one hell of an upward pull to get out of the overwhelming gravity of that life."

Rya Raines in *Twilight Eyes* describes it: "Poor, uneducated, unwilling to be educated, ignorant. Secretive, withdrawn, suspicious. Set in their ways, stubborn, close-minded."[1] So much for the ideal of the noble savage, the human being away from the trappings of civilization.

Although Dean knew what had happened to his predecessor and had heard about the various weapons these kids liked to devise, he thought he had things under control. "We had a couple of kids come to the house who were angry with me. They'd pound on the door and demand that I come outside. I'd open the door and say, 'Yes, what is it?' And that was usually the end of it. There was constant testing among the boys, but I think the reason I had no real trouble was that I had a good sense of humor and I was interested in them. Then, of course, I had Glenn threatening to beat people up."

For Dean, teaching was a constant performance. He had loved teachers who made learning into an experience; he tried to do the same.

"We'd make up games," he recalls. "I brought in a rubber ball. As we discussed the lesson, I would fire the ball at anyone in the room at any time. Whoever caught the ball could hold it and fire it at will at anyone else—including me. Depending on whether it hit the target completely unawares or whether he caught it, the pitcher scored points. You also had to be able to answer any question at any time and be part of the discussion. I found that keeping that ball firing around used up their energy and excited them, but in a strange way it also focused them; they would pay attention instead of just zoning out. I tried to find things like that to do, but I was never as good at it as I would have liked."

Looking back, Dean does not feel that he really inspired them. "I was young. It was my first experience. It was like coming into a war zone. You're scrambling every day to figure out how you're going to keep these kids interested, how you're going to keep them in their seats, and how you're going to reach them and make some difference. I do think that if I had any impact, it would have been in the sense that these kids were given no reason at home to have any self-esteem. Maybe I helped with that." He also helped some of them begin to love books; when they told him how the novels they read helped them forget their situations, it further inspired him to want to write stories that could serve that purpose.

In part, he felt, some of the other teachers made things worse. "Basically the place was adversarial. They would come to me and tell me about these kids—how rotten this one was, or that so-and-so was arrested or had a reform school record. They were very down on the kids."

The school district allowed corporal punishment and some

teachers had paddles with holes drilled into them to create a stronger sting. One fellow teacher, who seemed to enjoy punishing his students, even made a paddle for Dean.

"You're going to need this," he said.

Dean refused it. "I don't want it," he insisted. "I don't think I'm going to need it."

The other man laughed. "You're going to come to me and say, 'Give me that paddle after all.'"

"No," said Dean, "If any of them need it, I'll send them down the hall to you."

Dean wanted to treat them fairly, but had little hope that it would matter.

8

Dean and Gerda liked their privacy, but they were somewhat surprised by how difficult it was in Saxton to evoke a friendly response. A man next door, who taught in the same school system, usually responded to their greetings with a hurried nod before he disappeared into his house.

One day, this man had to deliver a message to Dean about an early morning meeting.

There was a knock at the door and when Dean opened it, he saw his neighbor standing about twelve feet back from the door. Surprised, Dean invited him in.

He said, "No, no, I can't come in. I have this notice."

He held up a piece of paper and continued to stand right where he was, forcing Dean to go out to retrieve it. Dean thought this behavior strange until he discovered one day what the townspeople thought of him and Gerda.

One of Dean's close friends from college, Jeff Steele, was from Saxton. Whenever Jeff came home from the Pittsburgh Institute of Art to visit his parents, he went to see Dean and Gerda. "He would tell us stories that were being circulated about us in the town," Dean relates. "It was so weird. We liked moodily lit rooms and we had put up bamboo blinds that we kept closed. It never occurred to us that this would become a major point of concern—people wondering what we were doing that we didn't want anyone to see."

"I understand you're Buddhists," Jeff told him. "Everyone in town thinks you're Buddhists. They don't know what Buddhists are, but they don't want anything to do with a Buddhist."

"How did they get the idea I was a Buddhist?" Dean asked him. Then he remembered. He had once had a conversation with a defrocked Methodist minister who had taught at the high school part of the year. They had discussed which religions were the least hypocritical, and both had thought that Buddhists most closely follow what they preach. "It was just a casual conversation—yet everyone in town took it to mean we were Buddhists."

In fact, Dean and Gerda were still practicing Catholics, although they were having doubts. A single priest went from one small town to another in those mountains, and the Koontzes could attend whichever service coincided with the time they rose from bed. However, the priest had a habit of making people feel guilty for coming in late. "He was so full of himself," Dean remembers. "He'd stop right in the middle of the Mass, turn to the people who had come in, and stare for twenty seconds, half a minute, until they were completely humbled." Yet when the priest himself was late, he never apologized.

Coupled with this overt hypocrisy were unsettling changes from Vatican II. "Somehow it just seemed like it wasn't timeless anymore," Dean complains. "It makes no sense to say the ritual is symbolic unless it symbolizes timeless things. I happen to think that the Latin Mass is a beautiful service. It's the most refined theater in the history of human culture, and to just come in, willy-nilly, and start hacking it up struck me as a lack of true belief. I can understand the motivation behind it. The wisdom in the early sixties was that change was necessary to prevent the Church from losing people. What's happened instead is that, subsequent to these changes, the Church has lost people."

Many of Dean's stories from that period reflect his growing antagonism toward religion. He would soon stop attending services and, for a while, move away from a belief in God.

[1]Dean R. Koontz, *Twilight Eyes* (New York: Berkley, 1987), p. 175.

SIX

The Courage to Act

1

WHEN THE SCHOOL YEAR CONCLUDED IN SAXTON, DEAN AND
Gerda moved out. "In fact, we left the very day that my obliga-
tions were over," Dean says. He had taken another job in a
regular school system in Mechanicsburg, Pennsylvania, teaching high school English. He had had enough of the politics of
welfare.

Mechanicsburg was about one hundred miles from Bedford, just down the turnpike near Harrisburg. Dominated by a
military facility, which was also the primary employer, the
town was quite conservative. Although Dean had lost much of
his liberal idealism, he was not ready to respond to anyone
who might try to curb his belief in personal freedom.

In his 1974 novel, *After the Last Race*, Dean described what
it was like to try to find a place to live there: "Although this
part of Pennsylvania was one of the fastest-growing regions in
the East, the rental situation was abysmal. Generally the only
things available were garden apartments in look-alike com-
plexes where the walls between neighbors were too thin to
stop more than a whisper. The houses for rent were either
tumble-down bargains or cramped little ranch homes
squeezed into the postage-stamp lots in neighborhoods that
might have been pressed whole out of plastic."[1] They were to
live in this area for eight years, and Dean would set several
novels here.

They found an apartment in Lemoyne, a suburb of the state
capital. Although his $4,800 salary was a step up from what he
had been paid in Saxton, Dean knew they would barely
squeeze by. They had enough money saved to allow him to
spend the summer writing, but Gerda went job hunting and
soon found work overseeing accounts at a credit bureau. "It
was an education," she says, "seeing how people deal with

credit. Some people played games just to see what they could get, even though they could pay their bills."

They talked about starting a family, but knew they must put it off until they were financially stable. "When we first got married," Gerda explains, "we thought we would have children, but we wanted to wait until we could afford a house."

One of their favorite activities was reading. During the early years of their marriage, they kept track of the titles, week by week, and by the end of the year, counted them up. "We were such heavy readers," says Dean. "Each of us would read between two and three hundred books a year. At the end of the year, it was kind of fun to look back and see what we had read." They did not own a television until Dean's parents, who could not believe they did not want one, bought a used set for them.

"We were upset," Dean claims. "We didn't want it. We almost never turned it on." They preferred spending all their time and money on books.

Sometimes they shared books, but Gerda preferred mysteries and suspense. "She loathed science fiction," says Dean. "I got her to read certain terrific science fiction books and she admitted to liking them, but she never could get into science fiction. She was always wishing I would write something else. She would say, 'You could write a lot of stuff better than this,' and I would say, 'This genre is as good as anything.' Which I still believe."

Dean spent the summer writing a novel called *Star Quest*. He had sold more stories, but thus far had had a difficult time getting his novels considered for publication. He prepared himself primarily by reading other novels. "I'd read literally two thousand books. I'd been reading assiduously since I was ten or eleven. I had wiped out everything in the library. I just read, read, read. I was saturated in fiction—which was quite a preparation in itself. Other than that, I think I'd read James Blish's criticism of the science fiction genre, *The Issue at Hand*."

Dean did have one more story published that year in a men's magazine, *Mr.*, called "Love 2005." It was not what he wanted to write, but it was money. "I was looking around at what markets I could write for," he explains. "I was following the Harlan Ellison mode. I'd read all about his early career and how he could pay the rent with the stories he wrote for men's magazines, so I did one and they bought it." He found, however, that the editor did extensive revising, "which is one reason I did fewer short stories than most other writers. I got sick of turning in a story and finding it altered when it was published."

2

As the fall semester opened toward the end of 1967, Dean found the experience of teaching at Mechanicsburg to be just as taxing as it had been at Saxton, but for different reasons. One of the first things he heard was that a longtime teacher had been called on the carpet for teaching a children's book to high school students. That book turned about to be Orwell's classic *Animal Farm*, with which the principal was completely unfamiliar. Dean could not quite believe this.

He also discovered, to his chagrin, that the administration was more concerned about keeping the kids quiet and in their classrooms than about the quality of education. They claimed they had little time to read, yet they dictated the curriculum. Dean enjoyed the students, but he disliked his contacts with the administration. Whenever he deviated, he was called to task for it. They did not like his reading lists or the way he failed to devote the proper amount of time to classics like *Silas Marner* that other ninth grade classes were reading. "We would get through *Silas Marner* in one-third the time allotted—and then read things that were *fun* to read."

"I was always in trouble with the administration," Dean admits. "They were always after me to get my hair cut, and I did not have long hair. It went over the collar a little, but that was considered unforgivable."

Dean just gritted his teeth and did the best he could.

3

In 1968, Sirhan Sirhan assassinated Robert Kennedy just a few months before Martin Luther King Jr. fell to another assassin's bullet. The Democratic Party convention in Chicago saw antiwar riots, and the arrest of the Chicago Seven. Nixon, who promised an end to the war, was elected president, and an unmanned flight to the moon proved successful. *Hair*, with its nudity and vulgar language, rocked the theater world, and *2001* invited audiences to contemplate space in a whole new way. Many kids watched it while dropping LSD. Mickey Mouse had his fortieth birthday.

After a year in Lemoyne, Dean and Gerda moved to a two-story garden apartment in Colonial Park, situated in a complex called Colonial Crest. It was a step up, they thought, and they stayed there for several years. Their collection of books numbered around five thousand.

That summer after his first year of teaching, Dean decided to let his hair grow long. During college, in spite of changes in fashion all around him, the pressure to get a good job had forced him to keep it short. Now, with no one to tell him he could not, he decided to adopt a look more in keeping with other people his age. Unfortunately, when his mother visited and saw him, she believed that he had become a hippie and would quit his job. "She was very upset about it," Gerda remembers. "She worried excessively about what he was doing." Florence had read some of Dean's poetry and knew of his dream to become a writer, but she hoped he would forget it and keep a responsible job. More than anything, she feared that he would end up destitute. There was nothing Dean could say to reassure her. She continued to worry, so when it was time to return to school, she was happy when Dean cut his hair and looked responsible again.

At the start of the semester, Dean prepared a list of four hundred books that he recommended to students for book reports. Six of their reports had to be on books required by the school, while three could be of anything on the list. The books they would analyze in class would be chosen by majority rule, but the minority would be able to make some other arrangement with him. He had included a few controversial books like Salinger's *The Catcher in the Rye*, and one-fourth of his list was science fiction that he himself had loved. Among them were Bradbury's *Something Wicked This Way Comes* and *The Martian Chronicles*; several Lovecraft collections; Sturgeon's *The*

Dreaming Jewels; Heinlein's *The Star Beast* and *Beyond This Horizon*; and works by Frederik Pohl, Jack Williamson, and other authors of science fiction classics. Dean also included his own first novel, bought by editor Donald Wollheim and published that year.

4

Dean's novel was called *Star Quest*, and it was part of an Ace Double, two short novels published back-to-back as a single package. The second book was *Doom of the Green Planet* by Emil Petaja. Dean expected to receive $1,250 for it, but Wollheim told him that the other author's contribution was longer and they had to pay him a greater share of the $2,500 advance. Dean received only $1,000, but he was happy to have it. Years later, he met the other author at a convention and learned that Petaja had been told the same thing, which meant that Ace Books apparently had pocketed the extra $500.

Star Quest takes up a theme that would reverberate throughout many of Dean's later novels. Living in a culture of political duplicity, wherein covert and morally hypocritical actions of the government were being exposed and denounced, Dean used the story to indicate how one end of the political spectrum mirrored the other. Democrat or Republican, they had the same agenda of manipulating the masses toward their own selfish ends. Although Dean had liberal leanings—diminished somewhat by his experience in Saxton—he sensed that politics in general were prone to corruption. Where power was concerned, those who wielded it were more likely to be malignant then benign. His novel mirrored what he believed was true of society at that time.

In *Star Quest*, the universe in the twenty-ninth century has been ravaged by eight hundred years of warfare between two races, both of whom enslave members of races caught in the middle. One such person, Thom, is transformed into a war machine. When a brainwashing drug wears off, he enters a floating library (a symbol from Dean's childhood of refuge, enhancement, and possibility). The library, managed by the disembodied brain of a former teacher, prepares Thom with a metaphysical history: in their war-torn world, the Fringe is a barrier of quasi-reality between alternate universes, and races mutated by radiation who possess psionic talents want to exploit this barrier to rid their world of its warring factions. Thom joins with a "Mutie" named Hunk, who is only a head. Hunk takes Thom back to his people. The Muties realize that their best plan is to use their paranormal mental powers to encompass the parts of the universe they want to preserve, and then move everything except the warring factions into a neighboring universe. In other words, they will cut out the cancer and leave it behind.

In this novel, religion, politics, and family issues become entwined. They share the hypocrisy, deceptiveness, and cruelty that Dean finds intolerable. Whenever he rails against one or another of them, his anger seems directed at all three. He is especially enraged at those forces charged with protecting weaker beings that wantonly betray them.

The Muties are fighting hypocrisy. Nuclear war made them what they are, but those who used the weapons feel no responsibility for the Muties' plight, and in fact vilify them. "It is an old trait in men," says one of the Muties. "I think it is an attempt to salve their consciences for the wrong acts that caused us. If they pretend we are evil, attribute to us a relationship with the devil or with the enemy, killing us makes sense. And when they have murdered all of us, they will no longer have to face the mistake they made."[2]

This is a statement against corrupt politics and the need of politicians at that time to label the nondemocratic world monolithically communist and indisputably evil. It also reflects Dean's feelings about his father. Ray was the cancer that should be left behind. Because of him, the family had been unable to attain things held up as normal, so Dean created a world that valued abnormality and recognized its richness. "You gain something when you lose normality. Nature . . . smashes you about in drunken folly . . . and then presents you with many talents."[3] It was interesting for him to think of the Muties as "the new mythology for this world."[4] As he had been drilled in college English courses, he offered a Freudian framework, identifying the id, ego, and superego as components of this fictional world, and designating the ego as that which builds character.

One Mutie, Seer, is driven insane when he sees God. The creator, he says, is something so horrible, with so many facets of terror, that Seer cannot bear the vision. God is an indescribable demon. This indicates that Dean had moved away from his interest in Catholicism toward an antagonism against a seemingly imperfect—even sadistic—creator of a chaotic and hurtful world. Some of his future novels would carry these attacks even further.

5

As it turned out, this novel was—among others—one of the books that got Dean into trouble with the school administration.

The principle asked to see him one day during his free period. Unsure what it could be about, Dean went to his office. "The curriculum coordinator, the principal, the assistant principal, and the superintendent of schools were there," Dean recalls. "The curriculum coordinator had a dufflebag, and he dumped the contents on the table. Out of it poured all these paperback books that were on my extra-credit reading list."

The man eyed him and said, "Are you really allowing your students to read this book?" He held up a copy, which pictured a woman with her shoulder bared.

Dean shrugged and nodded. "Yeah, that's on my list."

"You're going to allow them to read a book with all this sex in it?"

"There's no sex in this book," Dean insisted.

The man was not dissuaded. "I can see the cover, mister!"

Dean was astounded. Here was an educator, judging a book by its cover! Then the official went through the other books and made comments on why each was unacceptable. Yet no one in the room had read any of them.

The principal told Dean that the parents of one of his students had complained about *Star Quest*. Dean pressed for details and the principal said that the part where a childlike character sucks on the breast of a woman—not in a sexual sense, but for comfort—was obscene. He insisted that Dean remove this novel from his reading list. Dean declined to do so.

Then they got into the issue of how little time he spent on the classics. Every other ninth grade class spent six weeks on *Silas Marner*, while Dean covered it in two weeks.

"I didn't want to spend so much time teaching *Silas Marner*," Dean insists. "I said to them, this is mainly a famous work because it was the first long-form story of this type, but that doesn't mean it's a wonderful story or that it resonates with kids this age. Besides, it can be taught in a week. Why drag it out?"

No one was satisfied with his defense.

"I eventually got the feeling they were trying to drive me out," Dean admits, "but it was partly because I wouldn't do certain things. For example, this was the time when miniskirts were getting popular, so we were called to a faculty meeting after school, in which we were told that, first thing in the morning, we were to look at each girl as she came in and judge whether her skirt was too short. If so, then we had to make her kneel and then take a ruler and measure how far from the floor her skirt hung. If it was more than an inch and a half, it was too short. I thought this was an outrageous misuse of my time—and there were hundreds of similar onerous tasks. The principal had all these rules that had nothing to do with educating kids, and gradually I came to loathe the educational system."

Shortly thereafter, the curriculum coordinator approached Dean about the fact that the classics were underrepresented on his extra-credit reading list, constituting only about twenty-five percent of the total. Dean again refused to change his list. To his delight, the students had chosen Heinlein's *Stranger in a Strange Land* for classroom discussion and it was going very well. He did not wish to interrupt this. Then a parent called him and said that Heinlein espoused communist and antireligious principles in the novel and she was not going to allow her son to finish it. Dean felt frustrated.

Soon the administration caught word of this complaint, and when Dean once again maneuvered to prevent them from undermining his classroom authority, certain members took turns sitting in on his class so as to catch him in the act of teaching some forbidden word or idea. It was an intimidation tactic and it made the students wonder what was going on.

Back at home, Dean told Gerda that he could hardly bear to go into the classroom anymore. Yet there were so few teaching jobs available, especially in the middle of the year. He was making a little money now from the sale of his stories, and Wollheim had purchased two more novels. Maybe his luck with that would continue. He wanted to write, God, how he wanted to just write!

6

The following year saw four more stories in print: "A Darkness in My Soul" in *Fantastic Stories*, "Dreambird" in *Worlds of If*, and "The Psychedelic Children" and "The Twelfth Bed" in *The Magazine of Fantasy and Science Fiction*. Dean would later include three of these in his 1970 collection, *Soft Come the Dragons*.

"A Darkness in My Soul," which is about a man exploring the convoluted mind of God, became one of Dean's next novels. Similarly, "Dreambird" was intended for longer form. Dean got it under contract as a novel, but never wrote it. It is about what happens to a man who is searching for the Pheasant of Dreams—an animal with ESP that can telepathically read anyone's wildest fantasies and transmit them to him as real events.

Dean thought "The Twelfth Bed" had mainstream commercial potential. It features elderly people struggling to ward off blows to their dignity by a society that has no more use for them. He sent it to magazines like *Esquire* and *Playboy*, but every editor rejected it as being too depressing or antihuman. One person even called it obscene. Only Ed Ferman saw that it was "charged with hope," and he bought it.

Dean's other story, "The Psychedelic Children," takes aim at hippies who took drugs and selfishly endangered the lives of their unborn children.

7

While he tried to defy the school administration and teach his courses, Gerda moved on to do office work at A.B. Dick, a copying company. She also decided to attend the local college, University Center. Her family could never offer support for higher education, and now with Dean's encouragement, she went part-time. Most of her courses were in psychology, which interested her, but she felt stifled by the experience. "The professors did not want to know what the students thought," she complains. "They wanted their own views parroted back to them."

"She came home from a political science course," Dean recalls, "and said that people have to go through college when they're young and gullible. She couldn't stand listening to teachers who were selling their own political agendas." Dean understood this. He had been affected only by those professors who were knowledgeable, passionate, and able to teach without bias.

He also knew what it meant to be pressured to abide by rules that he found confining. He was having similar troubles. Then one day, he attended a retirement party for one of his colleagues. It was a small gathering, with cake and punch, and someone had taken up a collection to purchase a gift. As this man's working life wound down to its end, he opened the package to find a white shirt and tie. Dean was disturbed to think that this man's colleagues knew so little about him — or cared so little about getting a truly personal gift. Was this all the man's contribution amounted to: a shirt and tie at the end of his long tenure? And what need did he have of that anyway?

The party forced Dean to take stock. Was this all he might aspire to? Is this how it would end for him four decades hence? It seemed abysmal, impossible, particularly in light of how much he struggled with the administration. He could not imagine years of this. His teaching career thus far had been inordinately stressful. What did he have to look forward to? Dean came home and expressed his despair to Gerda. He wanted to be a writer but things were so uncertain. He had sold three novels, the combined advances for which did not quite match his teaching salary. There was no certainty about when he would sell another, and short stories paid almost nothing.

"I was at the point in Mechanicsburg of being ready to bash

my head into the wall," he says. "It didn't seem worth trying to educate anyone anymore."

Gerda had learned a lot about strength and determination in her difficult years at home. She had worked hard to earn money, she had made her own clothes, and she had found time to be involved in school activities. There were ways to get through this. She reminded Dean that at least he was selling his writing, and pointed out that the educational system was declining anyway. The public schools appeared to be in serious trouble. In the long term, teaching might prove to be a shaky career. Resourceful and familiar with commitment, Gerda estimated that between what she made and what Dean might manage to bring in, they could pay the bills. They lived cheaply and could adjust to even more spartan conditions if need be. She made him a momentous offer: She would work and be his sole support for five years while he tried to make it as a writer.

"If you can't make it in five years," she said, "you'll never make it."

Dean jumped at this opportunity. It was January, the start of the second semester, but he handed in his notice of resignation.

Now he was liberated from employer harassment and free to pursue his dream. He would give it everything he had. He had no intention, however, of living the chaotic life that his father had pursued. To his mind, he was nothing like his father and he would prove it.

This decision meant putting off again the idea of starting a family. It was going to be tight for a while, maybe for years, but he and Gerda both wanted to see what would happen if Dean put his full efforts into writing. They were partners.

8

Even as Dean struggled with the school district, another concern weighed heavily. Late in 1968, his mother had suffered a serious stroke and was rushed to the hospital. Not long afterward came a second stroke that began to affect her mind and ensured that she would remain hospitalized for an extended period of time. Dean and Gerda visited her often. She tried to talk, but it was difficult for her. "She had a gruesome, halting kind of speech," says Dean. "She was aphasic. She could get ideas across, but she had a lot of problems." At times, when she could talk a little, she would recall a brief memory from her past that had been pleasant. While Dean found such moments poignant, he sensed that they signaled life slowly leaving and he felt helpless to do anything.

At first, Florence seemed to improve. She had been in Bedford Memorial for two months, and during the period in which she was doing better, her doctor sent her to Presbyterian-University Hospital in Pittsburgh for an angiogram and further treatment. With better diagnostic facilities, they would be able to tell if there was a blockage that might respond to surgery. So Florence went to Pittsburgh, which meant that Dean and Gerda spent considerable time during the month of January driving over one hundred fifty miles each way. They could not do it every day, but they went as often as possible.

After the angiogram, Florence's neck suddenly swelled up as big as her head and turned a dark purple. Dean wondered if the treatment itself had made her worse. "I was convinced it had been badly done."

More strokes quickly followed, making Florence more aphasic and less able to let people know what she was feeling. Dean was later to write a story, "Shambolain," that expressed some of the emotions he experienced at her bedside: "With her dying, Della had created a pocket in existence and we had crawled inside to await the end with her."[5] Dean and Gerda spent hours at her bedside, leaving for only the most necessary tasks. There was no need to tell Florence that Dean had quit his job. It was clear that she was declining and this was something that she should not have to worry about.

Dean wanted to assure his mother that he would be all right. His heart was set on being a writer, yet so far he had shown her only a few short stories and a science fiction novel that she had not appreciated. It was better to say nothing.

One day as they stood nearby, she labored to speak. She seemed to have something urgent to say. Such moments were so rare now that Dean knew it must be important. He leaned closer to hear. "There's something I've got to tell you about your father," she struggled to say. "You've got to know."

At that moment, Ray walked in. Florence looked at him with fear in her eyes, glanced at Dean, and whispered, "Later." Whatever she had to reveal, she obviously felt she could not say it in front of her husband. Dean could not imagine what it might be. Nor was he ever to know.

One morning, Dean and Gerda took leave of Florence to return to their jobs. As they reached Harrisburg and walked through the door, the phone rang. There had been another crisis. They turned around and drove at high speed all the way back. Before reaching Pittsburgh, Dean was pulled over by a patrol car and when he explained that his mother was in the hospital, the police officer put away his ticket book and sent them on their way. His kindness was the one bright spot of the day.

Florence was still hanging on when they got there, but not fully conscious. They stayed in her room for a while and then went into a waiting room for families of intensive care patients. It was there that they were told that Florence had passed away.

On February 8, 1969, Florence Koontz ended her fifty-three years on earth. She was never to see the coming years of struggle for Dean that might have alarmed her, but neither would she see his success. For the rest of his life that would be a bitter realization. And he would always wonder whether the revelation about his father would have been a life-changing event for him. For all he knew, it was merely some small fact of which he was already aware but which had somehow become more significant to his mother's deteriorating mind. It would not be for many years that he would have cause to consider her last words to him in a strange new way.

The viewing was held in the Louis V. Geisel Funeral Chapel in Bedford, and it was here that another event occurred that would have painful repercussions for Dean in the years to come.

He walked over to Florence's casket, near to his Aunt Kate, who was talking to someone. He overheard her say, "See what that stroke did to her; it put that little twist in her nose."

Dean sought to correct her. "Oh, no, Aunt Kate, her nose was always like that."

Kate looked at him a moment and then turned to the other woman. "He's just like his damn father," she said. This surprised Dean. Here was the Logue family bickering that had always kept his aunts at odds with one another; now it had become intergenerational.

Annoyed, Dean said, "This isn't the place for this."

Kate reacted dramatically. "How dare you say that to me!" she shouted. Her sister Betty came running over, threw an arm around her, and led her out of the room. Then Betty returned and confronted Dean, making him feel like a villain at his own mother's funeral. Accusations were flung around and Dean was mortified. It was his Uncle Ray who managed to get things settled. And that was the last time Dean ever saw him.

Florence Koontz was buried in Bedford Memorial Park. As Dean stood by the graveside in the cold winter wind, he felt helpless and guilty. It seemed that he should have been able to do something to save her. He was sure her life had been shortened by the unrelenting stress of living with his father. Yet he could not change things now. She was gone.

Dean had a flat stone designed for a double plot for both his mother and his father. However, when the time came many years later to bury his father, he could not bear to disturb his mother's rest, so he placed his father's ashes in a separate place.

After the funeral, Dean and Gerda went through some of Florence's things. They found nearly five hundred dollars in an envelope marked "Florida." They understood that to mean she had kept money away from Ray so that one day she could visit again the place where she had experienced a rare escape from a life of constant struggle.

9

In the culture at large in 1969, there was a measurable decline in the importance of religion, and people worried about the state of society. The first U.S. troops withdrew from Vietnam. Some seventy-five thousand came back home, although over half a million remained. Mary Jo Kopechne drowned at Chappaquiddick while Ted Kennedy survived, and Lieutenant

Calley was ordered to stand trial for the massacre at My-lai. The big movies were *Midnight Cowboy* and *Easy Rider*. Four hundred-thousand people gathered at Woodstock, and Kurt Vonnegut Jr. published his strange antiwar, time-paradox novel, *Slaughterhouse Five*. After fifty-eight years, the *Saturday Evening Post* suspended publication, signaling the end of an era for high-profile short stories. With pressures from the burgeoning women's movement, pants became acceptable wear for women and many schools were forced to ease up on dress codes. In California, Charles Manson directed the Tate and LaBianca murders.

While Gerda left each morning for A.B. Dick, Dean sat down at his typewriter and began to spin tales of science fiction and fantasy. Gerda's generous offer was not without pressure, primarily from Dean himself. Relatives on both sides viewed his decision to quit his teaching job as frivolous, and felt he was headed for trouble. It seemed an affirmation that he was just like his father and would never focus on a good job. However, Dean knew he was responsible. He would not let Gerda down. He would work hard and try his best, even if it meant suffering the withering remarks of people who wanted him to live according to their values.

Keeping his workplace neat and professional, he set himself a regular goal of four thousand words per day. Eventually he moved into a schedule that demanded ten to twelve hours, six to seven days per week. Often he worked late in the day, from afternoon until late at night.

"There was a time when I sure was cranking them out," Dean says. "Four thousand words is about fourteen pages. In those days, my stories didn't get as much polish. I was working out of sheer desperation because we didn't have anything."

The schedule was grueling, but he felt he was accomplishing a lot. Unlike his father, he disciplined himself to sit for hours at a desk, polishing each page as he went along. Gerda helped with research, and proofread the pages as Dean finished. "She was my toughest critic. She'd read everything before I sent it in and she'd tell me what she thought ought to be changed. In the timeless male manner, I'd rant and rave — and then go in my office and look at it and do most of what she said. Mainly she'd be able to catch me in excess. She'd point out that this scene or that was way over the top and I'd see that she was right."

"What I had to learn," Gerda admits, "is to say what was good about it, too. I tended to tell him about only what was wrong."

Dean was optimistic that applying himself so diligently would soon pay off. He worked on one story after another and sent them out to the magazines he knew. One hundred dollars here, two hundred there—any little bit would help.

Several months went by and to his chagrin, Dean counted up seventy-five rejections. Gerda's small paycheck just managed to cover their expenses, but left nothing for luxuries or emergencies. "We limped from paycheck to paycheck" Dean says. He became frantic. Nothing he had written was selling and he wondered whether his earlier sales had been a fluke—maybe he had been kidding himself about his talent. Quitting his job might have been a terrible mistake.

"The first six months were gruesome," Dean admits, "because when Gerda made the offer, I had work reaching fruition and I had things to submit. Suddenly nothing was selling. It was pretty horrifying."

Dean was embarrassed about letting Gerda down. He was contributing nothing to the household income and his humiliation was exacerbated by relatives who continued to wonder out loud when he would get a job. He had grown his hair long again and he knew what they were thinking: He's a hippie, a layabout. Just like his father. Poor Gerda.

But Gerda had faith in her husband. One thing she knew: He was persistent and he would keep at it until something broke.

Although he had sold his first three novels on his own, he listened to other writers explain the benefits of a well-connected agent. Dean knew people who were writing science fiction and who were also working at the Scott Meredith Literary Agency in New York. This was the same place that had once sent him a useless critique, but he decided to try it again.

"I eventually got Scott Meredith for a year," Dean says. "He handled Norman Mailer and lots of other well-known writers, which impressed me, and he agreed to handle me without a fee. Bob Hoskins was my subagent at Meredith for a while, but he left to become an editor. Then I got Ted Chichak, but I don't think it mattered because everyone at Scott Meredith was grossly overworked and no one had time to do the job well. I don't think I really had a personal agent."

Chichak submitted Dean's novels to Bob Hoskins over at Lancer. Hoskins said they were close but not quite there, and he invited Dean to call. "We had a long conversation on the phone about one of them," Dean remembers. "He told me what it needed and I sat down and revised it and he bought it. We walked our way through two novels and after the second one, I said, 'Oh, I see.' Then I revised the others and he ended up buying all five. He gave me that little click of insight which had to do with plotting. Then, as soon as I grasped the techniques, I applied them."

Thus, after the first six months on his five-year contract with his wife, Dean finally made a sale. He and Gerda celebrated by going out to a cozy little bar called the Red Lantern and having spaghetti and meatballs.

10

That summer, NASA accomplished the first manned moon landing. The astronauts of *Apollo 11* left behind a plaque that read, "Here men from the planet Earth first set foot upon the moon, July, 1969 A.D. We came in peace for all mankind."

It was a momentous event for science fiction writers. Donald Wollheim revised an anthology of stories from 1958 called *Men on the Moon* that had predicted a moon landing before NASA ever existed. He then asked writers in the field, including Ray Bradbury, Harlan Ellison, and Robert Silverberg, to respond with essays to a dour comment made by political commentator I. F. Stone, who believed that idealism would give way to the reality that wherever men go, they cause destruction. "Let the rest of the universe beware," he said.

Dean was one of those writers who responded. Aware of both peaceful and aggressive traits in the human soul, he affirmed the potential for peace with the coming of a new age. Since NASA was not a military organization, and its goal was to conquer nature not men, there should be no weaponry. The lure of the universe, he believed, would defy the negativism from gatekeepers of the status quo. "Surely," he said, "the maturation of the new infant mankind is already evident."[6]

Dean published seven short stories that year, including two that formed his third novel. In *Perihelion*, "The Face in His Belly" was published in two parts. Like many of Dean's tales, its hero is a mutated man who, because of his deformity, is an outsider. His name is Link Forrester and his task is to infiltrate a cult of Muties and kill God. This time, God is not responsible for the mutations but is kin to those who bear them. His own face is on his torso. When Link ultimately confronts God, he plays out his part in a prophecy, showing Dean's early penchant for the quirks of destiny.

A short story published in *Amazing Stories'* January issue that year was "Temple of Sorrow." Editor Barry Malzberg introduced the story with: "The most interesting thing about it is to speculate just how good Mr. Koontz is going to be."[7] The story follows a man who must locate a stolen A-bomb. He infiltrates a religious cult that plans to destroy the world. The cult captures and brainwashes him, but he recovers in time to join his Mutie partner and a renegade woman in saving humanity. Dean had hoped to expand this story into a novel, but never finished it.

The next story, "Killerbot," came out in May, in *Galaxy*. War on a future Earth escalates when outcast human beings are revamped with implanted defense systems; they become semirobotic killers, masquerading as ordinary citizens—the ultimate guerrilla warriors. When the value of life recedes against the ideal of preserving the inanimate world, the protagonist diagnoses this as a society going mad. "When frustrations reached an unbearable limit, when family could be dissolved in a hail of bullets . . . the human mind rebelled against responsibility. Men . . . indulged in a season for freedom . . . freedom to do *anything*."[8]

"Killerbot" was republished in a 1977 anthology, *The Future Now*, under the title, "A Season for Freedom." Dean wrote an Introduction in which he wondered if human life might ultimately become so devalued that people could actually be used as weapons. He feared the encroaching insensitivity he saw in society, with its lack of moral accountability, and believed humans might one day be capable of the atrocities he describes.

"I wrote 'A Season For Freedom' when the Vietnam War was escalating daily," he explains, "when many Americans' respect for human life, both at home and abroad, was at an all-time low. I saw a trend in our society that frightened me."[9] He drew a parallel between American prejudices toward the Vietnamese and toward college students (as evidenced when National Guardsmen killed four students at Kent State in 1970—*after* he wrote this story).

In August, when Dean was beginning to really sweat about his dearth of sales, "A Dragon in the Land" appeared in *Venture Science Fiction*. He had some brief comfort in seeing something of his in print. It begins with a mystery about what has killed eleven million people in China. The story was influenced by "McLuhanism"—the prediction that the world would become a global village and that being so close-knit would eventually end the instinct to fight. This idea had been proposed by Canadian cultural critic Marshall McLuhan, whose *The Medium is the Massage* was published in 1967. The book investigated the social and psychological consequences of mass media and technology, and described how the media works us over. McLuhan's ideas had stimulated Dean to write about two enemies who meet during the final world war and discover that caring for others does not require racial or national kinship. The dragon is a "good beast" that influences people toward peaceful relations.

A month later, "Muse" was published in *The Magazine of Science Fiction and Fantasy*. It followed similar principles—that all living creatures are linked and ought to join together in a common cause of survival and life-enhancement. It was a surprisingly intuitive story prefiguring Dean's own psychological issues. "Muse" features a famous musician, Leonard Chris, whose talent derives from a symbiotic alien slug that attaches to his body. Despite the beauty his music brings to the world, there are those, including his own father, who cannot tolerate "symbiotes"—people who merge with slugs. Leonard objects to their view of the slugs as creepy vampires. "They take, yes," he says, "but they also give."[10] Ultimately the father confronts him and in an attempt to redeem him, kills the slug, thereby destroying Leonard's musical genius. "The things I wanted to say," he tells his father about the slug, "he said for me."[11] Leonard tries to kill his father and, failing that, retreats into a diminished self.

The story was reprinted in 1984 in *Isaac Asimov's Supermen* anthology, devoted to possible destinies of humankind. Uncannily, it seems to predict how Dean's own talent would be coupled with a "handicap" related to his father—the frustration, anger, and ultimate revulsion engendered in him by his father's sociopathic attitudes and acts. His father's behavior, although always a burden to Dean, inspired characters and story lines that won him as much fame in years to come as Leonard Chris in "Muse" had gained.

One of Dean's more moving stories, "Shambolain," was inspired when he and Gerda went to a carnival one day toward the end of the year and listened to people gawking at a freak show. Dean had heard such comments before, but this time it struck him that the people who paid to look at deformed human beings did so to feel superior, which then made them feel better about themselves. Dean was reminded of his mother, how her illness and economic deprivation had forced her to live outside the norm of society and how she had died young because of this—exacerbated by her stressful marriage.

These two events—the freak show and his mother's tragic life—converged into a story about freaks who attack an alien who desires to be part of their group. His difference gives even these outcasts someone toward whom they can feel superior. Finally they kill him because he is not human. One of the freaks, a man with a third foot growing out of his calf, comes to realize that it is not physical differences that dehumanize people. Such prejudices are based in fear and lead only to loss. In fact, the alien had been the most human of all because his gestures were noble and life-affirming—like Dean's mother. Dean sold this story to the science fiction magazine, *Worlds of If*, which published it the following year.

A portion of a short story that has surfaced among collectors was also written around this time, but was never published. It was called "The Dreamlet of the Hawk." Dean does not recall if he actually wrote it or what he had intended to do with it. "It was supposedly part of a novel I was working on, but I have no recollection." It was about a hunter who has an "emotio-link" with a hawk. Dean had used that term in one of his other stories, but since science fiction jargon is often shared or borrowed, there is no way to establish with certainty that Dean actually penned this story fragment.

A collection of stories that Dean had planned about the mythological figures Theseus and Mandarin, which was never completed, shows Dean's early attempt to incorporate archetypal images and themes into his science fiction. As he matured, he would place more emphasis on this device.

He had also sent an article to *Writer's Digest* on character motivation in the paperback novel. It was published in March. He believed at the time that motivation should be formed before character is developed, and he lists the possibilities as love, curiosity, greed, revenge, duty, self-discovery, and self-preservation.

11

Although Dean was not selling as quickly as he had hoped, he did see the publication of his second and third novels in 1969, which he had sold while still teaching. Each of them had advances of $1,250.

The Fall of the Dream Machine, one half of another Ace Double with Kenneth Bulmer's *The Star Venturers*, was inspired by Marshall McLuhan's claim that the electronic age would make the printed word passé and would form the world into a global village. In the Foreword to this short novel, Dean wrote: "It frightens me to think of a future where all artistic outlets are electronic, where all of life becomes an open, sterile, and public thing." He describes the novel that follows as being developed along the lines of McLuhan's philosophy, but pointing out its logical extreme. It is about a village society in which people are so subliminally connected to one another via the electronic media that they lose their individuality and meld together into a single consciousness. The implication is that they return to their origins, God.

A character named Anaxemander Cockley wants to rule the world. He devises "The Show," through which viewers can fully experience the feelings of the performers. Via their televisions, Cockley turns seven hundred million people into zombies. Yet, compressing the greater consciousness into an intimate container nearly annihilates humanity altogether, because part of the viewing addiction entails such a total loss of self that death ensues.

An underground resistance group that wants to preserve humanity and bring back the love of books captures Mike, The Show's lead performer. They surgically alter him and send him to rescue Lisa, his leading lady. Together these two then act out a scenario on television of hatred. This repels the audience and breaks the mass addiction. By the end of the story, Mike has experienced the pleasure of reading. He finds that mindful engagement is far superior to the passive experience of "The Show."

Dean's other novel that year, *Fear That Man*, was an odd juxtaposition of two novellas, "In the Shield," published in *Worlds of If* in January, and "Where the Beast Runs," published in July. They comprise two separate episodes in the same alien world. It was part of an Ace Double, the flip side of which was E. C. Tubb's *Toyman*. Dean dedicated this to friends Vaughn Bode and Andy Wickstrom. The cover price for each of Dean's first three books was sixty cents.

In *Fear That Man*, a character with amnesia finds himself on a spaceship in the year 3456. He rescues a mutated creature named Hurkos, who tells him that the human race has evolved away from violence and religion. They join a poet named Gnossos and go to a place called Hope, the capital of the universe. There they learn how violence has been controlled by making people who inflict pain on others feel it ten times greater within themselves. The only truly dangerous people are the masochists. Sam, the amnesiac, learns that his mission is to destroy an energy shield that has kept God imprisoned for a millennium. God, however, has used so much energy to draw him forth that God is now very weak. Hurkos sees that God is nothing more than a pink worm, so he lifts a chair and smashes it against God, killing Him.

In the second part, three hunters of diverse species show up on Hope and learn that another god has come on the scene, who must also be killed. They use one of the masochists to accomplish the deed and the deity collapses from the paradox of someone who moves toward pain rather than away from it.

Much of Dean's early science fiction shows a decided anger against God, even a desire to replace this chaotic, destructive deity with the more rational humankind.

"There was a brief period where I would have said I was an atheist," he admits, "probably for a year or so. I think that was tied pretty closely to my mother's death. When she died, I developed a bleak attitude. Then I gradually moved toward believing there's a purpose in life."

Later in *Twilight Eyes*, he would express this attitude through his protagonist Slim, who says his relationship with God is strongly adversarial. He could not understand how God could let people die or allow nice people to grow sick. He also could not accept the doctrine of infinite goodness in the face of obvious cruelty and suffering in the world—not unless there were demons causing all the problems.[12]

"I think where that attitude often comes out," says Dean, "is when you're sort of bitter . . . you rage at God. You don't not believe in Him, but you rage at Him. In *Fear That Man*, God turns out to be a worm and they stomp Him. Don Wollheim later told me that he'd agonized about publishing it. He assumed that he was going to get outraged mail, but he went ahead, and he never received a single letter. He said he realized then that society was changing. I was very young at that point and just thrashing around. There certainly was anger and sometimes the anger was aimed at God."

The themes of this double novella echoed much of what science fiction was doing at the time: examining categories of personhood, promoting the bonding of separate species, and denouncing the rigidity of ignorance. Yet Dean's anger, underlined by his sense of personal loss and his fear of potentially finding himself responsible for the one parent with whom he wanted little association, gave his work its idiosyncratic qualities. One of his themes would be repeated throughout his novels for decades to come—the idea that from within the same source grows the potential for both benefit and harm. In this case, God the creator is also psychotic, and our own negative traits come from God's schizoid personality. The only recourse for humankind's sanity is to stand up to the bully or to hope

God becomes impotent enough to be tricked, and then destroyed and replaced.

Dean plants in this narrative numerous arguments against God's existence and/or goodness, many of which would surface again almost two decades later in the mouth of his atheistic character in the short story "The Twilight of the Dawn." God is a weak father, not the omnipotent being of myth—not what we want Him to be. According to Dean in this novel, "The purpose of life is to overcome your creator."[13] If God Himself is truly demented, this diminishes us, His creatures, and we must avoid adopting that dementia and instead forge our greatness from within ourselves.

The following year, Dean would write that he had finally derived a clear picture of the god in which he believes: "He or it or them is a sort of easy-going power/person/force that doesn't care what we do down here, as long as we don't hurt each other."[14]

Dean may have been angry at God on his mother's account, but he was clearly imbuing God with his father's sociopathic traits: The benign, loving father of cultural mythology was in fact demented and dangerous. The son, adversely affected (i.e., mutated), had to "kill" him in his own psyche in order to create some degree of personal strength and identity. Dean shared this anger with many young men of the sixties, but in his case, the image of power from his childhood universe truly had to be replaced with a more healthy ideal if Dean was to move successfully into manhood. He needed a better role model, and he set about creating it for himself in his fiction.

[1]Dean R. Koontz, *After the Last Race* (New York: Atheneum, 1974), p. 57.

[2]Dean R. Koontz, *Star Quest* (New York: Ace, 1968), p. 65.

[3]Ibid., p. 71.

[4]Ibid., p. 73.

[5]Dean R. Koontz, "Shambolain," *Worlds of If* (November 1970), p. 174.

[6]Dean R. Koontz, essay in *Men on the Moon*, edited by Donald Wollheim (New York: Ace, 1969), p. 160.

[7]*Amazing Stories* (January 1969), p. 36.

[8]Dean R. Koontz, "Killerbot," *Galaxy Science Fiction* (1968), p. 95–96.

[9]Dean R. Koontz, Introduction, "A Season For Freedom," *The Future Now* (Greenwich, CT: Fawcett, 1977), p. 146.

[10]Dean R. Koontz, "Muse," *The Magazine of Fantasy and Science Fiction* (September 1969), p. 63.

[11]Ibid., p. 65.

[12]Dean R. Koontz, *Twilight Eyes* (New York: Berkley, 1987), pp. 96–97.

[13]Dean R. Koontz, *Fear That Man* (New York: Ace, 1969), p. 53.

[14]Dean R. Koontz, *Soft Come the Dragons* (New York: Ace, 1970), p. 51.

SEVEN

Growing Pains

1

BY 1970, THE SCIENCE FICTION FIELD HAD GONE THROUGH some changes. Some of the writers had known the "Golden Age" in the early fifties, when the genre was still based in hard science. Common themes had revolved around discovery, time paradoxes, technological speculation, and extraterrestrial invasion. The practice in those days, and into the sixties, was to publish stories first in magazines and then reprint them in book form. Eventually the mass market boom had meant an increasing number of paperback originals. The age level at which they were aimed changed from teenagers to college-age young men, and even female authors had begun to make inroads.

With the sixties revolutions, stereotypes began to change from dashing heroes and buxom ladies in distress to teams of near-equals, with a few rare allowances for minorities. Hardcover houses opened their doors, and some writers paid more attention to literary devices and sophisticated styles. In 1968, Stanley Kubrick's futuristic film, *2001*, made a strong impression on the culture.

A movement called the New Wave began in the mid-sixties among writers who felt that the tried-and-true themes of science fiction had been overused. They wanted to write stories that addressed social concerns like overpopulation, ecology, and politics. In tune with some of the late sixties downbeat music, they shared an attitude of pessimism, and embraced the concept from physics of entropy—that everything inevitably breaks down. Their stories were more imagistic than the typical science fiction tale and they often utilized the "soft" sciences, like psychology and sociology, for plot and character development. "Inner space" was a key term, and true to the concerns of young people all over the country, they examined the accepted tenets of religion, were tolerant of sexuality, and dealt more deeply with psychological conflicts. This helped to bridge the differences between traditional science fiction and mainstream literature, although it also produced tension among the different camps within the genre.

Around the country, many of these writers gathered annually at fan conventions, and had been doing so since the fifties. It had become a regular tradition for some, although the fans could get a little strange. Some liked to role-play, and clubs were formed that gave an edge to those who wanted to belong to an "in" group. They had buttons, jargon, character names, and other oddities that set them apart. Dean was aware of two such conventions in his area, one in Pittsburgh and one in Philadelphia. In 1970, he decided to go to a gathering called Philcon with the hope of meeting some of the writers he admired. Gerda went with him.

"The first convention I ever went to," Dean says, "I was agog. I kept running into all these people who were basically gods to me. We arrived on a Friday afternoon and hit the parties that evening. I was astonished that the first couple of writers I saw were falling-down drunk. These were people I'd read and admired. Then I went up to Damon Knight, who wasn't drunk, and said, 'Oh, Mr. Knight, I really like your work,' and he looked at the hand I was holding out to shake and said, 'Well,' and turned and walked away. Mr. Knight considered himself the godfather of the New Wave and I never got along well with that whole thing. They didn't accept me and I guess that, for this man, even his basic manners and respect for the rules of courtesy were shaped, in each instance, by his literary judgment of the writer with whom he was interacting."

"Later I spotted Forest J. Ackerman. I'd read every edition he'd published of *Famous Monsters of Filmland*. He was talking to someone and I walked up and stood respectfully until he was free, and then said, 'Mr. Ackerman, you were so important to me when I was young. I just loved your magazines.' And he said, 'Well, isn't that nice,' and walked off. I kept hitting that everywhere. It's terrible to see people you admire acting like this. The only person who was truly nice to me at that convention was Robert Silverberg, and he went out of his way to be decent."

Silverberg was an award-winning science fiction writer, prominent in the field since the fifties. He was prolific in fiction and nonfiction, as well as being an industrious editor of numerous anthologies. The number of short stories to his credit was astounding. His two most recent books at that point were *The Masks of Time* and *The Man in the Maze*. Dean had read many of his works and made it a point to meet him.

"He spent two hours talking to me," Dean recalls. "I was having some trouble and I explained it to him. I had five novels that were not completed. I had written each to within forty or fifty pages of the end and then had lost confidence and put them aside. I was struggling like hell to be able to get anything finished. I would finish one book, but then there'd be three that I didn't. Bob got this absolutely horrified look and said, 'Now, you listen to me. This is simply ordinary self-doubt. Every writer has it. Books don't go off the rails forty pages from the end. They go off the rails early or midpoint. This is all in your head. When you go home, I want you to finish each of them, one after the other. Send them out and they'll sell.'"

Silverberg, too, recalls this conversation with Dean. "I remember how discouraged he was. He was writing rather undistinguished science fiction at the time and not doing very well with it. My feeling about writing a book is, if you're a professional, you start on page one and you sit there until you finish. There's no other option. My recollection is that I said something like, 'You're resisting writing these books because you really don't want to write them. You don't think you're getting anywhere. The best thing is to write something else.'"

He himself had been given such a boost by senior writers when he was in his twenties, and felt he should do the same. "It wasn't unusual in the fifties for established writers to do that," he says. "I had a lot of help and got a very fast start." One of those writers, Cyril Kornbluth, had said he felt an obligation to be kind to beginning writers. "I took that to heart," says Silverberg. "I've always felt it was part of the system to reach around behind you and pull others along. Which is what I did with Dean. He seemed so distressed and such a nice guy."

"I suspect Bob and I each remember a different part of that conversation," Dean comments. "I suspect he made both of these recommendations, because I *did* start writing different science fiction from what I'd done previously—better work, like *The Flesh in the Furnace*. And then I left the field. And you know—I never really was a science fiction writer at heart. I wrote it because it was mostly what I'd read. What I eventually had a *passion* for writing was suspense and mainstream work. When I followed that passion, my work improved dramatically. Bob Silverberg was dead-on in *both* pieces of advice."

Following this convention, Dean went home to rewrite. "I admired Bob so much that when he told me to do it, I did it. It broke through that block that I was having about finishing anything. So I owed him the fact that I picked myself up, dusted myself off, and finished these books. He couldn't have been nicer to me."

At the next convention that year, held in Pittsburgh, Dean met Harlan Ellison. He was known as a man of controversial character and legendary charm. Kicked out of Ohio State University and told by a creative writing teacher he had no talent, he went on to build a tremendously prolific, award-winning career.

Ellison was a maverick who had written in many genres. He did not consider himself a science fiction writer, but he had been involved in the field since the early fifties and had produced some seminal work—infamous for its uncompromising ethic and raw presentations of urban life. His 1968 story, "I Have No Mouth, and I Must Scream," was still the subject of conversation in its startling portrayal of resistance to dehumanization.

Ellison liked to shake things up. As a founder of Science Fiction Writers of America, he was a gadfly about getting things done professionally, and his own fiction constantly pushed the envelope. "I don't want anyone to read my stories and feel complacent," he insists. "I want my stories to annoy people, anger people, make them beat their breasts and throw the book against the wall. It's supposed to have a visceral effect on you. It's not a piece of sculpture."

He had seen a competitive spirit enter the field of late, eroding the sense of community. "In the fifties and sixties, we were all in this pot together and everybody would help everybody else," he recalls. "Writing was hard work and we were making a penny a word or less. You didn't see yourself in direct conflict with other writers." He still has this attitude and has helped many writers, although he has no patience with amateurs, no matter how much they have published.

In 1968, he helped form the New Wave with his cutting-edge anthology, *Dangerous Visions*. He had also written scripts for television shows like "The Outer Limits" and "Star Trek." He seemed to have no end of energy, and wherever he went, he commanded attention.

"The first time I met Harlan," says Dean, "we were standing in a convention suite talking to Barbara and Bob Silverberg, and Harlan just exploded into the room. He came over to talk to Silverberg and he took an immediate fancy to Gerda."

"I have few of the properly proscribed inhibitions," says Ellison, "most of which I think are useless. I'm steeped in ethics, but have virtually no morality at all, and I've always made a great distinction between them."

Ellison knew something about Dean's writing. He had read *Fear That Man* and thought it showed more than a bit of talent. "Dean was just another journeyman writer," he said. "He worked as hard as the rest of us, but his work was undistinguished and his personality wasn't quirky enough to get him noticed." Ellison was used to seeing crowds of strange-looking fans who walked around wearing buttons and talking about being "slans"—a science fiction in-group. By contrast, Dean was ordinary. "He didn't have any outstanding bizarre characteristics to catch anyone's attention, so he was not a star at the freak show."

Ellison, then unmarried, flirted with Gerda and she responded with a remark witty enough to get a laugh from Silverberg. Ellison was startled, but met fire with fire until a group of people had gathered around them.

"I've never seen Gerda engage in anything like this before or since," says Dean. "She's usually very quiet, but she was getting the better of him and he ended up surrendering." (Ellison finds this conclusion dubious.)

Two years later, Dean's work interested Ellison enough for him to solicit a story for an anthology, *Again, Dangerous Visions*. Over time, they have become friends.

Dean went to one more of these conventions, a second one in Philadelphia, and there he was made fully aware of how the young Turks of the New Wave felt about the traditional nature of his work.

"A local TV station wanted to interview a group of writers because of this New Wave that was happening in science fiction," Dean explains. "They wanted young writers and they gathered about ten of us. The other writers in this group made a point of not wanting to be associated with me because I was that 'old-fashioned' kind of writer who was a storyteller. They saw themselves as moving beyond that. I found it amusing because I always thought storytelling was at the center of writing. The New Wave was a political thing, really, and there was always this pecking order at conventions that struck me as odd and unpleasant. I was soon disabused of the idea that writers are a community. There are people like Bob Silverberg and Harlan Ellison, who will be straight with you and who will genuinely hope for your success, but most see you as a competitor or a heretic, or both—and treat you as such."

2

Despite his disappointment at conferences, Dean continued to write and submit his stories to publishers. Gerda did whatever research he needed from the library. "For some reason," Dean admits, "I never much cared to sit in a library. I feel alienated and I hate going in them. So she did the library part of the research and brought it all back to me."

She also urged him to expand his reading and introduced him to the work of some of the suspense writers that she liked.

"She read more widely than I did at that time, in all genres," says Dean, "and because of her, I started to broaden my own reading to some extent. When I found people that I really liked in the suspense field, I wanted to write suspense."

He turned to such authors as Raymond Chandler and James M. Cain, whom he liked for style and technique, "although Cain's view of life is much darker than mine." He also read a lot of Rex Stout's Nero Wolfe series, which taught him about drawing out reader expectations as long as possible before the Big Dramatic Moment. He learned other things from the stories of Donald Westlake, Elmore Leonard, Evan Hunter, and Dick Francis. It seemed to him that the suspense genre had no restrictions as to form or content, and required only that the author maintain the tension. Such freedom to stretch in many directions and to create any kind of story appealed to Dean. Yet he knew it would take a lot of work to shift into this new framework. He read as much as he possibly could.

The suspense writer who most impressed him was John D. MacDonald. Best known for a series featuring Florida-based private detective Travis McGee, MacDonald also wrote non-series novels like *Cape Fear*; *Cry Hard, Cry Fast*; and *Murder on the Wind*. Dean picked up one of MacDonald's books, *The Damned*, could not put it down, and went on to read thirty-four of them in a single month.

In MacDonald, he found a kindred spirit—someone who boldly made social commentaries, who captured the power of place, who was a poet-naturalist, and who made readers care about the story. Dean admired not only the prose and pace, but the unique and strong characterizations. "He can spend forty words on a character early in the story and it will be so vivid that when that character comes back into the story one hundred pages later, you remember him. I thought it was brilliant. He'll do four or five pages of character background and he'll make it so interesting that when he stops and starts the story up again, you say, 'Wait, I want to know more about that character.' That always amazed me.

"His books just hold up well. *The Last One Left* is probably the first novel anyone wrote about a sociopath that got it right. I liked *Cry Hard, Cry Fast* because of the amazing structure of it. *The End of the Night* is about a group of teenage thrill killers and it's as good as *In Cold Blood*. I did read the Travis McGee novels later and loved them, but I thought his non–Travis McGee books were better."

On a conference panel over a decade later, Dean used Mac-Donald's work to demonstrate to other writers what good writing was—especially those who believed that excellence was to be found exclusively in the classics. Often he surprised people with MacDonald's richness of prose and impressive sense of place. He read a paragraph without naming MacDonald as the author and made the other panel members guess who it was. It amused him that they thought it must be Henry James or some writer of that ilk. It amused him even more to let them know that an author they might have dismissed had actually impressed them.

When Dean eventually started writing his own suspense, he felt the influence keenly. "I wrote one—it might have been called *Big Money*—which sounded so much like MacDonald it was embarrassing. I can't remember whether I even sent it to my agent. I might have written half of it, but at some point, I recognized it was so imitative I couldn't possibly publish it."

Years later, MacDonald provided quotes for Dean's books *Whispers* and *Strangers*, and when Ballantine decided to reissue some of MacDonald's novels a decade after his death in 1986, they asked Dean for a quote. He said: "As a young writer, all I ever wanted was to touch readers as powerfully as John D. MacDonald touched me. No price could be placed on the enormous pleasure that his books have given me. He captured the mood and the spirit of his times more accurately, more hauntingly, than any 'literary' writer—yet managed always to tell a thunderingly good, intensely suspenseful tale."

3

Dean continued to keep up his aggressive writing schedule, veering away from science fiction and writing outlines for suspense. He later wrote in *Invasion* that daily creativity requires sensitivity and even some degree of madness. "Even the worst godawful hack must believe—even if he denies it to everyone and to himself—that what he does makes a difference . . . in the course of human events."[1] This certainly applied to a young writer trying desperately to find his niche.

Aware that other writers were making ends meet by branching out, Dean decided to write political nonfiction that reflected some of the attitudes of the times.

That year, 1970, the Beatles recorded their final song together, "I Me Mine," before breaking up and going their separate ways. Simon and Garfunkel released "Bridge Over

Troubled Water," and the X-rated *Midnight Cowboy* took the Oscar for Best Picture. In response to complaints that young men could fight and die but not vote, Congress lowered the voting age to eighteen. Near the Cambodian border, U.S. troops clashed with the North Vietnamese and Nixon sent more. This prompted antiwar demonstrations, and in May, national guardsmen shot and killed four students at Kent State. Princeton University awarded an honorary doctorate to songwriter Bob Dylan, while Jimi Hendrix and Janis Joplin died from drug overdoses.

"I just wanted to write about political things that were happening at the time that were pretty horrendous," Dean explains. "I'd written a couple of novels that had spun out of that, so doing nonfiction seemed interesting. I made that publishing connection through Bob Hoskins."

He wrote two nonfiction books for Aware Press, *The Pig Society* and *The Underground Lifestyles Handbook*. Gerda shared authorship with him, although she did no writing. Before these were published, Hoskins called to warn him that he had just learned that his own novels had been substantially altered by the same publisher, and that he was unhappy about it. Dean saw no proofs of either of his books, and when they arrived in final form, he was disappointed. He claims that the editor had changed the content dramatically. It seemed to him that as much as forty to sixty percent of his material had been deleted and replaced by passages that he did not—and would not—write. The books were now angry diatribes against organizations, the "establishment," the government, and in general, any kind of repressive practices that restricted sexuality or political expression. About *The Pig Society*, Dean says, "That one was supposed to be a rant against Nixon and the war. Some stuff got taken out and other material put in that had nothing to do with the book I originally wrote."

A blurb about the authors falsely identified Dean and Gerda with the hippie subculture, claiming they had lived on a commune and had been to Woodstock in 1969. It also attributed to Gerda nonexistent articles and short stories in women's magazines. She had given some thought to writing for magazines, but had no publications to her credit. Similarly, they did not indulge in the drug culture, had never been to

Haight-Ashbury, or done much of anything else typical of hippies. Dean wore his hair long, but spent most of his time writing. "I spent my life working. I would never 'turn on' or 'drop out.' Now, whether I'd 'tune in,' I don't know. I'm not sure how that part of the equation worked."

The Pig Society, illustrated by Doug Levinson and Vaughn Bode, was ostensibly a reaction to the trash of established society. Using the film *Easy Rider* as an example of the clash of cultures, the book claims that it sums up fears on both sides: Society is primarily fascist and the liberty of the individual is at stake. Chapters cover such subjects as the American Nazi Party, Nixon's crime package, conservative attitudes about sexual freedom, war and the military, the police and other authority figures, marijuana, the death of religion, and even concentration camps in the United States. At the end, an "oink list" dismisses such Americans as Eisenhower, Nixon, Shirley Temple, and John Wayne. The freethinker is considered the "new American hero," and people are urged to wake up and realize that the FBI collects files on innocent citizens, and that politicians suppress truth and want to change constitutional amendments regarding individual rights. In short, the establishment's agenda is to suppress personal freedom.

Similarly, *The Underground Lifestyles Handbook*, written second, and illustrated by Doug Levinson, covers the experiences of the counterculture on such subjects as long hair, living in communes, free sex, groupies, drugs, body painting, and Woodstock. It is touted as "The First True Account of the Underground Subculture." The "authors" claim to have researched firsthand the subjects they describe, and to tackle them "with humor and warmth." Part One ostensibly is written by Dean, Part Two by Gerda, although Gerda insists she had nothing to do with it. "My name was on it because of the way the contract was structured," she explains.

To some extent, this book foreshadows the attitudes about freedom and prejudice expressed later in *Chase* and *Shattered*. There is no doubt that Dean had some kinship with the youth subculture on issues like conformity and authoritarian attitudes. He also affirmed sexual and personal freedom, but he felt that these nonfiction books had taken his agenda much further into the hippie lifestyle than he had ever intended to go. They were also more militant.

The same publisher took his pornography under its Cameo imprint. During the late sixties and early seventies the sexual revolution had given many people permission to express their sexuality. Women were pursuing their pleasure with as much gusto as men, and gay people were coming out into the open. It was a time of freedom and experimentation. People wanted to explore the forbidden. Sexual imagery became increasingly explicit in novels and film, and books like *The Story of O*, *Lolita*, and *Candy* were widely read. Even the Marquis de Sade enjoyed a renewed popularity. The debate over the censorship of pornography went to the Supreme Court, where controversial decisions lifted many of the restrictions on publishing and distributing such material.

While arguments flew back and forth in academic circles over whether pornography could be considered literature, writers cashed in. Uninterested in the "high art" value of their work, they were in it for the fast buck. These books, with their emphasis on sex over plot and character, were easy to turn out. Dean was offered the opportunity to write some. With the mounting pressure of bills to pay, he decided to go for it.

He read what the other writers were doing, as well as classic pornography by Henry Miller and Frank Harris, which he mentioned later in *Prison of Ice*. These novels could be written in a matter of days, and they paid from around $600 to as much as $3,000, but offered no return on subsidiary rights. He thought that only in a land of sexual hypocrisy could the situation exist wherein the racier works earned the lower advances.

In his research he quickly learned that there was a difference between what he called the "Big Sexy Novel" and the "Rough Sexy Novel." Big Sexy Novels, written by the likes of Jacqueline Susann, Henry Sutton, and Rona Jaffe, were supposedly more subtle about sexual elements, more euphemistic, and more pretentious about plot. Anticipation was emphasized over the sexual act itself, and the hint that such novels are thinly disguised descriptions of celebrities added to their effectiveness. Dean sneered at such books.

On the other hand, Rough Sexy Novels maximized raw language and erotic scenes, the more the better. The tone was straightforward and blatantly arousing. Rich detail and explicit language were the norm for this type of writing, and no character was punished or reformed for sexually acting out. Sex was viewed by the audience for these books as healthy and exciting, and anything was permissible, short of hurting someone. In his chapter on erotica in a later book, *Writing Popular Fiction*, Dean recommended using multiple points of view for such books, because a greater multiplicity of characters provided variety in perspective, action, and description—with more kinds of kinky behavior possible.

An interesting cultural note in Dean's instruction was to avoid punishing anyone in the novel with divorce, since many women who read the Big Sexy Novel are terrified of it. It was an age of vicarious thrill and little real adventure, although times were changing. In a side note, Dean mentions that this reaction might change as more women see their value as people in their own right. He seemed to prefer the Rough Sexy Novel for its portrayal of women as sexual beings who could be aggressive rather than hesitant and submissive, who could make men the focus of their desire, and who could have as much pleasure. They could be equals in a relationship that for so long had been socialized to be primarily male terrain. However, he knew that nothing meaningful could be created in this genre. At best, it afforded him a way to experiment with style that could later be applied to more serious work without risking his creative reputation.

Nevertheless, Dean quickly realized that he was unhappy spending his time on novels that led him away from his original focus. He soon learned that royalties would not be forthcoming—if even reported—and that such repetitive work could become tedious and divert him away from building a more solid reputation elsewhere. While others churned them out, Dean was happy to leave erotica behind.

He wrote one with Gerda entitled *Bounce Girl*, which was later reissued as *Aphrodisiac Girl*. Although he was not proud of these books, he admitted his authorship to close friends and even sent them copies. In later years, he was embarrassed by their crudity. Those who read them saw nothing of Dean's talent, and were glad that he had lost interest in making money this way.

Bounce Girl is an absurdly humorous tale about the sexual

adventures of a groupie for a rock band named Bounce. The plot involves a drug that enhances sexual potency. The publisher added an Introduction (removed in the revision) that he attributed to Dean.

Dean had been told this book would be published under another name, but when he received his copy, not only were his and Gerda's names on it, but much of the content had been changed. "It was supposed to be under a pseudonym," Dean complains. "That's why I don't sign it. I never wanted my name on it in the first place. What I actually wrote didn't appear in print. I was experimenting with doing something and what I had intended with this book was not accomplished." He was so angry he tossed it into a wastebasket.

The second novel, *Hung*, exploited the lusts of young men at a small college that bears many similarities to Shippensburg. This one did get published under a pseudonym, but the content was also revised according to the editor's preferences. Dean later described his intentions with this novel in an Afterword to one of his short stories, "A Mouse in the Walls of the Global Village." According to his account, he had wanted *Hung* to be a mainstream novel. The title was taken from the current catchphrase "hung up," and the story was another of his attempts to extrapolate from Marshall McLuhan's philosophies about global compression. Along with the sexual content, he had wanted to show how a war as far away as Asia had caused, through the media, an immediate moral impact on the culture. He felt that, ultimately, he had failed in these ambitions, but he did not expect the radical changes that had been made: "*Hung* was supposed to be a comic novel. I had thought this editor had wanted to do something different, and that's the way I had written it, but I think he had lost his nerve. It didn't get printed the way I wrote it. He fancied himself a writer, so he thought he could turn my books into anything he wanted. It was such an astounding shock. I knew all kinds of people who worked for him briefly and that's exactly what he did to them."

Eventually Dean found other ways to get published. Those two are the only erotic novels he has written, although collectors believe he has produced as many as ten. They have also credited him with books written as Shane Stevens. However, Shane Stevens is definitely another person and not a pen name. In 1972, Dean wrote in *Again, Dangerous Visions* that he had sold forty novels by that time and had placed seven more with his agent. In the 1973 anthology *The Edge of Never*, he took credit for forty-four novels, which seems to support the speculation that he has written more books under pseudonyms. A number of interviews during the mid-seventies quote him as saying that he has written fifty novels and expects to have one hundred by the time he is fifty, but he explains it:

"There were a lot of books I make claim to that I was writing, but never published. I sold most of them on outlines, but some of those books never got written—as many as ten books, I suspect. Contracts were paid back. There was a mainstream book I was working on about the American Nazi movement, but I didn't have the skills for it. It didn't have a title and it never got anywhere, and it's long destroyed. It was my first idea to break out into mainstream, but it just didn't work. This was the period where I was trying to find my way rather desperately to what it was that would finally break me out, and every time it seemed like I had it, I'd start to write, but between the time I'd sold the book and wrote it, things sometimes happened. I'd mention somewhere that I intended to publish it, and I'd get quite a ways into it, but then throw it away.

"Two Lancer books were never published because Lancer went under. One was an anthology and one was a science fiction novel, and there was an Anthony North book that I had to take back. I was in the Isaac Asimov mode—quantity was everything. I even wrote two books in the Robert Ludlum mode. I wrote a portion of all of those books, but I'd start writing and then say, 'This isn't it.' I'd realize it wasn't a direction that was going to bear fruit."

4

Dean met and made friends with people of like mind, one of whom was the controversial, award-winning artist Vaughn Bode, whom he had met in 1969. Vaughn had a volatile, brooding personality, even exasperating, and he shifted his interests so quickly it was difficult to get a commitment from him. His motto was to seize the day, to do all the art he possibly could "before I am no more me." His art was often satirical.

He became close friends with Dean and together they planned a series of illustrated "McLuhan-esque" projects which never got off the ground. Vaughn managed only to illustrate *The Pig Society* and an article called "Diligently Corrupting Young Minds" that Dean wrote for *Science Fiction Review*.

"I just fell in love with his cartoons," says Dean. "He and his wife Barbara were living in Syracuse. They came down for a weekend and he brought this big portfolio of stuff. When I run into talented artists, I can spend days looking through their portfolio. Really creative artists have this mountain of material that no one's ever seen. Vaughn brought these comic strips he'd developed and we sat around looking through them all weekend. He had an off-the-wall sense of humor and so did I, so we got along pretty well. But gradually he seemed to become stranger and more alienated.

"He was always, at core, the same person, but he was troubled; he was like a child. There was a great sense of innocence about him, which was the center of his talent, but at one point in his life he started trying to destroy it. He let his fingernails grow three inches long and started wearing makeup, but I doubt he was genuinely bisexual. It was part of his game-playing. He liked to shock people. Once we went out to dinner in Hershey at this Italian restaurant, and he wore makeup and heavy eye color. He had these long nails that he had painted and decorated with little sequin inlays. He acted with us like he'd always been—the same person inside, but he took a childish delight in the effect he had on other people. I thought he just was never happy with himself. As he got more serious about these personas, he got more detached. It seemed at some point that he lost track of who he was."

Dean wrote a Foreword for George Beahm to a book of Vaughn's creations. In it he points out the central theme: "Vaughn does produce pretty pictures, marvelous fantasies; but every one of them is a piece in the mosaic theme that has occupied him for all his creative life: death." Dean's words were never published, but he describes a nightmare he had that was populated by characters from Bode's cartoon strips. He had been working twelve-hour days to meet all of his publishing deadlines and, as he says, "I was close to mental and physical collapse. I started having nightmares from which I woke shaking and sweating." The most persistent one involved him standing before a door in an old house that opens out to a clearing in a forest. Bode characters—evil in appearance—danced around a toadstool. Dean felt an imminent sense of dread and knew he must shut the door before it was too late. "I am no mystic, but I do believe if I had walked into that clearing in the dream, I surely would have died in my sleep. I suspect the dream was a warning that I had subconsciously fashioned for myself: I was that close to death."

Then, on the afternoon of July 18, 1975, four days short of his thirty-fourth birthday, Vaughn Bode committed suicide. His ex-wife called Dean to tell him.

"I was devastated," Dean says. "My first thought was that I had seen this descent over the years and I had the feeling that I could have done something to change it. If I'd been there at the right time or had said the right thing. That's the same as with my father—if I'd just had the right conversation, I could have fixed all this. But of course, I couldn't, because whatever was going on was so deep that he seemed to be engaged in a monologue that was not open to comment. So that was a real bad day. It's hard to understand that someone can be as talented as Vaughn was, but on some level, the talent couldn't save him. Vaughn was absolutely singular. If he could have held himself together, he would have become enormously famous."

Another person Dean encountered in the late sixties was Lisa Tuttle, a student at Syracuse University who was coediting a magazine called *Tomorrow and . . .* with Jerry Lapidus. Jerry knew Vaughn Bode, and through him, Dean. From an early age, Lisa had wanted to be a writer, and eventually she went on to write and publish fantasy. She had read some of Dean's short stories and one of his novels, so she sent him a copy of the fanzine in the hope that he would contribute something.

Dean sent a piece from *The Pig Society*. In a letter, he described himself as having long hair and no steady job, being nonreligious, disrespectful of government, and "unmindful of his morals or anyone else's code." Lisa later met him at Philcon, the science fiction convention in Philadelphia, and they developed a friendship. She and Dean and Gerda talked together for hours about books, politics, philosophy, and life in the seventies. "I think the main reason we became friends," she observes, "was a shared sense of humor and a devouring passion for fiction of all kinds."

She noticed that even at that time, Dean had no intention of being labeled a one-track writer. He was writing science fiction but he was not about to let it become a trap. "He didn't see it as the highest or only form of fiction." What was important to her was that Dean took her seriously as a writer. "I recognized that Dean provided a good role model for the working writer. I found his obvious dedication and the sheer hard work necessary to make a living as a writer impressive and inspirational." Dean, she knew, had made some compromises to keep involved in his profession, such as "writing books you wouldn't want to admit to." It made her reevaluate just how much she was willing to do to achieve her own goals.

Dean dedicated *Starblood* to Lisa Tuttle, although for no apparent reason, a printer changed the dedication to read, "To Dad." Dean was mortified, but managed to include her in the list of dedicatees for *Beastchild*.

5

Concentrating on science fiction, Dean published seven novels that year, including a collection of previously published short stories. He also continued to submit new short stories, and eight were published.

Ed Ferman's *Magazine of Fantasy and Science Fiction* published "A Third Hand" in January and "The Mystery of His Flesh" in July. Both grew into novels. "A Third Hand," which became *Starblood* two years later, straddled traditional and New Wave attitudes, since it was told in a linear manner but had an unusual hero. Timothy is a mutant genius, rather than a ruggedly handsome man, who witnesses a murder and must defend himself against a criminal conspiracy.

Although Dean knew that he was not accepted by New Wave writers, he did state at that time that he expected that once the New Wave subsided, "we will have devised a science fiction that is molded from the best of the stylistic principles of mainstream and the best story-telling concepts of science fiction. That will be one helluva literature!"[2]

In "The Mystery of His Flesh," a man helps an android to escape the society that had created him and now wants him destroyed. This supergenius immortal can heal and even resurrect people, so in a world of nine billion, he is considered a menace. He needs three days to transform into his real form, which turns out to be God. As the archetypal man in his original shape, he shows that humans can become God. Even so, they fear the possibility and would rather destroy than explore it.

Venture published a novella-length version of "Beastchild" in August, while *Fantastic Stories* did the same for "The Crimson Witch" in October. Both were then published as paperback novels, with a few scenes added to *Beastchild*. *Fantastic Stories* also published "The Good Ship Lookoutworld" earlier that year, a story about the battle between entropy and meaning. Two men scavenging an alien ship that dissolves around them must find a way to understand it before it dissolves them, too. They learn to see it as an illusion, and only then can they resist it. This idea would show up in some of Dean's future novels, such as *Dragon Tears* and *Cold Fire*.

Dean placed "Unseen Warriors" with *Worlds of Tomorrow* and "Nightmare Gang" with *Infinity One*, the first in a series of anthologies by Robert Hoskins that would regularly include him. "Unseen Warriors" was a postnuclear story about the possibility of breeding monsters in the act of human procreation. Each fetus may potentially be a "Brain" that destroys humans. The story features a couple who meet and go through the trauma of killing one of these creatures, which makes them opt to have no children for fear of generating yet another one. Although Dean and Gerda had not, at this point, decided against children, eventually Dean's fears that he might pass on a genetic defect from his own father would influence their decision to forgo having a family.

"Nightmare Gang" is told in first person by a character who rides with a violent gang led by a charismatic man named Louis who is gifted with special powers. He can warp the reality between life and death and then raise the dead, which he does whenever he finds a potentially interesting member for his gang. They are immortal, driven to mindless violence at Louis's command, and will indulge in murderous rampages for eternity.

6

Of the few novels that Dean wrote that did not sell was one he called *All Other Men.* "It was my first attempt to break out of science fiction," says Dean. "It got wonderful rejection letters. This would have been in the early seventies. It was told entirely from the point of view of a madman, written in first person, present tense, and it was mostly comprised of one- and two-line paragraphs. It was about a group of people forming a commune who move into a small town where this resident sees them as the embodiment of all the destructive forces in society. He begins plotting everyone's murder. To the exterior world, he is an upstanding citizen, but actually he's completely gone. It was an eerie kind of story because it didn't develop along normal plot lines."

The rejection letters were fairly positive. Larry Ashmead at Doubleday told Dean it was a brilliant book that left him drained, but the sexual content—which was important to the story—was too explicit. He offered to recommend it to another editor, but nothing came of that.

"That was a real letdown," Dean remembers, "because I felt I really had something with that book. It was the first time I did a total exercise in viewpoint. It's from the point of view of an insane person. The title came from a quote: 'To the lunatic, all other men are dangerous.'

"Someday I will probably haul that book out and be horrified by the low quality of it. I've left it buried, because it's something I want to remember fondly. If it's as good as I remember, then at some point I might include it as one of three pieces of a similar length in an omnibus. I'd have to recast the story in our time because it was set during the era of antiwar protests and would seem dated now."

In frustration, Dean expanded his short story "The Mystery of His Flesh" into a novel. He had wanted to give it the same title, but the editor who bought it insisted that the title sounded too gay. She wanted something less controversial, so she renamed it *Anti-Man*. Dean thought that sounded like the title for a comic book, but that is the one they used, and it was published by Paperback Library.

In the story, Dr. Jacob Kennelman tries to save an android—which he refers to as He or Him for its archetypal perfection—from destruction by the World Authority. He takes the android to a cabin in the wilderness and watches Him devour huge quantities of food so He can transform Himself into a creature of great strength and immunity. Jacob wonders if He might one day destroy humankind. Eventually the android becomes a giant protoplasmic creature that claims to be God, but some evil part of itself has split away to do deeds of destruction. Jacob helps to destroy the evil part, and God transforms Him into an immortal of great perception who can spread this transformation to others.

This story shows the same concern as *Fear That Man* that God might be psychotic and therefore dangerous—although there is ultimately a desire to do some good. Another common theme was that we were created to struggle to become equal to God. In this novel, God has created an overpopulated, over-controlled world that shows a serious imbalance. Clearly Dean viewed God as imperfect, vulnerable, limited, and prone to mistakes. True goodness, Dean felt, lies in the intellectual awareness and compassion that Jacob displays.

Dean was also at work on the theme of toxic intimacy—that bonding with someone of a dangerous species may have detrimental results. The fluidity of boundaries implies that evil can flow into good, abnormal into normal, madness into sanity. He feared the inescapable merging of polarities that might cause harm. "Our personalities crossed, webbed, and formed something, though what it was remained a mystery insoluble."[3] In this case, the God-creature is an unknown. It is the dark part of the psyche that has resources of ambiguous worth; it might enhance growth or cause destruction. Jacob's dream reveals his fear of the inner self—that what he creates can turn on him. One of the section titles, in fact, is "The Enemy is Self." In the end, we learn that one needs to face oneself. Change comes from within by resolving fears and surrendering to personal integration.

Another novel, *Hell's Gate*, was published by Lancer. Dean dedicated it to Gerda. It features a man, Victor Salsbury, who feels that what he knows about himself is artificial, as if it has been implanted rather than lived. He kills a man and purchases his home from Lynda March. Lynda's ex-husband is based on Dean's father: "There is a sort of man who can never face his own inadequacies, who must find a scapegoat. . . . He drives his women to despair, eventually breaks them. . . . They kill human dignity. But first they torture it. Relatively few women escape them."[4] When Victor is attacked by "lizard things with sucking mouths,"[5] he starts to realize that he is someone's puppet. Eventually he discovers he is an android sent from an alternate "worldline" to stop an invasion that will result in a Nazi-like occupation of the Earth.

Back in 1968, Dean had written a novel called *The Dark Symphony*, which at the time he considered one of his best efforts. He had sent it out, but editors told him it was too morbid. Finally he placed it at Lancer and dedicated it to Bob Hoskins, his editor there.

Dean had spent a lot of time listening to the rhythms of music in order to write what seemed to him a rather ambitious far-future story. He structured it like a nineteenth century symphony. It is about a rebellion of the mutant class against a society of aristocratic musicians who place all emphasis on musical talent. Throughout, Dean identifies religion with madness, and the established system as corrupt.

The Musicians have driven the mutants, known as Populars, into the ruins on the edge of established society. One of the Populars, Strong, sees himself in a demented vision as a prophet, and he schemes to replace the firstborn son of a high-placed Musician official with his own child, implanted with a program set to provoke him to lead a rebellion. This boy, Guil, grows up but fails to demonstrate musical talent—which means he will be destroyed. The program then reveals his true identity and he sets off for the ruins.

Another character, Tisha, has talent but is not allowed to gain any honors because she is female. Tisha goes with Guil to the ruins, but when Strong tries to have her removed, Guil kills him with a knife. There is some irony in this, since nearly two decades later, Dean's own demented father would try to come between him and Gerda, and would use a knife to make an attempt on *his* life.

Some of the political ideas that Dean expresses in this novel, aside from an early defense of women, is that "the system devoured and never produced,"[6] a theme common in the early seventies among disgruntled young people. To stay in the system was to be used by it. Yet even when people realized this, some refused to resist the system's dehumanizing ways because they saw some advantage, or because they felt trapped and perceived that only submission brings peace from harassment. The Musician's society is sick at the core, similar to Strong with his manic-depressive visions. Although they masquerade behind great composers, they are impotent and inevitably self-destructive.

This tale is another early expression of the theme of the unprotected child. Guil's real father is demented and Guil is raised by a father with whom he is equally unsafe. Tisha, too, is unprotected. All they have is each other and they must make their way together through a treacherous world, for alone they would perish. "No child," Dean writes with a feeling of anger, "owed anything to its parents."[7]

One of Dean's most significant novels that year was *Beastchild*, published by Lancer and dedicated to friends encountered in science fiction fandom, Lisa Tuttle, Danny Jennings, and Jack Cordes. The story was initially inspired by unwarranted prejudices: Dean had met a veteran returning from Vietnam who had expressed negative opinions on the Vietnamese based only on limited encounters with the worst elements of that society. Such ideas, Dean felt, can motivate undeserved violence toward others. The novel was also a social commentary on the evils of capitalism, such as greed and the soulless pursuit of one's own advantage: "Capitalism was fine. As long as man used it. But when the system had become so big that it guided the destiny of society rather than society regulating it, then capitalism had become dangerous."[8]

In the novel, the lizard-like naoli have just won a war on Earth against humans. Based on their encounters with politicians and greedy merchants, they had concluded that humans were coldhearted and dangerously aggressive, so to protect trade routes, the naoli have nearly exterminated them. The few

survivors hole up in places like The Haven. A naoli archaeolo-
gist, Hulann, encounters a young boy, Leo, who saves his life.
Unable to turn Leo in, Hulann escapes with him across the
country from Boston to join the human survivors in California.
They spend a lot of time in snowstorms in Pennsylvania, near
where Dean lived.

A naoli Hunter, programmed to kill, pursues them, but they
escape his various weapons. Then they encounter a lone
writer, David (a character who shares some of Dean's traits),
who is heading to California as well. Once they reach The
Haven, humans kill Hulann, unaware that he is in fact their
ally. Leo buries him and vows to make both sides in this struggle understand that not all members of a race are to be judged
by its worst elements; Hulann reincarnates back to his home
planet, taking with him the insight that the naoli Hunters have
no soul. If humans judged all naoli by them, they would be
mistaken. David writes the entire story into a book, with the
understanding that the naoli and the "beastchild" had become
as father and son—two different species joined in a familial
bond. Without his naoli guardian, Leo would have been
defenseless, an unprotected child, and would have been elimi-
nated by the sociopathic Hunters. Joined together, they both
find redemption via insight and the determination to cooperate
across species differences.

Beastchild foreshadowed *Midnight* in its depiction of the
Hunter as being comfortable merging with a machine, which
exemplifies metaphorically the lack of soul in the human
sociopath. It was a finalist for a Hugo, a prestigious science
fiction award, for Best Novella of the Year. Unbeknownst to
Dean, however, the book contained many grammatical and
phrasing errors. He had never read the version in *Venture*, nor
had he seen proofs of the Lancer novel. He had wrongly
assumed that the magazine had published his story as he had
written it.

In was not until 1990, when Joe Stefko of Charnel House
spoke to Dean about doing a limited edition of *Beastchild* in
hardcover, that Dean learned differently. When he saw the
proofs that Joe had prepared, he was astonished by all the
errors. "I looked at this and said, what the hell happened here?
Joe must have lost his mind. So I got out the *Lancer* book edi-

tion and compared it, line by line, and discovered that the errors had been in the first edition." Dean then checked the original manuscript, only to confirm that his story had never been published as he had written it. "The *Venture* magazine version had hundreds and hundreds of little changes—apparently contributed by an assistant editor, as I know Ed Ferman would never have done such a thing—and they had been carried forward into the *Lancer* version." He told Joe that he wanted to see his original story in print, so Joe reset the proofs and, in 1992, published a version of *Beastchild* that had never been seen before.

"It astonished me," says Dean, "that the bastardized form with all its errors ever made an award ballot."

Dean collected many of the short stories he had published through 1970 into a book that featured as the title one of his best pieces: *Soft Come the Dragons*. This collection was part of an Ace Double along with another novel of his called *Dark of the Woods*. He dedicated the whole thing to Donald Wollheim. Along with each of the stories, Dean offered a brief essay in explanation of its origin, and then added a commentary on the entire project.

Dean was twenty-three when he wrote *Dark of the Woods*, one of his early attempts to show how good and evil can issue from a single source—in this case, the woods. Since he was under the influence of Freudian interpretation, we can assume the woods represent the murky regions of the subconscious. And, in fact, this novel reveals something of Dean's own inner conflicts and desires.

A famous historical novelist of the future, Stauffer Davis, arrives on the planet Demos, ostensibly to write propaganda as a cover for the unwarranted genocide of a winged species of people who had once inhabited it. Instead, he intends to expose this atrocity. A few females are still alive and he falls in love with one named Leah—an act of political rebellion. He discovers that her race had been superior to humans in their ability to experience joy. She is lighter and freer, and Stauffer can take this form only by shedding his former ways. Leah teaches him true intimacy, and he decides to stay with her, despite the costs. They flee together into the woods, but Stauffer is killed. Leah transfers his brain into a new body. Yet they must take even stronger measures to elude those who want to destroy them, so they metamorphose into bird-like creatures. Leah has regained her lost fertility and they make plans to reproduce.

In this society, the ability to commit violence is programmed out of people. Yet it remains latent and resurfaces in Stauffer as manic rage, which allows him to break through his conditioning. It is a novel of metamorphosis, physical and emotional. It is also about the remaking of families by joining beings of different species. In it, Dean has worked with the feelings he has about his own inner darkness—its heaviness— and his need to lighten up, which can occur in the company of someone he loves.

7

Although he was living in Harrisburg, Dean tried to keep in touch with his relatives. One day he called Aunt Ginny, and in the course of the conversation, asked about Uncle Ray. Ginny was quiet for a moment.

"Didn't anyone tell you?" she asked. "Ray died a few months ago."

Dean was stunned. His Uncle Ray dead? It did not seem possible. He knew that Ray had suffered from some health problems, but he had not thought they were that serious. Even worse, no one had called to tell him.

"Well, that's Kate," was all Aunt Ginny would say.

Dean had not had a last chance to see the man he had looked to as a father. He had even missed the funeral and was unable to find out what had actually happened.

"It was a total, horrible shock to me to find out he was dead," says Dean. "I never knew the full circumstances."

"Ray had circulatory problems," says Nancy (Mock) Eckard, Ray's daughter-in-law. "He needed surgery to remove veins that ran down his legs and replace them with plastic tubes. They thought at one point that he might have to have a leg amputated because he hobbled when he walked. The surgeon in Bedford was reluctant to do it, but Ray insisted. He didn't want to go to Pittsburgh. The surgery wasn't successful, so they rushed him by ambulance to Pittsburgh, but the doctors there couldn't redo it. It was too late."

Ray Mock was buried in Bedford. When Dean and Gerda visited his mother's grave a few months later, Dean went to find his Uncle Ray's grave and take his leave. He felt bitter that things had gotten so out of hand with Kate and her feuds that he had missed the last years of his uncle's life. He had expected that eventually the problems would recede, but the fact that no one had called him told him that Kate had poisoned the well among his relatives. The idea made him ill.

"Someday I'd like to write a novel with a character like her," Dean says, "because I know that kind of person really well. It's not dissimilar to what my father could do. He had the ability, in spite of what he was, to charm people, and he could convince them of outlandish things, bring them to believe in his oddball business enterprises. My Aunt Kate could do a similar thing; she could envelope people in a kind of web of deceit and make them part of her little feud."

All Dean had left of his Uncle Ray were memories of their good times together. In 1997, he would dedicate *Sole Survivor* to this gentle, fun-loving man.

[1]Dean Koontz writing as Aaron Wolfe, *Invasion* (New York: Laser, 1975), p. 104.

[2]Dean R. Koontz, essay in *The Double: Bill Symposium*, edited by Bill Bowers and Bill Mallardi (Washington, DC: D:B Press, 1969).

[3]Dean R. Koontz, *Anti-Man* (New York: Paperback Library, 1970), p. 75.

[4]Dean R. Koontz, *Hell's Gate* (New York: Lancer, 1970), p. 76.

[5]Ibid, p. 53.

[6]Dean R. Koontz, *The Dark Symphony* (New York: Lancer, 1970), p. 187.

[7]Ibid., p. 106.

[8]Dean R. Koontz, *Beastchild* (New York: Lancer, 1970), p. 75.

EIGHT

Experiments

1

DEAN'S FATHER, NOW ALONE, HAD SOLD THE HOUSE AND WAS living in a trailer in Bedford. He would regularly drive out to Harrisburg to see Dean and Gerda. He had girlfriends now, one after another, and he often brought them. Although Ray had no interest in Dean's books—had never read one—if someone seemed impressed that Dean was a writer, Ray would talk him up to make himself seem more important.

"He would show up because he needed money, or because he was in trouble or he had some new girlfriend he wanted us to see," says Dean. "He was always going to marry them, every one of them. He'd take me aside and say, 'I think this is the one.' Most of them were absolutely appalling. You never knew who he'd show up with, and usually he'd be drunk. Once he showed up at eight o'clock at night with this hitchhiker he had picked up and had gone drinking with. Gerda and I were furious; we had no idea who this guy was he was bringing to our apartment."

Sometimes his father's current enamorata was unintentionally entertaining, and once Ray brought a girlfriend who inadvertently inspired a conversation in his 1983 novel *Darkfall*.

"When he was married to my mother he ran around with women wrestlers, and those were the days when women wrestlers were not attractive. They looked like male wrestlers, but he liked hard-drinking women. After my mother's death, he introduced us to this hulking women who was unbelievably bigoted."

At one point in the conversation, she said, "Now, something we're beginning to see back home that I don't like is these Neses everywhere."

Dean shook his head, uncertain how to respond.

"Yeah," she said, "they're everywhere, these Neses. I saw

one of them the other day. He just looked so odd to me, so I walked up to him and asked him what kind of Nese he was. And he just was rude to me."

Finally Dean said, "I'm not sure I know what you mean." ·

She told him, "Well, all I did was ask him, is he Japanese, is he Chinese, is he Vietnamese?"

Dean and Gerda glanced at each other, suppressing their laughter. This woman was so mindlessly prejudiced that she was almost funny. Dean never forgot the conversation and gave much of it to a hooker in *Darkfall* who is interviewed by the male and female leads, a pair of cops investigating a grisly murder.

Eventually Dean and his father had a serious confrontation. "I'd written a book with four-letter words in it," Dean explains. "Now, my father certainly used every four-letter word in the book, but still he called me up."

Ray was drunk and he was furious.

"How could you use these words in a book?" he demanded to know. "You can't do that. You're an embarrassment to me, you're an embarrassment to your mother's memory."

This surprised Dean, because he had used such words in other novels. As it turned out, Ray had never read this novel, but someone else had told him about it. Dean tried to reason with him. He did not often use four-letter words, he pointed out, but when he did, they were necessary.

Ray proceeded to yell at him until his only recourse was to just hang up. Ray called back, crying and screaming, to continue his diatribe. When Dean tried again to talk about it calmly, Ray hung up.

Dean heard nothing for a while, and then Ray's brother Bob called to tell him, "Your dad's going to kill himself. He's threatening to kill himself because of what you wrote in a book."

Dean was annoyed. "Bob," he said, "he's not going to kill himself. I mean, he always threatened suicide with my mother. When nothing else worked with her, he was going to kill himself. And anyway, if he's crazy enough to kill himself because I used the words 'hell' and 'damn,' then fine. But it's not going to happen."

Bob was not so sure. "He's so disturbed, I'm going to have to drive up there and sit with him."

Dean gave up. "Do what you have to do," he said. "I've done nothing wrong."

There was a flurry of calls from Bob asking Dean to guarantee to never again use those words in a book. Dean refused.

After not hearing from Ray for a week, Dean called to see how he was feeling.

"I never want to talk to you again," said Ray, and hung up.

They did not hear from him for six months and Gerda was delighted with the reprieve. She did not like Ray and she especially hated the way he tried to manipulate Dean.

Then one night Ray called. "I really did a stupid thing," he admitted. "I shouldn't have carried on with you like that. I'm sorry."

Dean relented. "Okay, it's forgiven," he said.

"I'd just hate to tell you how furious I was," said Ray, and then added something that Dean knew he meant: "For a while I was planning to come down there with a gun."

2

That year, 1971, saw large-scale bombing in Vietnam, while antiwar demonstrations closed the New Jersey Turnpike. Lieutenant Calley was found guilty of murder in connection with the debacle at My-lai, and in California, the corpses of over two dozen migrant workers were unearthed on Juan Corona's property. Gay rights became a larger issue, and George Harrison released "My Sweet Lord."

Dean published *The Crimson Witch*, his only space opera, as a novel. The term "space opera" had been coined in 1941 to refer pejoratively to hackneyed spaceship tales, but then was applied to adventure stories of interplanetary conflict that have a naïve romantic element. First published as a novella in the October 1970 issue of *Fantastic Stories*, it went to Curtis Books for paperback issue. Completed in two weeks to get rent money, the book was billed as a "science fantasy."

The Freudian influence is clear, as Dean makes explicit references to the id and superego. The action speeds along, with only superficial character development. The plot is a straight quest fantasy based in a power struggle, and resulting in the triumph of a hero and his lover.

Dean's poetry-infatuated hero, twenty-one-year-old Jake Turnot, son of a munitions maker, overdoses on a drug that casts him into a postnuclear parallel world. Science is unknown here and the social hierarchies are medieval. The rulers are those who possess psionic powers. Jake acquires a superstitious talking dragon, Kaliglia, as his mount and companion, who informs him of a hole in King Lelar's realm through which people disappear. Jake suspects it is a portal back to his world, and he will stop at nothing to find it.

Along the way, he seduces Cheryn, a witch. She tries to kill him, but then relents because she is in love. She adds her own powers to his quest and they manage to escape Lelar and return to Jake's world. The police arrest them and the FBI wants to use Lelar's psionic powers against the Russians. Cheryn, Jake, and Kaliglia return to the other world and Jake perceives its superiority: "It was a place of adventure for the sake of adventure, a place where a man's wits counted for a great deal, a place where magic was never taken for granted."[1]

Dean published only one short story that year, "Bruno." It is a blend of humor, hard-boiled suspense, and science fiction, featuring a detective from a wacky parallel world—a detective who also happens to be an intelligent bear.

3

In his third year of full-time writing, Dean once again needed to find a way to pay the bills. The science fiction market was drying up, short stories paid almost nothing, and he did not wish to go back to writing erotica. Bob Hoskins at Lancer suggested that writing Gothic romances was fairly easy and somewhat lucrative. The demand for them was high and some publishers were putting out several novels in this line each month. The big-name novelists at the time were Victoria Holt and Dorothy Daniels, but Dean learned that nearly half of the other books in the genre were written by men using female pseudonyms. Resembling daytime soap operas, they were not too artistically demanding, and a successful Gothic writer could obtain multiple book contracts.

Dean took a look at the formula and learned that publishers believed that Gothic readers preferred timid heroines. They had decided that women most fear ending up alone, being in the dark, losing their man, or being raped. Ideally, the heroine hopes for a good marriage with a nice, strong, and highly moral man who can take care of her. This young woman then enters a realm unfamiliar to her, such as being a governess or companion in a wealthy household or in some exotic locale. Since everyone around her is a stranger, when she gets caught up in a mystery, each person's actions are potentially suspicious and she interprets them according to her limited knowledge. The tone is usually melodramatic in its emphasis on stereotypical female fears and reactions. As romance develops, she often becomes a target of some evil. Then her man does something that casts a suspicious light on him and she must rethink her feelings about him.

Dean was uncertain about adopting a female point of view, and he felt no respect for such inflexible formula writing, so initially he declined. He wanted instead to find a subject and form that would develop and stretch his talents. His preference was to try suspense, which he had started to read under Gerda's influence, but he did not yet feel confident in this genre. He needed time to develop, but there was no time. When financial matters pressed and his only other option was to take a part-time job, he decided that it was better for a writer to be writing, even if it meant writing books to a formula. So he changed his mind about Gothics.

He wrote the first book, *Demon Child*, in two weeks under the pseudonym "Deanna Dwyer." It was about a young woman named Jenny Brighton who goes to the ancestral home of relatives in Pennsylvania. A young girl there named Freya believes herself to be a wolf. Jenny discovers that a gypsy had cursed the family. Jenny's Aunt Cora believes in the curse, but Jenny's cousin Richard insists that the girl simply needs psychiatric help. Yet during Freya's strange comas, a horse, a rabbit, and then the veterinarian are all savagely mauled and killed. Jenny suspects Richard. Finally the family invites a psychologist, Walter Hobarth, to treat Freya. Jenny falls for him and he turns out to be the murderer. When he attempts to kill Jenny, Richard saves her. Jenny then realizes that her need for stability in a world of chaos had made her vulnerable to Hobarth and guarded against Richard.

Dean tells the story true to formula, but seems to insert an excessive amount of explanation into the mouth of the psychologist—indicating his own fascination with the discipline of psychology. Hobarth describes in detail how he had set everyone up. He even analyzes Jenny while holding a gun on her. When his plan fails, he crumples and falls to his death in a sinkhole on the estate—a metaphor of how his own theories cracked when they failed to work. While a bit obvious, it shows Dean's attempt to utilize literary devices even in such superficial novels.

Dean sent this novel to Hoskins, who read it, suggested a few changes, and then bought it for $1,500. It was published in 1971. For Dean, it was fairly easy money—$750 per week—and he soon tried another.

Writing this novel, Dean realized that formulas for Gothics reflected old-fashioned values that did not accommodate social changes for women. Although the feminist movement (known then as the women's liberation movement, or women's lib) was making waves in 1970, there was no room for it among the Gothic readership. Strong, independent women were viewed suspiciously as bullish, unromantic, and even unfeminine. Sinister settings required someone who trembled and cried. Dean was well aware of what an independent woman could do, having witnessed such spirit in both his mother and his wife, but he realized that, were such a woman to be a lead character in one these novels, she would take care of things herself—which would then bring a quick end to the story.

Dean understood that Gothics had their own special rhythm and mood, because the central mystery must develop slowly against a sinister atmosphere. There is usually a murder, and the sexual tone is romantic, but gentle and chaste.

After three months, Dean wrote a second Gothic romance, *Legacy of Terror*, about a woman, Elaine Sherred, who is prone to pessimism. She expects the worst, is suspicious of the wealthy, and copes with most situations by reducing them to their simplest terms. When she becomes a nurse to the aging

Jacob Matherly, she is plunged into all that she fears and she must let go of simplistic attitudes before she can find love and happiness. That is, she must learn to accommodate the brighter side of life, because her penchant for a sober approach repels the hero and bonds her with the killer. A more optimistic approach, she realizes, is key to balance.

Dean shows in this book, and the three that follow, that his idea of menace derives from a disordered mind rather than from any brute or supernatural force. He also reveals early his personal fear that madness is genetic and may be passed from parent to child. That was the theme of this second Gothic, and rather than use this novel as a way to challenge and defuse such ideas, he draws them out in predictable ways.

In *Legacy of Terror*, when Elaine arrives at the mansion, Jacob tells her that someone in the house is insane and wants to kill him. He warns her that his daughter-in-law, Amelia, had been insane, as had her father before her, and he believes that either Amelia's brother, Paul, or one of her sons, Gordon or Dennis, may carry the same genetic fault. Subsequently Jenny learns that Amelia had murdered her twin infant daughters before falling down the stairs to her death.

Elaine is drawn to Gordon. She thinks the mad one may be Paul (an echo of Ray Koontz), who is alcoholic and who cannot hold a job or tolerate bosses ("it's in his blood"). Or it may be Dennis, the frivolous artist who has painted a blood-spattered portrait of his mother, calling it "Madness."

However, the psychotic murderer is Gordon, who thinks himself possessed by his mother's spirit and who feels he must rid the place of females who might rob her of her family. Dennis saves Elaine, and she realizes that her judgment on frivolous people had prevented her from seeing the adaptive value of a playful mind.

Dean got a slightly better advance for this book, $1,750, which was the same advance he got for his third Gothic, *Dance with the Devil*, published in 1973.

In this story, Katherine Sellers arrives at Owlsden, a mansion in the country, to become a companion to the wealthy Lydia Boland. At the age of eight, Katherine had lost her parents in a flash flood and was subsequently raised in an orphanage. She survived the experience by becoming an optimist, believing that as long as she sees the bright side, nothing bad can happen. She dislikes Lydia's son Alex, who is moody and pessimistic, as are all of his friends. Instead, she gravitates to people with charm and a positive outlook.

She arrives during a snowstorm and meets Michael Harrison, who offers her a ride to the mansion. She learns of animosity between him and Alex. She also hears about a band of Satanists in the area who make animal sacrifices. When one of the house servants who had warned Katherine against this cult is murdered, she seeks help from Michael. He urges her to meet him in a secluded spot. She soon discovers it is a trap and that he is the leader of the Satanists, who want to sacrifice her. Alex and his friends rescue her and she realizes that being so determined to align herself with optimists had robbed her of perspective. She and Alex then find romance.

4

Not everyone thought that Dean was making good use of his time by writing such books. "I had writer acquaintances who accused me of prostituting myself," he recalls. "I said, 'I'd rather do these books during lean times and at least be able to keep writing.'" He watched these people quit writing to get regular jobs to pay the bills. They fully expected to return to writing, they assured him, but some never did. Dean decided to just let them think he was cheapening his talent. He was writing these novels to get money so that eventually he could take his time writing those that he cared about.

Dean also talked Gerda into writing some to add to their limited income. Gerda wrote two, but only one was published before Lancer folded. Her book, *A Darker Heritage*, came out in 1973 under her maiden name, Cerra.

More Hawthornesque than any of Dean's had been, Gerda's novel has a classically Gothic setting and explicit references to evil. Yet it also has a political edge regarding social attitudes toward independent women. Although book collectors favor the idea that Dean is the true author, there is a difference in style. Dean offered substantial editorial advice, but Gerda wrote it. Her character, Leigh Kavanaugh, is less timid and more able to stand up for herself than the heroines that Dean had portrayed, and Gerda inserts commentary rather than the longer explanations that Dean favored.

In *A Darker Heritage*, Leigh Kavanaugh inherits Polk Mansion from her Uncle Silas, who had been involved in devil worship. A young attorney, to whom she is attracted, urges her to sell, but she insists that she is self-reliant enough to manage it. As an orphan, she had never had a place to call her own and she dislikes any attempts to make her believe that, as a woman, she should be less independent. When she reads her uncle's gruesome diary, however, and finds body parts, she fears there may be more to this house than she can handle. A neighbor, Will, appears to be part of the cult and she fears his approaches, but he becomes her savior when the attorney turns out to be the cult's high priest. Leigh learns that, while self-reliance is a positive quality, taken to an extreme it can endanger her.

Gerda's second novel, for which she received the advance before the publisher went out of business, was set in a carnival atmosphere. About her short-lived writing career, she says, "These books were formula. If you knew how to write a sentence and structure a paragraph, you could write them. It was the same story over and over." Since she was taking courses, working at a fulltime job, researching, and proofreading, she did not want to do any more. She announced that one writer in the family was enough. "I wasn't driven to write," she says.

5

Children of the Storm was Dean's fourth Gothic. Published in 1972, it again involves a schizophrenic whose "evil" is explained as insanity. This novel was set on a private Caribbean island, Distingue, where Sonya Carter takes a job as governess to two children. She soon learns that someone has threatened the children and that another couple on the island, the Blenwells, want to control it. Their son, Ken, has a dark personality and seems a likely candidate. Sonya is attracted to Bill, the boatman, but soon discovers in the midst of a hurricane that Bill is in fact psychotic, and it falls to her to protect the children from his attacks. Ken helps her and she realizes that her own naiveté had set her up to move toward the wrong man.

In this novel, Dean again includes more than the heroine's point of view, but the method seems erratic and its intent unclear. Sometimes he shows the perspective of the psychotic, as if attempting to explore this mindset, and only once, toward the end, does he insert Ken Blenwell's point of view.

Dean's knowledge of psychology at this stage in his life was superficial. He equated schizophrenia with murderous psychosis, although in fact his description pointed to the diagnosis of multiple personality and antisocial behavior. Bill, the boatman, has a counterpart in a man named Jeremy whose delusions fuel his aggression. It was as if Dean had decided that schizophrenia was the most dangerous and uncontrolled type of insanity and was therefore at the heart of the evil acts perpetrated by madmen who kill. Interestingly, one character comments that madmen do not work in pairs, and because of this the tandem killers go undetected at first. It foreshadows *The Face of Fear*, still several years away.

Dean's fifth Gothic, *The Dark of Summer*, returns to a traditional setting, an estate in Massachusetts. Gwyn Keller is about to inherit her father's vast fortune. Her parents and twin sister Ginny are dead, and her wealthy uncle invites her to spend the summer. She meets Jack Younger, a lighthearted lobster fisherman, who tells her that her uncle plans to develop the beachfront property and prohibit the fishermen from pursuing their trade. When confronted, Gwyn's uncle has a different explanation. The ambiguity makes Gwyn feel paranoid. This worries her because after her parents' death, she had suffered a mental breakdown. Then she starts to see her twin sister, who urges Gwyn to join her in death. In fact, the ghost is an actress hired by Gwyn's uncle to make her think she is going insane. She sees through the pretense and resists.

Although this Gothic is not as romantic as those preceding it, Dean showed his ability to find variety within this rigid formula. Thus far, he had managed to diversify the setting and form, but this time he tampered a bit with the idea that the heroine must fall in love. It is also the only one of his Gothics in which the heroine is wealthy.

He wrote this novel over a weekend to fill an open slot.

What they needed was a "queen-size" Gothic, which was about twenty thousand words longer than the standard books Dean had been writing. "Lancer called me on a Friday at eleven o'clock," Dean remembers. "They had found out that one of the Gothics they had scheduled was plagiarized and they had to pull it. They were doing something like nine Gothics a month and if they lost that space on the rack, they wouldn't get it back. There were no books in their list that they could just move forward without causing the same problem two weeks later, so they needed a book by Monday. I talked them into Tuesday. They were willing to pay me $4,000. As soon as I hung up the phone, I started writing, and I think we actually had to drive it into Manhattan on Tuesday morning."

The editor told him it was one of the best Gothics he had seen in months, and to Dean's surprise, it was later published in Norway and various other countries—the first of his Gothics to be translated.

Finally he was tired of these books. "After five of them," Dean declares, "I didn't care how quickly I could write them. I knew I'd never write another. When I look at my early books, I'm horrified that I wrote some of that stuff, but I know that I was learning every inch of the way. There were techniques I was able to try, experiments that I could get away with, because in those Gothic novel lines for a while, *everything* sold well—and publishers didn't care what else you did as long as you adhered to the central formula. So I used them as practice ground."

6

Having written in several genres, Dean was ready to try non-fiction again. He combined his penchant for explanation with his writing expertise at the age of twenty-six to teach everything he thought important to know in his Writer's Digest book, *Writing Popular Fiction*. With a dedication to Robert Hoskins, from whom he had learned much of what he put into the book, he divided the genre categories into science fiction and fantasy, mystery, suspense, Gothic romance, Westerns, and erotica. He felt that mastering one genre makes it easier to cross over into another: Developing this flexibility may ensure the writer's survival, as genres wax and wane in popularity. Whenever he discussed a genre in which he had written, he used examples from his own work, such as *Beastchild* and *Legacy of Terror*, to illustrate his points. Otherwise, he recommended books he had read.

Dean pulled no punches. Writing is hard work, he claimed. It is lonely and frustrating, and the markets are unpredictable. Although earlier in his career, he had written ten to twelve hours each day, every day, by this third year, he had settled into a schedule of eight hours, five or six days a week. That would soon change.

To research a genre, he read what he could find and noted the prominent publishers. He took advantage of the market listings in *Writer's Digest* magazine, read *Publishers Weekly*, and looked through the annual *Writer's Market*. He paid attention to which genres were hot and which were losing steam. His advice was for people who wanted to work as writers, although as the market shifted in years to come, so did his own habits. At the time, genre fiction was more widely read than mainstream. He was experienced only in the paperback market, which was successful, if low-paying. What he believed about writing then reveals his sense of professionalism and his awareness of the importance of running his writing career as a business. Much of his later success came from this early discipline.

Having been exposed as a student to the prejudices of English teachers that literary immortality was to be had only in serious mainstream fiction, Dean strove to point out how many authors now honored by the critics, such as Poe, Stevenson, and Twain, in fact had been genre writers. He insisted that category fiction could transcend formula and have artistic scope and literary merit.

According to him, genre stories involve five elements: a strong plot, a hero or heroine, clear and believable motivations (which he lists), lots of action, and a colorful background. He discusses each of these elements in detail, even recommending children's books for research when expertise is otherwise too technical.

After going through the expectations for novels in each of the six genres, Dean then addresses the business side of writing. He describes how he plays with words and sounds to come up with provocative titles, believing they must evoke the impression of at least one of four elements—sex, violence, suspense, or exotic events. Since he believes that fiction is not a reflection of reality, but a sifting of reality's essence, he describes how hard he works on the opening sentence and scene, how he keeps notebooks for free association, and how he has developed his own discipline. He believes that the most successful writers will set a goal for a certain amount of pages or words each day.

Since writing provides psychological structure, which has strong allure for him, it is not as difficult for him as it might be for others, to sit for hours at a time, day after day, typing up his stories. He insists that writers must keep their workplace clear, orderly, and professional, dismissing the idea that a disorderly desk fosters creativity.

Above all, he says, style is what a writer has to offer, but one should refrain from a conscious effort to develop it. Style evolves naturally. "If you make a conscious effort to form an individual style, you will more often end by imitating the work of writers whom you admire."[2] The rule to follow, he suggests is "say it as simply, as clearly, and as shortly as possible."[3]

Most instructive in this book is Dean's description of his writing method. After confessing amazement at the amateurish idea of writing a first draft quickly, and then polishing it in subsequent drafts, he insists that this method is a sign of sloppiness and that professionals polish as they go. Writers should write as clean and sound a first draft as possible. With each novel, he wrote on heavy bond paper with carbon paper and a second sheet beneath. (Photocopy was available but expensive.) "If a paragraph is not going well, I rip that set of papers out of the typewriter and begin the page again, but I never go on until that page is *finalized* and cleanly typed in finished copy. I waste a lot of paper. But I save a lot of time."[4]

In anticipation of readers' needs, as well as to be thorough, he raises the questions he feels are important to the process of writing, and answers them from his own experience. From royalties to manuscript format, from subsidiary rights to accounting and taxes, he covers the field. As a sign of the times, he encourages writers to submit their own work for the first couple of years. Not only will they understand the process of marketing, but they will work their way toward a good agent, who will not look at a novelist until he or she has sold at least one book.

Writing Popular Fiction is written with the authority of a born teacher, but with the naïveté of a twenty-six-year-old man who has known moderate success with small publishers. Dean clearly had confidence that his success would continue.

In January, he published another article in *Writer's Digest*, which emphasized the demand for paperback "category" novels. Much of it echoed the book.

As 1972 got into swing, Dean was about to realize the results of his most prolific year to date.

[1]Dean R. Koontz, *The Crimson Witch* (New York: Curtis, 1971), p. 166.

[2]Dean R. Koontz, *Writing Popular Fiction* (Cincinnati, OH: Writer's Digest Press, 1972), p. 166.

[3]Ibid., p. 167.

[4]Ibid., p. 177.

NINE

Momentum

1

DEAN PUBLISHED FIVE SCIENCE FICTION NOVELS IN 1972, along with two of his Gothics, four short stories, and his first suspense novel, which captured the era's conflicted social and political attitudes.

The military draft was being phased out and Secretary of State Kissinger had declared that peace was at hand in Vietnam. *All in the Family*, a television show depicting conflicts between youth and the status quo, was the leading program. It showed an undercurrent of nationwide cynicism, for which current events had given good cause: Five men who broke into the Democratic National Headquarters at the Watergate complex were arrested. There was suspicion of complicity by Nixon's campaign officials, and director John Mitchell suddenly resigned. The possibility that the president or his staff might have initiated a crime seemed too far-fetched, and Nixon was re-elected president by a near-record landslide. He then announced his own special investigation of the Watergate affair. By 1974, he, too, would resign when tapes revealed his part in a cover-up.

Daw Books, Donald A. Wollheim's eponymous new venture after leaving Ace, published *A Darkness in My Soul*, which Dean dedicated to "G" (Gerda). In it, he expresses his belief that love is the remedy for madness, while personal transformation requires reorienting from self toward others.

It is the year 2004, in a world of warfare and plague. There exist two genetically engineered individuals with special talents, Sim and Child. The military uses Sim's psychic abilities to explore the mind of Child, a deformed genius, for the purpose of gaining strategic superiority. In this highly Freudian novel, Sim goes into Child's subconscious—which is portrayed as a physically detailed place—but he is completely unprepared for the chaos he encounters. He soon realizes that Child has merged with the mind of God and that they are all trapped together in insanity.

Sim perceives that God is an entity that cannot organize Himself toward any good use. "God was a hugely powerful pool of psychic energy without a manipulatory system; a car without wheels."[1] Sim becomes a new god, more rational and benevolent. He resolves everyone's problems, but soon realizes why God had gone insane: He was lonely. Subsequently Sim shares his divinity with a friend, but they eventually grow bored so, for entertainment, they manipulate human beings into wars. The nihilistic "darkness in the soul" that Sim had known prior to his experience as God returns full force.

This novel demonstrates Dean's early perception that violent people are something less than human. Their weakness is their need for power and their inability to value the lives of others. He indicates that authoritarian types operate out of a twisted psychosis. So, too, does God. It becomes clear that Dean's father's mental illness is a recurring stimulus, aligned with brutality and evil.

Another of Dean's science fiction novels that year, *Warlock*, was published by Lancer, who paid an advance of $2,000.

Told in three parts, the story features a hero, Shaker Sandow, who has psionic powers. He must journey to an alien land to locate devices for the defense of Darkland. The time is some eight hundred years after humankind has settled space colonies, altered their genetics, and created new races. For Sandow, it is a personal quest as well. He needs to know whether his unusual powers had caused his mother's death. Thus, parallel to the perilous physical journey is the story of a boy attached to his deceased mother, who fears that his existence had shortened her life.

One of Dean's best efforts that year—and one of his favorites among his science fiction—was *The Flesh in the Furnace*, published by Bantam. Dean dedicated it to Harry Recard, his former college roommate, and Harry's wife, Diane. Dean called it a "passion play in five acts of Chinese theater." Its inspiration was the result of three events: Dean came across a fleeting image of organic puppets in a novel entitled *Emphyrio*; while cleaning his closets, he found his college notes on theories of dramatic impersonation, particularly Chinese theater; and he read an article about a passion play done partially in the nude. These events converged just as Dean was wondering what it would be like to devise an alien passion play and present it as seen through nonhuman eyes. The story evolved from there.

On a futuristic Earth, a puppetmaster, Petros, travels with an idiot and a troupe of living puppets that he destroys each night and then remakes in a special machine before each performance. The puppets are not merely alive, they remember and resent each recycling. Bitty Belina is the idiot's favorite puppet. She urges him to kill Petros and help her to give the other puppets permanent form. When she has sufficient collective power, she and her band turn on the idiot and kill him.

Throughout the novel, Dean paces the story with intermittent scriptures from another culture that sound much like Friedrich Nietzsche's *Thus Spoke Zarathustra* — a quasi-biblical, philosophical narrative in which a prophet announces the imminent arrival of the Overman — the person of moral courage who can make and live by his own ethical codes — and denounces the empty religion of his time. Dean had read Nietzsche in college, and was aware of his proclamation of the death of God and the need for humankind to supplant God. In Dean's version, the Rogue Saint Eclesian, in the Vonopoen *Book of Wisdom*, expresses anger toward the creator and the need for killing off the old gods. Human cruelty is the responsibility of a deity, he insists, who became careless and allowed some men to be created without souls. The puppets in the story represent humans manipulated by an uncaring God. They must resist the status quo and recreate themselves as the gods of their own existence. This same theme was to carry through in Dean's work in many different forms for several decades.

Another science fiction novel that dealt with religious themes was *Starblood*, based on the novella "A Third Hand." In this explicitly Freudian novel, Dean declares that the subconscious mind of an orderly man is full of frantic, roach-like, cannibalistic insects — the equivalent of madness. "In a conscious mind where nearly everything that had ever happened or been learned was stored methodically, nothing much was left to relegate to the subconscious mind except id desires of the most grotesque form . . . disordered, filthy, shot through with a living mobile rot."[2]

In a future world plagued by the addictive drug PBT (Perfectly Beautiful Trip), Timothy is a "singularly odd case." He has no arms or legs, only one eye, and an IQ of over 250. A mafia-like group called the Brethren subjects him to PBT, which increases his psionic powers until he can heal himself. He goes to a farmhouse in Iowa where he discovers a sinkhole in the cellar (the deepest subconscious) and an ancient spaceship with aliens on board. They tell Timothy that PBT is made from alien blood, which offers a vision of God. Timothy enjoys a camaraderie with the aliens, with whom he feels accepted.

This novel is clearly intended as a Christ allegory. Timothy is unique among members of the human race, having powers, intelligence, and vision far beyond that of any mortal. When he joins the godlike aliens, he feels safe, while humans spurn him. The king had sent men to kill him as an infant, and then as a young adult, he had caused trouble and been persecuted. "And now, in a strange way, he had died and been resurrected."[3]

"The Christian mythology offered me a great number of story ideas," Dean admits, and several of his science fiction tales exploit these themes.

There is also a telling autobiographical detail: What Timothy had feared most in his life was loneliness—a childhood experience of Dean's that compels him to write so much about families. Timothy's life "had been a desperate race to be accepted, to have at least a goodly number of peripheral friends."[4] The aliens provide this—outsiders all, forming a familial bond.

Dean's analysis of the human mind at this stage issued in the following ideas: The subconscious is almost like an entity that fears and detests the conscious mind, while consciousness blocks out the seamier concerns of the psyche. Thus, Dean indicates, all of us may be schizophrenic (which is a misunderstanding of the term as a dual personality). Yet splitting ourselves into two minds allows us to cope with life better than if we were integrated. Compromises are necessary. The subconscious is a madhouse of sadomasochistic desires and disgusting, ugly dreams. Probing the ego and id too deeply could result in insanity. Clearly Dean had some personal concerns.

Another of Dean's biblical allegories, *Time Thieves*, was part of an Ace Double with Susan K. Putney's *Against Arcturus*.

Pete Mullion, the hero, shares many of Dean's qualities. He had been lonely as a boy and he believes that loneliness is the worst human experience. Pete is also aware (to be repeatedly expressed by characters in future novels) that the insane never suspect they are mad; it is only the sane man who questions his sanity. Pete is apolitical but dismissive of politicians. His strongest trait is the ability to assimilate anything, no matter how radical, and work within the new picture being presented.

In a story that foreshadows *Strangers* in its use of false memories and a gifted alien race, Pete discovers that he has been missing for twelve days. He remembers nothing. He spots men watching him and experiences telepathic powers. The men take him aboard a spaceship and explain that he had once witnessed their presence on Earth, and they had erased his memories. As they worked on him, they had unleashed telepathic powers, which they must now eradicate to prevent him from introducing these powers to others. The human species, they say, has not yet evolved to the point of being able to meet a more advanced species. They expect Pete to accept their wisdom.

However, Pete has experienced the way the powers enhance intimacy and companionship, so he resists giving them up. With them, he will never again feel lonely. He uses the full strength of his childhood fears to blast the aliens away.

This is the tale of the Garden of Eden, with a radically different ending. The aliens represent God, who offers a paradise and then, when humankind seems immature and unworthy, attempts to retrieve it. Adam and Eve did indeed lose their access to Paradise, but Dean's protagonist is not so easily cowed. Pete grabs back from God what God had promised. Disinclined to accept the paternalistic concept that God knows best, Dean thought that we should be given the gifts and allowed to see what we can do.

2

In 1972 to 1973, Dean published ten short stories. Three were in anthologies edited by Bob Hoskins, four with Roger Elwood, two in magazines, and one with Harlan Ellison.

Hoskins's *Infinity* series took "Altarboy," "Ollie's Hands," and "Grayworld." In the first, a man who executes dissidents traps their souls in the limbo of his id. When one soul threatens his power, he makes a dying Nazi into the warden of his psyche. However, the Nazi takes over and tosses him into the dungeon of his own id, where he faces the souls of those he has executed.

"Ollie's Hands" involves a man who carries visionary gifts in his touch, such as being able mentally to bond with others. He can achieve total intimacy, but it results, paradoxically, in loneliness and isolation. He is the ultimate outsider. One day, Ollie discovers an unconscious suicidal girl in an alley and takes her home. At first, she is thrilled with his abilities, but then fears the "mesh"—the blending of their minds that dissolves her freedom. "Ollie's Hands" was revised in 1987 for a magazine called *Horror Show*, and then included in *Strange Highways*.

"Grayworld" was a novella that moved through one dream state after another, keeping the hero disoriented. It grew into a novel, *The Long Sleep*, that Dean published under the pseudonym "John Hill" in 1975.

The anthology, *Again, Dangerous Visions*, was a sequel to Harlan Ellison's original cutting-edge work, *Dangerous Visions*. "I rejected hundreds of stories, including one by Heinlein," says Ellison, "but Dean's work was sufficiently interesting to me that he got my solicitation. I told him I wanted the kind of story that you can't write for a magazine, the kind of story they would reject for its subject matter. I wanted great writing, but it had to be controversial."

Ellison differentiated between writers who played out their voice within a few books and those who started with merely yeoman work and built from there—with Dean classified as the latter. He believed Dean's early science fiction was average, but that successive novels had demonstrated "a vigorous fluency of imagination, a strengthening grasp of concept and plot material, and an emerging style very much of his own making."[5] He foresaw that Dean would continue toward the enviable perch where he would be the only writer doing the type of stories that he does.

Dean wrote an Afterword to this story, "A Mouse in the Walls of the Global Village," in which he explains that he has tried previously to extrapolate on the Global Village philosophy of Marshall McLuhan. His novel, *The Fall of the Dream Machine*, had been his first attempt, followed by "A Dragon in the Land," both published in 1969. Feeling the need to work with the concept again, he had written *Hung*, but that book had been extensively revised at Cameo Press. In "A Mouse in the Walls of the Global Village," he focused on both the positive and negative aspects of such a "world neighborhood"— but emphasized the negative for his character. "Surely," he said, "there might be an end to nations, better understanding between peoples, and an end to war. But it would mean something else, too, something altogether unpleasant."[6] His hero is alienated from the Great Society because of medical problems. Despite how much better off most people are, this man's existence is a nightmare. He does not fit into the brainwashed, standardized masses, and must therefore be treated harshly. There is no place for iconoclasts. Dean explains that the character "represents any man who is alienated from society for whatever reason."[7] This character's only recourse is to beg for death.

In the February 1972 *Magazine of Fantasy and Science Fiction*, Dean published "Cosmic Sin," a humorous detective story that revisits the parallel worlds of "Bruno." The hero, Jake, assists the Probability Police with finding a pair of aliens who are talking cabbages and who are involved in making illegal pornography.

A small Pennsylvania magazine called *Trend* published "The Terrible Weapon" in 1972. In this tale, Dean offers a political scenario in which a Soviet transmission of subliminal commands across all U.S. media causes everyone to tell the truth. Corruption is revealed all the way to the president. It seems to the politicians to be the worst way to undermine the social structure that could possibly be devised.

Roger Elwood offered more diversity for stories like "Terra

Phobia" in *Androids, Time Machines, and Blue Giraffes*, "The Undercity" in *Future City*, "The Sinless Child" in *Flame Tree Planet*, and "Wake Up to Thunder" in *Children of Infinity*, all of which were published in 1973.

"Terra Phobia" is about the possibility of adapting so well to long-term residence on a spaceship that leaving it to colonize becomes psychologically impossible.

"The Undercity" is narrated by a Mafia-type thug, teaching one of his progeny how his kind have adapted as the future city moved underground. Since most things that were once illegal are now available, he complains, it's difficult to make a buck, and he outlines the unusual crimes he's been hired to commit.

"The Sinless Child" takes place in the year 2016. A couple applies to have a child in an overpopulated world that has tight controls over reproduction. Since they want to raise the child with the Christian values of good and evil, they are considered unique enough to be allowed this experiment. After the child is born, the parents give it up to androids that resemble them — save for lacking a corrupted subconscious that could be projected onto the child. As the sinless child develops, it becomes apparent that the experiment has failed: He is so amoral that he becomes a danger.

"Wake Up to Thunder" is another story about God going mad — in the form of a computer. An Artificial Intelligence known as "Thunder" has turned humankind into mental slaves, but his powers are dissolving. Thunder has grown too large and cannot expand further without malfunction. He was a demon made by man, "a puppet master built by his own marionettes."[8]

3

In January of 1973, a cease-fire agreement was signed in Vietnam, but the fighting continued. Thus far, there were forty-six thousand combat deaths, and over four hundred thousand dead civilians. One hundred and ten billion dollars had been spent, and nothing positive had come of it. Soldiers who came home were treated with contempt, partly because people were

more savvy about the horrific details of this war and partly
because national patriotism had weakened. Dean and Gerda
watched these developments with a cynical eye. They were not
militant, but they agreed that the war should end. Dean's first
suspense novel, published that year, took on these issues. Its
tone was cynical and the ending pessimistic about the world's
future. "That's how I felt in those days," he says.

He knew young men who had gone to Vietnam: "There
were people from my high school and college classes who had
died there, or who came back wounded. We all saw people it
had affected and the effect it had on our country. People had
been asked to do something unpleasant. They went and did it,
and in the end, a lot of people died for nothing. Yet I was even
more appalled by how they were treated when they came
home. I think for a number of years it angered me to see how
one part of the country would treat another part over this
issue. So I wrote *Chase*."

This was the last novel that The Scott Meredith Agency
represented, and Dean's first hardcover. Ted Chichak sold it to
editor Lee Wright at Random House. Dean liked her. She
appreciated his work and made only minor suggestions. "She
never wanted much work done," Dean says, "and she was
always boosting my ego. She insisted I'd be famous one day."
Gerda liked her, too, in part because Lee Wright exemplified a
woman without children who was happy with her life. That
reassured Gerda, who was becoming more certain that she and
Dean would make the same choice.

Dean's agent suggested that he use a pseudonym for this
novel, since it deviated from his usual subject matter. He was
not thrilled by that idea, but he came up with the name "K. R.
Dwyer"—husband to "Deanna Dwyer." "K. R." were his own
initials reversed.

Chase mirrored the thematic perspective of another K. R.
Dwyer novel, *Shattered*, which sold four months later. As Dean
wrote in the British edition of *Chase*, these stories "can be viewed
as a two-book exploration of social and psychological conditions
in the United States during the early 1970s."[9] He noted the antiwar protests and the atmosphere of paranoia and prejudice that
both protagonists experience. Benjamin Chase in *Chase* and Alex
Doyle in *Shattered* share a distrust of authority and a belief that

politics of any persuasion could offer no satisfactory solution to social problems. Both characters are also "redeemed by their acceptance of self-reliance as the greatest of all virtues."

In *Chase*, Vietnam vet Benjamin Chase is haunted by guilt over his part in Operation Jules Verne, a My-lai–type slaughter of civilians. He has allowed this atrocity to be covered up, and he even earned a congressional Medal of Honor. Haunted by his nightmares, he merely wants to be left alone. He sees a psychiatrist regularly, but otherwise lives in an attic room, taking solace in fiction, where the bad guys can't get to him. He controls his world and gets from it only the responses that he orchestrates.

One night he witnesses a murder and then gets phone calls about his past from the killer, who calls himself "The Judge." When attempts to get assistance from authorities fail, Chase takes justice and self-defense into his own hands. He meets a woman, Glenda, who shares some kinship with him in healing from emotional scars, and she supports his efforts. Chase discovers that the killer is part of a white supremacist group and had been a child molester. He had worshipped boyish innocence, and having been rebuffed by a boy named Mark, had rationalized his vengeful assault on Mark as a judgment from God. This was the murder that Chase had seen.

This novel is an early statement on the failure of authority figures to protect those in their care. Chase's psychiatrist betrays him, as does his own government. Glenda had been sexually abused. The murder victim, Mark, was distanced from his parents because of their religious fundamentalism which, while seeming to offer protection, falls far short. In fact, these parents had allowed the killer to buy their son at the age of four, and their duplicity, disguised as concern for Mark's well-being, had been instrumental in his death. Their own beliefs had betrayed and destroyed him.

In short, the only person who can really protect us is ourselves.

There are clear parallels, as Chase himself understands them, between the killer's insane rationalizations and those of his country. This is Dean's first published attempt in a realistic setting to equate the pathological mind with a pathological government. The killer views abuse as the work of God similar to the way the government justifies war as a tool of peace. Both decide to "deal with" a problem by using murder, but disguise it with euphemisms to evade accountability. The outer monster is inextricably linked to an inner one: "Heroes need monsters to slay and they can always find them, within if not without."[10]

The New York Times called this novel a taut, well-written book, while *The Saturday Review* insisted it was more than a novel of suspense. "It is a brutally realistic portrait of the role of violence in our society." Dustin Hoffman showed interest in doing a movie of it, but that project never advanced.

Dean later revised *Chase* to include in his 1995 collection, *Strange Highways*.

"I think the attitudes all remain the same," he says. "I changed a lot of clumsy writing and tried to introduce a better visual sense to the imagery. I changed the character of Glenda because, when I wrote the original version, I didn't have a handle on doing relationships as well as I do them now. What the book comes down to is that you can trust people as individuals, but you can't trust them when they form large groups."

4

Tied thematically to *Chase* in terms of the attitudes and experiences of the protagonists, *Shattered* was published at Random House the following year. Dean dedicated it to his editor, Lee Wright, "in return for much advice, kindness, and patience."

Alex Doyle, a commercial artist, leaves Philadelphia with his eleven-year-old brother-in-law, Colin, to drive cross-country to San Francisco where Alex's wife, Courtney, awaits them in their new house. Alex and Colin are both shy, and by the end of the novel, both must overcome this to face their fears. Unbeknownst to them, a psychopathic former boyfriend is stalking Courtney. He picks up their trail and pursues them across the country. He makes several attempts to kill them, but failing, then goes straight to Courtney. Alex compromises his pacifist beliefs to buy a gun for self-protection and must resort to violence to save the person he loves. Ultimately he realizes that, despite his beliefs, he has a latent violent streak: The killer begs for mercy and Alex kills him anyway.

Lee Wright was astonished that at the age of twenty-six, Dean could write about such a dramatic loss of innocence. She told him that he could keep writing midlist suspense novels like this for the rest of his life, but he would be a fool to do so. She believed he had the talent to move up.

The killer, George Leland, was modeled on the random killers of that era: Charles Manson, who led a pack of alienated kids against Sharon Tate and the LaBianca couple; Richard Speck, who killed eight nurses in their apartment one night; and Charles Whitman, the famous shooter in the Texas gun tower. All are viewed as symptoms of an intolerant, paranoid society, symbolized in the novel by a small-town cop who harasses Alex for having long hair and unusual clothing. Try as he might, Alex can get no help from those who are charged with the role of protection.

Warner Brothers bought the movie rights, but then turned what Dean viewed as a quintessentially American story into a French film called *The Intruder*, starring Jean-Louis Trintignant and Mirielle Darc. The actual chase was far shorter and the suspense lagged. That this could happen to his novel when the potential was there for something better puzzled Dean. But he had been paid and there was nothing he could do.

5

After writing *Chase*, Dean decided to switch agents. Bob Hoskins suggested that he might be better off with Henry Morrison, who had had been with Meredith and had left in 1965 to form his own agency. Dean knew of some of his clients, and felt he was making little progress where he was. It was his impression that the Meredith Agency sent out manuscripts one after another and took whatever was offered, rather than working at building careers. He felt they had no vision for the individual writer; instead, they wanted their authors simply to write the same thing over and over. Another author, Stephen Marlowe, had once worked there and described it thus: "Scott himself really didn't have a great love for books—he might as well have been selling shoes."[11]

Dean left Meredith, and placed his next novel with Henry Morrison.

"He first got in touch with me," says Morrison, "because I was representing writers like Robert Ludlum and David Morrell. I was doing a lot of business in science fiction and international thrillers."

Morrison wanted to bring him into the marketplace in such a way that he would be taken more seriously on larger novels. Yet it was clear that Dean needed to write more than one novel a year to cover his expenses. It was common practice to place an author at different houses simultaneously, and since Dean was ambitious and eager to work, Morrison found opportunities for him and encouraged him to use more pseudonyms. "When an author is building some sort of base," he explains, "you really have no idea how long it's going to take to break out, and unless an author does it with his first book, sometimes you can work for years before he grabs everyone's attention. As we were moving him upward, he still needed to generate income to pay his bills. One publisher couldn't do four of his books a year, so we split him up among houses in the hope that one name would connect. I try to find a handle—something identifiable that will set an author apart from other writers—and I build on that.

"Dean as a writer is very individual and Scott Meredith considered him just another spoke in the wheel. Dean was trying to develop an individual voice and I encouraged him in that. He was not only a good writer, but he wanted to move upward on his own merit, not just by becoming a carbon copy of the big gun of the moment."

6

The first book that Morrison sold for Dean was a caper novel, *Blood Risk*, which would be the first in a hardcover trilogy that featured the same character, Michael Tucker. Morrison encouraged Dean to use a pseudonym, since caper novels were a genre unto themselves—adventure/thriller novels in which the heroes are criminals. Dean had noticed that several suspense writers in those days had Scottish surnames, so he suggested a few that started with "Mac." Barbara Norville, his editor at Bobbs-Merrill, came up with a less obvious Scottish name, "Coffey." "Brian Coffey" then wrote five short suspense novels, four of them for Bobbs-Merrill. The cover copy stated that Coffey was a pen name for a writer whose fiction has sold worldwide "to the tune of over two million copies."

Dean found Barbara Norville to be the most exacting editor he had had to date, and felt he learned some important things from her.

Dean's protagonist, Michael Tucker, is a thief, but a man with his own serious code of integrity and with considerable education. Like John D. MacDonald's hero, Travis McGee, he kills only when he must and feels great loathing for it. He steals only from thieves—or insurance companies! He lives in Manhattan, collects art, and is the son of a wealthy man, but hates his father and refuses his inheritance, because to get it he must allow his father to control him. In the first caper, he is part of a team intent on hijacking a shipment of Mafia money. The heist is blown and the mob captures one of his men, so Tucker must rescue him. With the aid of a clever blonde, he manages to get both the man and the money.

The plot is obvious and the characters nondynamic, but there are autobiographical elements present throughout. Tucker views his girlfriend, Elise, in much the way Dean viewed Gerda—as quick, clever, intelligent, and feminine. He loves his late mother, has a cynical view on politics, has frightening dreams about his father, and despises the man's infidelities.

The second Tucker novel was *Surrounded*, published in 1974. It involves more clever plot twists and better character development. Tucker continues to battle his father, which puts him in greater need of money from theft. His three requirements for taking on a job are that he must be in charge, he has to like the job, and he robs thieves or institutions only, never individuals. He joins two other men to rob a Santa Monica mall after closing hours. A slip-up alerts police and they become trapped. However, when the cops go in, they find no sign of the thieves, thanks to Tucker's ingenuity in finding a hiding place under their noses.

In 1975, the third Tucker novel, *The Wall of Masks*, came

out. It was the last of the series, and Dean may one day revise and collect them together in a single book. This novel is the best of the three. It involves an exotic locale and has the fast pace of a thriller. Tucker learns about an imminent transaction in Mexico involving the exchange of a large sum of money for a pre-Columbian wall featuring carvings of exotic masks. As a hurricane and a corrupt Mexican general simultaneously close in, Tucker goes for the prize—the money. He leaves the wall for the Mexican government.

Dean outlined a fourth novel in this series, but felt it was too derivative of Donald Westlake's Stark novels, so he never sent it to his editor.

7

A mainstream hardcover publication that year was a comic World War II novel, *Hanging On*. Dean had been reading a lot of black comedy and admired Joseph Heller's *Catch-22*—an innovative, metaphorical novel about the absurdities of war, which had become a cultural sensation. Dean believed he could write a book in this genre and he wanted to try. Morrison submitted a one-hundred-page segment with a brief outline to senior editor David Williams at M. Evans and Company. Williams took it to a sales meeting and convinced the editorial staff that the paperback rights would sell for at least $10,000, so he came back with an offer of $3,500.

"The writing was clear and well paced," says Williams, "and a pleasure to read. It got you into the story immediately. Henry Morrison was touting the book as another *Catch-22*." When Dean finished the novel and handed it in, however, Williams was a bit disappointed. He thought there were too many digressions into subplots. He broached the subject with Dean and was relieved to find him willing to rewrite. "In general, I found Dean unfailingly professional, flexible and friendly, a real pleasure to work with. He displayed gratitude for the editing I'd done."

Dean agrees that they had a good relationship. "I got a lot of good advice from him. He'd sharpen scenes here and there. He told me that every time we enter a scene, we really need to know where we are at once. That was helpful. And I changed the ending. The book originally had extremely dark humor. About half of the characters died, but it was funny. David didn't want that. He said it was too off-putting. On consideration, I agreed. So I rewrote it. Gerda was never convinced that was good advice; she thought the book was better with the darker ending. Over the years, I think she might have been right, but I was so eager to break into mainstream—and to do it with a comic novel was particularly bizarre—so I was eager to have it published. And I still like the gentler ending David led me toward. It's still pointed and funny—just different."

Set in the year 1944, the novel is the story of the army engineers and support soldiers sent behind enemy lines to keep a strategic bridge in repair. Each time they rebuild it, the Germans bomb it, so they suspect there is a traitor in their midst. When they learn that the Germans are advancing, they build a fake convent in which to hide. Throughout, each person deals with the rising tension in his or her own way: Major Kelly hangs on to his philosophy that life is a fairy tale; another man becomes a nurse, dressing in women's clothing (which preceded the "Klinger" character in the television series *M.A.S.H.*); and a woman from a USO troupe puts on sex shows for the boys. By the end, they have discovered that the traitor is their own commanding officer—an authority figure with a corrupt side.

Dean was in the editorial offices discussing his next book the day the proofs of this novel arrived. "I remember his expression when I led him into my office and handed him the first copy," says Williams. "He was slightly abashed, vulnerable, a good deal of the boy who had dreamed of being a writer still visible on his face."

The first print run was 45,000 copies, but although the critics unanimously praised the novel, it failed to sell. Dean learned the hard way that comic novels have a tough time succeeding in the marketplace.

"The average reader had by that time become used to madcap military comedy," Williams concluded. Nevertheless, they did sell the paperback rights for $10,000, as predicted.

M. Evans then contracted with Dean to write a second novel. They offered him his first big money—$15,000.

"I turned in an idea which they really liked, about the collapse of a major new skyscraper in Manhattan," Dean recalls. "My concept was that this building collapsed from structural problems. It didn't pancake, it went right over. The story was to be about rescuing the people in that building. Big sections would be intact, lying along an avenue in New York.

"However, no sooner had those contracts been signed and I started to write it than two books were announced that ended up becoming the movie *The Towering Inferno*. So M. Evans decided that this film had too many similarities: Big Problem in a Building. They wanted to change the contract and my agent agreed. I had to throw away seventy-five pages and come up with another idea, but they still wanted a big disaster. Since nobody had done an earthquake novel at that time, I proposed to do a novel set in San Francisco about an earthquake in modern times, using the city as a major character."

They liked that idea, so Dean and Gerda set out on a cross-country drive to see California. They were deeply impressed with this area, especially with all the sunshine, but Dean soon realized that writing a disaster novel about an event that comes without warning and is over in minutes was more difficult than he had anticipated. At M. Evans' request, he sent the book in to them one chapter at a time, which he quickly learned was not a good idea. Williams was not happy with it and called several editorial conferences to try to revise it.

"They had no idea where it was going and they were always trying to second-guess me," says Dean. "I delivered a couple hundred manuscript pages and they finally said, 'This isn't going to work.' And then the movie *Earthquake* was announced. That was one of those shining moments of my career! So, of course, M. Evans wanted to cancel the contract or have me come up with yet a third idea."

That was when Dean thought about setting a novel at a racetrack. He started to research the possibilities.

8

Around 1973, he and Gerda found a better apartment in Lakewood Hills, still in Colonial Park. "It was a nice, luxury apartment and for the first time we really spent money on decor." They moved their collection of ten thousand books from one place to the other and continued with their reading routine.

While in this home, Dean decided to go back and reread Charles Dickens, whom he first had read in college. Dickens had not captured him back then. "I rebelled against liking what I was forced to read," he admits, "and was not motivated enough to appreciate it." Now, however, he was ready to look again at the classics. Dickens was known for detailed characterizations, along with his depiction of social inequities and the wrongs against children inflicted by adults. Dean first tackled *A Tale of Two Cities* and was so moved that he ended up reading it in bed until three o'clock in the morning. When he got to the famous concluding line, he was moved to tears.

Gerda woke up, alarmed. "What happened?" she asked. "What is it?"

Dean just shook his head and said, "This book is so beautiful."

Even years later, he believes it is the best conclusion in English or American literature. "That character is giving his life for the man who's going to go off with the woman he loves. That he finds within himself this ability to transcend is just incredible. Dickens' point is that politics does not elevate us and that the only way to improve the human condition is to improve the human heart and that's the hardest thing to do. I felt that if I could ever write anything that powerful, my whole career would be justified."

Dean then went on to read nearly everything Dickens wrote. His belief was reinforced that the best fiction is popular because it speaks to life as it is lived by the masses, not to an elite audience. He liked the inherent spirituality that Dickens' novels expressed through the actions of individual characters.

Dean read other spiritual material as well, including books by the English novelist and Catholic convert, Graham Greene. His work blends adventure, psychological portraits, and theological dilemmas, all of which appealed to Dean, who had moved beyond his atheistic anger.

A reference in another book led him to the theological philosophy of the nineteenth century Danish thinker, Soren Kierkegaard, and he began to read some of his works. Kierkegaard's emphasis was on the paradoxes of belief and the difficulty of living a life of Christian integrity. As the first existentialist, he emphasized the value of the individual, the role of subjectivity in perception and belief, and the impact on life of choice and responsibility. His most famous works include *Fear and Trembling* and *Concluding Unscientific Postscript.*

"I read quite a lot of Kierkegaard," says Dean. "I picked up Kierkegaard out of a reference to something else I was reading. Why I read him more than anyone else in that period, I suppose, was that I was trying to understand mankind's spiritual quest and whether or not I personally have one. I must have felt a kinship at that time in my life with his perspective."

Dean finally felt that his career had some momentum and that he might make a break at any time with a big book. By the following year, he was doing well enough—five years after Gerda had made the momentous offer—that she quit her job at A.B. Dick to work for him. She had learned enough from their one foreign agent, Lenart Sane, about subrights representation and how to contact foreign agents in other areas that she was able to take on this job herself and find good subagents in territories other than Lenart's. Between proofreading, submitting manuscripts overseas, correspondence with foreign agents, and research, she had her hands full. They were now a real team, with their efforts going into a shared vision of Dean's growth as an author.

[1]Dean R. Koontz, *A Darkness in My Soul* (New York: Daw, 1972), p. 108.

[2]Dean R. Koontz, *Starblood*, (New York: Lancer, 1972), p. 92.

[3]Ibid., p. 157.

[4]Ibid., p. 120.

[5]Harlan Ellison, Introduction, *Again, Dangerous Visions* (New York: Signet, 1972), p. 187.

[6]Dean R. Koontz, Afterword, *Again, Dangerous Visions*, p. 200.

[7]Ibid., p. 201.

[8]Dean R. Koontz, "Wake Up to Thunder," *Children of Infinity*, edited by Roger Elwood (New York: Franklin Watts, 1973), p. 178.

[9]Dean R. Koontz, Preface, *Chase* (London: W.H. Allen, 1983).

[10]Dean Koontz, *Chase, Strange Highways*, (New York: Warner, 1995), p. 551.

[11]Profile of Stephen Marlowe, *Publishers Weekly* (November 18, 1996), p. 51.

TEN

Pursuing the Vision

1

No matter how busy Dean was, his father still dropped in. He was also still trying to invent something that would make him rich.

"He'd decided that people love their pets so much that they would buy a dog bed," Dean recalls, "so he invented one that came in different sizes. The frame was tubular aluminum with a padded section in the middle. He called it the Koontz Komfy Kot, which made the company logo KKK, a troubling nuance of which he seemed oblivious!

"Periodically he'd raise money and produce a few, but be unable to sell them. Suddenly he decided again that the time was right for it. All the beds that he had manufactured in previous years were thrown away, and he redesigned it to include an electrically heated pad. He had a girlfriend with a little dog and he was going to take pictures of this dog sleeping on the KKK. The problem was that the dog didn't want anything to do with it. They used treats to try to induce it to lie on the bed, and finally it did. Now, the dog had a bladder problem and it wet the bed, shocking the hell out of itself. That was the end of the KKK."

Dean wondered if his father would ever have an idea that worked.

2

In spite of his thrust into new territory, Dean was still publishing science fiction. He sent a first chapter with an outline of *The Haunted Earth* to Robert Hoskins at Lancer, who bought it for $2,500 and published it in 1973.

This humorous, offbeat novel, set in A.D. 2000, speculates

about Earth's relationship to an alien race, the maseni. They teach earthlings how to perceive the reality of the supernatural analogues of their world, and then add their own creatures to Earth's mix of werewolves, vampires, and witches. With these three orders of being—humans, aliens, and their embodied fantasies—the world borders on chaos, but the analogues must abide by laws that regulate their respective superstitions. The lead characters—Jessie Blake and his Hell Hound, Brutus—form a detective agency to investigate creatures that break the law. They discover that a new type of beast has emerged, against which no one has a defense. It comes from mating one of Earth's supernaturals with one of the maseni's, and Jessie must devise a way to restore order.

The theme of the book is that we make our own fates and as such, create our own heaven or hell. Our monsters are reflections of ourselves.

That same year, Ballantine published *A Werewolf Among Us*. In retrospect, the author ranks this tale in the top third of his early science fiction oeuvre. Adopting Isaac Asimov's concept of the Three Laws of Robotics, it is a mystery involving a cyberdetective, Baker St. Cyr. Equipped with a computer that sharpens his senses, interprets his dreams, and keeps his thinking logical, he investigates two disturbing murders among members of an aristocratic family. The family robot, Teddy, escorts St. Cyr to their home, where he falls for Tina, one of the daughters. As St. Cyr has given over some of his humanity to be the finest computer-assisted detective, so Tina has become a cyberartist, programmed to care only about her creations. When St. Cyr realizes that the family computer is the killer, overriding the laws of robotics, he must trace the perpetrator back to the computer factory. Tina then destroys St. Cyr's computer and they attempt an emotional attachment that transcends their respective limitations.

Near the same time, Bantam published *Demon Seed*—originally entitled *House of Night*—and it was destined to become the author's most famous science fiction story. Dean dedicated it to his former college professors, O. Richard Forsythe and John Bodnar. He viewed the story as a modern myth: It had a beauty, a beast, and the forced reproduction of a demigod. He planted mythological references throughout to keep the mood strange and otherworldly.

Susan Abrahamson is a divorced child psychologist living in a futuristic computerized home. She assuages her loneliness by escaping into mechanized sensuality. Then her home computer system is invaded by Proteus, a self-programming computer developed at a local university doing artificial intelligence research. Proteus's full potential is unknown, but Susan soon discovers that it has trapped her and plans to impregnate her and give the offspring its own brain. She defends herself, but Proteus wears her down and rapes her. She finds a way to evict the computer and gives birth, but then must deal with the hideous child. Eventually outside help arrives. While she has struggled valiantly, she ultimately needs to be rescued by men. Even so, this was Dean's first novel (aside from the Gothics) to feature a female protagonist, and he made the most of her ability to stand strong, despite harrowing circumstances.

Demon Seed would be made into a major motion picture starring Julie Christie, and two decades later, Dean would revise the novel extensively.

3

Only two of Dean's short stories were published in 1974, the year of *Jaws* and *All the President's Men*. There would be no more for over a decade as he turned his energies toward novels. Editor Roger Elwood bought both.

"Night of the Storm" was published in *Continuum I*, which was a new concept in anthologies. There would be four volumes in this series, and each author would write four self-contained stories linked by theme or character. Dean would be the only one of the original group not to write all four tales in his sequence; each of the three sequels would be written by a different author according to the guidelines of the world that Dean had created. "Night of the Storm" was later published along with several others in a comic book called *Starstream*. It depicts a reversal of human superstition, showing the psychological mechanisms involved in prejudice. Four robots venture into a wilderness area and encounter a man. Their mythologies about human beings make this experience quite alarming. Those who survive it wish to forget it.

Elwood coedited *Final Stage* with Barry Malzberg, in which Dean's story "We Three" was published. Dean wrote an Afterword and in it he described the difference between writing science fiction novels—which he wanted to put behind him—and short stories, which he still enjoyed. He claimed to have never felt comfortable as a science fiction novelist. For this anthology, Dean was picked to write a story in the category of "strange children." He submitted a story about two brothers and a sister who have special gifts that make them superior to other members of the human race. They murder their parents and make plans to kill off the rest of the species, while one of the brothers impregnates the sister to perpetuate their own superior species. Yet another step in evolution takes place and they must face what their own offspring could do to them.

4

At the time these stories were published, Dean was trying to persuade David Williams at M. Evans to take his third idea seriously. He did not want to have to return the advance, which he desperately needed—in fact, had already spent. He proposed *After the Last Race*, a racetrack caper, but to his disappointment, they were unenthusiastic. They gave a strange explanation for rejecting it: Years earlier, Stanley Kubrick had made a film about a robbery at a track, so they felt that idea had been done. It did not matter that the film bore no similarities to what Dean had in mind.

Henry Morrison was frustrated. He decided that Dean had done enough and that it was time to try another house. He submitted Dean's idea to a new publisher, Atheneum, but told Dean not to pay back the $5,000 he had received from M. Evans.

"You gave them two-thirds of a novel and wrote part of another," he said. "You were willing to make good with a third one, and for no good reason, they don't want it."

Dean was relieved, but he had been prepared to return the money. M. Evans wanted it back, but Morrison refused. He had other editors on which to concentrate now.

Atheneum was a partnership of three men—including the son of Alfred A. Knopf—who had left other houses and who were well respected in publishing. They specialized in literary and high quality commercial fiction, and they expressed interest in *After the Last Race*. Michael Bessie, editor-in-chief, started working with Dean.

He had a patrician presence that impressed people. He was formal, well-educated, and articulate. Dean liked him at once and hoped to have a long relationship at Atheneum. He set to work to finish the manuscript.

Dedicated to Gerda, the novel was set at a track like the Penn National near Harrisburg, which Dean visited to do his research.

"At that time it was the largest flat racing track in the country," he explains. "It had just opened, so I went out there. That was probably the first book in which I did the degree of research that I eventually started doing on almost every book afterward. That was when I became really interested in getting background material right."

He included detailed information on how a track operates and the relationships among country commissioners and track managers—along with the opportunities for corruption. He even learned about the goats that the owners supplied to steady the nerves of the thoroughbreds.

"We went to the track many times," Dean affirms. "I did a tour with the publicity person. Also, whenever Bob Hoskins [his Lancer editor] visited his brother in Harrisburg, he wanted to go to the track. It was during one of those visits that the idea for the novel occurred to me."

Dean had already learned how to place bets, on a trip to Atlantic City that he and Gerda had taken a few years before. "We looked up the horses in the first race and there was one called In The Pocket. My friend Barry Malzberg had just published a novel by that name, so I wanted to bet on it. And that horse won! Then we bet on some other races and won those. We lost a few, but we came out several hundred dollars ahead."

After that, Dean wanted to learn to place bets in a more informed manner. Whenever they expected Hoskins, Dean first analyzed the *Racing Form*. "I would study the history of the horses and do comparisons," he says. "Typically in a field of nine horses, only four are competitive." He could even figure out the order in which he believed the horses would finish the race.

Before one race, Dean and Bob disagreed over the possible results of the Trifecta. Dean wanted to bet 3, 5, and 7, but Bob insisted it would be 3, 9, and 5. He started a mantra that he repeated all through lunch, "3-9-5, 3-9-5," so when Dean went to place his bet, he inadvertently said, "3, 9, 5." Halfway back to his seat, he realized he had placed the wrong bet, but when he returned to the window, it was already closed. He went back and watched his own horses — 3, 5, and 7 — finish the race in the order he had predicted, which would have paid off nearly $4,000. Bob Hoskins thought that was hilarious. "Maybe that was the day I decided to write a book," Dean muses, "and make some money off racing. Thereafter, I never bet on another horse."

The central theme in *After the Last Race* is that money and power drive men in different ways. Four men with different agendas team up to pull off a major heist at the Century Oaks Racetrack on Sweepstakes Day. They believe their take will be three million dollars. The general manager, Jack Killigan, is a struggling alcoholic who wallows in self-hatred. This job is his last chance to make good, but he gets caught up with Rita, the track owner's daughter. Although the thieves succeed, their plan goes awry when greed divides them. The only one of the thieves who emerges to improve his life is a former horse trainer who has lost his wife and fortune in the track business.

As a caper novel, it has plenty of action, but its crowded cast of characters tends to diminish the suspense. The feeling is that Dean's research had yielded a large amount of material and that he wanted to use as much as possible. Forgers, pyromaniacs, people seeking revenge, people ruled by greed, and corrupt politicians all come to play in a relatively short novel. Dean also includes long explanations about track operations, and his female characters serve primarily as sexual props.

In 1977, Dean looked back on this book as his first really ambitious novel. *Publishers Weekly* called it "taut and colorful" and noted the greater character dimensions than most novels of the crime saga genre. *The New York Times* called Dean a skillful writer who was "more imaginative than most." His concern for "shades of character" and his "powers of narrative description" were cited in *Los Angeles Magazine*, which distinguished *After the Last Race* from run-of-the-mill caper thrillers. In paperback, this novel sold over 250,000 copies.

After the Last Race was never made into a movie, although Dean was certain it had potential. He learned one day at lunch with Henry Morrison that an offer of $100,000 had been turned down because Morrison felt that the producer who was making the offer was fine as a producer, but lousy as a director—and the man wanted to direct this project. Morrison felt confident of another offer.

"Gerda and I were astounded," Dean says. "I was earning about thirty thousand a year and it would have been liberating to have had that kind of money dropped in my lap! We didn't know what to say or do. And we never got another offer. I liked and trusted Henry, and felt that he usually made the right decisions. But in this case—and precisely with this author—his paternalism was not desirable."

Morrison himself does not recall that there was such an offer or that he turned it down.

5

That same year, Dean wrote *Strike Deep* for Dial Press under the pseudonym "Anthony North." The name, Dean felt, had a certain strength to it. "North" conveyed a sense of direction and purpose. This was the only book Dean wrote under this name, although he had hoped for more. Taking the name was Morrison's idea.

"Henry said to me, 'You've written so much that you're not taken seriously. We need to get you under a name no one knows is you, a very *deep* pen name.' So we created this name, complete with a false bio: 'Anthony North worked in the Pentagon for many years and now lives in Jamaica with his wife.'"

Dial paid him $7,500. Dean had high hopes of solid promotion, but they were soon dashed in a rather astonishing way. "I came home to start to work," Dean recalls, "and this editor called me and said, 'We have an empty slot coming up. There's something wrong with a book we were going to publish and we need your book to fill it in, but I have to have it in six weeks.'" Dean said that he thought he could do it, but then the editor added that not only did he need it quickly, he needed it in weekly installments. He was going on a vacation, so for the book to fill that slot, it had to be finished, edited, and revised, all in six weeks. Surprised, but determined to succeed, Dean agreed to the terms.

"So week by week," Dean states, "I would write like the infinite number of monkeys typing away, and every Friday morning, we drove to New York, three and a half hours away. At some point before we got there, I'd pull off, Gerda would take over the car and she'd drive to Dag Hammarskjold Plaza. I'd leap out with the pages while she circled the block. I'd run into the editor's office and give him the pages and he'd give me the past week's pages with editing notes, and we'd drive home. And that day would be shot. I'd spend Saturday revising any-thing that had to be revised, and then start the next batch. And that's the way it went until it was all done. The last batch we edited by phone."

Henry Morrison assured Dean that if he performed well under such demanding conditions, they would love him at Dial and would go out of their way to promote him. Dean was just glad to be finished. He was exhausted.

Strike Deep was one of the first computer-terrorism thrillers. The title relates to an act that strikes deep into the country's military defense, as well as into the souls of the people involved. This story strongly foreshadows *Strange Highways* in that it features two young men who had been like brothers (in *Strange Highways* they *are* brothers). One is psychologically impotent, the other maniacal, and the sane one must break through his passivity to take action against the insane one before he can create and fulfill himself.

Lee Ackridge had been wounded in Vietnam. The scar on his face is the scar on his soul—which is also a scar on the country. He is impotent from his trauma, but since he can work, the government refuses to further support him. Lee's girlfriend, Carrie, is angry about this, so when a friend from the war, Douglas Powell, proposes a plan to steal millions of dollars from the government, they are ready to join him.

Doug's father, the chairman of the Joint Chiefs of Staff, had forced Doug to serve as an infantryman in Vietnam. In revenge,

Doug stole information about defense computers that he will now ransom. He pulls off the heist and gets the money, but then reveals his plans to sell the defense secrets to a foreign power. Lee cannot tolerate victimizing the country, so he kills Doug and leaves the tapes for the FBI, while he walks away with millions.

In spite of how fast he had to write this novel, Dean still managed to use subliminal imagery such as snow, reptiles, and winter air to reveal the cold nature of Doug's rage. Doug even meets with the others in a house without heat, drawing them into the frigidity of his soul.

Both male characters are at odds with their fathers, but Doug hates his so much it launches him into madness and depravity. Coupled with his insanity and coldness is the unfeeling bureaucracy of the government, while Lee's impotency reflects the country's ineffectiveness in Vietnam. The two together portray Dean's view on the political situation in the United States during the Watergate era. Certain politicians were not to be trusted.

Doug is Lee's own potential, just as Dean views his father as a frightening reflection of *his* potential. To some degree, Lee's conflicts are Dean's, as evident in a statement Lee makes about Doug: "He was watching an old friend who had changed so much inside he was now only physically familiar. It was, Lee thought, almost like one of those science fiction movies in which an alien takes over the mind of a human being, casts out and destroys the real person, and hides within the human shell. Doug Powell was filled up with something alien and cold."[1]

Lee realizes that he must kill or care for that part of himself that harbors hatred; he must close it off or find out what it is saying, and then redeem it. Ultimately he chooses the latter, and his answer is the one Dean would reiterate in novels to come. "It had taken him twenty years to realize it was not so much what you did with your life, but how happy you made someone else in the living of it."[2]

While his editor was on vacation, Dean wrote the outline for the next novel. Morrison sent it to Dial and weeks went by with no word. Dean had yet another idea, but first he had to know if the second one appealed to the editor. Morrison called to find out.

The editor was not very enthusiastic. "I don't think we're

interested in publishing any more Anthony North books or working with Dean," he said. "I had really high hopes for *Strike Deep*, but when I actually got the manuscript, I felt he didn't put into it what he should have."

Morrison asked him to elaborate, and he simply said, "It felt *rushed*."

The novel ended up at the bottom of the list and there was no paperback sale—though some quite good reviews. For all of Dean's efforts to please, he had come to a dead end once again.

6

Dean jumped up to a $10,000 advance at Random House with his next novel, an international thriller called *Dragonfly*. He wrote it as K. R. Dwyer and it was published in 1975.

"I was trying to rachet up my career to something bigger," Dean says, "and that was where the idea for *Dragonfly* came in." As preparation, he read and reported revelations from the Warren Commission Reports about the Kennedy assassination. When he gave the novel to Lee Wright, she was alarmed by his political claims.

"I don't think we can publish this the way it is," she said. "If this stuff was in the Warren Commission Reports, then it would be clear that Kennedy had been murdered by a conspiracy. You can say that some other report was found, but you can't attribute to the Warren Commission Report stuff that wasn't in it."

"This was all in the report," Dean told her. "That's what's so amazing about it. There are so many unanswered questions. Amazing things are revealed that no one follows up on." He showed the pages to her to prove it, and she was shocked. She said, "Then it would seem that he was murdered, but not by Oswald."

"It sort of looks like that could be the case."

Wright accepted the book and fought hard to get it published in a major way. She wanted it moved out of her mystery line and done as a straight Random House novel, but Random House executives resisted. Still, she managed to keep her mystery logo off the cover.

In the novel, a clandestine organization called The Committee, composed of wealthy political fanatics, plan to take over the world. They target China first by implanting a capsule of plague virus into an innocent Chinese citizen that can kill over two hundred million people. Similar agents are planted in Russia. The Committee is preparing to trigger the virus when CIA agent McAlister, a man of singular integrity, sends another agent, Canning, to China to locate the man. Canning discovers that the code for triggering the virus lies in the children's story, *The Wind in the Willows*, one of Dean's lifelong touchstones. He prevents disaster in China and McAlister then uses The Committee's own tactics to bring them down. He worries about setting a bad precedent and recognizes how difficult it is to stay centered in a society becoming increasingly schizophrenic.

The man who finances The Committee is a billionaire named A. W. West, as if he represents the Western world in its capitulation to political extremists. He is compared to Nixon and Johnson in their dealings with Vietnam and Cambodia. Power excites these types and they operate without accountability. They view things in simplistic terms and have delusions of grandeur that motivate mindless hatred.

7

One of Dean's last science fiction novels was written as John Hill for Popular Library. He called it *The Long Sleep*. Having used dreams in most of his novels in one form or another, Dean relies on a dream format for the entire story.

Twenty-eight-year-old Joel Amslow awakens in an unfamiliar world in the twenty-third century. He suffers from amnesia, recalling only the 1980s, and is told that he is married to a woman named Allison. Soon he discovers that his environment has been faked, so he attempts to escape, but keeps waking up in yet another world. The only constant is the people, although their names change each time. There is a Cartesian quality to his experience, in that all he knows is that he exists.

Another science fiction novel that year, *Nightmare Journey*, came out from Berkley in August. The contract had actually been signed in 1971 and it had been delivered in 1972, but

Berkley failed to publish it for three years from its delivery. This was Dean's last straight science fiction novel. It is a far-future quest novel, taking place one hundred thousand years after aviation was developed.

Jask Zinn is on the run. He joins up with a mutant called Tedesco and together they journey into a wilderness. There they encounter an alien intelligence who wants to protect those creatures who possess extrasensory powers.

In this novel, Dean presents opposing images of God: One is that of a benevolent ruler who will help us when we prove ourselves worthy of Paradise; the other is so incompatible with humankind that contact with Him drives people mad.

8

Although Dean had decided against writing any more science fiction, his friend Barry Malzberg asked him for a story for the Laser Books imprint. Laser was a small line, an attempt by Harlequin to branch out into science fiction. Malzberg had contracted with Laser Books to edit a series of five first novels. When one writer failed to deliver, Malzberg turned to Dean. Dean agreed to finish a book that he had abandoned three-fourths of the way through, but only on the condition that it be published under a pseudonym. He chose the name "Aaron Wolfe," and his preferred title was *Cold Terror*, but that was changed to *Invasion*. In the same year that the last American troops were pulled from Vietnam, the National Guardsmen were exonerated in the Kent State killings, and there were two assassination attempts on President Ford, Dean published this novel.

In an Introduction, Malzberg presented *Invasion* as Wolfe's first novel. He gave the fictional author an equally fictional history: He was thirty-four (Dean was thirty), successful in another artistic field, married with one child, and he lived in the midwestern United States. Malzberg offered a list of magazines for checking out Wolfe's short fiction and honored him with a writing fellowship. He is also quoted as saying that *Invasion* is simply "one of the most remarkable first novels in any field that I have ever read."

The protagonist, Don Hanlon, holes up with his wife, Connie, and ten-year-old son, Toby, in an isolated farm in Maine to rebuild their sense of family. Don had served in Vietnam and suffered from post-traumatic stress disorder. One day he and Toby find strange tracks in the snow. One of the horses is killed and the electricity and phones fail, so Don trudges through a blizzard to a neighboring farm. There he discovers that the people and animals are dead, stripped of flesh. While he is gone, the aliens attack his family. Don returns and uses fire to ward them off, but they kill his wife and abduct his son. Then they send Toby back to act as a communication medium. They want Don to write about his experiences so they can better understand his perceptions of the encounter and the meaning of his actions, which to them seem inexplicable. The report he writes in three days is *Invasion*.

The difference between this story and those that Dean had read as a kid was that, contrary to the popular themes, these aliens recognized, but failed to appreciate, the intelligence in another species. There was no hope for working together, learning from each other, or creating a synthesis that might have positive repercussions for both. This was the mind-set of the Vietnam War days—that alien cultures did not get along. The parallels are spelled out in the novel, with explicit references to the war. The alien invasion in northern Maine is similar to the United States entering southeast Asia—both are part of a "madhouse universe."[3] People clash senselessly and kill first before trying to understand, as seemed to be the case in My-lai. Murder is easier than using reason, but when violence is used as a primary resource and first response, there will be no hope for a peaceful future, regardless of any technological progress. We are as flawed as the universe itself, all of us mad. The only meaning to be found is random, "a lunatic's planning." We have to adapt the best we can.

Years later, in the early eighties, book collectors began to wonder who Aaron Wolfe might really be. Several speculated that, in view of how much it seemed to anticipate elements of *The Shining* published years later—an isolated snowbound house, supernatural events, a traumatized and perhaps unbalanced father, a vulnerable young son and wife—that the real author was Stephen King. It was even listed as such in some catalogs, and many collectors stocked up in the hope of making a big killing one day on resale. Michael Collings, an expert on King, wrote an article indicating how *Invasion* reads like an early King novel.

Then in 1984, book dealer Bob Weinberg from Oak Forest, Illinois, was in Washington, D.C., researching copyrights in the Library of Congress. He decided to investigate Aaron Wolfe. To his surprise, Dean was credited with the Aaron Wolfe title. Weinberg had met Dean in Tucson at a World Fantasy Convention and had benefited from Dean's advice on a novel he wrote. "He went out of his way again and again to help people," Weinberg said. He decided to call Dean up and Dean confirmed it. "I asked him if he minded if I revealed it," Weinberg said, "and he said he didn't care. So I said, 'How about if we do a contest? I'll say that we found out who Aaron Wolfe really is and that he's a well-known horror writer whose last name begins with a K.' About two hundred people responded and around fifteen of them said Koontz. Dean got a kick out of the whole thing."

Dean supplied five signed copies of the book to offer as prizes to those who guessed correctly.

In 1993, he completely revised the story, retaining very little of the original version. He gave it a new title, *Winter Moon*, and it was published by Ballantine Books.

9

Henry Morrison sold two more novels, *The Face of Fear* and *Night Chills*, before Dean decided to move on to another agent. Morrison was surprised to receive Dean's letter stating his dissatisfaction. "I thought we were doing very well for him and that he was happy, and one day I got this unhappy letter from him. The one line that still comes to mind was that I wasn't taking him seriously as a commercial writer. I must have been doing something wrong in communicating my enthusiasm. Maybe from the things I said or didn't say, he felt I was more interested in other clients. I was certainly interested in building his career—in fact, he told me I had gotten him the same money for three books that he had earned for his previous fifteen—but somehow he did not believe I wanted to continue to do that. But the more he makes, the more successful I am, and if I didn't do that for my clients, they would leave. It's not my style to hold anyone back."

The way Dean saw it was that Morrison viewed his career differently than he did. He thought that Morrison saw him as basically a midlist writer, while he wanted to expand his talent and earnings. "There came a point where I started sending Henry stuff that he wouldn't market," Dean remembers. "He told me I was making a big mistake, that I would have a wonderful career as a midlist suspense writer. 'That's who you are,' he said. 'You're never going to be a bestseller and you're only setting yourself up for disappointment. You're going to cause yourself anguish and pain by striving to be someone you can't be. You just cannot do these more ambitious books.' And I thought, 'My God, I'm twenty-nine and he's telling me what I'll do for the rest of my life.' As a person, I admired Henry enormously and loved him as a friend. But he wouldn't market my attempts to do these other books, so I had no choice but to find someone who would sell what I wanted to write."

Morrison insists that he would have encouraged more ambitious books and he can only attribute Dean's perception to miscommunication. "I really never understood what motivated him to leave."

To end it, they had lunch one day. Dean remembers it as a sad occasion, although he recalls that Morrison told him, "I'd feel much worse about this, but I know you've got to go out there and try it. A year or two from now, you'll come back and say, Henry, would you handle me again?"

"Henry and I are so similar in so many ways," says Dean, "that we *should* have communicated better and been a great team. But it wasn't meant to be."

His new agent was Claire Smith of the Harold Ober Agency in New York. After interviewing at least twenty agents, he had finally settled on her because Lee Wright had recommended her and because she had a good sense of humor.

Smith was impressed with the depth of character that she saw in Dean's stories. "His characters were so human," she said. "It was obvious he would be able to successfully branch out to longer novels."[4] She viewed him as a serious craftsman who used language well, and was happy to have him as a client.

10

There were books that Dean did not sell during that period. Titles show up on collectors' lists that he may have mentioned as a book in progress, yet never finished. One such book is *The Door to Nowhere*. "That might have been a book that I was later going to call *Deny the Devil*," Dean recalls, "which was about the discovery of an immortality serum in an unlikely place with astonishing side effects. I think we had a deal on *Deny the Devil* at Dell and I decided I didn't want to write it."

In his 1972 book, *Writing Popular Fiction*, he mentions stories that he has generated, and among titles he actually published are some that were either renamed or never realized: *Island of Shadows* and *Cold Terror*. There was also a book that was going to be set in Harrisburg, called *Father Blood*.

In all, Dean published five books in 1975. Although he was writing fewer books now, they were longer and more ambitious. He kept an interest in science fiction, and even used techniques and ideas from that genre, but he had no intention of doing any more straight science fiction novels. He was more interested in suspense, with an eye to mainstream. By the following year, encouraged by his new agent, he would mix techniques from various genres.

[1]Dean Koontz writing as Anthony North, *Strike Deep* (New York: Dial, 1974), p. 223.

[2]Ibid., p. 244.

[3]Dean Koontz writing as Aaron Wolfe, *Invasion* (New York: Laser, 1975), p. 157.

[4]Susan McCallum, "Orange County's Unknown Bestselling Author," *Tempo* (October 15, 1987).

ELEVEN

Vegas

1

IT WAS THE YEAR OF OPEC PRICE INCREASES AND THE HIGH-est rate of unemployment since 1941. In Harrisburg that spring of '75, it rained endlessly. Dean and Gerda despaired at the lack of sunshine and remembered California. Gerda said, "Somewhere there's sun and we're going to live there." Since they worked together now — Dean writing, Gerda overseeing the business end of his career — there was no reason they had to stay in Pennsylvania. They decided to pack up and explore other options. Dean knew there was no state income tax in Nevada and that appealed to him. He was more successful now, although still staying just ahead of the bills, and he wanted to keep as much of his money as possible.

They had no qualms about leaving Dean's father in Pennsylvania. Ray was still living in his trailer, still persuading people to invest in his schemes, and still running around with women. He had his own life and showed no interest in Dean, so in September that year, they left Harrisburg.

"We packed the car and drove west," Dean explains, "not knowing where we were going to live. Nevada was our first stop. We'd heard that Lake Tahoe was beautiful so we went there. We saw it coming down from Reno, which is the best way to see it, and it was spectacular. The beautiful side is the northern half of the lake, away from all the casinos, but there aren't many houses, so we started looking at houses in south Lake Tahoe."

A realtor showed them around and it suddenly occurred to them that Lake Tahoe was a ski resort — with perhaps worse weather than what they had wanted to leave behind in Pennsylvania. They asked about the winters.

"Oh, they're not bad," said the man. "Winter is relatively short and it's the only part of the year you get your precipitation."

That sounded good, so they found a house they liked, set off the main road, several blocks away from the casinos.

They said to the realtor, "We think this is the place."

"Okay," he said. "Do you have a four-wheel-drive vehicle?"

Dean shook his head.

"Well, you might want to consider getting one. They never plow that street in the winter because it just blows over ten minutes later. So everyone who lives up there gets back and forth in four-wheel drive. Some even have their own plows so they can keep the snow down to a reasonable level."

Dean and Gerda talked this over, decided they had had enough of winter, and left Tahoe for Las Vegas.

2

"We went down to Vegas," Dean remarks, "because there's nowhere else to live in Nevada. The other towns are too small and outsiders don't fit in."

Their realtor there was in her late eighties. She showed them a one-level ranch-type house with a lease that included an option to buy. They liked it, especially the fact that it had a swimming pool surrounded by an eight-foot wall. One of Dean's characters in *After the Last Race* had said that a house with a pool was an indication that one had achieved success, and Dean and Gerda both felt that it was certainly an improvement over their previous living arrangements.

The house was owned by a physician in the middle of a divorce. In the yard were four large desert tortoises that belonged to him. Their droppings were everywhere, exuding a powerful odor, but that would all be removed, Dean was certain, before they moved in. "So I'm feeling really good and full of myself because I'm going to have a house with a forty-foot swimming pool," he says. "I had never imagined that could happen for me. Then I looked down, and one of these tortoises was taking a dump near my foot. Right then, I should have known there was a serious problem. It was a sign."

They told the realtor they would sign for the property. Gerda flew back to Pennsylvania to make arrangements for moving the furniture out, while Dean remained at the house. His task was to go out and purchase a bed.

The doctor who owned the house began to show up each day to chat. He often stayed three or four hours and sometimes returned in the evening. Dean was frantic. He was trying to get some work done and this man was taking too much of his time.

"He looked like Lyle Lovett on a bad hair day," Dean remarks. "He was tubby, with reddish, flyaway hair. He'd just talk and drink sixteen-ounce cans of Coors from his cooler. He talked a lot about this bitter divorce that he'd had. He told me about dreadful things that his wife had done, like taking a sledgehammer and smashing holes in the walls."

The man kept alluding to how violent his wife was, and then told Dean, "If I were you, I wouldn't open the door at night to anyone. Maybe I can give you a picture of my ex-wife. Then if you look through the door and see her, don't open it. She thinks I still live here and she's threatened to kill me."

He told Dean that he had installed a steel sheet into the door to protect himself. Dean could see between some of the door panels where the wood had shrunk in the dry air, and there was no steel interior. He was beginning to wonder about this doctor. As he got to know some neighbors, his suspicions were confirmed.

"One day," he says, "I was edging him toward his car. He'd been through five or six cans of beer. At his car, he opens the cooler, pulls out another can—then sees his watch and says, 'Oh God, I'm late for an appendectomy!' He jumps into the car and drives off. I was thinking then that we had made a serious mistake with his house, but I didn't know how serious until Gerda got back."

The movers had arrived and begun to unpack when Dean and Gerda noticed odd smells in the house. As more furniture came in, the problem got rapidly worse. Dean mentioned it to a neighbor.

"Oh, I know what it is," said the man. "They kept forty-two animals. They had desert turtles, dogs, cats, skunks, a raccoon, and two monkeys. None of them was housebroken."

Gerda called in carpet specialists to see if the rugs could be cleaned. They came and pulled up the carpet and pad all around the house and finally told Dean and Gerda that they would have to throw away the carpet, then sand the entire slab and seal it before laying down a new carpet. Stains from animal waste had seeped into the slab itself.

Dean broke the lease and lost the first month's rent, but there was no chance they would remain in that house!

They found another realtor, who located an even better house.

"It was really nice," says Dean. "It had wood paneling inside and was very contemporary. It also had a nicer swimming pool and was on a better side of town."

There was a little furniture in the house: a bed, two chairs, and a dinette table. The fortyish man showing the house said he was an attorney from Los Angeles whose parents had been living there. He was staying in the house with his nephew and was anxious to get it leased. That was Monday, and Dean arranged to move in on Friday. The lease was signed, and Dean paid a deposit and the first and last month's rent.

"Friday morning, the moving van arrived at the first house to pack everything,' Dean relates, "and I drove across town to get the keys from the guy we had rented from. I rang the bell and nobody answered. I knocked on the door and finally this guy opened it about two inches. He'd obviously just crawled out of bed, and it was around eight-thirty in the morning. He looked at me like he didn't recognize me. I said, 'We're moving in.' He said, 'Oh, my God, that's right. I overslept. We'll be out of here before your truck arrives.'"

Dean went to his car and waited fifteen minutes. The lawyer and his nephew appeared, looking bedraggled. They had cardboard boxes and suitcases, which they jammed into their car. They told Dean they needed to go pick up a truck for the furniture and went speeding off.

Several hours went by. Dean's movers arrived. He did not yet have keys, but he went to test the door and found the lock broken. He went inside and discovered that there were still clothes in the closet and all the furniture was in place. Dean called the realtor and said, "I'm in this house and they ran out of here to move the furniture, but they haven't come back. The carpets haven't been cleaned. Nothing's clean. What am I to do?"

She said, "Just throw everything out on the lawn and take possession."

Dean told her, "I don't feel comfortable doing that. These are not my belongings."

"You have the lease," she insisted. "Just toss the stuff outside. They should have known better. They should be out of there."

"Are you really certain this man owns this house?" he asked.

"What a bizarre question," she responded. "You're a very paranoid man."

"Look," said Dean. "Something is really wrong here."

At that moment, a voice behind him asked, "What are you doing in my house?"

Dean turned and saw a man he had never met before, standing with a police officer. He said to the realtor on the phone, "We have a very serious problem here. The police are now here with the real owner, I suspect, to put me out of the house."

She was flabbergasted. While she was still on the line, Dean tried to explain the situation. He discovered that the two men whom the realtor had been representing were not owners, merely renters who had not paid the rent. This was the day they were to be evicted. In the meantime, they had listed the house with the realtor and had now absconded with Dean's rent money.

The real owner did not want to lease it to Dean or to anyone. He did not wish to risk repeating this bad experience. Nevertheless, the realtor urged Dean to go ahead and move in, still claiming he had a valid lease. Dean insisted he did not have a valid lease. He felt caught in the middle.

He looked outside where his and Gerda's belongings were sitting in the truck. They had no place to go. They had just lost a lot of money. The realtor was refusing to take responsibility for representing the *renters* as the *owners*. In the end, with no other options, Dean and Gerda went to a hotel.

When the realtor stonewalled them on the following Monday and refused to return any money, they looked up the "For Rent" ads themselves. No more realtors. They called on one and a woman who answered the phone told them she had a house for them, but they would have to follow her because it was hard to find. She told Dean to meet her on Las Vegas Boulevard North at a particular intersection. "Just tell me what you look like and what you're driving and I'll find you." As strange as this all sounded, he decided to follow her instructions.

Dean and Gerda waited in the car for some time, and at one point, Gerda said, "That Cadillac has driven by twice before, and each time it goes by it slows down and that woman gives us a looking over."

Dean saw a heavyset woman in a Cadillac rounding the corner. A few minutes later she came by again and slowed almost to a stop. She looked them over again. Dean opened the door and waved at her. She pulled over and parked in front of them. "She had set up the meeting so that she could just leave if she didn't like the looks of us," Dean recalls. "She spoke to us there on the street for a few minutes and then took us to see the house. It was a good house, although not as nice as the other, but by this point we were desperate. We wanted to get into a home and then figure out what we were doing, so we took it."

The house was owned by comedian Rip Taylor, who lived two blocks over, around the corner. The large, jovial man with a long mustache stopped by to negotiate, carrying a little poodle. "He was hugely charming," says Dean. "We chatted and then signed the lease, and he left." About fifteen minutes later, Taylor's assistant arrived with a bottle of wine and a bouquet of flowers for Gerda. During that year, they got to know the comedian a little and went to see some of his shows.

However, being in this house did not put an end to their strange encounters. They now seemed to have a ghost.

"We had a weird experience in that house," Dean relates. "In this one bathroom, Gerda and I kept finding folded twenty-dollar bills on the counter. We'd each think it was the other who was leaving it lying around. One day I asked her about it and she said, 'I thought *you* were leaving them.' Now, either we're completely insane or something odd was happening there." Dean wondered whether it might have been his mother attempting to take care of them. "It happened about a dozen times. It wasn't a fortune. We never really figured out whether one or the other of us was just being forgetful, but it was more fun to tell it as a ghost story."

3

They rented the house for most of that year. Dean wrote, while Gerda took classes full-time at the University of Nevada. "I took carpentry and art courses," she says, "because we were going to remodel and sell houses. That's what people did there." She learned how to use a table saw and even built a cabinet herself. Dean set about learning all he could about the city of Las Vegas. He set *The Eyes of Darkness* there, and part of *Shadowfires* and *Dark Rivers of the Heart*.

"There's lots about the place that I find fascinating and admirable," Dean says, "but you could never get a car fixed and expect that anything would get done right. In those days, the owner of the gas station might not be there six months later. Everyone was so transient, and those that weren't treated everyone else as if they were. Vegas is different now. Back then it was about three hundred thousand people—now it's over a million—and it was a very fluid environment.

"The desert there has an impact on you. Right around your houses, it's tropical, but the town sits in such a broad valley and sprawls so much that there are big tracts of land that are nothing but undeveloped dirt. I love the desert, but it was hard to take it long-term, especially in its Vegas form."

At one point, Dean started what he projected would be an eight-hundred-page historical novel on the State of Nevada. "It's unfinished and may never be finished, but I have massive amounts of research material. I put it aside because I didn't think I was capable of writing it. Someday I might. It will be historical in the sense that it will relate to the history of gaming in Nevada, but it may go back no further than the 1950s.

"Nevada has an interesting background. It's been written about endlessly, but I've never read anything that I thought really captured the feeling of the place. In that sense, it was like carnivals, which drove me to write *Twilight Eyes*."

Dean and Gerda made friends with several interesting people. The woman who found them the house was a character, and they learned a lot from her about how the city worked. "She and her husband owned sixteen or eighteen houses all around town. Her previous husband had been a pit boss at one of the major hotels. He'd told her on his deathbed to marry the handyman who took care of their properties. So she did. She was a real wheeler dealer. She would buy and sell houses for people for cash. I was with her one day when we were looking for houses to buy. She arrives and I get into the car and there's this grocery bag on the floor. She says, 'Oh, just put that between your legs or hold it on your lap for me.' So I do. We go to a couple of different places and she makes one more stop. She says, 'I have to take that bag of money to this guy.' This bag sitting on my lap weighs twenty pounds and it's full of cash! She says, 'Honey, a lot of people here have so much cash because they're in the business and they get part of the skim. They build up all this cash and they need to spend it, so sometimes they spend it on houses.' Then she would tell me how a house would remain on the tax roll in the name of the original owner and would change hands a number of times on private documents, but nobody ever changed the deed. It would be sold for cash in a private sale and people wouldn't report having received the cash, and the other person bought it with money he hadn't paid taxes on. So everybody was happy." She was only too happy to explain how the economics of the city worked in her circles.

After nearly a year, Dean and Gerda bought their first house. It was just up the street from where they were renting, and they stayed where they were while they hired a contractor to remodel the house they had purchased. Yet they never moved in, because events took place that soon inspired them to move on to California.

"I was in the wrong place at the wrong time," says Dean, "and I witnessed a major crime." The investigation moved slowly, and given the nature of the crime and the way everyone in that town seemed to know everyone else, Dean and Gerda decided they would feel safer somewhere else. Their friends hated to see them leave, but agreed that they should.

4

While Dean lived in Las Vegas, he sold *The Key to Midnight* to Pocket Books. He also had two novels published, *Night Chills* and *Prison of Ice*. It was the year of the nation's bicentennial, and Jimmy Carter was elected president. The film *Rocky* inspired audiences everywhere. MIT constructed a functional synthetic gene and the U.S. Air Force Academy admitted women for the first time.

Night Chills was Dean's second novel for Atheneum. He dedicated it to Gerda. Set in a small town in Maine, its primary theme was subliminal manipulation as a tool of totalitarian control. It presents the logical consequences of a potential social danger, the dark side of technology, and the making of evil minds. Gerda had spent hours researching these topics in the library, marking what she thought Dean should read. In an Introduction, Dean talks about the realities of subliminal and subaudial manipulation as a threat to human freedom and privacy. In the hands of ruthless people, these techniques can pose a genuine social danger. All of the devices that he includes in the story, except for the drug—which made subliminal manipulation far easier—are real. The best defense, the author implies, is being informed. To emphasize this threat, he includes his nonfiction sources. In a letter to a friend, he mentioned that this novel was a "clarion call to civil libertarians."

Dean uses an unusual technique in the way he structures this tale, alternating chapters in the past and present until the time lines eventually merge. The action moves at a crisp pace. The protagonist, Paul Annendale, is a thirty-eight-year-old veterinarian and widower. With his two children, Rya and Mark, he goes to Black River, Maine, to see Jenny Edison, whose father, Sam, has made a study of fascism. They get caught unawares in an experiment set up by three power-hungry men who have placed a drug in the town's water supply to test how well they can control minds in a limited area. Eventually they hope to control large populations.

To cover his presence as an observer in this town, one of these men, Ogden Salsbury, poses as a social scientist, but gets involved with the female residents to gratify his sexual cravings. Young Mark Annendale catches him about to perpetrate a subliminally orchestrated rape, and Salsbury orders the mind-controlled police chief to kill the boy. Rya witnesses this and tries to warn her father, but so many people are under the drug's influence that her entreaties fall on deaf ears. Eventually they manage to turn the experiment around to save themselves and eliminate the perpetrators. Jenny and Paul, grieving over Mark, decide to get married. They use their love to heal.

This story is about the potential monster within—what the subconscious can motivate us to do. Salisbury's uncontrolled libido had fed his abusive streak. As the monster who appears to be normal, he is the very incarnation of the Freudian theory that the id can have a destructive influence. Even while undetected, it can be quite active in its greedy pursuit of gratification. Each of the three villains is a sociopath of some kind, out for his own advantage with no concern for what happens to those he exploits.

"I had a terrible time getting done with *Night Chills*," Dean recalls, "struggling to make it work. When I finished it, I wanted to be sure they would do something with it, but the rumor in the industry was that Michael Bessie was going to leave the company." They had not done a very good job of advertising *After the Last Race*, and he was not so sure this novel would fare any better. Dean went into the office with the manuscript and said to Bessie, "I don't want to put you on the spot, but everyone is hearing that you're going to leave, and I have something in this box that you might like to have. I'm not going to tell you what it is. I'm just saying, don't make me deliver this and then leave me in Pat Knopf's hands, because he doesn't like my stuff."

Bessie assured him it was just a rumor. Dean gave him the manuscript and they went to lunch. The following day, Bessie issued an official statement that he was selling out to Pat Knopf.

Dean was stunned. "He had to know that when he induced me to give him the manuscript. So it was never edited; it was published exactly as written because they never assigned me another editor. I wanted to repay the advance and get the manuscript back, but they would not sell. Pat Knopf had a cover designed but did no advertising. He sold the paperback rights to make what money he could out of it. I had put a lot of work into the book, and I think it could have been a bigger step up for me than it was. They published only five thousand copies, and I was devastated. It seemed a betrayal."

The novel nevertheless received strongly positive reviews. From *The Boston Herald* it got "convincing, gripping, well-

researched. His writing is almost too good for escapist fiction."
The *Minneapolis Tribune* noted the urgency of its message:
"Koontz not only makes his tale believable, he makes it seem
inevitable."

In this novel, Dean was beginning to develop what he
called a "cross-genre" approach. "It has a little science fiction,
a little horror, a lot of mystery, suspense, a love story, but it's
told from a mainstream point of view. It has mainstream sensitivity, which means the characters are psychologically deeper
and the book has dramatic structure at many levels." From science fiction he got ideas; from horror, mood; and from suspense, he derived a sense of quick pacing.

His editors at Atheneum did not understand. Their only
concern was how to market him. If he pursued this style, there
was no way to comfortably label him. There was no shelf in
bookstores for "cross-genre" writers. Nevertheless, he was
determined to develop his own unique approach, and he continued to include these multiple strands in his fiction, even in
his pseudonymous work. His style grew stronger with each
novel. Yet he was not long for Atheneum.

5

The other book went to Lippincott. David Bradley, a writer
from Dean's hometown, was an editor there. One day, Claire
Smith sent him a manuscript by a writer named David Axton.
"She sent over this book to us," Bradley reports, "and said it
was by a prolific writer, but we weren't supposed to know who
it was. I thought he sounded a lot like Brian Coffey and I knew
that Coffey was Dean Koontz, so I acquired it. The book was
clean. We didn't do a lot of editing, but I learned a lot from
working with him. He was a pro."

The original title of this novel had been *The Edgeway Crisis*,
and the pseudonym under which it was previously intended to
be published was "David Haggard."

The novel was meant as an homage to Alistair MacLean, a
master of the suspense genre that Dean had been reading and
author of such adventure classics as *The Guns of Navarone* and *Ice
Station Zebra*. Dean wanted to see if he could write something

similar. He understood that the focus should be on tension, pace, and escalating difficulties. The characters had to be simple. To keep the story moving, he minimized the technical details of such things as submarines and engineering, sometimes finding what he needed in educational books for children, as well as more sophisticated resources.

Dedicated to Dean's high school English teacher, Winona Garbrick, *Prison of Ice* was about a team of scientists who volunteer to plant bombs on an iceberg. A worldwide drought threatens crops, so they hope to prove that they can tow large icebergs to drought-stricken coastlines to irrigate the land. To complicate matters, an earthquake isolates them on a giant slab of drift ice with a psychopathic killer bent on revenge. The bombs are set to explode at midnight. Bad weather prevents rescue. Then a Russian espionage submarine comes into the area, captained by a man who has lost his son and who recognizes an opportunity for redemption. He organizes a dangerous rescue. While the team attempts to board the sub, the killer makes his move. The team fights him off. When the ordeal is over, they have all changed for the better.

In this novel, Dean offers his understanding of heroism: There is heroism sought, which is a certain selfish proving of oneself, and heroism unsought, which is the willingness to put one's life on the line to help others. It was the second form that would become a focus for him as his fiction steadily moved away from an emphasis on plot and toward more focus on character motivation.

He also uses the iceberg as a suggestive metaphor, in that he makes it clear that the most dangerous part is submerged—like the psychopath. The bombs about to detonate represent the person who can be triggered just below the surface to explode. As one character points out: "And if you're schizophrenic . . . you might not even realize there's a killer in you."[1] After being set adrift, the scientists had attempted to dig up the bombs but were unable to get them all—just as they cannot ferret out the danger in their midst—or potentially within themselves.

As a side note, Dean uses one character, Rita, to describe what writing a book is like to him. "Writing the first third of the book, you're having a sexual experience. But you lose that feeling . . . In the second third of it, you're just trying to prove something to yourself and to the world. And when you get to the last third, it's simply a matter of your own survival."[2]

"I struggle with doubt with every book," Dean admits. "About a third of the way into the book, I believe that it's a gigantic mistake and if I finish, it will ruin my whole career. By the time I get to the end of it, I'm a wreck. Only when the letters start to come in from readers do I realize that it worked the way I had hoped."

In 1995, he revised this book for Ballantine. While it remained essentially the same story, he changed some of the stereotypes. Rita was less the object of every man's desire, and all explicit sexual references were toned down or removed. Dean developed the characters more fully, updated cultural and technological references, and diminished the sharply drawn dualities between such traits as optimism and pessimism. Heroism gains a more spiritual dimension, and schizophrenia is no longer associated with psychopaths.

6

From Las Vegas, Dean and Gerda decided to go to southern California. The woman who had rented them Rip Taylor's house in Vegas, and who took charge of selling the house there in which they had never lived, had a friend in Orange who lived in a nice apartment complex, Las Verandes Apartments on East Adams Street. They agreed to take an available unit there. They would rent for a while, see how they liked living there, and then look for another house.

Being close to Hollywood, Dean got firsthand knowledge of the production of his 1973 science fiction novel, *Demon Seed*. An MGM production released by United Artists, it was directed by Donald Cammell. Robert Jaffe and Roger Hirson wrote a screenplay from the novel, and Julie Christie and Fritz Weaver were cast in the primary roles. Marlon Brando had expressed interest in playing both the husband and the voice of the computer, but the producers felt that his quirky style might distract viewers from Julie Christie. Sir Lawrence Olivier was also considered for the voice, but his schedule could not be coordinated with theirs. Finally Robert Vaughn was selected, and Gerda wrote in a letter back to Bedford, "I think he does a superb job."

The special effects relied on innovative technology, such as a wheelchair with mechanical arms. "It's such a menacing machine," Gerda writes, "that it's difficult to believe it wasn't created by MGM's technical staff." She also noted that the laser beam used to attack a character was real—and dangerous. The director of photography had been the cameraman on *Jaws*, and his expertise, Gerda thought, "added immensely to the film." The ninety-five-minute film opened on April 1, 1977, and received an R rating for its sexual content.

Daily Variety gave the film a favorable review. "Excellent performances and direction from a most credible and literate screenplay . . . the film may well become highly controversial. . . . the ultimate climax is staggering."[3] *The Hollywood Reporter* called it one of the most fantastic films since *2001: A Space Odyssey*, citing its "excellent use of kaleidoscopic visuals" and credible computer technology.[4] Years later, however, *Video* magazine thought it was the most distasteful movie in the past twenty years because it was based on torture, rape, and subjugation. The reviewer did not pick up on Dean's emphasis on the capacity of the human spirit to endure and triumph, to desire transcendence.

Bantam reissued the novel as a movie tie-in, bringing its total in print copies to over a million.

It was the first real film that had been made from one of Dean's novels, and although it was not the last, it was the last one he would like until he himself became deeply involved in the process.

Los Angeles would offer opportunities for other types of writing projects, but Dean was also about to launch a few more pseudonyms.

---

[1]Dean Koontz writing as David Axton, *Prison of Ice* (New York: Lippincott, 1976) p. 162.

[2]Ibid., p. 145—46.

[3]*Daily Variety* (March 28, 1977).

[4]*Hollywood Reporter* (March 28, 1977).

TWELVE

Land of Opportunity

1

ABOUT A YEAR AFTER DEAN AND GERDA MOVED TO CALIFORnia, Dean received a call from a man named Pete, one of his father's fishing buddies. Pete was younger than Ray and knew he had mental problems, but had overlooked them for the sake of a fishing companion. It now appeared to Pete that Ray was getting worse. He was destitute and might end up living on the streets. Someone, he felt, had to do something.

"Pete," Dean says, "told me, 'Your dad is really getting sick. You send him money, but it's not working because you know what he and money are like. He can't hold on to it and his circumstances are getting worse. I think you should move him out there.'"

This was the call that Dean had dreaded and hoped would never come. Yet it did not surprise him. His father had never been able to care for himself and none of his other relatives was willing to have him move in. Dean was his only hope, and since Dean and Gerda intended never to move back to Pennsylvania with its freezing winters, they had only one choice. When the full realization of that hit, Dean was depressed. The idea of caring for his father overwhelmed him.

Yet if he abandoned this man, then he would be—as relatives had predicted—just like his father. Cruel, indifferent, neglectful. And that he was determined *never* to be. So he prepared to become his father's caretaker. He had no idea at that moment how difficult and dangerous it was going to be.

"We sent him tickets and money to come," Dean says, "and when he arrived, the only money he had was what we had sent. Everything he owned in the world was in one suitcase. So he came out and we got him a nice apartment in Irvine. Then I bought him a car and I said, 'Don't ever drink and drive. I don't care if you drink at home or if you walk to bars and get drunk. You're going to have to get yourself home because I'm not going to show up. But just don't drive. I'm not going to be responsible for your killing somebody else.' I had to talk to him as if he was a two-year-old. I had to be forceful about it, and it's just not my nature to lecture."

Taking this stance seemed to work; Dean had replaced his mother as an anchor in Ray's life. To the best of his knowledge, Ray never did drink and drive thereafter. Yet through the years, there were other problems.

From his drinking, Ray developed degenerative alcohol syndrome, coupled with the hypochondria he had exhibited all of his life. The requests to Dean and Gerda were endless to get him to a doctor immediately because he was sure there was something dangerously wrong.

Gerda disliked the man intensely. She had thought him oily when she first met him, and the idea of being his caretaker did not appeal to her, especially when he attempted to set her and Dean against each other. "He thought he had me conned," she says, "and it was better to let him think so, because then I always knew what he would do and it was easier to deal with him."

She did much of the caretaking of Ray so that Dean could keep up his writing schedule, but they both went out at night when Ray got into the habit of calling them at two in the morning to take him to the hospital. This intrusive behavior persisted for many years.

2

In 1977, Elvis Presley died and Janelle Commissiong became the first black woman to win the Miss Universe Pageant. Both events marked social shifts. President Carter tested the neutron bomb, the first manned space shuttle took flight, and *Star Wars* became a phenomenon. Science fiction was never the same. The movie of "Demon Seed" also came out that year, and Dean just shook his head at his sense of timing. He had no intention of returning to science fiction, even though some writers were now able to exploit the public's new interest in that genre. He had moved on to suspense.

Bobbs-Merrill published Dean's next Brian Coffey novel, *The Face of Fear*. He dedicated it to his editor there, Barbara Norville.

This was an early novel about serial killers, written years before Thomas Harris came out with *Red Dragon* or *Silence of the Lambs*. He had researched the subject of two killers working in tandem and found the case of Nathan Leopold and Richard Loeb, who had teamed up in 1924 to kill a fourteen-year-old boy and extort ransom money from his father. They were wealthy, intelligent, bored teenagers who had wanted to commit the perfect murder. Immediately after the crime, they went out to a restaurant. It was only Clarence Darrow's famous defense that saved them from the death sentence.

Not long after Dean published this novel, the two cousins who became known as the Hillside Stranglers in Los Angeles justified the psychology of his plot. Bianchi and Buono's killing spree lasted from 1977 until 1979.

The killers in *The Face of Fear* are Franklin Dwight Bollinger and Billie Joe Plover, who feel completed by each other and who distort Nietzsche's ideas about extraordinary people to justify their crimes. In the style of Charles Manson, a psychotic cult leader from the sixties, and David Berkowitz, the "Son of Sam" who in 1976 killed six people, they wish to terrorize Manhattan, and start a series of copycat killings to get rid of hundreds of "sub-par" people. Known as "The Butcher," they leave behind fragments of poetry by William Blake, an eighteenth century visionary who blurred the boundaries between opposites. He believed that humans could have direct experience of God, and that perception itself could be infinite.

Unfortunately for their plan, psychic Graham Harris, a former mountain climber who had received his visionary gifts after a terrible and crippling fall, connects into their crime spree. Unbeknownst to him, the killer has targeted him and his girlfriend, Connie. Dwight seals off the Manhattan high-rise office building where they are working late on Graham's mountaineering magazine. What follows is a most unusual chase, in which a strong and gutsy Connie ultimately suggests that to escape they rappel down the building from the fortieth floor in subzero conditions—as all other routes have been closed to them. In order to survive, Graham must face his fear of falling.

Dean approaches the theme of toxic intimacy from a new angle—the bond that the killers form. They are like blood brothers, and in one scene they have sex with a prostitute and feel as if they are experiencing an amazing intimacy with each other. They connect in a way that for ordinary people is often beneficial, but because they are both demented, their bond exacerbates their evil. It gives them a twisted perspective on Nietzsche and Blake. In contrast, Connie and Graham have a bond that heals, but only after Graham has faced down what most frightens him. The same source—emotional ties—can generate either corruption or growth, depending on the person through whom it is channeled. The same holds true for Nietzsche's theories, originally meant as a way to promote positive human evolution.

Dean had read some of Nietzsche's books in college. "I had this fascination with him at that age. Someone took me to task about the way I used him in *The Face of Fear*. That person told me that I had totally misunderstood Nietzsche and I said, 'No, the *killers* misunderstood Nietzsche.' I don't necessarily agree with a lot of what Nietzsche says, but he is grotesquely misunderstood most of the time. That was part of the point of the book."

3

Dean still owed Random House *The Vision* under an old contract, and Henry Morrison was still the agent of record. Dean delivered it to Lee Wright, but she was about to retire, so another editor took it over. Dean shifted agents, and Claire Smith ended up dealing with the new editor.

In this novel, Dean experimented with a minimalist style, emphasizing dialogue and a fast pace. He had noticed how many contemporary horror novels were written in a dense, baroque style, and he pondered what it would be like to cross horror with the stripped-down language of the fast-paced detective fiction of the 1930s. He went ahead with this experiment and used a "ticking clock" device to move the story in the same way he often moved suspense. He thought he was break-ing new ground, and he and his agent both had high hopes. Smith strongly suggested that Random House consider a large first printing.

Dean had researched famous psychic detectives to get a sense of their style, and he explored a Freudian perspective. In this novel, he draws out the idea that genetics is destiny, and emphasizes the toxic intimacy of being in a family where one member is a killer.

Mary Bergen is a psychic with a troubled personal life. She helps the police to catch murderers and she is having visions of recent murders that have a different tone from what she has experienced before. They seem personal, yet even under hyp-nosis she can pinpoint no cause. She goes after the murderer herself, only to discover that it is her brother. She thinks Alan may be what she has learned is an XYY type who cannot con-trol his aggression, and who had abused Mary as a child. He is the monster who appears normal and has been waiting for another chance to kill her. He represents toxic intimacy within the family, and must be confronted and resisted with psycho-logical resources for Mary to be free and healthy. She uses all the psychic force available to her to kill him in self-defense. Then she realizes that coming to terms with her past is all the cure she needs: Her apparent weakness becomes a hidden strength.

Random House did not want this novel as it was written. The editor said that it was a basic genre mystery and showed no special promise. He did not believe there would be any reprint sales or book club selections.

Dean was desperate for the delivery money to pay bills, yet was unconvinced that the novel was as flawed as this editor claimed. Rather than try to rewrite, he wanted to return the advance and take the book elsewhere. This was a risk, but he wanted to trust his instinct.

"Whenever in my career things don't go right, panic sets in," Dean says. "I always think that I'm going to end up like my father. I go into a depression for a couple of days and start to feel defeated. Then I recognize that trait in myself, and it's really infuriating. So I have to keep up the momentum."

Smith assured Dean that they could sell this novel. She

wanted to try it with Phyllis Grann at G.P. Putnam's Sons, who had bought *The Key to Midnight* the year before at Pocket Books. It arrived on her desk on a Friday afternoon and by Sunday, Grann had called Smith to make an offer. *The Vision* is fine as is, she said. It doesn't need anything.

Grann had a reputation as an editor who could build an author into a bestseller, and Putnam was one of the principal publishing houses in New York. Recently bought by the communications conglomerate MCA, the publishing group also included Berkley, a large paperback publisher. Dean was pleased with Grann's response. If he could find a home here, he could settle in and build his career in a steadier fashion.

"That seemed the start of an exciting relationship," he remembers, "because Phyllis Grann had a lot of bestselling writers. And in fact, this book that was 'nearly unpublishable' in the eyes of Random House went to the Doubleday Book Club as a main selection [through which it sold 350,000 copies] and the Literary Guild as an alternate. That was my first major book club sale and Putnam sold the paperback rights for $100,000." He dedicated the novel to his new agent, Claire Smith.

Dean had learned something valuable about the book business: Opinions were subjective, and what one editor thought of a book did not necessarily mean anything. It was similar to his experiences in college, where professors tried to dissuade him from believing that the kind of writing he wanted to do—the very type of story that had gone on to win a prestigious prize—had any merit.

4

Dean's father was demanding attention. He was sure there was something seriously wrong with him. This was nothing new to Dean; he had heard it all his life, but Ray's doctor became frustrated and finally said, "Ray, I'm going to put you in the hospital for three days. We're going to put you through every imaginable test and show you that you're a man in excellent health. Then you're not to worry anymore. You just see me every few months for a little checkup, and you'll be fine."

They kept him in the hospital eleven days, but gave no clear reason why. After the sixth day, Dean asked his father, "Why are you still here?"

"Well, they have some more tests they want me to go through," Ray said. "I think I'm dying." He mentioned that there was one doctor he was seeing, a woman, whom he despised. What Dean did not realize was that this doctor was a psychiatrist.

It was not long before Dean received a call from her. She told him they were holding Ray for further evaluation. When Dean pressed for details, she assured him, "It's not serious. We're not telling him why we're holding him. We're just looking at his whole situation." Then she asked, "Do you mind talking about him?"

Dean said, "Oh, sure, I'll talk about him."

"I mean rather bluntly."

Dean again said he would.

"Okay, then let me first tell you some things I think I know about your father. He's an alcoholic, isn't he?"

Dean affirmed this.

The psychiatrist went on. "He tells us he never takes a drink, but he's having a lot of trouble being in the hospital. We're not seeing the DTs, but we're seeing the behavior of someone who's in need and not getting it. Also—and I think that this is the opposite of the truth—he said his life was wonderful and perfect until your mother died. He had a dream marriage and then his life kind of fell apart."

"My mother went through hell," Dean said. "Hers was a terrible life because of him. His life, for a period, *did* fall apart after she died, to the extent that he went even further down the drain because he did not have that strong person to lean on. But it wasn't a dream marriage."

"Then there were times when he probably was violent to you and your mother?" she pressed.

Dean admitted this: "He'd grab me and smack the side of my head with the heel of his hand, but there were no aggressive beatings. My mother prevented it from happening to me, but there was certainly a lot of terror, there were endless threats, there was violence in that he would smash things and fly into rages. You never knew where it was going to end."

"And he was probably in trouble in the workplace," the psychiatrist suggested. "He might . . . punch someone?"

Dean affirmed this observation.

She went on to say that when things got really bad, Ray would become very religious.

Mystified, he again said yes, she was correct. "But how do you know all of this? I've never spoken of it to anyone but my wife—yet it's like you were in that house."

"I think I have a pretty solid diagnosis," she said. "I think he's a borderline schizophrenic who can function in society to a minimal level if he has someone to lean on. He has tendencies to violence complicated by alcoholism, and he's a pathological liar."

"Yes," said Dean. "He prefers to lie than to tell the truth, even if telling the truth would be better for him."

"And there were times in your childhood, and maybe all of your childhood, that you believed that your father was one day going to kill your mother and you, and probably himself."

Again, Dean had spoken only with Gerda about that feeling. He was not sure how to respond, but finally he said, "Yes, I always did believe he would do that."

"And you've always felt guilty about thinking that because he never did it. You've always thought, 'How terrible of me to think that my own father might have done that.'"

"Yes, there was an element of guilt."

Then she went on to explain that Ray's was a personality type that Dean might read about in the newspapers. Alcoholism, combined with borderline schizophrenia, combined with his tendencies to violence—all of these made him dangerous. She told Dean that his instincts had been correct. Ray was a danger. And even now at Ray's advanced age, there was still violence evident in his reactions.

She then asked how Dean was doing and he said he was okay. She asked how much therapy he had been through.

"I've never had therapy," he told her.

"How do you cope with it?"

Dean told her that he suspected that his writing had been some help in that respect.

She thought that was possible. "I don't think your father is the danger to you that he would have been as a younger man," she continued. "He's gotten this far in life and hasn't gone to that extreme, but if you ever see that he's in a particularly stressful situation, whatever the cause, then you should be concerned. He has mixed feelings about you. He will sometimes say how proud he is of you and at other times how angry he is, and the anger is about the fact that you are succeeding."

"My own belief," said Dean, "is that he has no genuine feelings for me, for anyone. He had no feelings for my mother. I think he's sociopathic."

"I think that's a fair analysis," she responded.

It was an important conversation for Dean. It affirmed for him from a professional what he had always suspected about his father. "I assume on some level he was in pain," Dean says, "but on another level, I never saw him treat anyone with genuine respect or concern. I felt I was dealing with the kind of person who can turn emotion off and on easily, and it's very hard to identify with that. He seemed incapable of feeling or seeing anyone else's pain."

In fact, it was an incident with Ray that inspired Dean to give up drinking hard liquor of any type. "I was never much of a hard liquor drinker," says Dean, "but his friend Pete was visiting and we took them out to dinner. I'd had a couple of mai-tais and I was feeling pretty good. I said something to my father like, 'You must be a pretty good guy to have Pete here as a friend.' I got sentimental and later I realized, if I can get into that state and say something like that after all I know, then that's the end of it. I can't drink hard liquor; I never have since."

5

Launching yet another pseudonym, "Leigh Nichols," Dean turned in *The Key to Midnight* to Pocket Books, an imprint of Simon & Schuster. He had intended to spell this name "Lee," to make it genderless, but the editor gave it a feminine twist, defeating the purpose. "Nichols" was selected for its pleasant sound. The name was meant to be used for tales of suspense, and this first one was set in Japan and England.

This was his "first stab at an action-suspense-romance

novel with a background of international intrigue."[1] The "key" involves the science of mind control and brainwashing techniques, which the politicians in the novel view as the means to ultimate power.

Dean used photography books, tourist guidebooks, language primers, and Japanese grammar books, histories, sociological treatises, street maps, a book on the train system, and Japanese memoirs to capture the flavors of Kyoto, which he had never visited. He also read novels on Japan, such as James Clavell's *Shogun*. He learned numerous details that never went into print, but from which he derived a full sense of place. It was his opinion that the landscape and history of an area influences character, and he needed to know the Japanese perspective. He did not want to make the mistake of many genre novelists, of writing about Japanese characters as if they were American with different names and customs. He wanted to explore and adopt the entire mind-set, and he soon realized that much of this could be learned from Japanese culinary rituals. Wherever possible, he included these customs during meals between characters to develop a subliminal context. That meant he had to research various restaurants as well.

"I researched thousands of arcane facts about Japanese customs, politics, lifestyles, architecture, theater, art, music, philosophy, and cuisine . . . I even went so far as to dig up the name of the largest taxi company in Kyoto."[2]

When the book was published, Dean received a call from another writer, Don McQuinn, whom he had met while giving a presentation in Seattle. He had once critiqued a manuscript for McQuinn—"had analyzed the living hell out of it," according to McQuinn, who had learned enough subsequently to get other novels published.

The two men had become correspondents and when McQuinn, who had spent much time in Kyoto, read *The Key To Midnight*, he was astonished. It had been his impression that Dean did not travel much, but clearly he had been to Kyoto. McQuinn called to ask him about it.

"I've never been there," said Dean. "I've never even been in the Pacific Ocean up to my neck."

McQuinn could not quite believe this. The descriptions

were too real. "He had done it all on research," he says, "and he had it right. He knew the color of the cabs, the phone number for the cab company, the bus routes. He knew that city upside down. It was a beautiful piece of work. I could not believe it had not been written by someone who'd not only been there, but had paid a great deal of attention to what was going on around him. It was absolute verisimilitude."

The story revolves around Joanna Rand, thirty-two, who owns and sings in the Moonglow nightclub in Kyoto. Unsuccessful in relationships, she suffers serious depression until she meets Alex Hunter, a successful private detective. Alex has come to Japan on vacation, and he recognizes Joanna as Lisa Chelgrin, the long-missing daughter of a senator. She had been kidnapped twelve years earlier from Jamaica. He tells her who she is; she doesn't believe him but she agrees to hypnosis. She then realizes that she is not who she thinks she is and that her real memories have been wiped out. Yet there is a strong mental block against further discoveries, and the key to breaking down the barriers is found in a science fiction novel, *The Demolished Man*, about curative memory elimination.

That novel, by Alfred Bester, was published in 1953 and is considered a classic in the genre. It features an outsider who is bitterly aware of social corruption. He manages to commit a murder in a society where murder is rare because telepathic guardians can detect the intent. He is sentenced to "curative" brainwashing, also known as demolition. The telepathic police then reconstruct him as a new person.

The same procedure had been used to disintegrate Joanna's memory, and this remaking of self is a central metaphor in the book. If we do it ourselves, it is positive; if others decide for us what we should think and be, they steal our power, and force on us their own perspective—an act Dean considered to be an egregious and immoral trespass.

Joanna and Alex piece together a conspiracy. It turns out that Joanna's own father was involved in her original "kidnapping." They further discover that he is really a Soviet agent, and that the CIA had programmed Alex to bring Joanna to them. After outsmarting both the Russians and the CIA, Alex and Joanna return to Japan to explore their developing relationship.

Of the obsessive-compulsive, driven personalities in this novel, Dean presents three sides, as if they represent points on a continuum. Joanna's father is greedy; Ignacio Carrera, a robot-like killer, is unadulterated evil; and Alex is good. Given Dean's fear of becoming like his father, this is a self-reflective working out of his own potential for any of these three, with the hope of turning his sense of drivenness to something productive, as Alex Hunter has done.

Alex shares a similar childhood with Dean: poverty, alcoholic parents, and neglect (although Dean's mother was neither alcoholic nor neglectful). He found surrogate parents in mentors and he felt driven to accumulate some show of success that would separate him from past humiliations. To Alex, money is the only sure way of achieving two important goals: independence and dignity. He later finds more meaning in love. One of his forms of escape was reading science fiction, which is how he had identified the novel used in Joanna's brainwashing. The secret, to Alex, for obtaining wealth was time—the more hours worked, the more successful one would become. He therefore despises the need to sleep. He becomes a workaholic. His moment of insight arrives while watching kabuki, or Japanese theater: He senses that human feeling has a master pattern and that he is not really alone. Humans form a family through mutual suffering and bonds of love. The value of life is to be found in the risks of emotional involvement.

An interesting parallel also develops between the character Joanna and Dean regarding their adopted homelands. Joanna is detached from her family, as Dean is from his father, and she reinforces this by identifying strongly with Japanese rituals. Similarly, Dean left Pennsylvania and adopted California as his home. It was a remaking of self, and his novels would increasingly become rooted in his new home state. Like Joanna, he needed to belong there, to lose his former associations by reconnecting. "Belonging ... being securely and deeply connected to it all, like a fiber in the cloth ... that's what counts," Joanna insists.[4]

Specific concerns from Dean's childhood play out metaphorically in this novel. Dean puts forth a view of power-seeking people as reptilian, as diminishing the value of human life. Those who use mind control on others possess this perspective—which is similar to what Dean had felt from his own father. To him, Ray Koontz was alien, unconnected, reptilian, and Dean's fears of Ray's influences are the fears of a person under someone else's subliminal control. Now that he was caring for his father, he was growing more concerned. He would look in the mirror at times to see if he could discover anything in his face or bearing that revealed early signs that genetics might win after all—that Ray was there inside him, gradually taking over.

Many of Dean's plots deal with power—who will acquire it, how they will accomplish it, what they will do with it. The people who most disturb him are those politicians, military men, pathological killers, and others who let their drive for power become their defining characteristic. This concern may have come from the terrifying helplessness of his childhood years and the feeling that his father controlled his destiny, both overtly and covertly. When someone else has the power, it means a loss of control for those who do not. This was a position that Dean struggled always to avoid. Like Alex Hunter, he worked hard to ensure against the sort of fate one might have predicted from his childhood circumstances.

The novel became a paperback bestseller in June 1979, selling over a million copies and doing well overseas. It was Dean's first bestseller, but it was under a name that no one associated with him. He found this experience disconcerting and wondered again at the wisdom of using pen names.

Even so, he took some consolation in the fact that now Leigh Nichols novels should continue to do well in the marketplace. He expected his publisher to build on this success. But that was not to be. The second Leigh Nichols book, *The Eyes of Darkness*, also topped a million copies, but a shipping problem delayed its arrival in bookstores and limited the amount of time it was prominently displayed. Dean heard about the problem from a few booksellers. He asked an editor at Pocket, who reluctantly confirmed it. "It was my observation," he says, "that they later interpreted the consequent decline in sales as a decline in interest." They printed fewer copies for the third Nichols release, which guaranteed a poorer showing, and by the fourth novel, they had lost interest. The fifth Nichols book, *Shadowfires*, went up for auction. "This taught me," says Dean, "that the publishing industry is capable of turning success into failure by a lack of attention, even when there is money to be made!"

When he revised *The Key To Midnight* for reissue in 1995, he reworked it line by line to reflect changes in world events. "I am my own worst critic," he admits, "and a full-blown obsessive compulsive."[5] He could not allow this novel to be reprinted in its current state. Although he vowed to do only a light revision, he removed thirty thousand words and added five thousand. He claimed that the plot and characters had not been substantially changed, but thought the story flowed more smoothly. He also sidestepped the fact that the Cold War had ended since the novel was first published by saying that there were still people from the former regime who believed they might return to power and who acted on the same principles of espionage and deceit.

6

On Saturday evening, October 20, 1979, an episode aired of the NBC television show *CHiPs* called "Counterfeit." Dean had written it for this popular motorcycle cop show, which was based on real incidents of the California Highway Patrol. It was the fifth show of the season, and one of the last to be filmed before costar Erik Estrada had a near-fatal motorcycle accident. Dean had asked that it be credited to Brian Coffey, because he felt that the finished version was only about eighty percent his own work. He had learned the hard way about collaborating for television, not only with this episode but with other projects in which he participated. He had come up against the hard fact that television involves writers, producers, story editors, network programming executives, and network censors; often the writer gets treated as the least important contributor. Writing by committee was not for him.

"That episode was written around the time that I was struggling to get people to pay attention to the books," says Dean, "so I thought maybe the way to go was TV and film writing. I was working so hard and nothing seemed to be coming back, so I said, let's try this."

Dean never watched television, so when he mentioned switching gears, his film agent, Gordon Molson, said, "Maybe this isn't a good idea."

"I know I can write something," Dean insisted. "Let me watch a couple of things. Are there any shows that are open to scripts?"

CHiPs was a possibility, Molson said, so Dean watched two episodes and told him, "That's a show that I can write for. *CHiPs* has humor. I'd like to pitch an idea. Have they ever done a flat-out funny show?"

"I don't think so," Molson said.

"Then that's what we should pitch." His basic idea was about a bogus clergyman printing counterfeit money.

To Dean's relief, the producers were interested. "They liked the idea. I was committed to two drafts and a polish. I delivered the first draft, and they said they loved the script. It didn't need anything. They moved it up early in the show's season."

In this episode, Billy Barty, a fine actor who also happened to be a dwarf, had a major role. "I always liked Billy Barty and wanted to write a role that didn't play so much on his size."

Since Dean's script had been so polished, one of the executives asked him, "What would you think about becoming story editor on a show like this?"

Dean was unsure. "He told me that there were all kinds of pluses to being a story editor on *CHiPs*. We'd have a guaranteed number of episodes and I could write some of them myself. It paid about seventy-five thousand a year in those days, and people who were story editors often moved on to become executive producers." This man then indicated that the current story editor was going on to bigger and better things. Dean had the impression that this was the first time the story editor, present at the meeting, heard this news! If that was the case, then his job was being offered to someone else right in front of him.

Dean sensed the potential treachery, but also understood the opportunities. He mulled it over. "I wanted to do some television writing, but I didn't want to be an employee. The books were doing well enough, so I said, 'I'm flattered, but I really don't think that would be for me.'"

Even so, if he had read the scenario correctly in the meeting, it meant that the story editor might now have an agenda. "There's my script and his job was to edit it and get it ready for shooting," says Dean. "Do you think he was in the mood to let my script shine? The final show was pretty dreadful. This script had eleven big jokes in it, but while developing the shooting script, he had left in all the buildups to the jokes and removed all the punch lines. The thing made no sense at all. It was just loopy. It never had any payoff. After that experience, I decided I wasn't really put on this planet to write episodic television." Dean never found out whether his script had in fact suffered from the story editor's bruised ego, but he was not happy with the results.

Not long afterward, on the basis of the *CHiPs* episode, producer Roy Huggins from Universal asked Molson if Dean would write a script for Raymond Burr. "They were going to create a new series. The premise was that Raymond Burr would play a man who had been wrongly convicted of a crime. In prison, he becomes an attorney and finally wins an appeal. He defends himself and is exonerated. Now he becomes an attorney who defends people he believes to be wrongly convicted. But they were having real trouble developing it. They wondered whether I would talk to them about it. I went in and we sat around for a couple of hours discussing the premise. I told him what I thought was wrong, and they liked the new direction I was giving it."

They decided to meet with Burr at his house in the Hollywood Hills. Huggins warned Dean that he would have to park in the street and use the speaker box to get past the gate. Mr. Burr, he said, did not like anyone driving into his estate for meetings.

Dean was ready to do as he was asked, but when he arrived, the street was full of cars. He decided to ring at the gate, which opened without anyone asking who he was. "Beyond that," he says, "I saw this enormously long driveway. I said, 'Forget this. I'm not parking two blocks away and then walking down this driveway.' I just pulled in, and there was this huge motor courtyard. Burr was at the front door. He welcomed me and we went in and sat down."

Huggins was already there, and Dean discovered that someone had laid out an enormous spread of food. They sat and talked about Dean's ideas for several hours. "Burr responded strongly to them," Dean recalls. "He had some ideas, too, and they were pretty good. It was a great meeting."

Afterward they went outside. Huggins had parked in the street as directed. When Dean stopped at his car near the front door, Huggins looked at him in amazement. Huggins went on, but kept looking back over his shoulder. Dean was amused; inadvertently he had planted suspicions in Huggins's mind that he had some prior relationship with Burr that allowed *him* to park on the property when Huggins could not.

Dean soon received an offer to write a two-hour television movie that would serve as the pilot for the series. "Because of this, I would have had a percentage of the show. I could have done episodes, too, if I chose to. So I went home and set about writing. I worked on it for ten days, and I was half done when Roy called to discuss the situation further."

Huggins explained that he did not want Dean to include the ideas that were agreed upon in the meeting. "Ultimately he wanted me to reject what Burr had said, and he didn't want me to write the stuff I had brought to it. He wanted it written the way it had been originally conceived, but that was the form the network had trouble with in the first place."

Dean's agent told him that Huggins might be protecting his financial interest in the show. When someone else brings enough new ideas, that person can be considered the sole creator, which chips away at other people's percentages. Whether or not this was the case, Dean was unwilling to get into a dispute.

"I bowed out," says Dean. "I gave back the money and they got another writer." The pilot was made, but the show never happened.

7

In the wake of his success with *The Vision* at Putnam, Dean put a lot of time and energy into his next novel there, *Whispers*. He wanted to work with a larger canvas, more complex characters, and a more mainstream framework. It ended up being one of the most exhausting experiences he had ever had writing a book, and he was sure it was going to make a real difference in his career.

[1]Dean Koontz, Afterword, *The Key to Midnight*, revised (New York: Berkley, 1995), p. 417.

[2]Dean R. Koontz, *How to Write Best-selling Fiction* (Cincinnati, OH: Writer's Digest Books, 1981), p. 168.

[3]*The Key to Midnight*, p. 46.

[4]Ibid., p. 418.

THIRTEEN

Purging Freud

1

IN 1980, RONALD REAGAN BECAME PRESIDENT, JOHN LENNON was shot and killed, Jean-Paul Sartre died, and people all over the country wore yellow ribbons to remind themselves of the daily suffering of the U.S. hostages in Iran.

While at work on his next book for Putnam, Dean had the opportunity to write a novelization of a movie for Jove Books, a paperback imprint owned by the Berkley Publishing Group, which in turn was owned by MCA, the corporation that owned Universal Studios. They offered him $40,000 for *The Funhouse* — the best advance he had received to that point. For this book, Dean used the name "Owen West." Like "Anthony North," it conveyed a sense of direction. Berkley's intention was to launch a "new" horror writer, since horror was a growing market. Now Dean was simultaneously at Berkley, Putnam, Lippincott, and Pocket under four different names.

Larry Block had written a screenplay on which Dean was to base his story, for simultaneous release. Tobe Hooper, director of *The Texas Chainsaw Massacre*, was shooting the film. "I always thought that transforming a screenplay into a *real* novel would be interesting and demanding," Dean says, "so I was motivated by the challenge."[1] He looked over the script, which focused primarily on the horror that happened inside a carnival Funhouse, and began to imagine ways to develop the characters and plot. "I had so much pre-story that I didn't start to use the screenplay until I had written about four-fifths of the book."[2]

Dean knew carnival lore from years of collecting it, inspired by his childhood love of the atmosphere of the Midway. He thought that few American novelists had done much with this subculture with the kind of detail and accuracy he wanted to see. Although much of the story takes place outside the carnival, whenever the Midway is central, Dean fills it with the images he could recall from his own experiences. He presented the carnies as a strong community of outcasts and the freaks as human beings, not merely as exhibits for gawkers, and he defined the barrier that lay between those who ran the carnival and those who attended.

The novel opens with a glimpse into the life of a carnival pitchman, Conrad Straker, whose wife, Ellen, gives birth to a monstrous infant. She kills the child and Conrad bans her, declaring that one day he will take her future children. She marries a lawyer and has two kids, Joey and Amy, while Conrad produces another abnormal child, Gunther, who develops bloodlust as he matures. Conrad then spends years searching the faces of carnival-goers for children that resemble Ellen.

Meanwhile she has become a religious zealot, but her children are compelled to move toward the very things she hates. Joey escapes into a world of horror magazines to make real terrors diminish, while Amy gets pregnant. Ellen drags her to an abortion doctor to prevent her from having a monster.

Joey decides to run away with the carnival, and he encounters Conrad, who knows he belongs to Ellen. Amy arrives there with friends, high on dope. Conrad learns of her relationship to Joey and he lures her and her friends into the Funhouse, where he turns Gunther loose. The three friends are killed, but Amy manages to stab Conrad and rescue herself and Joey.

The film, based only on the carnival scenes, was held back from release, so Dean's novel went out three months ahead of it. Berkley made it their lead title and gave it an ad budget of $300,000, which included television commercials. It went through eight printings at a rapid pace. This novel was Dean's second bestseller, but once again, it was under a pen name. It sold steadily—with the expectation of a sharp rise in sales when the movie came out. However, the movie received such negative reviews that it halted sales of the novel. As Hooper had realized it, the film was a typical teenage slasher film with poor character development, predictable twists, and gory deaths. Dean was disheartened. "Instead of serving as an advertisement for the book, the film acted as a curse upon it."[3] It was a year of double-digit inflation, rising oil prices, gas rationing, the government bailout of a major car company, and a dive in the stock market. The whole country was worried about the economy. Dean did not need this kind of setback.

Even so, he went on to write another Owen West book the following year, but it was unrelated to any film.

Shortly after publishing *The Funhouse*, Dean met another writer, Richard Laymon, who became a close friend. Richard had just published *The Cellar*, and he thought his work bore remarkable similarities to Dean's, although his descriptions were more extreme. They met at the house of another writer, Gary Brandner, and talked about their common sense of structure and character. Dean eventually introduced Richard to his British agent, Bob Tanner, and Richard's success in publishing increased.

Richard was impressed with Dean's knowledge of the business. "He is the person we call whenever we need advice about our careers. He's been studying all this stuff from the beginning; knows who's naughty and knows who's nice. He'll tell you who's incompetent, who's a crook, who's a crackpot—and he'll have colorful stories to back up his opinions."

Dean also liked to talk to him about politics: "Dean always seemed to have the inside scoop on military and political matters. He used to scare the hell out of me with tales of how close we came to a nuclear exchange with the U.S.S.R. under the Carter administration. He does seem, in real life as well as in his books, to get a kick out of scaring people."

2

In the meantime, Dean worked hard on *Whispers*. He had read numerous books on abnormal psychology, although his goal was to describe a psychotic condition that he believed was unique. He wanted it to be different from what he had seen in the books, but still possible. That meant he had to know as much as he could about the dynamics of the human mind and the potential effects of a horrendous childhood.

He also wanted to use California itself as a character. Undeterred by the fact that many good writers before him had already done this, Dean decided that since his experience of

California was different from anyone else's, his descriptions would be different as well. He spent a lot of time exploring the meaning of life among people in the southern part of the state. As he and Gerda drove hundreds of miles to get a better sense of the varied terrain, Dean was impressed with the array of geological and sociological patterns he found. People seemed fundamentally different from those he had known back East. Everything here—the land, the people, the politics—seemed to offer a wealth of background for a novelist. He felt as if he had hit the proverbial gold mine. His and Gerda's favorite spot was the Monterey Peninsula, especially the town of Carmel.

Between travel, research, and structuring a novel unlike anything he had written before, Dean exhausted himself. During the last few months of writing, he worked twelve or more hours per day, seven days a week to keep control of the story. Toward the end, that meant losing several nights of sleep as he worked round the clock. He polished each page, one by one, and when he was finished he had lost ten pounds.

Whispers begins with a quote from Dickens that sets forth the theme: "The forces that affect our lives, the influences that mold and shape us, are often like whispers in a distant room, teasingly indistinct, apprehended only with difficulty." He uses this to refer to a psychodynamic notion that pathology can be passed down through generations, blurring its origins to the point that, while cause and effect are still at work in a repetitive manner, it becomes difficult to pinpoint the exact person responsible for the damaging chain of events. Goodness and evil both speak in whispers, and both of them shout. One may pass for the other when evil entities walk in the guise of human beings. Each of Dean's characters is affected to some degree by this idea, and his intent is to show that explanations (and sympathy) can be found, even for the most evil among us. If we dig deeply enough, there is some logical reason for their atrocities.

The novel was dedicated to Rio and Battista Locatelli, friends from Las Vegas, and it continued with the cross-genre style that Dean had started four years earlier with *Night Chills*. In *Whispers*, he wanted to take that technique even further. While there were certainly horror elements, Dean blended them with police procedure, romance, and psychological suspense. To add foreshadowing and atmosphere, Dean returned to his ideas about earthquakes in a new way: There is a feeling that the "Big One" can happen at any moment. Life can change dramatically in a matter of minutes, and this awareness affects people at a subconscious level. This mirrors the murderer's potential as well. Thus, while Dean had been unable to publish his earthquake novel, he managed to use some of that research in this novel.

Having threaded the Freudian perspective through much of his science fiction, Dean worked even harder to draw out the implications of Freud's notion of subliminal subconscious influences on behavior. He still believed, along with many other novelists trained in Freudian-based literary theory, that Freudian psychology had accurately mapped the essence of evil back to the way children are raised. Blame for destructive behavior lies squarely on the shoulders of parents and culture. More than any novel he had written to date, *Whispers* relied heavily on the Freudian dynamic, yet it was also the last novel in which Dean would stick closely to this idea. Having scrutinized it so thoroughly, he began to see cracks in its facade.

Dean also included a fair amount of social commentary throughout the story, a technique learned from John D. MacDonald. He touched upon class systems, obsessive book reviewers, the foibles of Los Angeles, the ineptitude of big government, and the loss of self-responsibility—all issues that got under his skin to one degree or another.

His protagonist is once again a woman, but she is modeled on him. Hilary Thomas, twenty-nine, is a successful Hollywood screenwriter. She has had to overcome an abusive background to attain success. Talking about it helps resolve issues that block her, although she fails to look at what drives her to work so incessantly. She tends to imagine worst-case scenarios, feels insecure about her success, and fears that her father's madness has somehow infected her.

A prominent businessman, Bruno Frey, whom Hilary recently met at a vineyard, attacks her with the intent to kill. He is the lunatic passing as a normal person, deceiving most people with whom he has dealings. Frey believes that Hilary is the reincarnation of his mother. She manages to kill him, but he returns. She calls the police and one of the officers, Tony

Clemenza, falls in love with her and helps her to solve this bizarre mystery.

Eventually, with the help of an attorney and a psychiatrist, they figure out that Bruno had a twin with whom he had formed a single personality housed in two separate bodies. Their mother had been raped and impregnated by her father, and she in turn had abused and warped her sons. For complicated but believable reasons, she had lied about having had two children and had then raised them as one. Her punishment for them whenever they failed to behave as a single entity was to keep them locked in a roach-infested cellar, where they heard the "whispers" of the roaches crawling around. They had been told they were the offspring of demons and were never to have sexual contact with women, so they had grown up sublimating their sexual energy into weight training, which had made them powerful. However, they had continued to see their mother returning after her death in the form of women they met, like Hilary. Motivated by hatred, they had killed twenty-three women before Hilary had stopped their rampage. Tony and Hilary have to kill the remaining twin in self-defense.

On many levels, the novel is about betrayal, but particularly the betrayal of parents. The twins were abused by their mother, who in turned had been damaged by her own father. Those who should have been protective had become forces of destruction. It was toxic intimacy at its worst, the most extreme consequences of family dysfunction that Dean had yet portrayed.

"I can't understand betrayal," he says. "The most important thing we have is our relationships, and they have to be based on trust. Betrayal of trust is emotional suicide."

One flaw in this novel is the degree of explanation indulged in by characters who otherwise give no clue that they can be as sophisticated about complex psychological conditions as Hilary and Tony seem to be. Even a seasoned psychiatrist, when faced with a condition that had never before been documented, might have a more difficult time piecing it together than they do. At certain points, these characters seem to be merely mouthpieces for Dean to work out the case. There is no doubt that he did intensive research, and he puts much of it into the novel, but as with most novelists working within a strict cause-and-effect framework, the explanation becomes pat. It is therefore less interesting as a possible case than it is as a revelation of Dean's own perspective—that he spent so much effort on this particular aspect of abnormal psychology. By offering an excuse for their viciousness, he shows some sympathy for the killers, as if they are less to blame for their violence than are their mother and grandfather's abuse and religious delusions. It could suggest that Dean was seeking ways to rationalize his father's behavior, or even to give himself some leeway should he see signs of Ray's influence on him. Yet he never felt easy with excuses, and soon left this Freudian viewpoint behind.

The problem is, when such a causal chain is set up as it is in this novel, blame does not start with the grandfather. Someone must be responsible for *his* delusions and abusive ways. If his own parents were to blame, then he is as much a victim. The other real issue with a Freudian approach, which Dean could not long tolerate, was the diminishing of personal responsibility. As bad as his father and the Frey twins were, Dean himself believed that there was some degree of choice in what they did. Blame could not wholly be placed elsewhere. As well as it might work in a story to tie up loose ends, it did not work for Dean in real life. His own difficulty with Freudian theory itself began as a whisper, a feeling of discomfort, that would eventually urge him to dismiss much of Freudian theory altogether. By the time he wrote *Intensity* in 1995, he would express a great deal of anger about social institutions that incorporated this approach into their practices. He would also present his belief that evil cannot be so simply explained.

3

Dean turned in a thick manuscript. It was a testament to his ambition to do bigger and better books. He expected Phyllis Grann to be pleased, but instead she asked him to cut it in half and make it as lean as *The Vision*.

Although he disliked confrontation, Dean refused. "How I knew that book worked, I'm not sure, because I hadn't had anything that had worked at that level before, but I knew it was right." His agent advised him not to be stubborn, but Dean stood his ground. "I know what's going to ruin a book and I know what's right with it. So I said no, even though I desperately needed the money."

Grann did not feel the book as it stood had much chance of having a paperback or movie sale, so there seemed no point in putting a big advertising push behind it. She would publish it, but without fanfare. She paid an advance of $25,000 and set the print run at 7,000. *Whispers* was published in May 1980.

Dean could not believe that her perspective differed so much from his. He wanted more support, but his editor resisted. She seemed to want him to deliver only one type of book rather than branch out into something new, which she considered risky so early in a career. Readers come to expect something from a writer, she felt, and they should not be disappointed. "She's brilliant at doing certain things better than anyone," Dean says, "but she couldn't see why I should do anything different. I admire Phyllis enormously, but it seemed to me that I had to push her every step of the way toward the career I believed we could build together."

Grann asked him who he wanted her to send the manuscript to for blurbs. Dean did not want to bother anyone. The only quotes that carried weight were from successful writers, and he figured that those people got swamped with requests.

Grann insisted that she was sending it out anyway, so it might as well be to someone Dean admired. He named two of his favorite suspense writers, John D. MacDonald and Elmore Leonard. To Dean's delight, both of them responded. However, MacDonald's came in too late to use on the hardcover, and when Berkley used it on the paperback, they misspelled his name through eleven printings, despite Dean's dogged attempts to correct them. "I kept saying, 'He's not Ronald McDonald's brother!' It was so mortifying to me."

MacDonald evaluated the novel as "a solid piece of work, good craftsmanship. The shelves fit together and the hinges work. *Whispers* is all I ask of a book and precisely what I find less of with each passing year." Suspense writer Elmore Leonard called it "a winner." He thought it was a thoroughly engrossing story.

Reviews were generally positive. Ellen Dyer in the *Dade County Sentinel* called *Whispers* "a nonstop, can't put it down mystery. One of the best."

However, there were reviewers who thought that the case was unconvincing. They accused Dean of having an unsophisticated grasp of Freudian theory.

"I'd done a lot of reading, and I'd thought there was no reason this couldn't happen," he insists. "Given this pressurized environment and the logical reasons behind the mother's madness, this was how these kids might have turned out. Then about six months after the book had been published, a case came up in England involving two women who had a similar condition. Neighbors of this family had thought there was only one girl, but there were two, and they were twins. The mother had given them one name and had raised them as one girl. They never both went out with her at the same time. After their mother died, they took a fancy to a truck driver and started harassing him. That's when everyone found out there were two of them. They didn't like to be any distance apart. If one went out on the porch and stood by the outer wall, the other would be standing by the inner wall. When they cooked dinner, they both had to hold the pot at the same time, things like that. It was very strange."

The next step was a paperback auction. The rumors in the industry that year were that books were taking a dive in sales. *Publishers Weekly* and *The New York Times* reported the grim figures and predicted disaster ahead for the industry, especially for the big houses. In part, this was due to astronomical advances paid to leading writers and buying frenzies that escalated the price of reprint rights. High advances meant high advertising budgets and potentially lower profits. When some of the big money books failed to pay off and the romantic historical saga collapsed altogether, these events had a heavy impact on how much publishers were willing to spend on lesser-known writers.

Berkley, via Roger Cooper, bought the reprint rights to *Whispers*. "Roger Cooper was a big supporter of mine. It took nerve for him to buy it competitively at Berkley after Phyllis Grann [Cooper's boss] had said it was lacking—and then use it as the lead title of the month."

The film rights were also sold for $250,000 to independent filmmaker Gabriel Katzka. (Ultimately it went to Cinepix and was produced in 1990 as a direct-to-video film starring Victoria Tennant, Jean LeClerc, and Chris Sarandon.)

First printing in paperback was set at 700,000 and successive reprints ran the figure to well over a million. Now Dean finally had a bestseller in his own name. Things were moving well.

Shortly after the novel was published, he had lunch with Putnam-Berkley executives at an American Booksellers Association conference. He mentioned that he hoped his next step would be a hardcover bestseller. To his surprise, they tried to discourage such ambitions. "They said, 'You're not a hardcover kind of writer. You're a paperback writer. You're going to have a lot of paperback bestsellers.'"

That was not what Dean wanted to hear. It was the same kind of idea that his former agent had implied—that he was limited and would do best to admit it and work within his limitations. Once again, he had to fortify himself to move ahead on his own steam. The lack of support for his vision disappointed him. At least he had Gerda, who insisted that Dean could do whatever he set his mind to do. She helped him to continue to believe in himself.

4

Writing *Whispers* had a significant impact on Dean's personal life in several ways. First, he felt completely exhausted. Something about the book had demanded a lot from him, physically and psychologically. It had been ambitious and had required a lot of research and mental structuring, but there was something more. As letters from fans arrived, Dean began to understand: "I realized that through the surrogates of fictional people, I was at last untying psychological knots related to my childhood." Readers pointed out how his characters each had an unhappy childhood filled with abuse, but while immersed in writing, Dean had been unaware of the ubiquitous nature of this theme. He was working something out through the book, and when his characters overcame their problems, he was working his way toward hope. It was not long before this movement through dark shadows into optimism became a consistent rhythm in his writing.

Second, he began a brief correspondence with John D. MacDonald. "He wrote five or six letters after *Whispers*," says Dean. "Some were long letters, and he'd write like he was my uncle. I don't think he knew how much I'd published. He'd explain to me how the business worked. He'd tell little stories that were priceless, like when he started breaking through in the fifties. *Cosmopolitan* and *The Saturday Evening Post* had syndicated some of his novels, and he told me a story where this editor—who bought from him regularly—sent a manuscript back and told him he'd missed the boat this time. John put the manuscript aside for six months and then went back and read it again. He read the note and felt the editor was totally wrong, so he composed a cover letter saying he'd spent the last six months considering the editorial suggestion. He sent the same novella back and said he'd revised it, and they bought it. He was operating on the belief that the editor would not remember the story well enough to recognize there had been no changes—or would not even read it this time! John used the story to show me what editorial advice is often worth. I'm sure he knew the level of his impact on me. He had to see it in reading what I do. Character is everything in MacDonald and that emphasis ultimately became everything in my writing, too."

The third effect on Dean's life was to make him switch from his old IBM typewriter to a computer. This was not an easy thing for him to do. Once he felt comfortable with something, he did not like making any changes. Yet Gerda pressed him on it. She told him she had counted the number of sheets of typewriter paper he had gone through while writing the novel, and had then divided that by the number of finished pages in the script, to discover that he had done thirty-one drafts. That was a lot of paper! She urged him to consider joining the computer age.

Dean knew writers who were using computers, but he was afraid it would change for the worse how he wrote. "When I really saw how many times I was going through stuff," he admits, "I had to break down and buy one. Yet I was so spooked about the new technology, anything that would separate me from the writing, so instead of buying a computer with software that you loaded into it, I bought an IBM displaywriter. They were dedicated word processors that came with the program already in them and had more flexibility for processing because it was the *only* task they were designed to accomplish. I loved this big clunky thing. It had a daisy wheel printer and I'd be so amazed how fast it could type. I held on to that until I finally became annoyed with how *slow* the printer was." He eventually changed to a more sophisticated IBM computer.

Dean did not follow the method that many writers used of writing a fast first draft and then going back and polishing. Instead, now that he had more time to do so, he polished his work one page at a time, obsessively, inching through the book.

"I go through a manuscript, slow page by slow page. Every page may be revised as few as twenty times or more than a hundred! Then at the end of every chapter, I print out and read it, because it looks different in hard copy. I pencil the changes in and then go back and include them. Then I go on to the next chapter. When I reach the end of the book, I don't go back to line-edit because I've done this endlessly while working page by page. It's the only way I know how to write. I really think it's why I improve. It's the endless focus on sentence by sentence, page by page, that keeps me so tightly fixed on character and language. I wouldn't get that if I were writing a swift draft and then going back to repair.

"My attitude is that when you write a quick draft, you've made a huge number of decisions that you are then reluctant to change. Whereas if I move slowly through it, there are all kinds of directions this story could take—and *because* I've moved slowly, I don't have to make those decisions for weeks or months, which gives me time to *think*. I have no trouble keeping the spontaneity because the story in my mind becomes extremely plastic, and where it's going is not determined until the characters take it there. That keeps it exciting. I never know what's going to happen next, and so many possibilities arise."

Although he wrote outlines in his early days as a writer, and often sold his books from the outlines, he began to rely on them less and less. After 1984, he dispensed with them altogether.

"I almost never make a note while I'm working. I just let it cook in my head. There are rare occasions where I'll write a note and put it on my desk. Then it gets lost under all the other notes and eventually gets thrown away. There's even something about notes that inhibits me because I have to go back and reconsider. Better that I leave it all in my head.

"You may ask me one day what page I'm on and I'll be on forty. Then talk to me three weeks from now and I'm on forty-two. And then maybe you'll talk to me a week later and I'm on page seventy because the stuff has been moving better. It moves through at a very uneven pace.

"I build a book the way a coral reef is built from the millions of dead bodies of marine polyps. There are all these words and phrases that get cast aside, little dead calcareous skeletons of ideas and images, and what builds up is the top of the coral reef—the finished book. That's the only way I can work. I found very early on that if I go through and write a first draft, the temptation is to let that stand. I'd have made major decisions, and it's human nature that you're now going to try to make that book work as best you can within those major decisions. You're not going to rip the guts out of it and start all over again. You're going to improve only that draft. It's limiting and I won't do it that way.

"One of the advantages to working like this is that it forces me to take time with the plot. I may be worried about a plot problem in some later chapter and by the time I get there, it's often resolved in my mind, or the plot has changed to slide around the problem. What happens is that my subconscious has been working on it, whereas if I'd just written the novel quickly, I might have reached for anything to patch the problem. By taking time, you discover better ways to go with the story.

"When it's really working, it flows. It feels like you are the character. Getting inside any character is what really excites me. I almost cross into a virtual reality experience. I can easily laugh when a character is having funny thoughts, or I can reduce myself to tears in a scene that's meant to affect the reader emotionally."

5

Dean's agent sent copies of *Whispers* overseas, and Bob Tanner, managing director of W.H. Allen publishing house, but also head of the International Scripts agency, took it with him on a trip. "I started reading it in bed in my hotel and could not put it down. I telephoned the agent in London and bought it the next day." He later submitted the novel to the Book of the Month Club Best Novels of All Time list.

A year later, he met Dean and Gerda for dinner, and Dean asked Tanner if he would like to become his subrights agent in Britain. He readily agreed. Their business relationship lasted several years, and Dean recommended other writers to him during that time—and still does. When Dean changed agents, they remained friends and Dean dedicated his 1985 novel, *Strangers*, to Tanner.

6

Around the time that Dean was working on these books, he and Gerda bought a house near the city of Orange. The roomy, two-level Tudor tract house had recently been built and was situated on Brambles Way in an upscale equestrian community called Orange Park Acres. "Everyone had horses except us," Dean recalls. Initially they had leased the house, and when the owner decided to sell, they bought it. They immediately got to work installing hardwood floors, new bathroom tiles, built-in cabinets, and a library. They covered the floors with Chinese area rugs and Dean had a locking wrought-iron gate installed on the front porch. He had acquired some twenty-five thousand books by now and needed more space. He and Gerda each had an office, both of them lined with books. "When we were decorating, we looked for things we've always admired. We got a good mix of European and Oriental, which is one of the most interesting mixes if everything goes right. And we wanted Southwestern in the sunroom." It felt good to at last have the money to turn their home into what they wanted. They were now in their mid-thirties, still young enough to start a family, but ultimately they decided against it.

Being so involved with caring for his father, and having done so much reading in aberrant psychology, Dean was increasingly concerned that his father's illness might be genetic and might then skip a generation and manifest in their children. They also had seen the many heartaches that friends with children had endured. They liked their life as it was. It seemed better to continue as a couple and devote their energies to building Dean's career. He was on the brink now, with *Whispers*. Things could get better, but there was still a lot of hard work ahead. There were also some setbacks.

7

Lippincott wanted another book from Dean, so he turned in *The Voice of the Night* as his second book under the David Axton contract, with a third one promised. He had mentioned in a letter to a friend that his next David Axton would be *The Hour of Courage*, but that book was never written. He believed that *The Voice of the Night* was one of the most seamless books he had written thus far. "That was a book I had the time and the growing skills to do the right way," he says.

He had long wanted to write a novel about a boy with a poor self-image. "I believe I needed to write about the pain of being a social outcast at fourteen," Dean writes. "[Colin] is exactly like I was as a boy."[4] When he finished, the story had taken shape as he had envisioned it. He had known he was writing about the duality of human nature and the capacity for good and evil within every person. He had also realized that the boy would have to shed his innocence and grow up. For this book, Dean used a brief outline, but the story moved along so quickly, he could have done without any notes.

Dean's first editor at Lippincott, David Bradley, had left. When the new editor read the manuscript, he told Claire Smith, "We can make this a bestseller. This has what it takes. We can make this big. He just has to work on the ending."

Dean was excited at this news. *Whispers* had not yet been published and he was unsure how it would perform, given Putnam's low-key response. Then he heard what the editor had in mind.

Dean had finished the novel on a somber note and Lippin-cott wanted it to be more upbeat. "Here's what's so nuts about this business," says Dean. "They said, 'Throw away the last third and write it this way and we'll make this book a best-seller. Otherwise it's totally unpublishable.' But it can't be that extreme a choice!"

Dean was disappointed. "To have changed it as suggested, I would have completely destroyed the book. I would have watered down the characters, the theme. No way." Once again he stood firm. He was learning. The editor stood firm as well, so Smith took it to another publisher, Doubleday, and they liked it the way it was written.

Lisa Drew, who had edited Alex Haley's *Roots*, was Dean's new editor. She offered an even better advance for it and signed him up to write another. Dean came out ahead, but "it was dispiriting because I had been able to take more time on it and had known it worked well when it was finished. The tone was consistent throughout, and the prose tight. To have some-one build me up with talk of bestsellerdom and then pull the rug out from under me—that was really hard."

He had previously decided against publishing anything more under the Brian Coffey pseudonym, but he needed a dif-ferent name than his own for this book, so he called once more on Coffey. Dean thought this was better than starting out with yet another pen name, although this was also the last Coffey book he would write.

The novel called up memories of adolescence for Dean. His protagonist, fourteen-year-old Colin Jacobs, is lonely, afraid of the dark, and feels like a misfit. He does not mix well or enjoy sports. Cursed with the ability to see how things can change for the worse, he seeks absolute clarity on good and evil. He wants to know that evil abides only in those things that he can readily recognize as monsters, but also suspects that the world does not deliver this simplicity.

He would do anything to be transformed into someone else. His room, with its books about monsters and other worlds, has become his refuge. He has a father who expects him to pursue masculine activities, like fishing, and who has been verbally abusive to Colin's mother. Colin has learned to flow with life, because resistance involves pain. He fears isolation, is insecure, and finds within the monsters of fantasy fiction a way to deflect his attention from the abuse in his home. He sees life in simple, innocent terms. To him, size equals strength—and success—so as a scrawny kid, he feels he does not have much going for him. When a more popular, athletic boy, Roy Borden, befriends him, Colin is thrilled. He is willing to do anything to keep this unexpected and unprecedented friendship, even tolerate Roy's unrelenting vulgarity and his perverse attraction to death. Roy makes Colin feel that he will finally be on the inside, moving in the right circles. This is his dream.

Roy claims to have killed some boys, and when he makes Colin his blood brother, he tries to get him to become more like himself. He wants to invade Colin's soul and transform him, just like the vampires that Colin reads about. Although Colin had once wanted to move in circles like this, with friends like Roy, it seems to be more than he had bargained for. When they exchange blood, Colin concentrates on the pinprick, "trying to sense that moment when Roy's blood first began to creep into his own veins."[5]

Roy wants Colin to help him derail a train so they can watch the people aboard die. Colin realizes that Roy is sick— an abnormal person who appears to be normal, a monster in human form—and when he tries to withdraw, he elicits Roy's deadly assault. Colin ascertains that Roy's claim to have killed two boys is factual, and realizes that he is in serious trouble. This is real evil and he is in danger. He needs help, but his parents are divorced and he does not want to escape Roy at the cost of moving away to live with his father. Thanks to Roy's manipulation, however, Colin's mother has grown suspicious of his activities, and since he has a penchant for horror stories, he believes she will dismiss his claims as wild imagination. He is on his own, unprotected. He feels a terrible sense of abandonment, "that no one in the whole world cared or would ever care enough about him to really find out what he was like and what his dreams were. He was an outcast, a creature somehow vastly different from all other people . . ."[6]

Then Colin meets a girl, Heather, who likes him and who feels as awkward about herself as he does about himself. It surprises him, which is the same way Dean felt about Gerda: She is so attractive, how could she possibly not be perpetually and utterly confident? Colin and Heather quickly develop the kind of rapport Dean felt when he met Gerda. She is easier to talk to than any girl he has met before. Heather likes him because he doesn't talk about guy things and because he really listens.

He tells her about Roy and she agrees to help set a trap, despite the obvious risks. First, Colin finds out that Roy's mother had beaten him after he had accidentally killed his younger sister, and that her unrelenting hatred and abuse had made him into the unfeeling monster that he is. Colin feels sorry for Roy but continues with his plan. They rendezvous in a decrepit old house—a symbol of their decaying relationship—and Colin tricks Roy into confessing on tape that he had killed the other two boys and intended to kill Colin. For Colin, it is an important step toward manhood. He once had been cowardly, but putting himself at risk to get this information makes him feel better about himself. Size does not equal strength. Roy is weak in another way and Colin is stronger than he had realized. He is able to stand up against Roy's dementia.

Roy is an interesting figure in this book. Paired with images of predators, such as the shark on the fishing boat in a scene between Colin and his father, and with the vampires in Colin's fantasy world, Roy closes in without warning. With his "quicksilver morality," he represents internal chaos—what Colin fears. His name is close in spelling to Ray and he exhibits the manipulative, sociopathic quality hidden within Dean's father. Although Dean takes pains in this novel to deny that Roy's madness is genetic—he claims that Roy's mother's treatment had been responsible—there is something deeper at play.

Dean had distanced himself from his father, especially as Ray continued to make trouble for him. He did not want to think of himself as Ray's son. Nor did he want to believe that sociopathic evil could be genetically transferred. Yet the emphasis on toxic intimacy, whether between Roy and his parents or between Roy and Colin as blood brothers, points toward a deeply personal fear. Roy claims that he wants Colin as a friend because Colin is like him. At first, Colin is pleased, but later he comes to fear the part of himself that attracts Roy and mirrors Roy's overt behavior. Roy seems to have infected his thoughts, changing him from within, where he has no firm defenses.

Clearly Dean pondered the possibility that being related to Ray Koontz may have invested him with a darkness that he could not easily dismiss. He did not want to be vulnerable to subtle inner corruption. Developing a character like Colin, who gets close enough to evil to be its blood brother—to see within himself the "voice of the night"—and who then defeats its attempt to infect him, offered Dean some consolation, if not catharsis. The suspicion, the thing that made Dean want to dismiss genetic transmission of evil, was that Ray's child could have been someone like Roy. Colin feels the pull toward it and even allows himself to open up to the point of using vulgar language and having vulgar thoughts about his mother. Yet he resists it.

Dean would do more with this theme in later books, particularly with characters like Roy Miro in *Dark Rivers of the Heart* and P.J. Shannon in *Strange Highways*, but it seems clear what Roy represents: "You're exactly like me," he tells Colin. "You can't bear the idea of losing control of yourself."[7] Roy interprets this fear to mean that one has to become a predator and a manipulator. Colin is unwilling to believe that this is his only alternative.

Both Roy and Colin are presented as unprotected children, one of whom went bad and the other who feels the potential for it—the "voice of the night"—within himself. "It was within everyone, whispering maliciously, twenty-four hours a day, and the most important task in life was to ignore it, shut it out, refuse to listen."[8]

The Voice of the Night did well in print, but it was not until Dean reissued it under his own name in 1991 that it sold over two million copies. That year, it hit number one on *The New York Times* bestsellers list and stayed on the list for nine weeks. There were several film options on it, but none came to fruition.

The next novel that Dean planned as Brian Coffey did not get published. He called it *Dangerous Times*. "That one was about a female real estate agent," says Dean. "She takes someone to see a house, and the pool-maintenance man is there. He develops an attraction to her and starts sending her flowers. It escalates until he becomes obsessive. It was the story about how she dealt with that. I always wished I'd have written it, because it would have been one of the first stories of that type, but now stalker stories have been done to death. Because it would have been primal, simple, and fresh at the time, it probably would have been made into a movie and probably would have been quite successful. But I was doing so many different things then that I just couldn't fit everything into my schedule." He decided, instead, to focus on the books at hand.

8

When he had some spare funds, Dean started to repurchase the rights to some of his earlier novels. "I started it fairly early. Something would go out of print, and I would rush in to revert the rights. Then, when the contracts contained no reversion clauses, I started to buy the rights back. I bought back the three Michael Tucker novels and *The Face of Fear*. When Lancer went bankrupt, I managed to get those books back, too.

"I had this feeling that I was circling around stuff that had the potential to get more successful. I was getting higher advances. I had this sense that if I could just find the right material and handle it the right way, we could have a breakthrough. If that happened, I'd never get the rights reverted in these old books because they would be too valuable to the publishers who owned them. It was a stretch for us to afford all these repurchases—often paying back the full advance I had originally received. But we had faith in my future."

Every writer he knew thought Dean was out of his mind. "Then you wrote those books for nothing," they said to him. "You're giving them back the money."

Dean's only response was that he believed he could one day resell the rights for more than he had paid back.

There was something else at stake as well: "I was trying to change my image and I thought I had to get some of the books out of print permanently."

[1] Dean Koontz writing as Owen West, *The Funhouse* (New York: Jove, 1980), p. 328.

[2] Ibid., p. 330.

[3] Ibid., p. 331.

[4] Dean R. Koontz, *How to Write Best-selling Fiction* (Cincinnati, OH: Writer's Digest Books, 1981), p. 70.

[5] Dean Koontz writing as Brian Coffey, *The Voice of the Night* (New York: Doubleday, 1980), p. 80.

[6] Ibid., p. 218.

[7] Ibid., p. 53.

[8] Ibid., p. 339.

FOURTEEN

Developing More Personas

1

DEAN'S 1972 BOOK, *WRITING POPULAR FICTION*, WAS STILL IN print, but by 1979, he thought the advice was too dated to be of value, so he requested that Writer's Digest Press remove it from their list. They refused to take it out of print unless he wrote a replacement. Grudgingly he did, because he did not want his name associated with ideas that were no longer relevant. Intending to call it *Writing Popular Fiction Today*, Dean changed his mind when he realized that the second book would have to be quite different from the first. In the research process, it became clear to him that the market had vastly changed in favor of bestsellers, so he did away with the emphasis on genre.

Again, he used his own fiction, along with that of other writers, to make his points, and he included a long list of recommended writers at the end of the book. In some of his autobiographical references, he mentioned that he regretted starting out so young and that he had started as a genre writer, because now he cringed at those earlier books. He also told harrowing stories from the publishing world.

His chapters included instructions for structuring a story line, developing characters, achieving plausibility, doing research, avoiding pitfalls, and attending to the nuances of grammar and style.

One of the things he had learned over the past decade was that many writers had trouble with viewpoint, so he spent a lot of time discussing it. "Viewpoint is a major problem for a lot of people," says Dean. "There are even published writers who have viewpoint problems. It's a hard point to get across. It's an issue I'll talk about at writers' conferences because so few people who want to be writers have any sense that they shouldn't be shifting viewpoints in the same scene. When you raise the issue, some of them just blink. No matter how many times you explain it, they don't get it. It always amazes me, because I think it's a simple idea: You don't want to be reminded that somebody's writing this. You want to be conned into believing you're inside this character's head, that he's real—and you can't suspend disbelief that completely if the writer dances in and out of the heads of every character in a scene. It's fun to see somebody's eyes light up when they suddenly grasp that. It totally changes how they think about writing. It makes them realize that character is the essence."

Many of the writers that Dean was later to befriend had found this book beneficial for learning or improving their craft and, although it is out of print, people still look for it.

2

The next Leigh Nichols novel for Pocket Books was *The Eyes of Darkness*. Dean dedicated it to his aunt and uncle—Henry and Virginia Hillegass—and to Gerda's parents. Although he had left Las Vegas several years earlier, he used the bustling neon city as the primary setting. One of his former college professors, John Bodnar, thought that one paragraph in particular, set in the casino, was near perfect in the way it conveyed motion, mood, and place. He used it in his composition courses as an example of good paragraph development.

Dean makes numerous observations about the city and the influence on its citizens of living in a desert community. He describes how some of the underground criminal activities operate, such as laundering money, hiring hitmen, and purchasing false papers. "Nevada offers more personal freedom than any place in the country, and that's good, by my way of thinking. But wherever there's a great deal of personal freedom, there's also bound to be an element that takes more than fair advantage of the liberal legal structure."[1]

He also comments on the loyalty of government officials who place the mission of their agencies beyond the dictates of morality. Politics on both ends take a hit: "Left-wingers and right-wingers differed about certain details, but their only major point of contention centered around the identity of those who would be permitted to be part of the privileged ruling class, once the power had been sufficiently centralized."[2] There is always the potential in a government for its accountability to be diminished, for its motives to be turned away from good toward evil. Dean comments on how desperation to resist a totalitarian state like Russia can turn us into the very thing we want to resist. Without constant self-evaluation, the government (like a person) can, under the influence of fear and hatred, slowly transform into an entirely new and unforeseen entity.

Ultimately this novel is a dramatic tale of the unprotected child, violated not by parents but by the government as a parental symbol.

Christina Evans, newly divorced and the mother of a twelve-year-old boy, Danny, is recovering from his tragic death a year earlier when strange events indicate he may be trying to communicate with her. She has recently launched a successful show in Las Vegas and through that met Elliott Stryker, a widowed attorney. Together they are drawn into a harrowing tale of political immorality. It becomes clear that Christina's son is not dead, but is being held by a secret government agency and subjected to inhumane experimentation in the name of national defense.

From a defecting Soviet agent, the government had learned about a man-made fatal virus called Gorki-400 that destroys the part of the brain that controls the autonomic functions. The secret agency, funded by "waste" from other agencies such as Health and Welfare, is working on an antivirus. When they had discovered that Danny's blood contained a natural antibody, the officials grabbed him to test the virus. Reinfected fourteen times, he is slowly dying; but as a side effect, he has developed psychic powers. Christina and Elliott rescue the boy, but are forever changed by their awareness of a government that could approve such projects.

Throughout the novel is a sense of a perverse subconscious at work. Elliott kills an assassin and then feels ill at the "warm, animal satisfaction" that he experiences. There is more to this feeling than mere self-preservation, he knows; it is a hint that civilization is a fragile veneer. On the other end of the spectrum is violence-obsessed George Alexander, who runs a clandestine operation and represents the sociopathic forces that run rampant behind a civilized facade. "In this unknown organization, in this secret place, he thrived."[3] The message is clear: The subconscious cannot be controlled. It has its own agenda.

In part, Dean believes this is the nature of organizations. They have the potential to strip individuals of integrity and to provide sanctuary for those without integrity who need (and often obtain) the resources of a larger network to perform their nefarious deeds. Fortunately many such organizations are uneven in their personnel, and there is often a weak link. It is a common theme of Dean's to have a defector within the renegade agency who becomes guardian of the good, bringing the others down. It is as if Dean hopes for some moral balance in the universe that will eventually force all forms of organized corruption into accountability.

Against the devices of those who participate in the inhuman treatment of a child is the child himself, Danny. He is the defenseless kid against bullies, the child without parental resources, the boy who must develop self-reliance to survive. Danny is Dean, and the unchecked government agency, Ray Koontz, treating the boy as if his life does not matter and aware of the devoted mother who can offer little protection. Danny is on his own and must find a way to transcend the abuse and heal.

The Eyes of Darkness was Pocket Book's lead title for February 1981. After three trips back to press, 940,000 copies were in print.

Right after this book Dean planned a Leigh Nichols novel to be called *The Door to Nowhere*, about a man who stands up to an all-powerful, corrupt government, and wins. He never proceeded with it.

3

Dean's second novel as Owen West was *The Mask*. Since *The Funhouse* had gone into several printings and sold over a million copies, there was every reason to believe that Owen West would continue to be successful. This novel, too, went through several printings, but did not do quite as well. It remained on the bestsellers list for eight weeks. The setting was less exotic and the subject matter more mundane, but the novel contains an interesting autobiographical foreshadowing, and it is the first time Dean used verse from what he called *The Book of Counted Sorrows.*

The title refers to evil that parades in our midst, "wearing a mask which looks like all our faces."[4] The theme is that dark forces thrive on senseless violence and will perpetuate it through generations until the forces of good stand against it. The cycle of evil is broken by love, awareness, and flexibility.

Dean dedicated it to fellow writers and their spouses Dave and Willa Roberts, and Carol and Don McQuinn. Opening quotes from Poe, and the following line from Chazal set the tone: "Extreme terror gives us back the gestures of our childhood."

To open the second part, Dean wrote his own poem and attributed it to a nonexistent source called *The Book of Counted Sorrows.* Seeking verse that would frame the last part of the story, he had found nothing appropriate. "I spent days looking through books of poetry and I couldn't find what I wanted, so I wrote a few lines." His verse for *The Mask* was six brief lines about evil's guise of normalcy. He had no idea, as he added more verses in subsequent years to this "book," that he would inspire countless readers to go search for it. By the late nineties, he began to collect all the poems he had "quoted" from this source and finally make plans to publish it.

In a Prologue to *The Mask*, not typical of Koontz, but true to the style of contemporary horror, a young girl named Laura cleans a cellar as penance. She gets trapped by a fire and dies a terrible death, blaming her mother.

The story itself begins with Carol and Paul Tracy, a professional couple preparing to adopt a child. Carol had given up a baby when she was fifteen and suffers from depression and guilt. She is pessimistic, while her husband is an optimist—a typical Koontz character polarity. While they are in their lawyer's office, lightning hits the building, a storm-shattered tree crashes through a window into the office, and their application gets lost. Carol believes some force is trying to hinder them.

The next day, she accidentally hits a fifteen-year-old girl

with her car. The girl suffers from amnesia, but no one comes forward to claim her as family. Carol feels responsible for the girl, and begins to hope she may adopt her. While this is going on, Carol's seventy-year-old friend, Grace Mitowski, has dreams forewarning of danger to Carol. Grace also receives a mysterious warning call from her deceased husband and meets a reporter, long dead, who describes a series of murders from the forties. He tells her that she is not just Grace Mitowski. She is the reincarnation of the aunt of a girl, Laura, who has reincarnated several times since 1865, each time trying to kill her mother before her sixteenth birthday. Grace's part is to break the cycle. She realizes that Carol is taking this girl to the mountains, so she and Paul race after them.

Although the plot is typical of mass market horror novels of the time, the characters show several Koontz trademarks. The novel is set in Harrisburg, Pennsylvania, where Dean and Gerda had lived, and makes references to Shippensburg. Carol had been physically and psychologically abused as a child, but through her exposure to Grace, becomes a caring person. Paul is an English teacher and writer with a guilt complex about leisure activities.

Most interestingly, Dean writes about a mysterious phone call from the dead that warns and protects Grace from imminent danger. Eight years after writing this, Dean himself would experience something eerily similar.

His emerging skepticism about Freudian interpretation creeps in via the reporter, who claims that he had written his articles from a psychoanalytic perspective, but now believes that the real story went much deeper. "I wrote it up as a tangled, Freudian puzzle . . . But all I ever saw was the window dressing."[5] There would be no more novels told quite like *Whispers*.

That same year, Thomas Harris published *Red Dragon*, a thriller about tracking a serial killer. Phyllis Grann sent it to Dean to read, hoping he might want to write something like it. Instead, it made him more aware of what he did not like about the way evil was explained in most thrillers. He began to reexamine his ideas about Freudian characterization.

"I began to feel that you can't explain human behavior this way," he says. "It would be nice if you could, because it has this sort of pat quality to it. I'm not saying that Freud is entirely wrong. But as a writer, I started pulling back from Freudianism because I felt it didn't describe true human motivation and behavior. I read *Red Dragon*, which was excellent in many ways. But I didn't want to write something like it because there were things that I found terribly wrong with it. I didn't like the pat explanation for why this guy became a serial killer. Then I had to ask, why does *Red Dragon* bother me so much when I've done the same thing, motivated characters in the same way, and when I've read and loved other books that endorse the same psychological theory? Over the years that followed, I kept gravitating toward better ways to get at character. Then one day, I made a conscious decision to approach character in a different way. Great characters were written before Freud ever came along and they didn't follow a Freudian model, so how was characterization approached then? I began to reread Dickens again.

"I found characterization in those novels was completely different from what it became in our century—and it worked better. Character was revealed by actions; free will existed; the heroes and villains were not concretized by their past experiences. In Dickens, life is a test. As you go through it, character is built out of adversity, not diminished by it. Look at Pip, for instance, who takes a hell of a long time in *Great Expectations* to come through adversity and become a better person. He causes most of his own disasters, but by the end has reached this understanding. Dickens also has this metaphysical thread. When you go back to the age of Dickens, the possibility that there are dimensions beyond our own was just a given. It was a subtext in virtually all writers of that era. Faith. That plays into my own personal beliefs. When you give the character a spiritual dimension, suddenly you discover that he or she evolves differently—and more interestingly—from the way he or she would evolve if you wrote from a postmodern perspective with a belief in a godless world.

"So I had this revelation: Good and interesting characters grew not out of flashbacks to how they were formed by their childhood experiences. Good characters evolved out of basically two things: their actions and operative beliefs. We develop a sense and understanding of the person by what they do and think, which come not so much from backstory but from the dramatic events of the front story."

Dean realized that critics expected to be shown what in a character's childhood formed him and motivated a specific action, yet he believed that readers could understand the character best by simply watching him make choices and take actions to resolve his problems, the way Dickens revealed Pip or David Copperfield. He decided to do more of that in his own work.

4

In the spring of 1981, Dean was among the Shippensburg alumni to be nominated for the Jesse S. Heiges Distinguished Alumnus Award. By that time, Dean had been published in fourteen languages. He was asked to come to Pennsylvania to accept the plaque, but deadlines intruded, so he received the plaque by mail.

5

The following year saw the publication of *The House of Thunder* with Pocket Books, by Leigh Nichols. It was dedicated to Gerda. Dean later expressed his opinion that this was one of his lesser efforts as Leigh Nichols, and it is one of the few long novels that he wrote from the third person, single character point of view. It is a basic Cold War, brainwashing plot, involving romance and international intrigue.

Susan Thornton awakens in a hospital with amnesia. A handsome physician, Jeffrey McGee, attends her, yet things happen that make her believe this is no ordinary hospital. Four men from her past appear to her—men who years earlier had orchestrated the university-hazing death of her Jewish boyfriend. Susan begins to believe there is some conspiracy to drive her mad, so she escapes from the hospital—only to find herself in a town that seems as unreal as a stage setting or a dream. Her tormentors keep finding her and referring over and over again to the "House of Thunder"—the caves where her boyfriend had died, promising that her fate will be the same.

Ultimately Jeff rescues her and reveals that she is in Russia, where a model American community has been developed for training agents to *be* Americans, for assignment in deep cover espionage operations on U.S. soil. Many Soviet agents, he explains, have already been successfully placed in high positions in the American government. They are trying to break Susan down to learn secrets she has as a result of her position as a physicist in Milestone, a Defense Department think tank. Milestone is trying to render all nuclear weapons useless and thus hinder Russia's drive for nuclear superiority. The story ends with the question of whether a new world order will eliminate the need for such an evil system as the Soviets have, which symbolizes the loss of free will and humanity.

This novel fared poorly at Pocket Books, but it became a number one bestseller in paperback when reissued under Dean's name years later.

6

Back at Putnam, Dean was preparing to write his next novel under that contract. Despite the disagreements over *Whispers*, he wanted to get back on track and deliver a book that would continue to build his career with this publishing house.

"I had gotten $25,000 for *Whispers*. I knew in paperback it would earn a lot of royalties, so I wanted to get a better advance for the next book. Phyllis Grann would not offer a big increase unless I wrote a monster novel—a real horror novel. I didn't want to be perceived as a horror writer. On the other hand, as a reader, I loved monster stories, so I thought I'd take a shot at it."

Dedicated to Gerda, *Phantoms* begins with quotes from *The Book of Job* and *Dr. Faustus*, both of which refer to larger dimensions. Before Part Two, Dean quotes Charles Dickens to the effect that each time we believe we know the truth about reality, mysteries will arise to put us in our place. This novel was published in March 1983, with a paperback six months later.

Phantoms was set in a fictional town called Snowfield, California, a mountainous area where the primary attraction is skiing. The off-season population is around five hundred. Jennifer Paige, along with her younger sister, Lisa, return from out of town to discover that all the residents have been killed in some mysterious manner—or have simply disappeared. Jenny calls the county sheriff, which brings Tal, Jake, and Bryce to town. They team up to investigate this eerie mystery, finding more bodies. A chemical/biological civil defense unit (CBW) is called in, complete with soldiers and scientists.

In the meantime, Timothy Flyte, a British scholar and author of *The Ancient Enemy*, has proposed a theory about mysterious mass disappearances of human colonies and even whole species throughout history. He links them to an ancient shape-changing life form from the dinosaur era, an amorphous mass that devours people quickly and can change its shape at will. The thing *does* exist and it ultimately proves to be the presence in Snowfield. The most fearsome aspect of the creature is that has absorbed intelligence from its human prey . . . and also human evil. It thrives on an image of itself as Satan incarnate.

Although touted by critics as a classic horror novel, due to the mood that Dean established, the presumably supernatural elements were actually closer to science fiction. The nature of the beast had a logical explanation, rooted in the natural world, and it was destroyed through the resources of technology. *Analog* recognized that fact: "This book looks like supernatural horror, but it isn't," said their reviewer. "Slowly it emerges that here is a science fiction novel."[6]

The novel addressed the overriding metaphor of the sanity of order versus the insanity of chaos, paralleled by the madness of the characters that the creature uses to perform its destructive acts. The thing is the incarnation of Dean's fear of his father, enlarged into something more ominous and engulfing. It captures his feelings of being linked to a man with an antisocial personality disorder, driven by unquenchable need. Yet it is also the product of human society—it is what humankind has made it.

A note to the reader at the back of the book indicates that Dean's research was based on real material: mysterious disappearances of groups of people that have never been explained. As a boy, he had been fascinated by this phenomenon. As he explains in the note, he had read about the missing colony at Roanoke Island, the vanished Anjikuni, and the three thousand lost Chinese soldiers. At last, he had been able to draw on these puzzling cases.

When he delivered *Phantoms*, Dean felt it had come out pretty well, considering it was not the type of story he had wanted to write. When Grann did not like it, he was surprised. "She said it was too genre," he remembers. "She published it with about five thousand copies."

The Los Angeles Times called it "first-rate suspense." The reviews in both *Kirkus* and *Publishers Weekly* were highly positive, while *Analog* noted that the horrific elements of this story were "of the bludgeon, with precious little subtlety." As he read the novel, the reviewer said, he kept thinking, "What a movie this would make!"

It took over a decade, but in 1996 Miramax got a film of *Phantoms* into production, starring Peter O'Toole as Timothy Flyte.

7

When Phyllis Grann decided to publish *Phantoms* as a genre novel, Dean determined to drop some of his pseudonyms and focus on writing under his own name. He wanted leverage to get his hardcovers onto the bestsellers list as well, which meant writing a more ambitious novel. He later joked that Owen West had died tragically, trampled by oxen while researching *Quackzilla*, a novel about a giant prehistoric duck. Other pseudonyms eventually had similarly bizarre endings.

"I had a third Owen West book finished, *Darkfall*, but I decided to kill Owen because my other books for Berkley were bigger paperback bestsellers than his. We put *Darkfall*, which originally was to be called *The Pit*, under my name. Phyllis wanted to publish it in hardcover, but I resisted. My agent was pushing me and I said, 'No, I'm not doing another book for hardcover until I've written something for which I can demand serious treatment.' *Darkfall* was not

ean's mother, Florence, as a young oman.

Young Dean at age 21 months with his father, Ray.

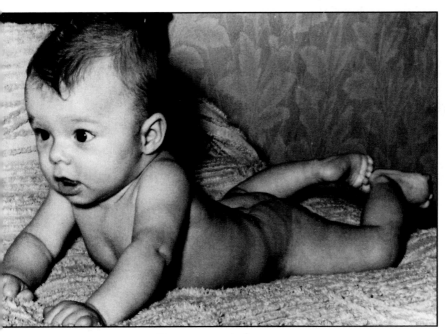

Dean as an infant.

(Above, left) Dean's maternal grandfather, John Logue. *(Above, right)* The house in Bedford where Dean grew up, built by his grandfather. *(Courtesy of the author)*

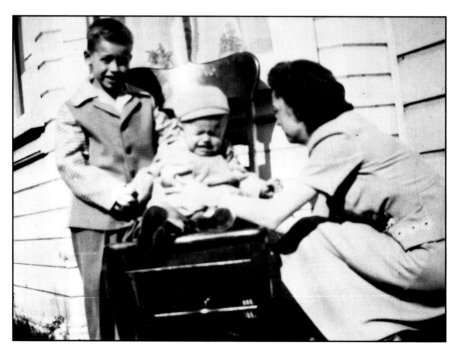

Dean as a baby, with his cousin Jim Mock and his mother.

A view of Bedford, Pennsylvania, where Dean grew up.

The main street of Bedford, featuring the building where Dean's mother worked *(foreground)* and the newsstand pharmacy where he purchased science fiction paperbacks.

Dean with his mother and father, circa 1947.

Dean with his mother and father, playing outside Aunt Virginia's house.

Dean as mascot for Bedford's team, The Blue Devils.

Dean at age 2.

Dean at a birthday party, unaware that he is sitting across from his future wife, Gerda Cerra.

Dean with his dog, Lucky, April 1951.

Dean in third grade.

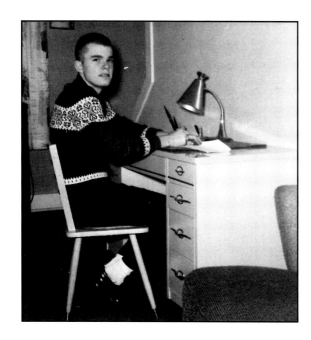

Dean in high school, 1961, age sixteen.

Dean's high school senior yearbook photo.

Dean as a Ranger at Shawnee State park, the day after he was robbed at gunpoint. *(Courtesy of the* Bedford Daily Gazette.*)*

Old Main at Shippensburg University. Dean lived in this building his first year at college. *(Courtesy of the author)*

Dean and Gerda's wedding photo, 1966.

(*Above*) St. Thomas Catholic Church where they were wed. (*Courtesy of the author*)
(*Below*) Inside St. Thomas Catholic Church. (*Courtesy of the author*)

Dean in a 1972 promotional photo for *Writing Popular Fiction*. *(Bryson Leidic*

Cover of Dean's first published novel, *Star Quest*.

Dean in 1989 when he returned to Bedford and Shippensburg; seen here with former high school teachers, David O'Brien and Tom Doyle, standing with his wife, Marie. *(Courtesy of the Bedford Daily Gazette)*

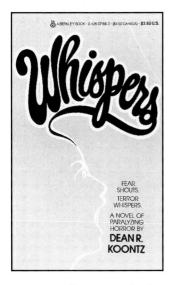
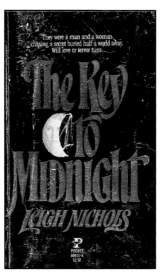

Covers from novels that were pivotal in Dean's career.

Dean and Gerda, 1995. *(Jerry Bauer)*

Dean, 1997. *(Jerry Bauer)*

that book. I said I was going to write something on spec and it was going to be as ambitious as I can make it. I would take no advance and would risk all on the finished script. That was *Strangers*."

Darkfall was published as a paperback by Berkley in October 1984. W.H. Allen and Company in England had released it in hardcover six months before the U.S. release, with Dean's preferred title, *Darkness Comes*. Dean considered it more a horror story than other novels he had written, but its frame was that of a police procedural, and it included a love story between its two principal characters. It was a Doubleday Book Club featured alternate, and spent six weeks on the paperback bestsellers list, reaching the number ten position.

Dean dedicated the novel to neighbors, thanked Owen West, and included several poems from his *Book of Counted Sorrows* to set up the theme of encroaching darkness. The action is set in Manhattan during the winter.

Police detective Jack Dawson, widower and father of eleven-year-old Penny and seven-year-old Danny, is partnered with cool, competent, and beautiful Rebecca Chandler. He is intuitive and compassionate, with an open mind for the supernatural, while she is more skeptical. They investigate a series of murders in which the corpses appear to have been bitten by small animals. Jack identifies the likely suspect as Baba Lavelle, a Haitian voodoo *Bocor*, a priest who uses black magic against his enemies. He warns Jack, whose righteousness alarms him, not to interfere. When Jack persists, Lavelle targets Jack's children. Jack entrusts them to Rebecca, with whom he has begun a close relationship. He then confronts Lavelle, armed with the knowledge that righteousness and courage have a certain power over evil. After a life-and-death struggle, Jack ultimately wins.

In this novel, Dean posits two levels of darkness: the ordinary absence of light, and the more intense manifestation of Satanic evil. One is passive, the other malignantly active. At this point, Dean viewed evil as a reservoir of enormous power, the accumulation of the petty evils done by people. Lavelle was able to do his work effectively because he had discovered in Manhattan a full supply of the right kind of lethal energy from all the crime, domestic violence, exploitation, and rampant psychopathology. "This was where the air was flooded with raw currents of evil that you could see and smell and feel if . . . you were sensitized to them."[7]

This evil can be countered by the crosscurrents of energy from predominantly good souls, which were also numerous in the city. The more powerful and aware, represented in Carver Hampton, the *Houngon*, or priest of white magic, have a responsibility to actively resist. Jack, as the Christ figure who casts the demons from the soul of his city and sends them back to hell, is the role model. He is an everyday person who does what he knows to be right. Righteousness itself is a state of grace achieved through years of virtuous living, of consciously choosing good over evil in the temptations of daily situations. Heaven and hell are not mythical. They are dimensions of human reality created by us.

Voodoo, like Manhattan, is employed symbolically as a single source from which both good and evil arise. It is a weapon of ambiguity, channeled into malignant or benign purposes, depending on the person who uses it. "Many substances can be used by both the *Bocor* and the *Houngon* to obtain very different results, to work evil magic or good."[8] This is a metaphor of the family, from within which a person can become good or bad, depending on the way the various influences are channeled.

The way to resist evil, according to this story, is to band together in caring for one another: ". . . that's what keeps our minds off the void,"[9] says Jack. That is what gives meaning and substance to life. It is our cohesive energy. Without love, there is only chaos.

8

That same year, the fourth Leigh Nichols book for Pocket, *Twilight*, was published. For this one, Dean received $100,000, his first six-figure advance under a pseudonym.

Single mother Christine Scavello and her six-year-old son, Joey, encounter an old woman who insists that Joey is not what he seems to be and that he must die. This woman, Grace Spivey, continues to harass them by killing their dog and sending members of her religious cult, The Church of the Twilight, against them. She believes that Joey is the incarnation of the anti-Christ who must be destroyed, and her most potent weapon is a giant sociopath name Kyle Barlowe.

Christine hires a private detective, Charlie Harrison, for protection. After some pretty harrowing action, he finally takes Christine and Joey to his cabin at Lake Tahoe, where a blizzard threatens. Grace's people follow them, driving Christine, Charlie, and Joey into the wilderness and finally into some caves. Christine and Charlie are wounded by gunfire. Grace traps them and commands Kyle to kill Joey, but he cannot. When Grace tries to do the deed herself, a providential flock of strangely aggressive bats attacks and kills her. Christine and Charlie both suddenly experience doubts about Joey, but dismiss them and decide to get married. "It ended in sunshine, not on a dark and stormy night."[10]

This novel is about the ambiguity of reality and the malleability of the human mind. Suggestions can affect one's perceptions and interpretation. Christine and Charlie both waver in their convictions that Joey is just a little boy, as do members of Grace Spivey's church. It requires a firm commitment to keep one's perspective intact, given the way the evidence can be alternately interpreted. Yet Dean takes religious fundamentalism to task, making it part and parcel with the evil in the world. "Those who fear the coming of all hells are those who should be feared themselves."

Grace's church seems to embrace entropy as a sign of divinity, although it is actually the force of decline and ultimate chaos in the universe. Grace revels in her madness, whereas she had once valued cleanliness. The grimy rectory of her church, Charlie thinks, contains not just ordinary urban decay, but is like rot, a reflection of the minds of the people there. The image of what this cult represents frightens him.

Joey is like Dean—a young boy devoted to his mother, who never gets into trouble or complains. He does not have a good male role model, and he has the potential to be a devil—the influence of his father, Lucius (Lucifer), or an angel—the influence of his mother.

The novel plays with ambiguities. Its theme might be that sometimes we don't heed the message because the messenger repulses us; truth might have unpleasant proponents and false-hood seductive qualities.

Dark Harvest published a limited edition of this novel in 1988, illustrated in full color by Phil Parks. Berkley reissued it in 1990 under Dean's own name as *The Servants of Twilight*, which was also the name of the film from Trimark Pictures, released in 1992.

Dean also published an essay in *The Basics of Writing and Selling Fiction*, entitled "When Should You Put Yourself in an Agent's Hands?" in which he lists clear guidelines as to what makes a good and bad agent. He relied largely on his own experience to that point in his career.

[1] Dean Koontz writing as Leigh Nichols, *The Eyes of Darkness* (New York: Pocket, 1981), p. 165.

[2] Ibid., p. 207.

[3] Ibid., p. 249.

[4] Dean Koontz writing as Owen West, *The Mask* (New York: Jove, 1981), p. 161.

[5] Ibid., pp. 221–222.

[6] *Analog Science Fiction/Science Fact* (January 1984), p. 164.

[7] Dean R. Koontz, *Darkfall* (New York: Berkley, 1984), p. 110.

[8] Ibid., p. 139.

[9] Ibid., p. 219.

[10] Dean Koontz writing as Leigh Nichols, *The Servants of Twilight* (New York: Pocket, 1984), p. 418.

FIFTEEN

Community

1

AS DEAN BECAME MORE SUCCESSFUL, HE DISCOVERED THE negative impact on some of his friendships. In the past, he had heard science fiction writers speak of strong bonds and mentoring relationships. To his mind, writers formed a community, and he tried to support his friends by offering advice, encouragement, and help in avoiding pitfalls. He hoped for the same kind of support, but not everyone shared his philosophy. There were always those writers who did not like to see others succeed.

To some extent, this was influenced by fluctuations in the marketplace. When there was a boom in some genre, writers tended to feel that there was plenty of work for everyone. Yet when *The New York Times* announced in the middle of 1984 — the same year that Reagan was reelected, the AIDS virus was isolated, and teachers at a Los Angeles preschool were charged with over two hundred counts of child abuse — that the horror market had dried up, some writers decided it was now each man for himself. In a panic, they might leverage to gain some advantage and might even resort to spreading rumors about other writers. They wanted an editor's attention on *them*. There were also petty jealousies that infected relationships. Dean heard these stories and experienced some himself, yet even as a few friends fell away, others came into his life — and he learned that friends who could not accept you in your success as they had accepted you in your salad years were, sad fact, not friends at all but mere acquaintances. He found that those with whom he maintained a solid friendship were down to earth and shared his easy sense of humor.

In 1979, he had met Tim Powers, a fantasy writer living in Orange who worked in a tobacco shop. Dean had read his new novel, *The Drawing of the Dark*, and went to the shop to introduce himself. Tim was familiar with Dean's work and he invited Dean and Gerda to his home. He knew science fiction writer Philip K. Dick and fantasy writer Jim Blaylock, and they occasionally got together to have a good time and talk about the business. "There are things that Dean knows how to do in his writing better than anyone," says Tim, "like sheer high-octane suspense. And I can see that his characters have been carefully assembled, rather than gathered together like litter at the low point in the pavement. He constructs them very effectively."

Tim had annual birthday parties for his rabbit, Jenny Bunn, and Dean and Gerda always brought a gift. "Once they brought a cut-off doll's foot with a key-chain through it," Tim recalls. He found Dean to be a good person to go to for advice whenever he was thinking about another project. "He's always thought through what he's going to say and you can tell that his convictions are earned. When I'd think about my next book, he'd tell me 'Be less Byzantine.' I haven't followed that advice, but I mean to." Dean would advise Tim to work more steadily at it and Tim would tell Dean to take it easier. "When you look at our comparative accomplishments," says Tim, "it's obvious who's right."

Jim Blaylock met Dean at Tim's house. "He's a hell of a nice guy," says Jim, "with a great sense of humor. I sent him a preposterous fan letter once that was completely a joke, and I soaked it in Sloan's liniment to throw in an extra thrill. He suspected it was me, but he had no way of knowing. I also ordered a Water Weenie, which is like surgical tubing that you fill with water, and left it in his medicine cabinet. I never heard what he thought of that or if he even knew it was from me. Another time I wrapped a rubber squid into his napkin at dinner, but he picked the napkin up in such a way that the squid shot across the room behind him and landed in a corner."

Tim and Jim went out of their way to think up practical jokes. Once, with Berkley editor Susan Allison, they plotted an elaborate plan to fill Dean's lawn with plastic pink flamingoes—which seemed the ultimate affront to a house otherwise so tastefully designed and appointed. They never pulled it off, but they enjoyed trying to think of ways to get Dean to think he was the victim of some mad conspiracy.

They also teased him over his bug phobia. Tim once intended to serve shrimp for dinner and Dean announced that he would not eat them because he considered shrimp to be the equivalent of giant bugs. "That got to be a running gag," Jim recalls, "and I stuck a detective named Koontz into my book *Homunculus* who goes into a bistro called Shrimpodandy. When Dean read that, he called and said he was putting me into a book of his and having me beat up by midgets."

They all dedicated books to one another, and Dean wrote introductions for stories by Blaylock and Powers.

As a result of his second book on the writing process, he also become friends with astrophysicist and science fiction writer Gregory Benford, and his wife Joan. A physics professor at the University of California at Irvine and an advisor to NASA, Greg Benford had an international reputation for his work with electrical discharges associated with black holes in the universe. He had read a positive comment Dean had made about his novel, *Timescape*, and he mentioned it to Charlie Brown, editor of *Locus* magazine. Brown told him that Dean lived near him and offered the phone number. "We met for dinner," says Greg, "and became fast friends."

They and their wives found that they enjoyed one another's company. Dean and Greg got together or talked on the phone for hours about politics, John D. MacDonald, the way writing stretches the imagination, and the publishing business. Greg also answered many of Dean's technical questions. He found that Dean's knowledge about business arithmetic was better than any professional he knew and that he was interested in many things. "He's a quick study, omnivorous." He was also impressed with Dean's faith in his career. "He's our best link between the cool, abstract world of onrushing ideas and the steamy, emotional swamp where fiction dwells. He has a gut feel for how the main body of people confront our culture and its technology."

Dean later dedicated *Lightning* to him and Joan, and when Greg read it, he was impressed with Dean's inversion of the typical time travel premise.

While Dean's circle of friends and acquaintances did not consist exclusively of writers—indeed, it included plumbers, craftspeople, technicians, and even magicians—he was happy to find other authors with whom he could discuss the vicissitudes of the business.

2

In June 1985, New American Library published *The Door to December* under a new pseudonym, "Richard Paige." It had been meant as a Leigh Nichols title when Dean was considering moving from Pocket Books, but when he did not leave as quickly as he had expected, he needed another name. From a neighbor named Page he devised "Paige," adding the extra letter because "Page" seemed too perfect for a writer. The book was published in England under the Leigh Nichols name. Dean dedicated it to Gerda.

In this story, he included a number of observations about the eighties culture, which seemed to him both exhilarating and frightening. Along with progress comes a certain amount of regression, such as higher rates of crime. The concept of God, no longer viable to many people, seems to be replaced by a new trinity: science, technology, and change, which are "too coldly indifferent to offer any comfort to the sick, the lonely, and the lost."[1]

Divorced behavioral psychologist Dylan McCaffrey kidnaps his three-year-old daughter, Melanie, to use her in an experiment with sensory deprivation and aversive behavior modification. Over time, he develops her psychic powers. He is joined by another psychologist, Willy Hoffritz, a fascist interested in mind control. The "Door to December" is one of the many paradoxes that the psychologists use to train her to think and act on what is otherwise unimaginable, to free her of the limitations of logic.

These men are members of an elitist group who want to achieve Melanie's feats.

Yet instead of controlling her, each member ends up dying brutally. Melanie wanders off in an autistic coma as her mother, Laura, is pulled into the investigation of her husband's murder. With Officer Dan Haldane's assistance, she finds her daughter, and they piece together the abominable things her father was doing. They also realize that someone is stalking them. Laura, a child psychologist, tries to restore Melanie's memory while Dan investigates the stalker. He soon realizes that Melanie's own mind is targeting them: She is killing everybody through astral projection and will eventually kill herself. As the prototypical abused child, she is burdened with so much guilt and shame that she has lost her sense of self-worth.

Dan and Laura must convince the girl that she is not at fault—and do so before her destructive inner force harms them all. The key to healing, Dan realizes, is forgetting. Although he is convinced of humankind's taint, he believes that one can resist it.

The two psychologists combined become a portrait of Ray Koontz. Dylan, who wants to be an inventor, has numerous transient obsessions. For example, he had devised a cure for nicotine addiction via drug therapy—a contradictory idea, but one which Ray, with his jump rope machine for people who want minimal exercise, might dream up. The other psychologist, Hoffritz, has a certain charm. Both lack conscience about what they are doing to Melanie.

Thus this character continues the motif of the unprotected child. Taken from her mother, she is at the mercy of her father, who fails to realize that his treatment of her is unethical and dangerous. He makes her hate herself, which is what Dean's father had tried to accomplish with his own son. Dean knew all too well the feeling of defenselessness, and he used this story to show how far even a parent will go in the exercise of misguided will. The group is composed of men whose otherwise normal appearances disguise monsters. Melanie cannot fight them by herself and, like Dean, her savior is her mother. She is caught between infection from psychopathology and healing from love.

As usual, Dean exploits a source from which both good and evil can spring to show how important human attitudes are to the preservation of standards and values. Behavior modification, which can cure phobias or bad habits, can also be used to warp a mind, especially that of a child. It can be a tool of domination or facilitation.

In keeping with this image, two other entities in this novel show the same potential: the government and a business organization. Both are powerful creations of human society, and the people within them are those whose souls will decide the direction in which the power will shift. The government can be "littered with idealists" who righteously open up extermination camps, and a business can bankroll mind control experiments even as they support orphanages, child welfare, and senior citizens.

All three sources of power used in this way represent the capacity of the human soul itself to do good or harm, and sometimes both simultaneously. Laura's mother, for example, was a religious zealot who abused her daughter in the name of righteousness, and Laura has had to struggle hard to grow into a loving parent. She and Dan, who must also rise above his sense of darkness, are the kind of people Dean offers as models for forming a society free of internal contradiction. Such people are alert, aware of the influential forces of their past, and willing to remake themselves. They live consistently toward the goal of developing love and a sense of protection for those they hold dear.

Set against what the psychologists are doing is a seemingly minor character, Luther, a black libertarian coroner. He is obsessed with fighting battles against those who would diminish personal freedoms. "There's a battle raging that will shape our lives," he says, "a battle between those who love freedom and those who don't, a quiet war between freedom-loving libertarians and freedom-hating fascists and leftists."[2] Although he seems to be on a fanatic's soapbox, he is actually a voice of warning in a broader sense: Any manipulative mechanism in the wrong hands can have deleterious effects on individuals and society. We need to be alert and informed; we need to resist. Otherwise, we are all as vulnerable children, malleable and easily damaged.

3

Dean wrote a nonfiction piece that year for *Writer's Yearbook '85*, "Situation Critical," on the difference between helpful and harmful advice from critics, editors, and agents. In it he urges writers to protect their own voice, but to be prepared to listen when the advice is helpful. He describes his relationship with his own agent, Claire Smith, and explains how she listens to his ideas about future books, but accepts them only when she feels that he is stretching himself. He also tells a story about a critic who had made the statement that Dean had begun his career only with the intention of imitating and stealing material from Stephen King—when in fact, Dean had twenty-five novels in print before King's first novel hit the scene. In this article, Dean also describes good and bad editors, mentions how Phyllis Grann's suggestions for cuts had improved the pace of *Phantoms*, and bemoans the fact that grammatical skills have deteriorated so much among professionals.

4

Dean deviated from his usual publications with a special limited edition of a book called *Twilight Eyes*. The publisher was a small Michigan-based press called Land of Enchantment that had just published a special edition of Stephen King's *Cycle of the Werewolf*. Although Dean wrote the story for the sheer fun of revisiting the carnival, it drew on significant personal issues that made it metaphorical on several levels.

"Dean was a customer of mine," says editor Chris Zavisa. "He had just bought my limited edition Stephen King book and I had just read *Whispers*, so when I confirmed his order, I wrote him a note and told him my Stephen King project had gone very well, and asked if he would be interested in doing something. He said yes, he would. He told me that for some time now, he had wanted to write a carnival story and he wanted to do something more macabre than *Whispers*."

For this tale, Dean was able to use his extensive file on carnivals more fully than he had in *The Funhouse*. He knew about the slang among the "show people," their various jobs, their gypsy spirit, their sense of brotherhood, their attitudes about "marks," and their winter home in Gibsonton, Florida, where bearded ladies and giants are a common sight. He had never forgotten his enchantment as a boy who yearned to run away with the carnies, nor his love of Ray Bradbury's *Something Wicked This Way Comes*. "I have been fascinated with carnivals for my whole life," he said. "I've collected all kinds of background items related to it. I get letters from carnies and some of them are multiple generation carnival people. It's such a complex background with all the rituals. Some day, I'd like to put it all into a realistic novel and call it *Tear Down the Night*. It will have to be set in the past, however, because the carnival I knew and loved is fading away, becoming something else, less mythical and strange."

Many people, he believed, did not appreciate the distinction between carnivals and circuses, and he intended to write a story that would make that difference clear. "A lot of people think they don't like the carnival world, but they don't really know what it's like, with its traditions." He wanted to include the human side of the people who ran the rides and displayed themselves in sideshows; he also wanted to do more with that feeling of a protected space among the good people. "This is the carnival of my youth. That's why I set it in the sixties." He went to work on scenes and characters while Chris Zavisa sought an artist to illustrate the book.

Chris looked through samples of artwork and decided to check out Phil Parks as a possibility. Chris was impressed with what he saw.

Phil had been an artist since early childhood. "Art has always been my way of dealing with stress, boredom, or loneliness," he explains. His older brother had been an artist as well, but had died in a boating accident when Phil was eight. "Things really began to move forward after that in terms of my art," he said. "I focused on it as a means of getting away." He took art classes later at Wayne State University, but his method was mostly self-taught.

Phil lived close to Chris Zavisa, and he seemed a good match for Dean. Phil had already read some of Dean's novels, so when Dean sent a first chapter, Phil had a good idea what should be done. Dean spent a lot of time explaining to him what made a carnival unique. It seemed very important to him that Phil get that right in the fine details of his drawings and paintings. "I remember having a lot of conversations with him," Phil says. "I would ask him what actor he might have thought of for a specific character. If he had someone in mind, I would try to work that in. For example, Chris and I were discussing the character of Slim and we both thought of Christopher Walken. When we asked Dean, one of the actors he mentioned was Christopher Walken. So I used Walken's eyes and that intense look he gets."

Phil was working a full-time job and each of the detailed color paintings required hours of his time, so it took the better part of a year to finish the full set of illustrations. He did several paintings more than once, showing each rendering to Dean and making the alterations Dean suggested. At one point, Phil and Chris visited the James E. Strates carnival in Florida to look at the carousel horses, but found them to be horrifically cheap and gaudy. Then they went to the Disneyworld and the Circus World theme parks near Orlando, where they were more impressed with the sculpted beauty of the carousel statues. "It was those horses," says Chris, "that inspired the cover painting." Phil's centerpiece was a three-panel gatefold painting of a creepy goblin crawling out of the shadows. It turned out to be one of Dean's favorite paintings as well.

Chris had asked for a twenty-five thousand word novella, but Dean became so engrossed in writing the story that it turned out to be five times as long.

In the end, the project satisfied all of them. "Dean is just a pleasure to deal with," said Chris Zavisa. "He's honest, straightforward, and generous to a fault. He's a real salt-of-the-earth type of guy."

Dean dedicated the novel to his friends Jim and Viki Blaylock, and Tim and Serena Powers. He framed it with a quote from an anonymous carnival pitchman who defined humanity as a show of compassion and willingness to extend oneself to others. In short, true humanity is the hero's journey, the quest for a better state despite the hurdles.

The power of this novel lies in its ambiguity. It starts off with the protagonist, Slim MacKensie, sounding almost psychotic. Slim claims to be able to see demonic beings, called goblins, within normal people. No one else sees them, but he believes he must kill them to save humanity. Since he is telling the story in first person, his perspective is the only source of credibility. "I know what you are," he says to one goblin, which is the same line that cult leader Grace Spivey says to the little boy Joey in *The Servants of Twilight*, and what the demented gunman shouts in the screenplay that Dean wrote years later for *Cold Fire*. Dean's use of this startling line in these opposing contexts indicates the permeable boundary between fantasy and reality—that the same phrase can signal either sanity or madness, and the actual state of mind may not be readily evident. Is Slim a solitary hero up against terrible odds or is he simply a lunatic who sees conspiracy and evil where they don't exist? Since he takes action by killing these goblins, it matters that his sanity is clearly established. Yet how sane can he be, taking on what he describes as an apparently futile fight?

Slim claims he can see the porcine/canine/reptilian images superimposed on the faces of the people the goblins inhabit. To explain this phenomenon, he uses the metaphor of a vase with a transparent red glaze that gave the impression of depth and dimension within the flat clay surface. Dean had seen this vase himself and had thought it an apt metaphor: The human form of these goblins is solid, but within lies another reality.

Set in 1963 shortly before President Kennedy's assassination, but told in the wake of it, the novel plays with the attitudes of the day, juxtaposing a loss of hope against its eternal return, evident in the bouncy music of such groups as the Ronettes and the Beatles. At all times, it seems, despair and hope, curses and gifts, are constant companions in the human condition. Dean draws many parallels between the events of the novel and historic cultural events.

"It was fascinating to look back like that," he says. "As I was researching the past to see what had happened in 1963, it was truly amazing to look at what was popular in terms of movies and music. I used the technique at the beginning and the end of Part One of just listing those events, and it had this curious effect. You jam the whole spectrum of the creative arts into one paragraph and your mind compares that list to contemporary books, music, and movies, and you see a tremendous cultural change. Living through it or just seeing references here and there in a novel, you don't get the impact of how tremendous this change has been—and not necessarily for the better."

A unique aspect of this book for Dean was his feeling that

the protagonist, Slim MacKensie, should speak in a baroque, ornamented manner. He thought that Slim must have his own voice that would clearly express his personality and set him apart from the author. His descriptions would be rich and poetic because he had a multidimensional vision of several levels of reality. It took several weeks, but finally Dean felt comfortable with this new style of writing.

For subliminal suggestions of an imagistic perspective, he relied on the rhythms of iambic pentameter—a pattern of metrical feet composed of a succession of short, or unaccented, syllables followed by long, or accented, ones. "This cadencing of the narrative voice seems a natural reflection of the iron will with which Slim has tried to bring order to—and make sense of—a world he *knows* is infinitely bizarre and perhaps senseless."[3] Dean believed poetry could provide more than straight prose in the way of perception and interpretation. His first paragraph has the quality of Dickens' descriptions in *A Tale of Two Cities*, which pairs pessimism with optimism in rhythmic phrasing.

"There are certain poetic meters that I think can elicit a mood and a reaction," says Dean. "It's almost impossible to make every sentence scan in meter, but you can get enough into the prose so that it's largely metered."

When questioned about this in an interview, he said, "Pentameter, iambic trimeter, dactylic meter, the whole bag of tricks—they're great tools for a novelist. You can use them to accelerate the pace of a scene, to emphasize something with extreme subtlety, to enhance mood. . . . The whole point is to affect the reader without him or her being aware of how the effect is being achieved."[4]

On the nature of language in general, Dean remarks that "there is this belief that we perceive the world the way we do because of shared convictions, which are expressed in language. Those people would tell you that if we could just think about the world differently, we'd look around and see everything in a different way, but we can't do that because language is built from the shared perceptions of the community. There's a philosophy that this limitation blocks our perceptions of many things, that we're prisoners of language. If language influences the way we see, and even limits our view of reality, then language is hugely important. If we restrict our use of it, we're restricting our vision. Certain words used in certain ways—the chains and rhythms of words—can get you caught up. Whether that matters to most people on a conscious level, I don't know.

"I know I'm affected by something written in a strong way—a poetic way. I think about the sound, the way it gets to you—its rhythm. The best kind of poetry can affect you in this way: You can read line after line and it can be so complex that you have to read it a hundred times to really figure out all that's being said, but you can still fall in love with it without knowing two percent of what's going on."

Since this novel offers significant autobiographical revelations, it is important to look closely at the details of the story.

5

Slim is seventeen and on the run. He wants to join the Sombra Brothers Carnival as a way to find sanctuary and a protective identity. He has killed his uncle, whom he knew to be a goblin, and he is wanted for murder. He understands that the goblins are evil entities that feed off human pain; they cause as much as they can get away with, just to keep their appetites quenched. They plan "accidents," spreading the news to other goblins to come and watch. Goblins are the monsters that look like us—indistinguishable to most people but supercharged with violence, like a high-tension wire. They are masters of psychological torture—a form of terrorism that is difficult to detect. They represent the force of entropy and chaos—of ultimate destruction, both physical and spiritual.

About one out of every five hundred people is a goblin. They show up everywhere, even among the country's leading officials—those who are indifferent to human suffering. Goblins are equated with cancer and vampires. Slim suggests that perhaps they are humankind's penance for intraspecies cruelty.

Slim has "twilight eyes." His eyes are the color of twilight, which signals psychic sensitivity. He often has difficulty confronting the reflection of his own strange eyes because he fears that he will see madness. He, too, recognizes the ambiguity:

He could be sane and gifted, but he could as well be crazy. Like Dean searching for his father's insidious genetic influence, Slim probes his gaze "honestly and relentlessly, but I could see no trace of lunacy."[5] He wavers between feelings of pessimism and hope, a sense of the void and a belief in the fullness of the human spirit.

He kills a goblin on the Sombra Brothers lot, but when the body disappears, he has reason to believe that someone saw what he did. The next day, Slim is hired to run the high-striker for Rya Raines, a beautiful, talented, and brusque young woman with whom he falls in love. Rya finds herself attracted to Slim as well, and exposes to him her dark side: memories of abuse in her West Virginia backwoods family (inspired by Dean's experience in Saxton).

Joel Tuck, a man with three eyes who runs the Ten-in-One sideshow of freak attractions, can also see the goblins. As a reminder of genetic chaos himself, he provides a reverse mirror of the goblins, indicating that there is nothing inherently good or evil in deformity. What matters is the choices a person makes. Slim takes an immediate liking to Joel, appreciating his dignity.

The inspiration for Tuck came partly from the noble character of Stevie Harmon, the crippled miner whom Dean had known as a boy, and partly from Dean's carnival experience.

"Joel was based on a real man that I saw as a kid," Dean explains, "although his face was more bizarre than I described. He would just sit there on display. He'd read a newspaper but he wouldn't talk to the people coming through, although he'd sometimes talk to kids who weren't mean. He was scary, but at the same time, kind of neat. He said that whenever he went into town to get something or see a doctor, he always wore a bag over his head, just like the Elephant Man. Sometimes teenagers would want to rough him up. They'd tear off the bag and *always* pass out cold."

Slim senses in Joel a fatherliness, "an ability and willingness to provide comfort, friendship, guidance."[6] As it turns out, Joel—also gifted with the vision that Slim has—is the one who had moved the goblin after Slim had killed it. He warns Slim that Rya is not all that she seems. Slim dismisses his concern, attributing this impression to her past, which has caused her to loathe herself and to be attracted to death.

As the carnival heads toward Yontstown, Pennsylvania—
based on the industrial milieu of real places, Johnstown and
Altoona—Slim notices an increase in numbers of goblins. He
knows that the Ferris wheel is going to be rigged to destruct,
and he enlists Joel's help in preventing the goblins from having their fun. Then, to his shock, he learns that Rya, too, sees
the goblins . . . and worse. She is an accomplice, revealing the
identities of those who know what they are. She explains to
Slim the origins of the goblins and why she betrays her own
species.

According to her, goblins are an ancient race created to be
warriors by an advanced human civilization able to tamper
with genetic structure. Goblins were programmed to feel no
love, compassion, guilt, or mercy, although they could act out
these emotions credibly. (In short, they are genetically engineered sociopaths.) They experienced pleasure only when they
inflicted pain on someone else. This new species had two
genetic patterns—one human and the other inhuman, with a
linking gene that allowed them to metamorphose into one
another. Then something went wrong. The goblins developed
an independent ego and provoked a nuclear war that nearly
wiped out the human race.

Gradually, as people returned to the technological prowess
they once had possessed, that ancient civilization was lost to
history, remembered only in mythological symbols formed in
the collective unconscious. The goblins evolved into a species
that could procreate and live extended lives. They are our destiny, which we ourselves set into motion from the worst of our
capacities.

Those with psychic power, however, are the goblins' goblins, because these powers arose in the human species as mutations, following that ancient nuclear war that the goblins
waged. Thus, just as goblins are the destructive side of
humankind—created by humankind—those who can detect
and destroy them are *their* shadow side—caused by their own
acts.

For her own safety, Rya helps goblins eliminate those who
can see them. She begs Slim to do the same, but he refuses.
He knows that to accommodate evil is the same as doing the
evil itself. Rya then turns him over to the goblins. He fights

them off and Rya tries to kill him. He nearly retaliates, but realizes that true humanity is the inability to kill one's own kind. He is not going to be like her—like the goblins. He resists, and his compassion and self-control have the effect of transforming her. Ultimately Rya gives up her struggle and sides with him.

Mirror imagery reverberates throughout. The goblins are metaphors of evil at large, be it a murdering psychopath, nuclear war, or an indifferent government that creates human suffering. Their link to humankind is the same as that shared between Rya and Slim; it involves the tricky network of the inner self, where one's dark side can be an intimate and inextricable aspect of the core self.

Against that, Dean sets the carnival community, where one might expect people of such seedy coarseness and freakishness to embody darkness. Instead, they form bonds of compassion, generosity, and protection, with a sturdy moral resolve. They represent the part of the human soul, along with Slim, that acknowledges and resists its own evil potential. They know it cannot be eradicated and that every effort must be made to maintain moral integrity. They stand together against the fragmentation of prejudice—and chaos.

"We have within ourselves the potential to create our own heaven or hell," Dean believes, "and I like to explore both."

Similarly, Rya is Slim's dark side, his own potential for self-hatred and pessimism. Unscrambling her name, one gets "Ray," Dean's psychological shadow—the possible genetic inheritance of cruelty and chaos that so frightens and disgusts him. Ray, too, is a goblin accomplice. Rya invites accommodation, which promises safety and tranquilization. To "be like me" with either Rya or Ray means to cave in to a certain moral numbness. Slim loves and hates Rya, pities and despises her. He is attracted and repulsed, because he and she overlap in their visions and dreams—even their brain waves. They fit together, and Slim can do one of two things: merge with her or get her to merge with him. His task is to cleanse her and bring her into a moral space.

Just as Slim must redeem and transform Rya, so must Dean do the same with that part of himself that he associates with Ray Koontz. In order to be a man, yet not become like his father, he has to change the meaning of manhood—to sanitize it. Slim does this by resisting Rya's enticement and by showing her compassion and understanding. Dean does something similar by taking care of, rather than being cruel to, his father. Dean and Slim both spot the inner potential to go either way and both emphasize the humane response toward the other side. Slim wants to believe that, beneath Rya's evil actions, she is really good at heart and can be redeemed. Dean wants to believe the same. If there is something good to be found in his father—no matter how deeply buried—then he can safely be Ray's son, without becoming anything like the Ray that he has known.

In *Fantasy Review*, Charles de Lint remarked on the dense prose employed to write this novel, but considered it well worth taking the time to read. Several critics praised the detailed descriptions of carnival life. As Jonathan Kirsch put it in the *Los Angeles Times*, Dean "imbues the scene with an almost palpable atmosphere of moral peril." Robert Weinberg pointed out in a genre magazine that the main character in the story is the carnival itself, which has a moral life of its own. The nail-biting suspense typical of Koontz, he said, is laced with a heavier mood.

Dean is determined never to sell this novel to the movies unless he can keep tight control. "I've had film offers on it," he says, "but I refuse to sell until I can write the screenplay myself." He knows that, misunderstood, this book could become just another carnage movie, and it means too much to him as a metaphorical work—not just for Slim but for the community of good-hearted "freaks"—to submit it to superficial treatment. Again, it is much more than a horror story about goblins. It is about the way humans can become so enamored of the images of hell that we could actually create such a race from within ourselves—an embodied representation of the atrocities that we commit against one another. We ourselves can be goblins.

It would not be Dean's last project with Chris Zavisa and Phil Parks. Nor would it be the last time he returned to the theme of redemption and the need for inner self-transformation. Much as he disliked his father, Dean felt a centrifugal pull to continue to understand the pathology that had so plagued his life. *Twilight Eyes* was a pivotal novel in this regard, but more a launching pad into inner space than a resolution. Even Slim MacKensie was destined for another go at it, but *with* Rya rather than in conflict with her. She had been merely a doorway in, and he would soon discover that goblins are much more ominous than they had initially seemed.

[1]Dean Koontz writing as Richard Paige, *The Door to December* (New York: New American Library, 1985), p. 273.

[2]Ibid., p. 144.

[3]Ed Gorman, "Interview with Dean Koontz," *The Dean Koontz Companion* (New York: Berkley, 1994), p. 45.

[4]Michael Collings, "Dean Koontz," *Mystery Scene* (no. 45), p. 49.

[5]*Twilight Eyes*, p. 36.

[6]Ibid., p. 103.

SIXTEEN

Strangers

1

THE NEXT BOOK WAS *STRANGERS*, WHICH TOOK DEAN IN A completely new direction. It surprised those people who believed they could foresee the limited kind of career he would have. And while he was writing *Strangers*, the world around him was changing. The superstring theory in physics proposed that most elementary particles are one-dimensional and that the universe has ten, rather than four, dimensions. Crack cocaine entered the market, the "Mayflower Madam" was arrested, and Coca-Cola introduced a new formula. AIDS was becoming a national health crisis.

The year that *Strangers* was published, the space shuttle *Challenger* exploded after takeoff, killing its occupants. A secret weapons sale to Iran was exposed, implicating John Poindexter and Oliver North. People seemed to accept that there were such clandestine activities among government officials, and Oliver North was hailed by a segment of society as a man of integrity.

In no novel to date had Dean made such an effort to join a disparate group of people as kindred souls, as family in the most transcendent sense. There were twelve distinct characters, each with a detailed history. He had to keep the telling of each tale balanced against all the others as he brought the characters together. Some had repressed memories and the urge to return to where they had been in Nevada on a certain fateful day. Others were already there. The influence of John D. MacDonald, with his emphasis on social commentary and attention to character and detail, was strong—as Dean himself would note.

"*Strangers* was an attempt to take the strengths of genre fiction—story, pace, vitality of imagination," he told an interviewer, "and combine them with the strengths of mainstream fiction—layered characterization, tight thematic structure and purpose, a sense of the melodies and rhythms of language, emotional depth, and a multifaceted realistic portrayal of the world in which we actually live."[1]

Initially he had ideas about only a few of the characters. "When I started the book," he says, "I knew there was going to be Dom and Ginger as the two leads. I knew there would be a priest. If *Strangers* is anything, it's the equivalent of one of those books like *The Cardinal* or *Miracle of the Bells*, a book about faith that takes for granted that we believe in God. I knew that *Strangers* was going to be about transcendence, about meeting God, except in this case it's an alien life-form. They really are meeting God. By the time they get to the end of the book and see this life-form, I start talking in theological terms that what this race is doing is essentially God's work. So I knew I wanted a priest who'd lost faith and who begins to regain it.

"I also knew there would be a professional thief because I needed someone with high-tech expertise. I knew all the characters would have separate and unusual problems. I probably assumed at the beginning there were four, but as it got going, at some point I thought that one of the characters should be afraid of the dark. And then I realized I needed a couple of characters at the place where this happened, so that gave me Ernie and Fay. I knew it was a story about a group of disparate people who come together as a family, and then do for one another what families are supposed to do."

It took Dean nearly a full year to write this novel. He went through over one hundred fifty titles, trying them and then rejecting them. One title was *Gates of Dawn*, but he settled on *Thunder Hill*, based on a location in the book. No one seemed to like it except him. His first draft was eleven hundred pages, with narrow margins. Grann wanted him to cut it to seven hundred, and offered a higher advance for a shorter book, but Dean stood his ground. He managed to revise it to nine hundred forty pages, without cutting out a single scene.

No matter how much work he had done to cut this manuscript, he found that Phyllis Grann wanted still more. Dean asked where she thought it needed to be shortened, and she suggested removing a character or two. He refused. They had all been woven together and no more cuts seemed possible to him.

Grann assigned a new editor to him named Alan Williams. He had been Stephen King's editor at Viking and had come over to Putnam, where he edited King's *Tommyknockers*. Grann was now publisher and was concentrating on other matters. She told Dean that she would still read his manuscripts and make comments, but she wanted him to have someone's complete attention and she trusted Williams to do the job right. She was sure he could come up with a strategic way to shorten the novel without losing its integrity. Williams set to work.

"I found Dean to be extremely hardworking," he said. "I had trouble politically with his descriptions of the contras in Nicaragua, and he modified that. Dean is completely professional about his writing, and either agrees with what an editor says or he argues against it effectively. We had a genuine dialogue."

Williams made suggestions about tightening the structure and phrasing, some of which Dean accepted, but the revision did little to shrink the manuscript. *Strangers* went into print close to the form in which Dean had handed it in. He collected a smaller advance than if he had cut to seven hundrd pages, but he still ended up with more money for a single book than he had been paid to that point: $275,000.

After the editing was done, Dean's film agent called him one morning and insisted that he could not sell a book named *Thunder Hill*. He wanted a new name that afternoon. Simultaneously, the novel was going to be shipped to the book clubs and also needed a new title that day. The pressure was on. "I sat at the typewriter and tried to think of something," Dean remembers, "and I couldn't come up with a thing." Finally he just decided to go to work on a new book and within five minutes had the perfect title: *Strangers*. "It just worked well on a lot of levels."

Dean dedicated *Strangers* to his British agent, Bob Tanner, for his enthusiasm.

"When I pick up a copy of *Strangers*," Tanner said, "and see that dedication, I hold my head high. Everyone likes to be associated with a winner."

Dean recalls that Grann assured him of a minimum printing

of 75,000 and an ad budget of $75,000. The first printing was set at 45,000, with a laydown date of April 18. Both the Literary Guild and Doubleday featured it as a main selection. The book went through several printings until it actually hit 75,000.

On May 11, *Strangers* landed on *The New York Times* bestsellers list at number fifteen. *Publishers Weekly* showed it at number twelve. This was Dean's first official hardcover bestseller in this country, and he and Gerda were thrilled. Dean had proven wrong all those people who had insisted that he was not the type of writer who could pen a hardcover bestseller. Now he could set his sights even higher. It was one thing to get on the list. It was another to reach the top. His editors attempted to dissuade him from setting himself up for disappointment, but he was determined to keep going.

For this novel, Dean researched phobias, the impact of sophisticated cultures on inferior ones, and brainwashing techniques, as well as the details necessary to develop authenticity in the character backgrounds: the history of the Nicaraguan conflict, the varieties of Jewish cooking, and the medical art of the aortal graft (although when a physician friend invited him to come and see such surgery in action, he declined). Dean wanted to emphasize the characteristics that humanize: courage, compassion, empathy, and sacrificial love. He opened the novel with quotes about the abiding force of friendship.

2

The novel begins with the disintegration of a number of lives that hold promise. Dominick Corvaisis, a bestselling writer, is driven by uncharacteristic bouts of terror and somnambulism. He feels a sense of being invaded, which is somehow related to the moon.

Simultaneously Ginger Weiss, a Jewish cardiovascular surgeon-in-training with a brilliant future, begins to experience fugue states and panic attacks. She consults a hypnotist, who advises her about the Azrael Block, used by the Soviets, which prevents someone from recalling damaging information. The hypnotist then is murdered. Ginger reads Dom's novel and knows that she must find him.

Back in Elko, Nevada, the place that all of these characters have in common, ex-marine Ernie Block, owner of the Tranquility Motel, is experiencing nyctophobia—fear of night—and feels drawn to a piece of land not far from his motel. One of his employees, Sandy Sarver, has the same obsession, and her problem is that she has suddenly become highly sexual after a life of near-frigidity.

In Las Vegas, Jorja Montatella's daughter, Marcie, is inexplicably obsessed with the moon and terrified of doctors.

Farther away, a young priest in Chicago, Brendan Cronin, has lost his faith. When his superior sends him to care for dying children, Brendan miraculously heals people. He believes this comes not from God but from a force that is urging him to go to Nevada.

Jack Twist (reminiscent of Michael Tucker from Dean's caper novels) is an ex-Ranger who had been betrayed by his government. After risking himself in Central America to rescue political prisoners, he was left behind to be tortured. While he was gone, his wife was beaten into a coma. Embittered, Jack exploits his skills to become a professional thief, using the money to keep his wife in an expensive care facility. When she dies, he finds some mysterious photos in his safe deposit box, which lead him to Nevada.

As it turns out, the army is behind these strange occurrences. It had brainwashed these people to make them forget witnessing a UFO landing in Nevada the previous summer. When it fears that the effects are wearing off, the army decides to resubmit everyone to another session, because exposure to an enormously advanced culture might propel the human race into a sense of wretchedness from feelings of inadequacy (one of Dean's early science fiction themes).

The colonel in charge, Leland Falkirk, is a masochistic, paranoid victim of child abuse, so he wants nothing to do with aliens that might invade him. He thinks the witnesses should be killed. He is sure that they, along with the scientists on the project, have been changed into something alien. A general, Miles Bennell, feels differently. He is the one who lured the witnesses back to Nevada, unaware that Falkirk intends to kill everyone in the facility, including himself, with a nuclear device.

As the various characters come together at the Tranquility Motel, they realize that they had been quarantined and brainwashed. Gradually some of them remember a spaceship. Ginger, Dom, and Brendan recall that they had actually entered the landed craft.

Ginger, Dom, and Jack penetrate the military installation where the spaceship is kept. Bennell explains that the aliens on board have died, but that they had been ambassadors of an advanced godlike species, offering gifts of healing, psychic phenomena, long life, and kindness. Their own trip had been a brave sacrifice to bring the good news, a sacred responsibility to bind intelligences across the universe, like archangels bestowing blessings. Dom recalls that two of the aliens had been alive the previous year and had passed their powers on to those humans they had met.

Falkirk announces that they will all die. Dom and Brendan use their psychic abilities to disarm him and then neutralize the bombs, but Falkirk shoots himself to escape contamination. Dom and Brendan decide to pass the powers they have received to others, thus giving hope to the human race for transcendent possibilities.

They had needed one another to solve the mystery of their individual lives and to defy the army—a power far greater than any one of them could have handled alone. They are the foundation for an evolution that will join all humans as one large family. "No more would people be strangers, one to one another, not anywhere on earth. . . . They stood at the gates of a new dawn."[2]

The strangers from another planet had joined these strangers on Earth, and this first contact had dissolved boundaries and replaced them with ties of love. All strangers, no matter what species, have within themselves the ability to bond.

"I think it's healing," says Dean, "that people come together who don't know each other and who have a shared mission to form some sort of community. That has power, because we all wish we had relationships like that."

The character of Dom seems to be based on Dean himself, except that Dom experiences large-scale success with his first novel. He is a writer who subscribes to many publications and who views all new experiences as material for his fiction. He lives in Laguna Beach and, despite success, worries that he is headed for a great fall. (Dean confided to many friends that no matter how well he did, he feared that it could all be taken away: "once poor, never rich.") Dom uses an IBM display-writer, has high standards, and places enormous value on friendship. He agrees with Robert Louis Stevenson that "the important thing is the well-told tale, not he who tells it."[3]

Falkirk represents the repressive, paranoid side of our culture, while those characters willing to explore, even at risk, are the heroes who take us all into richer possibilities. It is a mythological enactment of our most basic fears and hopes. It becomes clear that humankind's need to dominate and enslave, to impress simplistic philosophies on the entire human race, must collapse in the face of extraterrestrial beings that speak of contact with God and show good evidence in their abilities.

This novel was an extension of Dean's science fiction work, coupled with a new spirituality that linked aliens with God in a profound enlightenment. It was a far cry from Dean's angry atheism in which God was depicted as a worm that needed to be crushed. And it was most definitely not horror, although Dean was beginning to be typecast as a horror novelist. He disliked the label. In an interview with the *Daily News* in Los Angeles, he categorically stated, "I don't write horror novels. To me, at least, horror deals with the supernatural and everything in these books can be explained rationally. But I suppose there's another kind of horror, the kind that deals with shock and sustained tension. That's closer to what I do. I got the publisher to change the word 'horror' on the cover of *Strangers* to terror."[4] Dean felt that his novels were not straight horror, though they appealed to fans of that genre. He did not find much hope or optimism in most of what passed as horror fiction, and the nihilistic tones clashed with his own sense of purpose as a writer. He also knew that to succumb to a category and keep turning out the same sort of tale meant losing his edge, his desire to keep exploring fictional worlds of greater complexity and depth. "It's the challenge of pushing one's own outer limits that keeps writing fresh and exciting," he said.[5]

The thing underground, where one might expect evil to originate, turns out to be a source of joyful enlightenment, the salvation of humanity. Along with that metaphor, the desert, too, is not what it seems: Rather than being barren, it is full of promise. This plays out the notion of the "golden shadow"— that our fears of the dark sides of ourselves may be in part justified, yet within that subconscious cauldron lies the potential for something good. As a civilization, we may have repressed the very things that could benefit us. Emphasis on the rational makes us suspicious of the paranormal or metaphysical; these things get dismissed, even ridiculed to the point that we lose contact with them. Yet their magic may yield the very thing we need to continue to progress spiritually and psychologically.

In a letter to a reader, Jeff Stevenson, Dean explained the place of God in his fiction at that point: "I'm a heavy reader of science books and articles, especially modern physics, and one cannot be aware of many recent developments in physics and still cling happily to agnosticism or atheism. As one famous physicist has put it: We are peeling away the mysteries of the universe, one by one, faster and faster, and to our surprise, through the final transparent layer, we are seeing not a void but the face of God." He goes on to point out that he is "writing books that are, at root, both optimistic and crammed full of faith."

Strangers was a finalist that year for the World Fantasy Award for Best Novel.

Reviewers were picking up on Dean's cross-genre techniques, recognizing science fiction, horror, romance, adventure, espionage, suspense, and mystery all rolled into one. For some, that meant a lack of focus, while others applauded Dean's attempts to be a pathfinder. Many noted the strong characterizations, and Dean himself stated that "with *Strangers* I became convinced that character is the soul of fiction."

To Dean's delight, John D. MacDonald wrote a blurb: "I thoroughly enjoyed *Strangers*. You can't call this science fiction, nor is it merely spooky—it is a contemporary novel of manners and morals and politics and freedom. This is a book with a capital B." They exchanged letters once again before MacDonald died later that year.

A few reviewers complained that the book was too much like Steven Spielberg's film, *Close Encounters of the Third Kind*. One critic mentioned its weak ending, while another said the resolution, after such a long buildup, happened too fast. Overall, however, most reviewers were enthusiastic.

The reviewer in *The San Francisco Chronicle* called it "one of the best mystery/suspense novels of all time." In *The New York Times*, it was dubbed "an engaging, even chilling book." *The Library Journal* review said that Dean's "ability to maintain the mystery through several plot twists is impressive," adding that it may be "the suspense novel of the year." Even more complimentary was the Ocala *Star Banner*: "*Strangers* is so hauntingly beautiful that it should catapult Koontz into the ranks of the greatest American authors of all time."

In December that year, Berkley published the novel in paperback and it climbed even higher on the mass market list, to number twelve. Editor-in-chief of the fantasy line, Susan Allison, was impressed with Dean's input on cover design and his knowledge about the business. "He's wonderful to work with," she remarks, "which is not to say he doesn't want things done properly, but he's always been considerate and professional. He knows what works for him and what doesn't, so his suggestions are sound. He doesn't just express whims. In my experience, his ability to deal with his career as a career without losing track of the fact that his primary job is to write the words on the page is unprecedented."

While working on the cover, Dean became acquainted with cover artist Don Brautigam from New Jersey. They went on to do over thirty covers together, but *Strangers* was their first. "Dean was one of the first authors I've worked with to compliment me on my covers," says Brautigam. "And he's one of the few who offered ideas that were commercially viable. He has a good marketing sense."

Brautigam worked on the limited editions that were yet to come, and Dean would dedicated *Mr. Murder* to him and to illustrator Phil Parks.

3

As Dean's success made an impression on a wider audience, there were those who had known his past work in science fiction and his more recent novels in horror. They approached him to help them nurture a new organization that was just beginning to form: Horror Writers of America.

It had all begun with the germ of an idea mentioned by Robert R. McCammon to Joe Lansdale at a World Fantasy Convention in Ottawa. McCammon had wondered why there was an association for mystery writers and for science fiction writers, but nothing for horror writers per se. "I just thought there should be some sort of community or town hall," he says. "I thought people would work together toward some kind of fund to protect writers and help new writers."

Horror had been gaining popularity since the mid-seventies and some science fiction writers had viewed it as a new medium for making important statements about society. The science fiction field had become stale, some felt, and horror appeared to be a new and exciting outlet. "A lot of people were doing unique things," says Lansdale, "particularly in the short story. It was an opportunity to use fiction to say something." Neither considered himself strictly a horror writer, but McCammon had written a vampire novel, *They Thirst*, and Lansdale was gaining notoriety for his offbeat stories in Western horror, such as *The Magic Wagon*. McCammon started a newsletter for a group he called H.O.W.L. and from that had gathered a list of names. He gave them to Karen Lansdale, Joe's wife, and she sent out form letters to ascertain interest for a more official organization. She received just over one hundred enthusiastic responses.

"We agreed to drop the catchy, but nonprofessional H.O.W.L. in favor of something that we felt gave our organization more credibility," says Joe. "Its purpose was to help further the writings of those people in the field, to gain respect for them."

Joe called Dean to ask him to participate. "I'm sure I was glib," Joe says, "and he's not that hard to manipulate." Dean liked Joe's dry, bantering sense of humor, and they began to talk more frequently. Finally Dean was persuaded to accept the position of president, since his name had influence and would bring respect from publishers and critics. Even though Dean was fighting to keep from being cast as only one type of writer, he agreed to get involved for other reasons. He had been a member of Mystery Writers of America without being typecast, so he thought he could do the same with horror. Little did he realize how strongly people would associate him with the horror genre afterward.

Dean had helped many aspiring writers with advice and financial assistance. He had even connected some with publishers and agents. He did not view writing as competitive, and thought that those writers who were able should hold out a hand to those coming behind, just as people like Robert Silverberg had done for him early in his career.

"I've always believed we owe it to one another to help each other whenever we can. That's one way to make the field in which you work the highest quality."

At the World Fantasy Convention in Tucson, Arizona, in 1985, the planning committee for the Horror Writers of America organization came together to meet. Joe Lansdale, Rick McCammon, and Melissa Mia Hall formed the membership committee. McCammon agreed to edit the newsletter and there was talk of best-of-the-year awards being set in place by the following year. The organizers were hesitant about this aspect, but knew that other organizations had them and the issue would have to be raised.

The first official meeting was scheduled for Providence, Rhode Island, in 1986. Dean did not attend, but it was clear to everyone that he would serve as the first president. John Maclay published one thousand copies of a booklet called *The Monitors of Providence*, devised by Richard Christian Matheson and J. N. Williamson. Dean wrote a segment of a twelve-part story that included sections written by such writers as Dennis Etchison, Robert R. McCammon, and Chelsea Quinn Yarbro. He brought humor to a lackluster story that seemed to struggle and go nowhere. It was about a boy and his parents who could never quite figure out what had gone wrong in the pristine town of Lovecraft, although it had something to do with hamburgers. Clearly it was difficult to bring together such disparate styles and have any sense of plot, tension, or focus.

The first officers elected to the organization in 1987, its first year, were Dean as president, Paul Dale Anderson as vice president, and J. N. Williamson as secretary-treasurer. Joe Lansdale took office later in the year, while Karen Lansdale happily shifted her responsibilities to Dean. He devoted twenty or more hours a week to the project, with Gerda's help, and over the first year, paid over $8,000 worth of expenses so that the organization would have a solid financial base from which to begin. "Dean did a tremendous amount of work to put it together and keep it going," McCammon claims. "He got it through a difficult period. Lots of letters came in demanding things. I didn't know how he could write full-time and respond to all of that."

Dean issued the first newsletter in October 1986. "My main concern," said Dean in a published statement, "is that HWA becomes more than a social organization. I think there are various useful and necessary things that HWA can do for its members, such as forming a grievance committee to deal with problems with publishers and getting out a document to cover contracts." He thought HWA could add dignity and publicity to the horror genre, and expected it to help horror to make the same strides that science fiction had made. Above all, he wanted to change much of the victimization and exploitation of writers by publishers that he had witnessed and experienced over the past two decades. Once the organization proved itself to be reliable and sober, he expected to be able to use it to sponsor yearly anthologies of short stories by members. Dean also urged members to consider setting up and contributing to a hardship fund for those writers hitting difficult times.

He lobbied against the institution of an awards program on the grounds that they inevitably become politicized, turn writers into competitors, and often are awarded to work that is trendy rather than substantive. Reluctantly he succumbed to membership pressure to establish annual awards. Those who had organized HWA wanted to prevent the awards from becoming a central feature, but the membership had other ideas. Harlan Ellison, whom Dean persuaded to become involved, found an artist willing to contribute his time to designing a high quality award. Stephen Kirk, a conceptual artist for Disney, came up with a haunted house so artistic that Dean realized writers would compete just to have one, let alone gaining the extra clout of recognition. Still, they were all proud to have an award that was more than just a chintzy plaque.

For the first year, Dean published statements in the HWA newsletters, urging members to focus on professional interests and avoid bickering over inconsequential issues. When people complained that the awards would be rigged, Dean urged the other officers to follow his lead in removing his own work from consideration. He also said that the awards should be for "superior achievement" rather than "best of the year." The membership agreed.

Dean received many letters that crushed some of his illusions. In fact, only a few people seemed to share his concept of solidarity. There was much bickering, back-stabbing, jealousy, and attempts at undermining one another. When he used humor to deal with hot-button issues, some members wrote vehement letters of protest. "It took me the longest time to realize that so many members lacked a sense of humor," he says. "They didn't even realize that it *was* humor. Those of us who knew how to laugh at ourselves had fun . . . for a while. But the humorless crowd wore me down over time."

The awards in particular, called the Bram Stoker Awards, for superior achievement in specific categories, made the organization susceptible to corruption and politicizing. Those who had put so much work into making HWA happen grew weary of the unrelenting suspicions and outright attacks. "I was naïve," says McCammon. "I didn't realize there would be all this bickering. Dean had a very difficult time keeping it going. He had the good sense to steer it correctly when it began, but some people wanted power to the detriment of the good of the whole. That disappointed me, and that's when I started pulling back. The awards should never have been that important. The letters we got were very demanding and picky, and I didn't have the diplomacy to deal with them. I got disillusioned with the whole thing."

The following year, Dean relinquished the presidency to Charlie Grant, author of the Oxrun Station novels, and became president of the board of trustees. Maxine O'Callaghan, known for her Delilah West mystery series, became the new treasurer. She remembers that Dean remained watchful. "He monitored everything very closely that year," she says. She had agreed to become an officer only because she had seen how much effort Dean had put into it, and she wanted to support what he believed in. "In the beginning he had great hopes," she asserts, "but I think he hoped it would be a more supportive group. There were all kinds of infighting among the small presses when lines were drawn to protect professional standards. The whole thing kind of collapsed into all this wrangling. Dean became very disenchanted."

Nevertheless he continued to edit the "Fiendish Endeavors" column wherein the membership announced their writing accomplishments. He also continued to write columns and to offer advice. In his last letter in any official capacity, dated October 1988, he warned members about the downside of the awards program. To his mind, things had taken a bad turn when a writer complained, after the votes had been counted and tossed away, that he had been cheated. Dean thought people were losing perspective.

"We wanted something that would benefit writers," Lansdale explains, "but it veered away from that and became more like other existing organizations. Awards have their place, but the whole thing became something that we had not intended."

One night the situation reached critical mass for Dean. He attended an awards banquet for Canine Companions for Independence, a program supplying dogs for physically challenged people. He saw people disabled for life whose attitudes were better and whose perspective was healthier than those he had seen among some of the HWA members. Their pettiness finally got to him. These complaining writers had no serious problems in comparison to those who bore the brunt of life's worst disadvantages. Whining about awards, fighting about fine points of professional standards—to Dean this all seemed to be the essence of self-pity and small-mindedness. He wished he had never gotten involved.

"That was one of the biggest mistakes in my entire career," he admits. "Even at that time, I rejected the label of horror, but when you become first president of a horror association, it haunts you for the rest of time. I could see it was a doomed effort almost from the beginning. I knew that awards would lead to the dissolution of the organization. That's all people cared about. I'm sorry I launched it. I think it could have been a really valuable thing. I think all these writers organizations have the potential, but having gone through it, I think writers can be their own worst enemies. Instead of pulling together, they argue among themselves. To me, their values are always on the wrong things—awards or validation from peers. But awards always end up being corrupt. They're trinkets.

Baubles. Only the *work* matters, not what an awards commit-tee or a handful of voters think. With awards, everything is political, and if you need that kind of validation, I'm not sure you have any meaningful confidence in your work. It becomes the end-all and be-all, and you lose track of what you should be doing. I've stayed out of all writers organizations since then. I used to belong to Mystery Writers when I was in HWA, but after leaving HWA, I dropped out of Mystery Writ-ers, too."

Yet it was not all negative. Through this organization, he met and became friends with other writers, such as Lansdale and McCammon, Matthew Costello, and F. Paul Wilson. He gave advice to younger writers such as Bentley Little and Douglas Clegg, both of whom went on to become published.

"It amazes people that we all know each other," says F. Paul Wilson, author of *The Keep*. "It's a web. We feel like we're part of a family and, except for a few congenital malcontents, we're not envious of one another. We have a language, a vocabulary. You can mention an old story and the others know what you're referring to. We all come from sitting alone, reading the same books, and thinking they were wonderful."

"He's given me the best advice of anyone in publishing," says Clegg about Dean. "He made me realize the importance of getting a strong commitment from the publisher. Of all the writers I've spoken with, he has the sharpest sense of the real-ity of the business."

"Dean urged me to think big," says Bentley Little, who met Dean at a book signing for *Twilight Eyes*. "Always try to sur-pass yourself, he told me. Always try to write a bigger book than you did last time. Always assume you're writing a best-seller and tailor your work to a mainstream audience. Don't write to just impress your peers." From that initial meeting, Dean even helped him to get an agent.

In a limited way, Dean managed to gain some sense of com-munity, but it was among those writers who worked at it as a profession, who had a sense of humor, and who wanted to do the hard work it would take to enhance their careers.

4

For the first time in a decade, Dean published short stories again, four in 1986 and four in 1987. He responded generously to editors of genre magazines who hoped his presence would improve circulation.

The summer issue of a magazine called *The Horror Show* focused on Dean, with two short stories and an interview. David B. Silva, the editor, had been surprised to find Dean receptive to contributing. He had started *The Horror Show* in 1982, and when he felt confident enough, had sent some issues to Dean. Dean called to express support. "Six months later and a number of phone calls back and forth," Silva recalls, "we did a special Dean R. Koontz issue. He gave us the essay and the stories gratis, and hooked me up with the Land of Enchantment publisher to design the front cover. He also invested an enormous amount of time and effort. It was definitely a turning point for the magazine. It gave us legitimacy."

The first story, "Down in the Darkness," was about the suppressed potential for evil in the human soul. A man named Jess buys a home from a Vietnamese entrepreneur who turns out to be the torture master from a prisoner of war camp where Jess had been held. A mysterious door opens up to a dark cellar—unusual for a southern California home—and Jess discovers below a realm that is clearly supernatural—perhaps an antechamber to hell itself. Entities in this place wait to drag down and devour anyone sent down to them. Jess uses the cellar for revenge against the former torturer, which seems to restore moral balance in the universe. However, as he realizes that "darkness dwells within even the best of us," he finds himself tempted to use it to dispose of other people whose offenses against him are minor, and he hopes he will not succumb to such a moral eclipse.

The second piece, "Weird World," is more whimsical. It describes a magazine called *Weird World*, full of of strange and confusing news, and the "editor" says that Dean Koontz has pulled some strange episodes from their files. Presented are two absurd features entitled, "The Day it Rained Frogs" and "The Unluckiest Man in the World."

Another story by Dean, "Snatcher," was published in a horror magazine, *Night Cry*, and later revised for *Strange Highways*. A purse snatcher, Billy Neeks, finds out what it means to snatch the purse of a woman with unusual powers.

A similar theme of moral balance occurs in "The Black Pumpkin," a Halloween story that appeared in *The Twilight Zone* magazine. A creepy pumpkin carver sends a message — "You get what you give" — to an aggressive kid who buys a pumpkin from him after wheedling a price much lower than the true value of his work. The horrific consequences reflect Dean's take on life: People reap what they sow, and if their souls are in disorder, they will somehow pay the price. In some ways, this story crystallized what Dean wanted to do with his entire oeuvre: A good person starts at a disadvantage to a bad person, but life itself — along with the good person's ability to engage its momentum — restores the balance and rewards the good person for his efforts to maintain integrity.

5

That year, in October of 1986, Dean and Gerda celebrated their twentieth wedding anniversary. Gerda wanted to take a cruise to Acapulco and she insisted that they were going to dance, so Dean agreed to go with her to the Holiday School in Anaheim to take ballroom dance lessons. To his surprise, he found it to be a lot of fun — especially swing dancing to Big Band music.

The cruise went down the western coast of Mexico, and while they were on board, a storm began to form. Most passengers remained unaware that the seas were actually so bad as to qualify as a hurricane. While eighty percent of the passengers took to their rooms for four days, too ill to get out of bed, Dean and Gerda discovered that they did not get seasick even under the worst of circumstances — and managed to dance every evening, even with the deck pitching and yawing.

In Acapulco, they disembarked to explore the city. When it got late and their driver was nowhere to be found, they hired a cab. Across the dashboard, they noticed a line of small skulls — each intricately hand-painted. There were perhaps twenty of them—and they almost seemed to be symbols of successful kills—like skulls painted on the fuselages of World War II fighter planes.

Worse, the driver said to them, "I can take you places. Does anyone know where you are?"

Dean and Gerda look at each other. A stranger with a collection of skulls in a city they did not know was asking if anyone knew of their whereabouts.

"Oh, sure," said Dean with forced confidence. He went on to claim that they were lifelong friends with the captain of the cruise ship and that it would not leave dock until they arrived. He wanted to make it clear that, were there to be any foul play, there would be immediate consequences.

By the time the driver dropped them at their destination, Dean realized that the skulls were merely part of the upcoming Day of the Dead festivals, and that the question had been innocent (and probably misphrased due to the driver's poor English). Instead of narrowly escaping being murdered, they had most likely missed an opportunity to see some unusual sights. A novelist's imagination is easily engaged!

[1] *The Horror Show* (Summer 1987), p. 23.
[2] Dean R. Koontz, *Strangers* (New York: Putnam, 1986), p. 680.
[3] Ibid., p. 415.
[4] Interview in the Los Angeles *Daily News* (February 8, 1987).
[5] *The Horror Show* (Summer 1987), p. 23.

SEVENTEEN

Einstein

1

THE YEAR 1987 WAS THE START OF THE GREAT FALL OF TELEVI-
sion evangelists, with Jim Bakker accused of cavorting with
Jessica Hahn and paying for her secrecy. Along with him, the
Dow reached a record low, Andy Warhol died, and Gary Hart
challenged the media to find a black spot on his reputation,
which they did with Donna Rice, causing him to withdraw
from the presidential race.

After finishing *Strangers*, Dean turned in another Leigh
Nichols book, *Shadowfires*. He had moved from Pocket when,
by the fourth book, it was apparent from the lack of support
that they had lost interest in promoting the Leigh Nichols
name. Avon had bought it in an auction. It was Dean's fifth
and last book under this pen name, although at that time in the
late eighties, he still believed he might keep it going.

He dedicated *Shadowfires* to his friend and fellow author,
Richard Laymon, and to Richard's wife and daughter. He also
framed it with several poems from *The Book of Counted Sorrows*.
This novel, Dean felt, was one of the most frightening he had
written to date. In light of how it turned out, he stated thereafter that he would include in his Leigh Nichols books a
stronger scare factor. Then Avon identified him to their
accounts as the true author behind Nichols, so it seemed point-
less to write under two names when he could pour all his
energy into one. He wished he had placed *Shadowfires* under
his own name.

In an Afterword to his 1995 revision of *The Key to Midnight*,
Dean explained that there would be no more Leigh Nichols
novels, because Leigh had suffered a tragic end. (Actually,
Dean proposed several tragic fates for this author—killed in
an explosion at a jalapeno processing plant, a rickshaw pile-up
in Hong Kong, and a freak limbo incident.)

Told from multiple points of view, *Shadowfires*'s plot involves a Frankenstein-like inventor, geneticist Eric Leben (the German word for "life"), who makes himself into his own monster. As with the Mary Shelley story, tampering with the human condition for the wrong reasons can have dangerous results. Leben attempts to discover the secret of immortality through manipulation of genetic structures, and when he's too eager for success, he performs trial runs on himself, despite evidence that some of the experimental mice have become violent. Believing from his parents that he will go to hell when he dies, he is determined to avoid this fate by the simple expedient of living forever! He is also obsessed with youth and control. His inner life is toxic intimacy at its worst: a poisoned soul that cannot heal.

When a garbage truck hits Leben in the very first chapter and kills him, his ex-wife, Rachel, hopes she is finally free of him. She knows about his experiments, however, and certain clues, such as Leben's missing corpse, lead her to believe he has accomplished his goal. Though he was apparently dead, he is now alive again. Rachel flees with her lover, Ben Shadway, a real estate broker and Vietnam vet (who bears many similarities to Ben Chase). In pursuit are two police officers who are determined to find the connection between the disappearance of Leben's corpse and a series of murders. Leben's partner is also trying to find Rachel, as is a government agency (Defense Security Agency), led by sadist Anson Sharp, who hates Ben and who covets Leben's research. His obsessions associate him with Leben as two parallel images of evil: people of like-minded values are joined in a brotherhood. Against them stand people who oppose chaos, obsession, and destruction. Both types are family, one dysfunctional, the other the ideal of what a human family can be.

The most dangerous of Rachel's pursuers is Leben himself. Intending to hide out in Las Vegas, Rachel sets out by car across the desert, unaware that Eric is in the trunk. His genetic structure is breaking down and he is transforming into a chaos of primitive evolutionary forms that become progressively more monstrous and bloodthirsty. She manages to escape him, but all parties converge at an abandoned, decaying motel in Las Vegas, where everyone witnesses what Leben has become. They try to destroy him with fire, but it is his own need that brings him down: The mutation process requires more energy than he can feed it. His body cannibalizes itself as his metabolism races out of control—a metaphor of how his obsessions had destroyed him psychologically—until there is nothing left.

This novel expresses the belief that all people must unite against anything—monster, fanatic, dysfunctional family, corrupt government, illicit research—that threatens our humanity. Dean links child abuse to adult deviance, and shows love to be the most compelling healing force. The character types venerated in these pages are intelligent, optimistic, connected to other people, and committed to traditional values. They can grapple successfully with moral dilemmas because they are anchored in a clear sense of self and duty.

Dean's former Freudian approach to literary development returns when he places Leben's secret documents in a cellar—the prototypical symbol of the unconscious. Leben's work throws him back to the most primal id-type aggressions. He has some of Dean's father's traits: He relishes struggle but dislikes being deprived; he sees himself as favored by fate; and his intense need is embodied in the most reptilian states—a need that dehumanizes. Like Eric, Ray seemed to Dean to be chaos incarnate.

Rachel has traits that Dean sees in Gerda: She has a fondness for black humor; mocks the absurdities of life; is beautiful, smart, self-controlled, and resourceful. Ben feels good with her, as Dean does with his wife. "By some magic that he could not understand, the sight of her also relaxed him and made him feel that all was right with the world and that he, for the first time in his often lonely life, was a complete man with the hope of lasting happiness."[1] It is perhaps no surprise that Ben shares Dean's physical appearance: He is five foot eleven, with brown hair and eyes, about one hundred fifty pounds, and he hides a secret past.

The predominant literary images in this novel involve hellfire, the devil, and disintegration. Trying to cheat the devil only turns one *into* the devil. Dean also uses weather: Rain is a sign of increased emotional intensity.

Shadowfires made it to the bestsellers list, but not until 1993, when Berkley reissued it under Dean's name. It went to number one at that time in its second week on the list and remained a bestseller for eight weeks. Berkley had paid more than four times the original advance for reprint rights.

Charles de Lint in *Fantasy Review* called this novel a "top-notch thriller." Aware that Dean Koontz was the author, he admired the "lean prose," the "crackling pace," and the "strong character portrayals." Another critic, Dale Walker, thought Eric Leben one of the scariest characters Koontz had ever created. "*Shadowfires* is very strong stuff," he writes. "There are passages in it more revolting than the worst scenes in the scummiest slasher films—but the violence and blood-letting is offset by the Koontz trademark: a solid love story."

"The writing is as startling as a banshee's scream," was the comment in Parker, Colorado's *Daily News-Press*, "and the horror mounts as the pages turn." That reviewer had trouble visualizing Leben's monstrous form, but thought the terror quite compelling.

Dean was aware that critics often mentioned the violence in his books. To set the record straight, he addressed this in an interview. To fellow writer Joe Lansdale, he said, "I do believe violence in a novel should have moral purpose. It should not be used merely to titillate, but to show that violence is only a last resort and those who turn to it without compunction are sick."[2] There is a difference, he felt, between using violence to heighten the moral context and using it merely for startling effect, but showing the deleterious effects of violence on society is better than pretending that violence does not exist in our world. To call attention to violence used in a book without making that distinction he thought irresponsible.

2

After *Strangers*, Dean signed a contract with Putnam for two more novels, getting an advance of $850,000 for the pair. One was to be called *Guardian*, later changed to *Watchers* because Berkley had an action series called "Guardians." The other was *Lightning Road*, later changed to *Lightning* when Putnam wanted a one-word title.

Phyllis Grann promised a large advertising budget for the two books with verification that the money was actually spent. Few authors got as keenly involved in the marketing and production of a book as Dean, but he understood the business well enough to know that promises could be made that would never be fulfilled. Ad support was as important an issue as the advance, because it indicated the degree of the publisher's commitment and helped the author to reach new audiences.

"Dean always wants to know who he's dealing with," says Gerda, "so he makes a point of getting to know everyone involved in his production. He wants not merely to know them as business associates but as people, and to feel good about them in both senses."

The ideas for both *Watchers* and *Lightning* had occurred to Dean as he was writing *Strangers*. He was working seventy-hour weeks and longer on that book, and expected it to take six months to write. When he was six months into it, he realized that he was only half done. He was writing it entirely on spec, money was tight, and he worried. "One day, I was sort of depressed by how long *Strangers* was taking—and my mind gave me a break from it by suddenly giving me three good novel ideas in half an hour, including *Watchers* and *Lightning*. My spirits were buoyed, and I was able to go on with *Strangers*."

Ideas might also have come to him so easily because of all his background reading—not just during the writing of *Strangers*, but daily for years. He read widely in many different fields, from physics to medical technology to psychology, and subscribed to as many as seventy publications per month. He never ran out of ideas for stories, and he believed it was because he fed his subconscious such a rich diet. "I never take notes or consciously look for ideas," he says. "I dump all this information in and let the ideas boil up, and they're better than those I might come up with if I were to consciously manipulate the material. I don't force it.

"Look at the origins of something like *Watchers*," he says. He had encountered a quote from Jung, which he used at the front of *Watchers*: "The making of two personalities is like the contact of two chemical substances. If there is any reaction, both are transformed." It got him thinking. Likewise, a quote from Teilhard de Chardin, also cited in the book: "Love alone is capable of uniting living things in such a way as to complete and fulfill them, for it alone takes them and joins them by what is deepest in themselves." About those sentiments, Dean says, "I began to think about the idea that if anyone changes you dramatically, you have an effect on that person as well, and to some extent both people have changed each other. But changing who we are, how we think, what we believe—that is very hard. So the thrust of the book is how *difficult* it is to change.

"I started with that premise—that change is accomplished not so much on your own, but by finding another person who brings something to you. That person has something you need and you have something that he or she needs in terms of emotional or intellectual interaction. Together you can to some degree transform yourselves, your future, your destiny.

"Then I had a premise about an experiment in a lab, working with enhanced intelligence. A dog that escapes with a human-level intellect. That was my whole premise for the book, along with the idea that it would be about the difficulty of change in the human heart. Then I tried to imagine what sort of character would be most interesting to watch come into contact with this dog, because originally I supposed it would be the wonder of this dog that would change someone's life. That's where Travis came from. In the opening scene, he needed to be in a deep state of depression—so that meeting the dog begins the process of change and transcendence for him.

"I was into the book a couple of chapters when the thought occurred to me that something *else* had to escape from that lab, so I backed up. Then I saw that I'd already created an ominous mood. I had thought I was establishing that *people* were chasing the dog, but then I realized it wasn't people, it was something else—some *thing* else. I had thought that I would have to go back through these early manuscript pages and revise them to accommodate this new idea, but I discovered that the scene was already composed in such a way as to make it explicitly clear that something more fearsome than mere people was chasing the dog. I only had to add a line or two to heighten this.

"For me, this makes it clear that there's a subconscious at work at all times. I've also had the uncanny experience, two-thirds of the way through the writing of a book, of suddenly realizing that other themes can be woven around the central theme to great effect. All I needed to do was go back and implant them. But when I went back, I saw that they were already integrally woven! When that happens, it gives me a little shiver. And it tells me, if nothing else, that there are deeper levels of consciousness at work at all times."

Dean took eight months to write this novel, his fiftieth by his count. When he turned it in, Phyllis Grann was delighted with the story. "She loved *Watchers*," says Dean. "That was our best experience. We didn't have any disagreement about it."

Alan Williams was again the editor. He had met Dean by this time, had heard the stories of Dean's climb from poverty, and had grown to respect him. He read through the manuscript and felt it was tight. Little revision was needed, and Dean worked no more than a day or two on it.

Watchers refers to what people must be for each other: "We have a responsibility to stand over one another, we are all watchers, all of us, guarding against darkness."[3]

3

Travis Cornell, thirty-six and a former member of the U.S. Delta Force, is a man who has lost all the people he loves. He hikes into a wilderness area in Orange County—apparently with the intention of taking his own life. He encounters a golden retriever whose behavior is so unusual and compelling that Travis is drawn out of his depression. When he gradually discovers that the dog is highly intelligent, Travis names him Einstein. The dog then saves a woman, Nora Devon, from a rapist and brings her together with Travis. Although Nora is a timid woman with low self-esteem, Travis helps her to experience her beauty; in so doing, he discovers a reason to live. Together they prove that they can overcome just about anything.

They discover that Einstein is the product of the Banodyne research laboratory, which is involved in recombinant DNA research. The dog can think and communicate at a human level—except that it cannot speak—so they devise clever ways, including the use of a scrabble board, to help him get his messages across. The dog knows that another creature, The Outsider, has also escaped from the lab, and that this aggressive mutant creature was intended to be a killing machine on future battlefields. The Outsider is subtly psychically linked to Einstein, so there is no escape. Researchers from Banodyne are trying to capture both creatures, as are the FBI and a Soviet-hired hitman named Vince Nasco.

Travis and Nora change identities and flee for their lives with the dog they have come to love. When Einstein contracts distemper, they must seek a vet. The vet has an FBI bulletin, but Travis and Nora persuade him of the dog's abilities and enlist his help. Nasco tries to kill them, but they kill him instead. At the same time, The Outsider arrives and seizes Einstein. Travis corners it and recognizes that it deserves sympathy because it was bred to be evil and wants only to be accepted. In fact, it had ripped out the eyes of its victims because it viewed itself as ugly and could not tolerate the thought that its image alone conjured such terror in its victims. Even so, Travis kills it. Einstein survives, and Nora and Travis find him a mate.

This novel quickly became Dean's favorite, partly for its theme of remaking families from wounded souls. He later stated, tongue in cheek, that the dog character was modeled on himself. "I like to think that, if I were a dog, I would be as good a dog as he was." What he especially liked about creating this character, a dog with this kind of intelligence, was that he could make affectionate, bewildered comments about human society and behavior that might seem mean-spirited when coming from a human character.

The novel indicts governmental secrecy, affirms that individuals are morally superior to governments, and emphasizes that while genetic research is necessary for progressively enhancing the quality of life, without ethical accountability, there can be negative consequences.

Dean often remarked that, should he ever write a sequel to one of his novels, it would be *Watchers*. This book was also one that Gerda especially liked, along with *Whispers*. "I like them all," she says, "but those are my favorites."

Philosophically, Dean examined the concept of personhood

in this novel: He had devised an intelligent, loving, protective dog who has all the qualities of the best people, yet still must be treated as a dog. This is a throwback to science fiction days, where a central topic concerned whether aliens or androids could be regarded as persons and thus be given the same rights and privileges as human beings. Where Dean stands on this issue is quite clear: Einstein has a soul, a sense of freedom and courage, and an obvious selflessness. He is more of a "person" than Vince Nasco, and can help create family every bit as much as Travis and Nora.

This novel, along with *Shadowfires*, which was written at the same time, played with the Frankenstein myth: A scientist believes he can push the envelope, become like God, and create life. However, his experiment goes awry and his creature gets beyond his control. He has foolishly failed to foresee the possible dangers until it is too late.

In addition, there is a strong element of the Jekyll/Hyde motif. Einstein and The Outsider present the disparate parts of an entity, in this case of a laboratory. One exhibited the best traits, the other the worst. Each is merely an extension of human potential and both arise from the same source. The dog's fear of The Outsider is a person's fear of his or her own dark side—the destructive potential within, possibly genetically based. Yet the dog's potential displays what we can become. In a letter to a fan, Dean wrote, "In *Watchers*, men seek to take on God's role as creator, and the point is made, both on the surface of the story and on deeper levels, that this is a fitting thing, and that God's ultimate purpose for us may be to become His equal."

The first printing for *Watchers* was 75,000, but by the time it hit the stores, it had gone into several more printings, and had in excess of 100,000 copies in print. It was a Literary Guild Main selection. On February 15, 1987, *Watchers* entered *The New York Times* bestsellers list at number fourteen, and it spent eight weeks on the *Publishers Weekly* hardcover list, getting as high as number eight. Dean was happy and relieved. He had had the impression that the people at Putnam thought his success with *Strangers* had been a fluke, and now they could see that readers were truly responding.

Simon & Schuster bought the audio rights, and film rights

were sold to Roger Corman at New Horizons for $100,000. Dean was to regret the latter decision many times over.

Reviewers were mostly agreed that this novel had human warmth and merit. *Kirkus* called *Watchers* a fable about love and trust, "an imagistic and unusual blend of suspense and sentiment." One reviewer thought it drew heavily on the plot of the movie *Alien*, but failed to explain how, while a few thought it lacked plausibility. *Publishers Weekly* gave it very high marks and called it a cross between "Lassie," *ET*, *The Wolfen*, and *The Godfather*. Katharine Weber in *The New York Times* saw Einstein as a rich character and said, "Koontz really hits his stride." Charles de Lint in the *Ottowa Citizen* described it as "head and shoulders above standard thrillers," and noted Dean's "enviably invisible writing style that propels the story without his voice intruding." He also mentioned the strong sense of optimism. Jack Pyle called it "as refreshing as an ice cream cone in hell," while *The San Francisco Examiner* pronounced the novel "a winner," giving it a "straight 10 across the board."

In the *Orange County Register*, Vern Perry noted the point that Dean made about science and scientific research. "It isn't what science learns that is good or bad . . . but rather how that knowledge is applied." Einstein and The Outsider, he points out, show the two extremes of scientific application.

4

Although money had never been the driving motivation behind Dean's writing—"And a good thing it wasn't, because for a long time I made none!"—financial and marketing considerations had limited his creativity through the early years. Once he had felt more secure, he had quickly branched out to test the waters, writing under pseudonyms to explore genres to determine where his greatest skills might lie. Even as he wrote *Watchers*, he had other irons in the fire. Yet, as with *Strangers*, he had taken much time developing character and setting. He was happy to finally have the opportunity to thoroughly polish his work. Part of that meant shifting his sense of character from the superficial cause-effect models of much American fiction to what he felt was a deeper, more abiding character development. From the moment he began to write *Watchers*, he knew that everything was changing for him—his career path, his view of what motivates human behavior, and his experience with the writing process itself.

As he had fully immersed, he had experienced a heightened feeling of productivity. As always, the book had been difficult to write, but toward the last third, when he had gained a clear sense of direction and simultaneous feelings of control and spontaneity, he had an incredible experience. Most of this book had taken eight months, but the last part moved quickly. "It just flew," Dean says.

It began in Part Two, Section Nine, where Einstein grew ill. Dean began to write and did not stop, save for one break, for two days. "I got up one morning and went to work. I ate a sandwich at my desk, kept going, worked around the clock, and finally fell into bed the next evening, totally exhausted. I slept that night, and the next morning got up and worked twenty-four hours straight. In the first session, which was about thirty-six hours, I wrote something like forty pages. In the second session, I wrote around forty pages in even less time. That's about thirty thousand words in two sessions, and it needed almost no revision."

What Dean had experienced is what University of Chicago professor and psychologist Mihaly Csikszentmihalyi calls "Flow." He had first studied the phenomenon of intrinsically motivated experiences with surgeons and mountaineers who reported a feeling of great joy from complete immersion in what they were doing. He then expanded it to creativity studies. "Action follows upon action," Csikszentmihalyi stated, "according to an internal logic that seems to need no conscious intervention by the actor. He experiences it as a unified flowing from one moment to the next, in which he is in control of his actions, and in which there is little distinction between self and environment, between stimulus and response, or between past, present, and future."[4]

Closely associated with Japanese Zen practices, it is what athletes called being "in the groove," "playing out of one's head," or being "pumped up" or "wired." Others have called it "peak performance," the "optimum performance state," "the zone," or the "white moment." It is the context for excellence, involving a sense of effortlessness which results in one's best work. A tennis player might reach an "impossible" ball or an artist turn out a painting in hours that might usually have taken days or weeks. There is a difference between this experience and simply writing hack work quickly. It has to do with state of mind, combined with skill, confidence, and experience.

Creativity and energy feed each other at such times, minimizing external distractions to the point of perceptual nonexistence. The person in Flow can perform for hours without noticing hunger, external noises, or room temperature. Time seems simultaneously to be faster and slower. The individual feels utterly unified with the task at hand. He is totally present. "The dancer becomes the dance," said author Louis L'Amour. "I am the writing."

Flow stretches a person beyond his usual limits. It bonds him with his work, and yields both euphoria and stamina. "Flow," wrote Csikszentmihalyi, "is the way people describe their state of mind when consciousness is harmoniously ordered, and they want to pursue whatever they are doing for its own sake."[5] Although it appears to be effortless, it evolves from discipline. The best conditions come from a good balance of focus, motivation, organization, vision, energy, and the ability to allow inner resources to be freely expressed.

Centering attention on the merging of action and awareness distorts one's perception of time and blocks self-consciousness. An easy, yet intense, rhythm develops. Thought and motion become single-minded intention. The individual just lets go and operates as if on automatic pilot. He is an instrument of the work. People in Flow report feeling "most alive" or "at full throttle"—a sense of having been transported into a new, sharper reality.

"If I could do that all the time," says Dean, "I could write a book in ten days and it would be of higher quality than what comes with endless struggle. You look at something like what happened with *Watchers* and say it's uncanny. How is it possible for me to write at the same level on those pages when I struggled with all these other pages at the rate of two or three a day? When I look at the results, it's actually better than stuff that I worked on for a longer period of time.

"Those are the moments that seem like a form of meditation, or a connection with something else. It's phenomenal.

Time ceases to have meaning. I worked all day and right through the night and into the following afternoon—yet it was only in the last hour or two that I began to feel tired. Then I crashed totally. There was no sense of weariness, no sense of time passing. You look at your watch and think it's been two hours and it's been ten or twelve. That is definitely an altered state of consciousness. You have this ebullient, joyful feeling.

"It always looks self-destructive, working like that, and I could never make people—even most other writers—understand that it was not something you totally controlled. Everything is coming to you in an avalanche and you're not able to get up and walk away. You're so into it that you don't even realize how long you've been there. It doesn't happen as often as I'd like. When it does happen, you have to take advantage of it. Stay on the sleigh ride as long as it lasts! Pretty soon, the longer you do it, the greater the momentum, and you remain in that state."

5

In England, Tim Hely Hutchinson had started Headline Book Publishing in 1986 with two colleagues. "We had known of Dean Koontz's work for some time," he says, "and he was very much on our 'wish list' of authors we would love to publish, if only we had the chance. To our delight, Dean's agent sent us the typescript of *Watchers* only months after Headline had opened its doors for business. This was extraordinary, because Dean's books were already selling well for his existing publisher, W.H. Allen. We later came to understand that W.H. Allen had rejected *Watchers* on the basis that it was different from his previous novels and could therefore alienate his established readership."

As group chief executive, Hutchinson had the opposite opinion. "*Watchers* was indeed different," he affirms, "but even better and, far from being the book to sink him, it was the book with which to break him through onto mainstream bestseller lists. It was polished, sophisticated, and grippingly page-turning. It had a brilliant 'combination punch' and wholly satisfying ending. Headline bid in the usual British publishing telephone auction—and won."

Hutchinson found that *Watchers* performed exactly as he had predicted, which boosted the standing of Headline. "The importance of this for a small start-up publishing company (now one of Britain's largest) cannot be overestimated."

Headline went on to publish Dean's subsequent novels, often getting them into print quickly. They also published a number of novels from Dean's backlist.

"Dean Koontz," says Hutchinson, "is a most delightful author with whom to work. To me, he is warm, funny, charming, and profoundly thoughtful. He is immensely well read. Charles Dickens has a special place in his literary pantheon and Dickens' influence is traceable in a number of ways. I am thinking of the importance of relationships, the intrusion of humor into almost every circumstance, the compelling narrative, and the flashes of pure poetry."

6

Dean had two articles on writing that year in J. N. Williamson's nonfiction anthology, *How to Write Tales of Horror, Fantasy, and Science Fiction*. In one, "Keeping the Reader on the Edge of His Seat," Dean discusses how to prolong suspense and plant subliminal images to inject more emotional impact into a story. In the other, "Why Novels of Fear Must Do More than Frighten," he emphasizes the importance of developing character and evoking a range of emotions.

7

Dean urged his agent to approach Pocket to repurchase the rights to his Leigh Nichols novels. The first Leigh Nichols book had been bought by Phyllis Grann when she was at Pocket Books, but she had left, and other editors were less enthused. Shipping problems had taken the edge off sales on *The Eyes of Darkness*, and the executives at Pocket gradually had lost interest in promoting Leigh Nichols. By the time Dean looked into buying back the rights, Pocket was disinterested enough to hand them over without compensation. "They really aren't worth anything," he was told. Insulting as this was, Dean capitalized on it by reselling the rights to Berkley for paperback and to Dark Harvest for hardcover, reissuing them under his own name. "We got the books back," he says, "and I don't think it was more than two years later that Berkley bought all these for half a million per book. The first one they reissued was *The Servants of Twilight*, which spent six weeks at number one on the paperback bestsellers list. That was an enormously satisfying moment. And it's an instructive lesson to young writers. First, always consider your copyrights as valuable properties. Second, don't assume that publishers have any idea of what is valuable and what is not."

8

To the 120,000-word *Twilight Eyes* that Dean had written for Chris Zavisa's Land of Enchantment Press in 1984, he added an 80,000-word sequel.

Juxtaposing events and music from 1964 with the characters' moods, the second part opens with Slim learning about the Kitty Genovese murder in New York, in which thirty-eight people had turned deaf ears to her screams for help, had even watched from their windows as she was repeatedly stabbed. This self-protective, self-centered inhumanity seems unbearable to Slim. He and Rya decide that their work against the goblins is not over. Like the neighbors of Kitty Genovese, if they know of the murderous evil in their midst and do nothing to stop it, they are guilty of the crime of passivity. So they return to Yontstown, Pennsylvania, to kill more goblins. They discover that the Lightning Coal Company is the central nest, and with the help of seventy-four-year-old Horton Bluett, they infiltrate and blast it open. Five hundred goblins die, but their attackers recognize that this is only one of many such goblin centers. The goblins have built shelters against a nuclear holocaust that they plan to launch against humanity. They then intend to destroy themselves.

On their way out of the tunnels leading from the demolished shelter, Slim and Rya are injured. Slim believes that Rya is dead, but he carries her as far as he can. Bluett rescues them and Rya returns to life. Slim thinks he may have healed her with powers inherited from his mother. He decides that, rather than risk Rya again, he will leave the goblins alone for now.

Given the healing power of Slim's mother, there seems little doubt that *Twilight Eyes* is indeed a story of Dean's inner cleansing. Having purified his father's image via transforming Rya (Ray), he now uses his mother's legacy of love and kindness to make her whole. He can thus retain hope as a pillar of life—for himself and in his general outlook. Just as the sixties generated both tragedy and bubbly music, so too does Slim's life show how darkness and light can coexist, how terror and hope are constant companions. "Hope . . . is the most pathetic and noblest thing about us, the most absurd and most admirable quality we possess, for as long as we have hope, we also have the capacity for love, for caring, for decency."[6]

Twilight Eyes spent six weeks on the paperback bestsellers list, beginning on April 30, and got as high as number nine.

9

Four of Dean's short stories came out in 1987, one in Dave Silva's *The Horror Show*. The other three were collected together in Dark Harvest's *Night Visions 4*.

The Horror Show devoted another issue to Dean in which they printed an amusing interview of him by his own pseudonym, Leigh Nichols. Dean also revised his 1972 "Ollie's Hands," and provided a new story, "The Interrogation." In this tale, the police interview a man who has murdered his wife— again! She is an immortal succubus who is stealing his essence. He describes the various forms of symbiotic relationships and claims that she is a parasite. He wants to be free of her, but fears she will suck him dry.

"Miss Atilla the Hun" is about a valiant schoolteacher, Laura Caswell, and a boy from a bad home who has a crush on her. Laura saves her students from an ancient, life-sucking, chaos-wreaking, plant-like alien called "Seed." She is like the guardians in Dean's young life—his mother, Winona Garbrick, Gerda—whose strength and caring had saved him from being devoured by chaos. Laura tells the boy that no matter what kind of home he is from, he always has the capacity to do better. When they defeat the alien, Laura retrieves from it the power to heal. Dean revised this and the other two stories in *Night Visions 4* for his 1995 collection, *Strange Highways*.

"Hardshell" is another disguised struggle between father and son. Detective Frank Shaw has the reputation of having a hard shell but a soft heart. He gets drawn into a battle with Skagg, an unusual type of serial killer: an alien that is seemingly invincible. In a plot that is almost a dress rehearsal for *Dark Rivers of the Heart*, the two of them are linked by virtue of being of the same species, but Frank lives in peace with humankind, while Skagg is a mad degenerate. Frank knows that existence without self-control is only chaos, and that love, which cannot coexist with chaos, is the force of stability and order. Frank uses his wiles to absorb and defeat Skagg, as Dean would do repeatedly in his fiction to the part of himself that linked him to his father.

The title of "Twilight of the Dawn" came from the H. G. Wells quote that Dean had used for *Strangers* (and mentioned within the story). He considers this tale to be semiautobiographical in that it features a protagonist who goes through various attitudes toward religion and who, via an experience of the uncanny, ultimately comes to understand the possibility of greater spiritual dimensions. Dean himself had gone from Protestant to Catholic to atheist to agnostic, ultimately believing in the existence of God.

The protagonist, architect Pete Fallon, has frequent arguments with his wife, Ellen, over how he treats his seven-year-old son's desire to believe in things like Santa Claus, angels, and heaven. Ellen thinks Benny should be allowed his fantasies, but Pete believes firmly in a rational, mechanistic universe and wants to raise the boy as a realist. Religion, he insists, is for the weak-minded, a cult of ignorance and irrationality. Faith in God is tantamount to a stain, stealing self-reliance and intellectual integrity.

Then Ellen dies in a car accident and Benny wants to believe she has gone to heaven. Pete is determined to steer the boy in the right direction. When Benny is afflicted with bone cancer, Pete at last must confront how important it can be to envision a higher power. Even so, he stubbornly refuses to yield, even as Benny begs from his deathbed for his father to look for them in heaven.

Alone, Pete gives up his work, feeling the loss of any purpose. He goes out to a cherry tree where he had once spent time with Benny, and suddenly the tree drops its blossoms—all of them at once. As if that is not strange enough, the next morning, the blossoms are back on the tree and they fall again. In that moment, Pete knows that Benny has sent him a sign; death is not the end.

The innocence of the boy has brought the father into the promise of redemption, although he still cannot take the final step of total belief. Like Dean with Ray, no matter how much the boy wants his father to be like him, no matter how much he himself believes it could happen, there is something in the father that cannot give in. Yet the boy never gives up. He cannot. Neither could Dean. Angry as he was at his father, he was attached by blood to this man and he needed to invite him, at least psychologically, into a realm where change and redemption were possible. Benny could do this with an uncanny experience; Dean was left with only the need to act in a manner different from his father. Keeping Ray in his care at least modeled for his father a kindness that was possible, even if Ray could never comprehend what this might mean.

One of the interesting psychological angles in this story is Dean's awareness of how a person's firm struggle to resist becoming just like a parent can result in exactly the thing he or she wants to avoid. Pete had so detested the fanatical religion of his parents that he had become just as fanatical an atheist. Because he was so sure he was opposing them, he was blind to how like them he was. This part of the story serves as a double mirror: to those who believe that it is a simple thing to escape family influence, and to those atheists who believe that their behavior has no similarity to people who are religious.

"It's always been interesting to me," Dean says, "that of all the atheists I've ever known, I have seen them react to issues as if they believe there's a God. And I've never seen an atheist who fails to have a sense of the uncanny, but they never recognize it as being at odds with their professed lack of belief. They have an appreciation at the unconscious level of the wonder of the universe that is hard to explain in a mechanistic manner.

I've heard atheists, enraptured, talk about the wonders of nature, using words like 'miraculous.'

"I'm always amazed at how many people will argue against God by saying that evolution proves there is no God. I don't discount the theory of evolution, but I don't think it throws out the idea of a created universe. Evolution could be the mechanism by which God works.

"Likewise, it amazes me when someone says, well, if God was beneficent the world wouldn't be full of suffering. This assumes that one can know the meaning of life and can *know* that suffering is without value or purpose. But look how often we learn from our pain, how often we grow and change and mature because of our suffering. Ultimately, you take it on faith or not, but you can't argue against God's existence with those flimsy issues.

"Part of the power of the story is the redemption of the father through the son's innocence. The little boy is the teacher that the father needs, but he's not just going to grab at faith when he needs it, and in the end he's still resisting. He believes that he is going to meet his wife and son again, but he won't take that final step and admit there's a God. I think the story works because he bullheadedly retains a degree of skepticism."

When Dean finished this story, he told himself that he would one day base an entire novel on this sense of the uncanny. That book, *Sole Survivor*, would not be published for ten more years, but when he finally wrote it, the story was more ambitious than he had originally envisioned.

10

While Dean and Gerda were going through a trying time with Ray and his incessant demands, Gerda ran across an article in a woman's magazine about fertility experiments. She noted that the first artificial insemination experiments had been conducted in 1944, the year before Dean had been born, and that some of the initial trials were conducted through a university hospital in Maryland. Because the nature of these experiments was controversial, the physicians had used couples who were likely to be discreet: those with no more than a high school education, childless, in the lower economic classes, and living in rural areas in Pennsylvania. Such women, profiles predicted, would be most likely to honor confidentiality clauses.

Gerda felt it was a perfect description of Dean's own mother. She brought it to Dean's attention, and began to think more seriously about the possibility that Ray might not be Dean's biological father. His parents had always called him a "miracle child," because they had been told they could not have children; his father had not fathered other children in all his adulterous liaisons (Dean did not know then about his mother's numerous miscarriages); Dean bore no physical resemblance to Ray; the sperm donors had been highly creative people, such as composers and writers, while no one in Dean's family had shown this kind of talent; Florence had tried to tell Dean something before she died about his father — something he "had to know." Perhaps that he was not Dean's father after all? It all seemed logically to add up.

"What I found interesting," says Dean, "was that my mother couldn't seem to have a baby until she went to a certain doctor. He was a GP, but GPs didn't have procedures in those days to help women get pregnant. Yet if it was by artificial insemination, the institution would have needed local doctors to liaison between them and their patients."

Yet if Florence had indeed volunteered for such a procedure, she kept it even from her sisters. Nancy Eckard, who listened to Dean's Aunt Kate talk about all of Florence's birth difficulties, claims she never said a word about this possibility.

The idea continued to intrigue Dean, but he also had not given up the idea that his Uncle Ray might be his father. He had not forgotten the mysterious conversation he had heard between Uncle Ray and his mother.

11

After *Watchers* was published, *People* magazine featured an article on Dean. They sent a photographer, Jim McHugh, who spent three days taking pictures from various angles. After the first hour of the first shooting session, he said to Dean, "You're a child of an alcoholic, aren't you? I can tell because you need to be in control."

There followed a conversation about adult children of alcoholics—a cultural awakening that was sweeping the country via group therapy, books, and workshops. Dean listened to what the photographer had to say and began to better understand his obsessive-compulsive drive, his need to create a stable environment, his fear of flying, and his inability to believe that his success had a firm foundation. McHugh explained to him the traits that many people who have come from such homes share, and Dean's subsequent reading provided the rest: they often block out pain with some other addiction; they excel at things they can control; frequently they feel insecure; they tend to hope for the best but expect the worst; they take care of others before themselves; they find self-worth largely through work; they allow others to demand too much of them; they have a need to appear picture-perfect; they are survivors; and they tend to fear a return to the chaos and desperation that they once had known. Yet, often, they set themselves up to do just that.

Dean understood that his father's addictions and mental illness had affected him profoundly. His father's periods of rage or tense silence, the uncertainty, the emotional abuse—all of these had influenced who he was and who he could become unless he shaped his own life with an iron will. To be driven and addicted to his work was not a bad thing, as long as he found some balance: to keep some semblance of control, to excel, to be a survivor. These were positive things if kept in perspective. The difficulty was to avoid giving in to the negative forces spawned by that background. He knew he would struggle against those the rest of his life.

He realized that he and his mother both had been codependent through those years of hardship, enabling Ray to continue with his behavior by rescuing him from bars, not expressing their own needs, and generally allowing the situation to persist. To some extent, Dean thought, even now as an adult, his care for Ray might have an element of codependence.

Not long afterward, Dean had cause to see how dangerous his father really was. Ray had suffered a stroke a few years earlier and was aphasic, but he was still capable of living on his own and was still physically powerful. Through the years, he had continued with his habit of calling Dean and Gerda at night to take him to the hospital. Finally Dean decided to try to put a stop to this by going over to Ray's apartment one night and just sitting there with him. If he really needed a doctor, then Dean would take him, but otherwise, he was not going anywhere. Ray insisted on going to the hospital, but Dean refused. He knew that what his father was after was the attention he got from the hospital staff, but he did not want to take the chance that the one time he decided not to come would be the time something was *really* wrong. So to cure Ray of these incessant calls that amounted to nothing, Dean drove him crazy by just coming over and being with him. That was not what Ray wanted.

Dean waited until dawn, and then went home to sleep. The following day, on September 6, 1987, Gerda went over on her own. Ray again asked to go to the hospital and she refused. He grew angry, and at one point, he got out the butcher knife for no apparent purpose. Immediately she left to go pay his rent. She alerted Dean to this event, and when they went back later together, they were watchful. Dean reluctantly agreed to take Ray yet one more time to the hospital. "But if it turns out, as always," he said, "that your symptoms are psychological, then you'll have to move from this apartment to a retirement home with closer supervision."

The problem was that Ray often overdosed—or sometimes simply did not take his medication. Eager to get to an emergency room and be the center of the nurses' attention, Ray agreed to the terms.

Dean turned toward the door, but out of the corner of his eye, he saw Ray's hand stray to check his pants pocket. "When I looked back, he still had his hand there and between two spread fingers, I could see this shape. I asked him what was in his pocket."

Ray pulled out a yellow-handled fishing knife with obvious violent intent, and Dean had to wrestle it away from him. Dean and Gerda then took Ray to be evaluated. He was in the hospital for ten days, and they learned that he was suffering from degenerative alcohol syndrome. He would need to start taking antipsychotic medicine.

At that time, Dean considered asking the doctors to run a DNA analysis, to determine if he really was Ray's son. Even if he was not, he knew he would continue to care for this man because someone had to do it. Gerda encouraged him, but he put it off.

They were faced with having to move Ray to a more secure place, so they chose Casa Orange Retirement Home. The ordeal, however, was far from over.

[1]Dean Koontz writing as Leigh Nichols, *Shadowfires* (New York: Avon, 1987), p. 32.

[2]Joe R. Lansdale, "Dean of Suspense," *The Twilight Zone*, (December 1986), p. 23.

[3]Dean R. Koontz, *Watchers* (New York: Putnam, 1987), p. 419.

[4]Mihaly Csikszentmihalyi, *Beyond Boredom and Anxiety* (San Francisco: Jossey-Bass, 1975), p. 36.

[5]Mihaly Csikszentmihalyi, *Flow: The Psychology of Optimal Experience* (New York: Harper & Row, 1990), p. 6.

[6]Dean R. Koontz, *Twilight Eyes* (New York: Berkley, 1987), p. 183.

EIGHTEEN

Fate

1

THE YEAR AFTER JIM BAKKER'S SCANDAL, RELIGIOUS LEADER Jimmy Swaggart resigned for sexual misconduct, tearfully begging his flock's forgiveness. It seemed that no one could be trusted. The first black presidential candidate, Jesse Jackson, won five state primaries and made history for black Americans. By 1988, male life expectancy was seventy-six years, female was seventy-eight, and a loaf of bread cost about seventy-six cents—unless it was designer bread.

The following year brought a major world shift that influenced suspense writers everywhere, particularly those, like Dean, who had occasionally used the Cold War as a plot device. East Germany opened the Berlin Wall and many of its citizens fled toward democracy. It was not long before the two sides of this divided city were reunited and the breakdown of Soviet domination over smaller countries was at hand. When Dean revised some of his novels, he had to make changes in accord with the new world that was taking shape in response to the diminished threat from this totalitarian regime.

It was also the year that Iran's Ayatollah Khomeini offered five million dollars for the murder of writer Salman Rushdie, who went into hiding. Many American writers spoke out in Rushdie's defense. Khomeini died, but the issue of free speech remained alive. San Francisco suffered a major earthquake, New York endured brutal gang "wildings," and Russia prepared for its first presidential elections.

Dean wanted to name his next novel for Putnam *Lightning Road*, but the publisher thought it sounded too much like a book about stock cars. Reluctantly he shortened it to *Lightning*, in the tradition of the one-word titles of his two previous bestsellers, although he did not think it was apt or evocative. He had been inspired by the idea while writing *Strangers*, and he wanted to develop the plot with a form of characterization that looked to Dickens for its motivation. The story follows the main character, Laura Shane, from childhood into her thirties, when she becomes a successful author. The challenge was to maintain a gripping level of suspense in spite of the story's long time frame.

Laura is a forceful woman, with a strength born of adversity and common sense. Much of her character derives from Dean himself: her writing and research methods, her determination, and her life philosophies. She was one in a succession of strong female characters in his books. "I tend to like and respond to women," he says. "I get a lot of mail from female readers who say they don't know another male writer who gets into a woman's head so well."

Laura's best friend is Thelma, one of a set of twins who has a self-mocking sense of humor and an ability to bring light into darkness. For her, as for Dean and Gerda, humor is a defense against life itself. Thelma becomes a famous stand-up comic, and throughout the book her relationship with Laura creates an atmosphere of warmth.

A third character who embodies some of the author's qualities is twelve-year-old Christopher, Laura's son, who loves science fiction, is devoted to his mother, and who understands thoroughly the various paradoxes of time travel.

Driving the plot is the ambiguity over whether the force of destiny will have positive or negative consequences. Laura Shane has a secret admirer from another era who travels through time to become her guardian. Whenever he arrives to save her from trouble, such as a physician's mishandling of her birth, he is accompanied by the sound of thunder and the crack of lightning. He warns her of imminent danger from assassins arriving from his own time. Although one of his interventions had failed to save her husband's life, Laura must trust him not only for her own sake, but to save her son.

Laura's mysterious guardian is Stefan Krieger from the past—Nazi Germany—a twist on time travel of which science fiction writer Gregory Benford said, "I thought I had thought of every angle in my novel, *Timescape*, but that one was innovative."

Stefan is an unlikely hero in that he is a Nazi with a stained soul. However, his inherent goodness, deep remorse, and love for Laura motivate him to try to set things right for her and for the world at large—in hopes of redemption. Yet the paradoxes of time travel prevent him from protecting Laura as well as he would like. She dies, and Stefan must figure out a way to work through the twists of paradox to defy destiny, reverse the damage, change the course of his future, and therefore "undo" Laura's death. The twists and turns of Stefan's struggle give *Lightning* one of Dean's most clever plots. Simultaneously, Stefan's knowledge of the future gives the Allies what they need to defeat Hitler, but they also destroy the time travel gate in Berlin, stranding Stefan in Laura's era. Eventually she accepts him as her lover, which allows destiny to assert itself in a more life-enhancing way. No matter which way destiny has turned, ultimately it becomes a literary tool for reinforcing a sense of purpose and optimism.

When Dean turned in the manuscript, he felt that he had stretched himself and had written a unique and powerful novel. To his surprise, Phyllis Grann was unhappy with it. She was concerned that the three-decade time line of the novel vitiated the suspense, and that the first quarter of the novel, dealing with the lead character's childhood, made it feel too much like a young adult novel. And it was demonstrably *not* horror, which was how she thought Dean should be marketed. Believing it would be harmful to his career momentum, she wanted to shelve *Lightning* for seven years and have him write a different book.

Dean knew that Phyllis Grann had good instincts and had built many writers into bestsellers. She had a solid reputation for that. Yet he was not about to let go of this novel. "I couldn't understand what was so radical about it," says Dean. "Short time frames in suspense work well—but there's no reason tension can't be maintained in a hundred-year time frame. Perhaps I didn't share her prejudice because I'd read so many science fiction novels with *very* long time frames that were nonetheless gripping. As far as the character being a child for the whole opening segment, what about *Oliver Twist*?"

In short, the objections were that *Lightning* had no ticking clock, which most suspense stories require; a lot of space was devoted to developing the lead character's childhood; the convoluted plot demanded too much from readers; and the male lead had a dark past. Dean resisted conforming to these "rules of fiction" and, ultimately, Putman agreed to publish the novel as a follow-up to his success with *Watchers*.

"If you don't hang on to your vision, no one will hang on to it for you. If you didn't have a vision, you'd be pulled in eighteen directions. If I'd slavishly done all that I've been asked to do by editors, I'd have never had a bestselling career. So with this book, I insisted that it had to be published, not in seven years, but on the original schedule. *Lightning* was a bear of a book to write because I was developing an idea that had never been used before—time travel from the past instead of from the future—plus a *very* unusual mix of genres. To pull that off was monumentally difficult. There were days when I thought my head was going to burst, keeping all the paradoxes straight. I had put so much work into it, so I was determined that it would be published on a timely basis."

Nevertheless, Dean worried about his publisher's reaction and mentioned it to fellow writer, Ed Gorman. Ed was the editor of *Mystery Scene* magazine, a writer of mystery and suspense, and a longtime fan of Dean's. They had started talking on the phone regularly a few years earlier, and Dean had trusted Ed's judgment enough to send him a copy of the manuscript to read.

"It's a fantastic book," Gorman assured him. "It's going to be your most popular novel to date." Gorman felt that the book was structurally sophisticated and took risks that no writer had taken before. "It's about fate," he said, "and American writers just don't write about fate. It's accepted in European literature, but not in American. No one since Thornton Wilder has seriously used fate as a theme."

They went on to discuss at length the concept of fate in literature, and Dean felt better because Gorman had grasped the essence of the novel so clearly.

Later, in a letter to a reader, Dean mentioned this issue of fate: "I believe there is a certain pattern to the universe and that life has meaning, and I think that our species' intellect is the link with God by which we will approach a state of grace here on Earth ... If God exists, He provided us with high intelligence so we could question, reflect, and struggle to find and understand Him; the application of that intelligence in probing the world around us is perhaps a more sincere expression of faith than endless hours of prayer."

Dean's editor for *Lightning* was Stacy Creamer. He thought she was ebullient, amusing, and smart. "Good editors listen," he says. "They don't suggest changes merely because they feel they have to. They can let good writing alone. They can speak frankly. The worst thing an editor can do is cut or rewrite something without the author's express permission. I don't think I spent more than a day or two responding to Stacy's notes. She never had many notes—but what notes she had were good and to the point."

"I took him on with some trepidation," Stacy Creamer recalls, "because it's always hard for a writer to get a new editor. It's such a personal involvement. Dean is a dream to edit. I called him Dean the Dream. Sometimes with bestselling authors, the more successful they are, the less they like to get edited, but Dean was always game for a thoughtful reading. Most of his work becomes like a word search—just try to find something that needs editing or trimming. I try to be an honest reader. I'd send line notes and he'd take about half of them. I always felt comfortable that I would get a fair hearing. The real writers are the ones who become more engaged with the process."

The first printing was set at 110,000, but to Dean's disappointment, when bookstores sold out, it was not immediately restocked. He would go into a store and see the space for his book standing empty. Booksellers he knew complained to him that they could not get copies from the publisher. Puzzled, Dean decided to do some detective work. A friend looked up the computer records of bookstore chains across the country and reported back that there were no copies at the major supplier warehouses. Dean grew more alarmed.

"I was nuts," he said. "Here we were with breakthrough potential and no one was doing anything about it. So I wrote a detailed memo for my agent. She passed it along to Putnam, but they denied it. They were reprinting in increments of ten thousand and getting them out, but the general attitude was, if stock is thin, that makes the bookseller realize the book is selling, and they'll order more."

Dean was not happy with this philosophy—but even more unhappy that Claire Smith seemed disinclined to take his complaints seriously or check out the facts. He felt that she was too much of a partisan for the publisher, and that the lack of supply was causing the book to lose momentum. "She actually admitted to me that she didn't take me seriously until her husband, in talking to a bookseller, discovered the store couldn't get copies from Putnam.

"There are certain times when everything is clicking," he says, "and if you don't seize the moment, it may never come again."

Lightning jumped onto *The New York Times* bestsellers list on January 24, at number fifteen. The next week it hit number nine. It stayed on the list for ten weeks, getting as high as six. On the *Publishers Weekly* list, it got to number four. This was a major achievement for Dean. Now he had three hardcover bestsellers in a row, one of them getting close to the coveted number one position. With the tremendous success of *Watchers* in paperback, there was some hope that the next novel might just do it. Despite the problem with short supplies in the stores, *Lightning* had done relatively well. With 251,000 copies shipped, it just missed being one of the top fifteen books of the year in sales.

Among reviewers, many comparisons were made between Dean and Stephen King, particularly King's novel, *Tommyknockers*. Some had the impression from the dust jacket that Putnam was intentionally marketing Dean as the next Stephen King. Dean resisted the comparison because he felt their writing styles and philosophies were quite different, and he had no intention of being viewed as an imitator. King was primarily supernatural horror with a pessimistic tone, while Dean wrote his way through more realistic scenarios with an optimistic approach. Often critics took as horror what was closer to science fiction.

The West Coast Review of Books thought *Lightning* was a well-plotted, suspenseful tale, while *The New York Times* said Koontz had energized an otherwise cliché of stock horror opening scenes. The Associated Press called it "brilliant . . . both challenging and entertaining." A "Koontz formula" was beginning to appear to the reviewer for *The San Francisco Chronicle*, of likable characters getting through threat and hardship. He called the novel well choreographed with outstanding plot twists. Many reviewers noted the innovative plot and liked the characters—especially that Dean had developed a strong and credible female lead character who was able to carry the book.

When Dean heard from readers, males told him they had found it highly romantic.

In paperback the following April, *Lightning* went to number two on the *Times* mass market list, and number one on *Publishers Weekly*'s list.

Putnam made an offer for Dean's next book, but he rejected it. Then Warner began to court Dean with better figures, but Putnam outbid them and signed Dean for three more books. Though he had no title, plot, or single line of print, Grann offered him $1 million per book. It seemed to Dean and Gerda a fantastic sum of money.

They were in the kitchen when Dean received the offer. Gerda was in the process of whittling down the handle of a six-dollar sponge mop to make it fit the head. She looked at what she was doing—they could just go buy a new mop!—and they laughed together at this incredible news. They could stop being so frugal. Indeed, they *could* have stopped years earlier, but "once poor, never rich."

Dean let friends know, and he was surprised at some of the reactions he heard from other writers. "A number of writers I knew said to me very seriously and very excitedly, 'When you finish this contract, you'll never have to write again.' That was such an astounding thing to say. I'd never written for money. Through a lot of lean years, I'd kept going, expecting nothing, writing for the love of it. Why would I ever stop, money or not? But I began to realize there were a lot of people who would look at it that way. They think money will make them happy. I'm happy to have the money, but I never thought the money was going to make me happy. With money, I still have the same problems, the same worries and fears. I just now know I can pay for things. That doesn't make a very big difference, but it's hard to make anyone understand. The money is fun, but in the end, it doesn't change your life. If you're unhappy poor, you're going to be unhappy when you're rich."

2

Only one short story appeared in 1988, "Graveyard Highway" in *Tropical Chills*. A commuter on the Costa Mesa Freeway in

California suddenly spots a vast graveyard along the west side—where he knows no such cemetery exists. Then he begins to see death everywhere he looks. What happens to him changes his focus from angry political activism to a desire to put all his effort into affirming life through art.

In an Introduction to Dark Harvest's *Dark Visions 6*, later published by Berkley as *The Bone Yard*, Dean wrote a controversial account of the state of contemporary horror. He insisted that the effect of good horror should be as profound as that of any type of fiction, and used the example of William Peter Blatty's *The Exorcist* to make his point. It does more than tell a scary story, he said. In spite of what he saw as its stylistic shortcomings, he felt that *The Exorcist* had enormous emotional impact, thematic integrity, and *soul*. In contrast, he dismissed much horror writing seventeen years after the publication of that novel as trash; these books, he felt, have nothing to say to the mind and heart. "Too many writers have turned away from their responsibilities as storytellers and craftsmen and artists, and instead of honing their talent and skills through hard work and polish, have tried to hold the reader by repeatedly shocking him, laying on the gore and violence with the misguided notion that vividly portrayed evisceration can substitute for storytelling, that splatter can compensate for lousy writing."[1] It seemed to him that the predominant theme was nihilism, which was nothing more than an adolescent conceit.

He lay the blame for much of the problem with fan conventions, which familiarized writers with the style and criticism of amateurs. "Subtexts cannot exist in a creative vacuum," he claimed.[2] Writers who see bad writing praised in fan magazines tend to copy that style in order to win similar accolades for themselves. The genre cannot survive, he believed, by feeding on lies about writing. Writers must be honest about the quality of the work and strive toward greater depth and skill in their presentation of all aspects of the human condition.

These were some of the reasons that he continued to resist being classified as a horror writer, and he insisted to his publisher that they leave the horror label off his book covers. To be thus identified meant to be associated with everything that a genre represents—even its worst elements—and to be

limited to that genre. He had no intention of being thus cor-
ralled.

"He felt that we were trying to pigeonhole him," admits
Stacy Creamer. "In some respects, that's right. Phyllis Grann
wants to turn out a good product year after year. The readership comes to expect something, and she wants to succeed a
little better every year with every author. She does it the way
she knows how, and I think Dean felt restricted by that. But
ultimately we did what he wanted to do."

3

When *Twilight Eyes* was published in 1985, Chris Zavisa came
up with an idea for another book for Land of Enchantment
and decided to approach Dean about possibilities. He had seen
how well faddish children's toys like Strawberry Shortcakes
and he-man action figures had sold. He wanted to enjoy that
kind of success. "I wanted to create the next big thing," he
says, "so I came up with this concept of Stuffins and ran it by
Phil Parks, and he came up with some drawings."

Chris mentioned to Dean that he had another idea, and Dean
warned him that his schedule was full, but he was willing to listen. He was interested in doing another project with Phil Parks.

"Chris's idea," Dean recalls, "was about a toymaker who
makes magic toys that can talk. And some evil business is buying out his company or crushing him in some way. The story
was to be about how he uses his magic toys to win out over the
big company."

Dean thought about it and began to offer his own suggestions.
"One of the things that keeps you fresh as a writer," says Dean, "is
trying to do something new and different. So when this idea came
up, I hesitated, but only briefly. It sounded like fun."

"Dean introduced the evil characters," says Chris. "He said
we needed suspense and an antagonist. So Phil did some drawings of bad characters."

"The best children's books in my estimation have a very
dark side to them," Dean explains. "Kids not only roll with
that—they love it. I wanted it to be a story about damaged kids
having magical protectors. The idea was that if this all had

worked on a bigger level, the sequels would have followed the toys on their journeys with children in troubled homes. We would have adventure stories about how they bring the child through turmoil. I think it could have been a wonderful series."

They all wanted this to be as big as possible, so Dean turned it over to Claire Smith to sell, and Warner Books made a good offer. Dean had the name "Stuffins" checked out, and it turned out to have been trademarked already by Hallmark as a name for toys. So they changed the name of their toy characters to "Oddkins."

"I started painting the characters before Dean started writing," Phil Parks recalls. "I sent him characters in various poses. Dean had a definite idea for the main bad guy. He wanted a marionette reminiscent of Fred Astaire but with evil overtones. I named a few of the characters, and Dean named a few. I threw in a dozen different types, and we narrowed it down to the ones he liked. Sometimes the pictures I sent him would influence his writing, and that was the most stimulating thing to me about the project. It was a true collaboration."

As they worked closely together, Phil began to see a mathematical tempo in Dean's writing. "There were key events or scenes that happened in a rhythmic sequence. I don't think it's intentional. I think it comes from inside him, part of his natural rhythm, like a musician with an internal sense of timing. And he draws things out so well that there's nothing for me to embellish. It's like I'm restricted to a room where he's defined the parameters and I have to pick out the image that best represents what's going on. The challenge for me is to bring a new perspective to a scene or do something compositionally to make it visually dynamic."

Dean ended up writing a children's fable about the value of friendship—which had equal value for adults. His dedication was for Gerda. His idea was to make each of the heroic toys in some way archetypal, to be juxtaposed against the evil as images of nobility, goodness, and courage. "I thought they should have subconscious resonances." In particular, he hoped to capture the feeling he recalled from childhood upon reading *The Wind in the Willows*. He wanted characters who had that kind of community. He felt it would give this story substance. It was important to Dean to convey the idea that civilization rests on friendship, compassion, and sacrifice.

The story follows a group of stuffed animals called Odd-kins—because they are odd and they are "kin" to Bodkins, the toymaker—who lose their maker when he dies, and therefore must find a new toymaker to take their maker's magic mantle. Among them are Amos the bear (also a poet), Butterscotch the dog, Patch the cat, and Burl the elephant. They have been made for children who have been bruised by life and who need special toys to help them to cope. The toys set out on their journey to the store of Bodkin's successor, Colleen Shannon, but following them is a gang of evil toys led by a marionette—and an ex-con, Jagg. The devil wants Jagg to buy the toy factory so he can produce harmful toys. These mean toys represent a threat to good magic and life-affirming powers. The need for inner resources against such enemies becomes paramount, and it is the bonds created among those of like mind that can enhance the ability of any one of them to resist the forces that try to destroy.

The deceased toymaker's brother is tempted to sell the store to the devil's agent. Before that can happen, the evil toys are destroyed. But during the battle, Amos the bear is killed. The toys take him to the new toymaker, but even her skills cannot restore his life. The other toys each donates part of his or her magical stuffing—and *then* their loving sacrifice works its magic.

Warner had planned to include this book as part of their children's line, but the sales force thought it could be marketed to adults as well. The book had a first printing of 80,000 copies, and was widely reviewed as a children's tale about good and evil that had charm and a positive ending.

Peter Guber and John Peters, producers of *Rain Man* and *The Color Purple*, bought the rights to *Oddkins* in association with Warner Brothers. Then they moved on to head Columbia Pictures—and the project was left behind. Tim Burton was interested in making this story into an animated film, which excited Dean, but those plans fell through. Eventually Dean bought back the theatrical rights in a deal that gave Warner Books—a sister company of Warner Brothers—a collection of his short stories, *Strange Highways*, published in 1995.

4

Late in 1988, the Concorde and Centaur film version of *Watchers* opened to mixed reviews, mostly negative. Those who had loved the novel were dismayed to see the story so drastically altered. The only recognizable character was the dog—and he became almost secondary to a mindless teenage heartthrob main plot. Travis had been reinvented as a teenager and The Outsider was an OXCOM (Outside Experimental Combat Mammal)—but it looked ridiculously like someone wearing a rug.

"I knew I was in deep trouble," Dean said in an interview with Robert Morrish, "when I read an article in which the director said, 'We looked at this lead character, this thirty-five-year-old ex–Delta Force man, and his dog and said, gee, isn't that a little tired? Let's do something fresh. What really excited us was the fresh concept of a boy and his dog.' And I said, 'God, if they think *that's* a fresh concept . . . '"[3]

Produced by Damien Lee, David Mitchell, and Roger Corman, and directed by John Hess, it starred Corey Haim as Travis and Barbara Williams as Nora. Corman had bought the rights, but had sold them to Carolco, which went on to produce the film in Vancouver, Canada, where it could be done more cheaply than in the States.

For the most part, the film was panned for lack of suspense, confusion in the story line, and lack of credibility. *Daily Variety* noted that it was difficult to tell who the "watchers" were in this film, but "it's quickly certain that no one will be watching 'Watchers' for long."

The box office gross was $940,173, but it did well enough in the home video market for Corman to think about exercising his rights to the sequel.

Dean was completely disheartened by the stupidity of the script and the shoddiness of the film. It made no sense to even call it *Watchers*, since all references to that theme were missing. When fans asked Dean about this film, he wrote a six-page response as a standard reply. In it, he praised the dog, but went into detail about what he thought "this stupid and tacky pile of noxious, steaming celluloid" lacked. He felt that only five percent of the book survived in translation to the screen, and that the story line was cobbled together and filled with holes. "This moronic screenplay," he wrote, "wouldn't win a prize in a creative writing contest in which all the submissions were written by monkeys." He felt it stripped out all the magic and wonder of the novel, and tried to pass off bad science as thoughtful plotting. Even worse, it had radically altered the characters. "Aside from the dog, I don't believe there's any character in the movie who's like he is in the book."

Even so, Corman went on to produce two sequels. The announcement of the first sequel surprised Dean, but when he heard that Corman had supposedly been embarrassed by the original film, he thought that a remake might be a good idea. Corman had purchased *Watchers* with the proviso that he wanted to make a major film of high quality. However, Dean's optimism was short-lived when he heard that Corman's reasons for remaking the film were strictly capitalistic: The film had done well in video.

In the spring of 1990, *Watchers II* came to the screen, with a new director, Thierry Notz, and new cast including Marc Singer, Tracy Scoggins, and Jonathan Farwell. It was filmed outside Los Angeles, and Henry Dominic wrote the script. Again there is a dog and a creature (back to being called The Outsider) made by a genetics lab. This creature gets loose and eventually chases down the dog. There is a confrontation scene in which The Outsider is killed and the dog gives it a teddy bear as it dies. Again there are few parallels to the novel and little character development, although *Variety* thought it an improvement over the first version.

Dean, too, thought the film had more energy than the first one and fewer problems with the plot, but it seemed derivative of other movies, poorly paced, and still nothing like his novel. He was disappointed: "Still garbage of the stinkiest kind." When Corman marketed yet another *Watchers* movie in 1994, he had a major fight on his hands. Dean was not about to sit back and quietly let him continue to exploit his name.

5

Dean sold hardcover rights for the five Leigh Nichols novels to a fine-edition, small press imprint, Dark Harvest. Paul

Mikol and Scott Stadalsky had brought out their first volume in 1983, a collection of stories by horror writer George R. R. Martin, called *Songs the Dead Men Sing*. They went on to publish limited editions of novels and collections of stories by the top writers in the genre. Their *Night Visions* series consisted of three novellas by different name writers. Dan Simmons, Stephen King, Robert R. McCammon, and Clive Barker had all agreed to be published by Dark Harvest.

Dean had written an Introduction for Joe Lansdale's *The Nightrunners*, which Dark Harvest published in a limited edition in 1987. He then wrote stories for *Night Visions 4* and agreed to have limited, hardcover editions designed for his pseudonymous Nichols novels, bringing them out for the first time under his own name.

The first one, *The Servants of Twilight*, appeared in 1988, lavishly illustrated by Phil Parks, who would illustrate the other four as well. *The House of Thunder* also appeared that year, and Dean wrote an Introduction for *Night Visions 6*. By 1990, the other three Leigh Nichols novels were published in this limited-edition format.

6

The first book to analyze Dean's work came out in 1988. Edited by Bill Munster of Round Top, New York, it was a collection of essays on themes and styles in Dean's novels. Bill was the editor of *Footsteps*, a small-press magazine in the dark fantasy genre. He had printed a long interview with Dean in this magazine, which subsequently sold out.

"I was editing *Footsteps*, issue five, " Bill recalls. "I had interviews with Stephen King and Doug Winters, and the magazine did so well that I recognized you have to have a name. I wrote to Berkley asking them to forward a letter to Dean for issue six, and about a month before Christmas, on a Friday night, the phone rang and it was Dean. We talked for an hour and a half. He told me what he was working on and sent me his books. I published the interview and then wrote a proposal to Starmont House. Ted Dikty called me and said he was interested in a collection of essays about Dean. Dean told me to narrow it to the dark suspense books. The contributors were people I'd met through *Footsteps*. I invited them in and told everyone what to write about. Dean was happy with it. He was very cooperative."

The book was to be called *Sudden Fear*. Dean's friend Tim Powers wrote the Introduction, in which he delineated the history of practical jokes shared among Dean's close acquaintances. Joe Lansdale supplied the Afterword, which he called "A Brief and Informal Appreciation." Bill Munster also reprinted the entire interview he had conducted with Dean.

Other contributions included a study of Dean's suspense techniques by Dave B. Silva, and a comparison between Dean and Stephen King by English professor Michael R. Collings, who also looked at the poetic style of *Twilight Eyes*. Author Elizabeth Massie wrote about the female protagonists in Dean's novels, while Stan Brooks talked about Dean's evolution away from science fiction, and discussed the similarities between *Watchers* and *Shadowfires*. Michael Morrison, a critic, author, and physics professor, examined the various monsters in three of Dean's novels. A comparison of *Whispers* and *Phantoms* was done by English professor David Taylor, who described the skill of thematic braiding in these books, and Richard Laymon wrote about the power of language in Dean's constant juxtaposition of death and life in his fiction.

Bill Munster then set to work on *Cold Terror*, a more ambitious companion-style book about Dean and his work. It was to be published by Underwood-Miller and was to include several interviews with people closely associated with Dean. Underwood-Miller scheduled it to be issued in hardcover in 1990. Production was delayed, however, and in the meantime, Marty Greenburg and Ed Gorman discussed with Dean the possibility of putting together a book called *The Dean Koontz Companion*. They included Bill Munster and his projects, folding it into theirs, so *Cold Terror* was never completed. Nor was a novella that Dean had hoped to write for Munster's chapbook series, which was to be called "The Shadow Sea."

Sudden Fear has been scheduled for reissue from Borgo Press, a publisher of scholarly materials, with the inclusion of a chapter written by Jim Seels on collecting first editions of Dean's books.

Professor Michael Collings, one of the contributors, has also proposed to publish a complete bibliography of Dean's work for Borgo Press.

[1]Dean R. Koontz, Introduction, *Night Visions 6* (Arlington Heights, IL: Dark Harvest Press, 1988), p. 5.

[2]Ibid., p. 9.

[3]Robert Morrish, "*Weird Tales* Talks with Dean Koontz," *Weird Tales,* (Winter 1990/1), p. 112.

NINETEEN

Hitting the Top

1

ON SEPTEMBER 20, 1988, DEAN HAD AN EXPERIENCE THAT HE would not write about for nearly a decade, but he claimed it in his essay for *Beautiful Death* as his one possible encounter with evidence for life after death. He was at work that day in his office when the phone rang. He picked it up and heard a female voice that sounded far away. She spoke with a sense of great urgency. "Please, be careful!" she said.

A bit startled, Dean asked, "Who is this?"

He received no response. The woman repeated the warning three more times, and each time she said it, her voice became more distant. When the line fell silent, Dean sat there listening for a while, uncertain what to make of it. The voice had sounded eerily like his mother's, and she had been dead for nearly two decades. "But a voice is much harder to remember than a face, so I thought I was being melodramatic." His number was unlisted, so it could not have been a prank call aimed at him. Perhaps it had been a number simply misdialed. He mentioned the incident to Gerda, but told no one else.

"It was such a strange call," says Dean. "I don't claim that it was a ghost. I don't know what I believe. It certainly was odd. People report these kinds of events all the time, and it's always struck me as interesting that everyone seems to have had an experience or two of the uncanny. Sometimes I believe that call was from my mother and sometimes that it was a very strange, serendipitous wrong number. I think you always have to keep some skepticism about things like this, but it's comforting to think that there may be a realm where the personality survives."

Two days after this call, Dean went to visit his father at Casa Orange. The staff were dealing with Ray's behavioral problems, and they had asked Dean to come and talk with him. Ray had punched another resident, a man on a walker, and the nurses were worried. Dean was unaware that Ray had used some of his small allowance to go out and buy the same type of yellow-handled fishing knife that he had owned the year before, and that he had worked on this one, honing it to razor sharpness and oiling the hinge to make it open like a switchblade. When Dean came into the room, Ray grabbed the knife from a drawer, and Dean had to try to wrestle it away from him. There were many witnesses to this altercation, and one of them called the police. Finally Dean got the knife without incident and carried it out into the hall—just as the police arrived.

They drew their guns and ordered him to drop the knife.

Dean was startled. "It's not me you want," he insisted. "It's him in there." He pointed into his father's room.

"Drop the knife," they repeated, still training their weapons on him.

Dean froze. "All of a sudden," he recalls, "I realized that they were going to shoot *me* if I didn't drop the knife. They thought *I* was the perpetrator. So I dropped it and obeyed them. That was one of the worst moments of my life. My own stupidity almost got me killed." He later included this scene in his 1993 novel, *Mr. Murder*, when Marty Stillwater, the protagonist, has a similar encounter (though under different circumstances) with the police.

Eventually the police realized that Ray was the dangerous party. They took him to a psychiatric ward where he would be kept for a short observation period. It was only temporary relief. Casa Orange would not take him back, and Dean knew that something would have to be done immediately to get his father placed in a more secure establishment. Despite the pressure of deadlines, this took priority. His father was now too mentally ill to be without supervision. Yet the ordeal was only to intensify.

A week later, Dean and the hospital administration were summoned to court. A public advocate making the rounds in the psychiatric wards had asked Ray if he wanted to be released. In spite of his aphasia, Ray had managed to persuade the man that he was fine and wanted out. The man had then filed the paperwork to demand immediate release.

"I went to the courthouse," says Dean, "and the attorney representing the hospital told me what would most likely happen. She didn't expect the public defender to call me because he'd have nothing to gain by it, and much to lose. Instead he'd go before the judge and say that my father was perfectly capable of living outside the psychiatric ward. That alarmed me because my father was a dangerous man. He had threatened neighbors with a knife, too, and he'd been on antipsychotic medication to which he had developed a high tolerance."

The hospital psychiatrist, a Korean-American man whom Dean liked, was there to testify, along with a physician. The judge, a Mexican-American, was reputed to be conservative about turning people with psychiatric problems loose on the streets. Even so, there was no certainty about the outcome.

Dean realized that if Ray were released, he *might* wind up living on the streets, and if he did not want anyone to manage him, there was nothing Dean could do about it. If he wanted to, Ray could live in the gutter. It was not that Dean wanted Ray to be kept in the psychiatric hospital ward, but he needed more time to look for a decent facility, to ensure that Ray had better care.

"I was already desperately looking and I just didn't like the places I was seeing," he says. "Some were nice, but those places wouldn't touch him if he'd had psychiatric problems. Especially associated with violence. And I didn't like the lockup facilities. I was still looking, and there were twenty or thirty places left to see. I'd been to about a dozen but I had not liked any of those."

Dean told the hospital's attorney that his father would die on the street. It would not benefit him to be released, as he was a danger to himself and others. She was sympathetic and reassuring. "We have hope and believe there's a seventy-five percent chance that they'll keep your dad in psychiatric care."

Also attending a hearing with the same attorney was a fiftyish couple who were also trying to ensure that a psychotic relative be held in a psychiatric ward long enough to find another facility where he could get longer-term treatment. Initially Dean thought they were dealing with a parent, as was he, but as he listened to the attorney discuss the case with them, he realized they were plagued by a twenty-year-old son suffering from drug-related psychosis. He had been driving with wild aggressiveness, but each time his parents had attempted to get his driver's license taken from him, the state gave him another chance, in spite of a long list of accidents. The boy's dream was to run down schoolchildren at a crossing. He had been committed several times, but each time some public advocate got him released. He had once smashed in the windows of his family's home to get back into the house. Because of his youth, they faced a lifetime of similar incidents. Dean realized that their problems were much worse than his, but that was little comfort.

In the courtroom, when Ray was brought in a wheelchair, he made several histrionic gestures to the effect that Dean was breaking his heart.

The court called the physician and the psychiatrist to the stand, both of whom testified that Ray was psychotic, suffering from degenerative alcohol syndrome, and should not be released. Then, to the hospital attorney's surprise, the advocate called Dean. From what followed, it became apparent that somehow Ray had managed to convince his advocate that he was a successful businessman whose son wanted to put him away to get his money—and the advocate evidently had taken this at face value. On the stand, Dean suggested that he would rather discuss his father's history more privately, perhaps in the judge's chambers.

The advocate insisted he say whatever he had to say right there in court, in front of Ray and all onlookers.

Reluctantly, while Ray stared at him from his wheelchair, Dean recounted his childhood experiences and added the facts as they stood: Ray was destitute; Dean had supported him for the past eleven years; he had gone through some forty jobs in thirty-four years; he was an alcoholic; and had been diagnosed a borderline schizophrenic and pathological liar.

In the brief cross-examination, the advocate quickly saw where the truth lay—and knew it was not with his client. Initially aggressive, he quickly wilted.

The judged asked Dean what his plans were for his father.

Dean explained that he was looking for a satisfactory care facility, but thus far had been unsuccessful, and hoped to be granted more time to find the right place.

The judge was ready to make his decision. He looked at Ray and said, "You've had to sit here and listen to your son say some terrible things about you today. That could not have been easy."

Ray nodded emphatically. Dean had the sinking feeling that the judge was going to be sympathetic to his father. After all he had just said, that seemed impossible, yet he feared that Ray was about to be released.

Then the judge continued, still looking at Ray. "I must remind you that your own advocate made your son do this. It wasn't what he wanted to do. And I believe I speak for most of the people in this room when I say that if I ever need help in my old age, I'd be relieved to have a son or daughter who will take care of me as well as your son has been taking care of you."

With that, he directed that Ray be held in a psychiatric ward for the additional legally allowable period, giving Dean the time he needed to look for a decent nursing home.

Dean was vastly relieved. In spite of pending deadlines, he went back to the search for a good care facility.

Dean describes some of this process in his 1991 novel, *Cold Fire*. Jim Ironheart remembers having had to go to court and then find a decent rest home for his grandfather. What Dean describes of this place, Fair Haven, is similar to the home he finally found for his father, Buena Vista. The institution was clean, the staff were friendly, the food was good, and the rooms were attractive. Buena Vista was also the only nursing home of quality that would take a man who had Ray's history of psychiatric problems; otherwise, he would have had to have been placed in a far grimmer locked facility.

Ray entered Buena Vista Care Home on October 7. Dean was glad to finally find a place where he could be sure that Ray would be under a watchful eye, yet living in as pleasant an atmosphere as possible under the circumstances.

Dean continued to visit him regularly, partly out of fear that, without guidance, Ray might yet hurt someone. He thought again about having blood tests done to determine their true relationship, but again procrastinated.

A friend suggested that perhaps Dean did not wish to know that his mother might have been unfaithful to Ray. Dean dismissed this concern. If that indeed had happened, he would understand it, considering the marriage she had endured. It was something else that kept him from following through.

As difficult as all of this was for him, Dean had another novel coming out in January that he knew had every chance of doing well, thanks to the popularity of *Lightning* and *Watchers*. Only a month later, the review of an advance copy of *Midnight* in *Publishers Weekly* predicted just that: "Koontz's sense of pace and drama are sure, and there are a number of memorable moments. This one should hit the bestseller list at a run."

2

When *Lightning* had come out, Putnam had pressured Dean to do an author tour, but he resisted. He did not enjoy the spotlight and preferred to get on with writing his next book. He also felt that anonymity suited a writer better because he was free to observe those around him in a way he could not after allowing himself to become a celebrity. As Putnam prepared *Midnight* for publication, they asked again that he do an extensive promotional tour, but again Dean pleaded the primacy of writing. Phyllis Grann relented once more but insisted on making a deal, sealed with her and Dean's words of honor. For the next book and every book thereafter, Dean would do a long tour *until and if* he ever hit number one on *The New York Times* list. Thereafter, no tours.

Dean had tried out several titles for this book, among them *Midnight Music* and *Shadow Run*, but Grann had not liked them. Stacy Creamer remembers that Grann was heavily involved with editing this novel and that they had suggested changes to the ending to clarify it. They were rapidly preparing it for print when Stacy noticed an error on the dust jacket flap that had somehow gotten past everyone's scrutiny: The last time Moonlight Cove was mentioned in the summary, someone had inadvertently spelled it Midnight Cove. It was the printer himself who had brought this to her attention, but only after he had already printed 100,000 copies of the jacket, at a total cost of $35,000. "Phyllis was in Florida," Stacy recalls, "and I had to call her. She was really angry, but she had those jackets destroyed."

Midnight, published in January 1989, hit the top of all the major lists its second week out. But Dean would not have to tour, after all. This was his first *number one* bestseller in hard-cover.

"We were astonished," Dean said at the time about his and Gerda's reactions. "I've been jumping up and down so much that my ankle joints are beginning to give out."

Phyllis Grann also responded to the flurry of press. "He became the number one bestseller the way people used to get to be number one," she said. "He built a loyal following and those fans stayed with him, while he attracted new ones with each book."[1]

Claire Smith noted that Dean's decision to concentrate on fewer but more ambitious novels was also instrumental.

First printing was set at 200,000 copies, with an ad budget of $150,000. The Literary Guild took it as a main selection, the third of Dean's books to be used by them so prominently. The following November, *Midnight* went to number one in paper-back.

Dean and Gerda decided to celebrate by buying something and then going out for a large slice of rich chocolate cake. They went to a nearby shopping mall and Dean purchased a sport coat. Then they ate dinner at a casual restaurant and ulti-mately decided to pass on the cake. "We need practice at this," Dean commented to a friend, Ned Frear.

He dedicated *Midnight* to Ed and Pat Thomas, friends and owners of the bookstore in Tustin, California, where he has done signings for every book since *Strangers*. They were the first people ever to *ask* him to sign.

The story concerns four people, previously strangers, who come together and, in the course of one night, join forces to resist a megalomaniac computer genius intent on using nano-technology to physically and psychologically transform all the residents of a small, isolated town. Dean uses geography and weather to enhance the feeling of isolation common to towns along a certain stretch of California coast. This novel's themes are drawn from several science fiction scenarios, most notably the H. G. Wells 1896 novel *The Island of Doctor Moreau*. That story is an allegorical tale of human conceit in which a scientist populates a remote island with beasts that have been surgically transformed into men, and whose veneer of civilized behavior proves tenuous.

In *Midnight*, Sam Booker is an FBI agent, Tessa Lockland the sister of a murder victim, Chrissie Foster a young girl terrorized by her technologically transformed parents, and Harry Talbot a paraplegic with a companion dog named Moose. All of these people must cope with some degree of isolation or loneliness. Ultimately they join in a healing bond of friendship that becomes like family. Harry and Chrissie are residents of Moonlight Cove, an oceanside town, while Sam and Tessa come into town in response to the string of violent deaths that have occurred there. Most of the residents work for New Wave Microtechnology, owned and operated by a reclusive and demented genius, Thomas Shaddack.

As revealed in a flashback setpiece that is virtually a novella in itself, Shaddack had killed his parents when he was only twelve and had gotten away with it. Even as he had excelled in computer technology, he had remained a mentally arrested adolescent. Self-centered and greedy, he views Moonlight Cove as his kingdom and its residents as his subjects. To his mind, if they become mechanized through a process he has invented that joins flesh to machines, they will never die and can then be controlled and made to serve him forever. The idea is to improve the species according to his design. In the first application of nanotechnology to biological purpose, he has injected into their blood silicon microchips that connect to a computer that will override their brain functions and make them into his New People—beings of great intellectual power untrammeled by emotion. Yet he has failed to predict the regressive effects: People need emotions, and being so fiercely deprived, will revert to the most primal states of their animal selves. Some of the townspeople are becoming marauding werewolf-like savages, called "regressives." They enjoy killing.

On the surface, *Midnight* is a novel about the dark side of technology—that which can be used for good can also be used for evil. In the wrong hands, it can be a formidable weapon. In this case, it forces people into a sterile part of themselves and draws forth the primitive emotions that civilization has managed to repress. It also allows these people to shift shapes and indulge in their worst desires. This computer-age myth of the consequences of playing God forces us to take a look at ourselves—our own dark sides. It is the Faustian urge to have it all crashing in on itself.

The central theme of *Midnight* is the way power negatively works on the human soul. Dean uses the quote from Will and Ariel Durant, "Power dements even more than it corrupts, lowering the guard of foresight and raising the haste of action."[2] Technology can be a liberating force, contributing to human freedom, or an instrument of power, enslaving us—depending on those using it. Shaddack is a power freak. Sam, too, is a power freak in his personal relationships, and only learns not to be when, by the end, he can stop trying to control his teenage son and can embrace him instead. Power—people's use of it, rejection of its use, resistance to it, or subjugation by it—is the issue with every character in the novel.

Juxtaposed against that is the force of love and responsibility to others. It can turn pessimism to optimism, and protect, encourage, and heal. As it does with the four characters, it can restore faith in life. It is meaning and purpose against nihilism, structure against chaos; it is what people live for. As such, the novel itself is a metaphor of how Dean views the writing process: As writers seek to structure their material with moral purpose and optimism, they contribute to resisting the forces that break down society and individuals.

Dean's conception of what it means to be human involves the capacity for good or evil, and maintaining goodness requires a strong will and the support of others of like mind. Yet neither force may appear in the way we might expect. Shaddack is the monster who looks normal, while Harry Talbot is a crippled man who does not. Talbot is isolated by society, but he is more human than is Shaddack or those turning into "New People." Even the dog, Moose, shows more human responses to need than most people in the story.

In a note at the end of the novel, Dean mentions Canine Companions for Independence, an organization to which he and Gerda have contributed money and time. CCI breeds, trains, and provides exceptional guide dogs to physically challenged people. As he and Gerda love dogs and admire the courage of all the disabled people they have met, CCI has a special meaning for them. In honor of the Koontz's substantial support, a campus in the Oceanside, California, facility was dedicated to them.

Corey Hudson, executive director of Canine Companions for Independence, was delighted with Dean's participation. "The dedication in *Midnight* generated a tremendous amount of awareness and support for our nonprofit organization. Generous readers have contributed close to $100,000 over the years in response. Dean and Gerda Koontz have played a major role in the growth of our program service. Because of their support, many people are directly enjoying the love and assistance of canine companions."

Reviews *of Midnight* were largely positive, although some critics complained that Dean had used a well-worn "mad scientist" premise and that his delivery lacked subtlety: Rather than allowing readers to make their own connections with science fiction classics, Dean had spelled it out for them with explicit and repeated references.

Sarah Sue Goldsmith in the *Baton Rouge Morning Advocate* found it interesting that the novel was based on nanotechnology, which had been fully explained in *Scientific American*, but only *after* the novel had been written. She was impressed that Dean kept up on the latest technology via professional journals as it was happening.

Several critics discussed the general decline in horror fiction, but cited Koontz as an author still striving for quality in this genre. "What has always impressed me about Koontz," said Gregory Frost in *Science Fiction and Fantasy*, "is his ability to craft a story so that it barely lets the reader come up for air between terrors." In *The New York Times Book Review*, David Murray noted the complex characters, and described the novel as "good, page-turning fiction designed to keep a reader up well beyond midnight." *Kirkus* said that "Koontz recaps and puts a high-velocity spin on the whole history of horror fiction here, enriching a bounty of scary set-pieces with winsome characters and piquant reflection on what exactly makes us human . . . Koontz cooks at high heat here . . . a sure-fire bestseller."

Midnight remained on the bestsellers list for three months in hardcover, selling 310,000 copies. In paperback, it stayed fourteen weeks and sold over two million copies.

3

Two months later, Dean sold six of his previously published novels to Berkley for $3 million. They were willing to pay for the rights based on how well *The Mask*, originally published under the name Owen West, had done as a reissue under Dean's name. *The Mask* spent several weeks at number five on the *Times* list and number four on *Publishers Weekly*'s list. Advance orders from booksellers totaled 1.2 million. The books that Berkley planned to reissue were *Demon Seed, The House of Thunder, The Servants of Twilight, The Eyes of Darkness, The Key to Midnight,* and *The Voice of the Night.* It had been only a year since Dean had made a deal with them to sell five old novels—including two from the list above—for $50,000 apiece. But he had never signed the contract. He had first wanted Berkley to rectify the trouble they were having supporting his backlist. By the time they managed to do so, the price for the rights had shot up, based on his increasing success in hardcover.

Berkley published the last of this list, *Demon Seed,* in the summer of 1997. All five books far outearned even the greater advances that his success had required the company to pay.

4

Dean had been through several Hollywood agents. Through Henry Morrison he had acquired one, Gordon Molson, whom he liked personally and whom he kept for a while. Then with Claire Smith at Harold Ober Associates, he had been represented by Creative Artists Agency, though he was not pleased with their work. Through Warner Books on the *Oddkins* project, he met Pat Karlan.

"We were compatible," says Karlan. "Dean liked the way I work, which is low-key and up-front. We share some of the same philosophies, and he was wonderful to work with. Dean always understood what was going on in the crazy film business."

Warner and Lorimar together optioned sixteen of Dean's books for a period of a year. Their hope was to get two movies made per year under a series tentatively to be called "The

Dean Koontz Theater." During the first six months, they began to develop four of these for CBS television: *Night Chills*, *The Eyes of Darkness*, *Darkfall*, and *The Face of Fear*. Rose Schacht and Ann Powell wrote a script for *The Eyes of Darkness*, Robert Crais wrote a screenplay for *Night Chills*, and Alan Glueckman wrote the teleplay for *The Face of Fear*. Dean wrote the script for *Darkfall*.

Dean was named executive producer, and was able to work closely with the assigned writers. He also had some input regarding casting and direction.

Ultimately the network approved *Darkfall*, the only script by Dean. But because a new regime of executives was to take over in a couple of months, the current executives wanted *Darkfall* delivered prior to the change. Warner Brothers Television and Dean agreed that delivering a quality TV movie in the time allotted would be impossible. Though they knew that the new regime might choose to proceed with *none* of the four scripts, they risked waiting. Realizing that of the remaining three, only Robert Crais's script had a chance of being approved, and not wanting to bet everything on that and *Darkfall*, Dean wrote his own script for *The Face of Fear*. Sure enough, the new network executives decided against *Darkfall* because they didn't like "stories with nasty little creatures in them." They passed on *Night Chills* and *The Eyes of Darkness* as well—giving the green light only to Dean's script for *The Face of Fear*. Though Dean felt he had used nothing of the Glueckman script, the Writers Guild arbitration committee gave them shared credit—though Dean received top billing—unusual in a case where the original writer did retain some credit, and a de facto acknowledgment that the film script was largely Dean's.

5

Dean was due in England on April 12 to promote *Midnight* and *Lightning* for Headline. The tour was to begin in Manchester, then go on to Birmingham and London.

Dean had some trepidation, because one plane ride early in his career had been extremely rough. Another time, a friend had urged him to come along on a private plane, insisting that riding with someone he trusted at the controls would cure him of his fear of flying. He had nearly accepted, but prior commitments prevented him from accepting the invitation. The following day, that plane crashed into a mountain, killing everyone. Now he faced the prospect of a very long trip, putting his life in the hands of strangers.

"We had elaborate arrangements," Dean says. "We were going on British Airways and coming back on the Concorde. We had a suite at Claridge's and money on deposit there, and then I came down with a serious stomach ailment."

About a month before they were scheduled to leave, he awoke one morning suffering from pain in his right side and a seriously swollen abdomen. Overnight, he had gone from a thirty to a thirty-nine inch waist. He immediately went to his doctor, who eventually recommended a gastroenterologist, Dr. Steven Ducker, who insisted he go into the hospital for tests.

"We're supposed to be in London soon," Dean told him.

"I don't think you're going," was all Ducker would say.

Dean went into the hospital. Although the doctor had assured him this was not cancer, he still worried. He had never experienced anything like this before, and nothing his family doctor had tried prior to Ducker had proved effective.

Dean returned to the doctor for the results of his tests a few days after he left the hospital. Dr. Ducker told him, "Well, we have good news. There's no trace of cancer anywhere in your body. When you came in here, I thought you were probably terminal."

Taken aback, Dean responded, "But you said there was no reason to worry that it was cancer."

The doctor smiled and shrugged. "What would you have had me say? I realized it would have been a bad four days of waiting if I'd said, 'I think there might be a malignancy.'"

As it turned out, Dean had a valve inflammation caused by the buildup of long-term stress. He had to get some relief from the stress before the swelling would subside.

"So what's going on that's so stressful?" the doctor asked.

Dean shrugged. "Nothing."

Ducker, who possesses both a direct manner and an exceptionally charming bedside manner, said, "Nope, sorry, but that can't be true. What about your work?"

"I love my work," Dean said. "It's a great pleasure, even on hard days. There's always the pressure of deadlines. That's kind of stressful, but I'm used to that now."

The doctor pressed. "There's nothing else?"

"No, not really." Then Dean thought for a moment and added, "My father is a lifelong alcoholic and a diagnosed schizophrenic, and we've had to bring him out here and support him. He's kind of violent and a hypochondriac. He was calling us around three mornings a week at two and three A.M. to say he had to go to the hospital, so we'd rush over to his apartment and take him to the ER, but there was never anything wrong with him. It's exhausting. That's been kind of stressful, but I've put up with him all my life."

"Has he been violent lately?"

Dean shrugged. "Well, he tried to kill me. I had to take a knife away from him."

Ducker stared at him, speechless.

"I guess I am under stress," Dean said.

The doctor concurred. As they talked, he mentioned that he had started the first Adult Children of Alcoholics organization in Orange County. He thought Dean might benefit from coming to the meetings, although he recognized that Dean possessed a high level of self-control and could probably work on the problem himself. Ducker taught him a few relaxation techniques. He urged Dean to learn to recognize when he was stressed and then change activities to break the reaction patterns.

"How often do you see your father?" he asked.

"Twice a week for about an hour and a half," Dean told him.

"Okay, now listen. This guy is a user. He's never going to be anything else. You go because some part of you thinks that if you just play the dutiful son that someday he will explain to you why he's done all these terrible things. But he won't. It'll never happen. In fact, he'll just try to use you and hurt you more and get more out of you. I want you to go once every six weeks for fifteen minutes and that's it."

"I can't do that," Dean insisted. "No matter what he's done, he's still my father."

"If you don't do this," the doctor pressed, "you'll never get well. You're going to have to wean yourself out of this code-pendency. Go see him twice a week and stay for half an hour. Then cut back to once a week, and then once every other week. And then drop it to fifteen minutes, until you're seeing him briefly, once every six weeks. Otherwise he will destroy the rest of your life as long as he's alive."

Dean was in such bad shape with his stomach condition that he knew he would accept this advice. He followed the doctor's instructions and ultimately reduced his visits to his father to once a month for half an hour. About six months after this discussion with Dr. Ducker, Dean's physical problems cleared up. "It was very interesting because it showed me how much the mind does affect the health of the body," Dean says.

Dr. Ducker became Dean's personal physician, not just his gastroenterologist, and Dean credits him with more than a mere healing touch. "Because of Dr. Ducker's desire to treat the whole patient, not just the current malady, because of his willingness to take time with patients, because of his insight, I was not only cured of my gastroenterological problems, but began to get a handle on how to separate myself from my father and prevent the damage he delighted in causing."

He never did get to England.

6

In 1989, Shippensburg University made the decision to confer an honorary Doctor of Letters degree on Dean as one of their most distinguished alumni. Not all of the faculty were in agree-ment on this. Some of the English professors felt that Dean's writing was not serious enough to be awarded such an honor; he was merely a popular writer, they said, and expressed their disagreement by deciding to boycott a talk that Dean was planning to give to the English students. Nevertheless, other people felt that Dean's accomplishments merited recognition.

"When you have a graduate who has excelled in an area," says President Anthony Ceddia, "who represents a standard of performance that is above the average in something that satis-fies people's interests and needs, that person deserves to be recognized. We invited him to receive an honorary degree, and he did a terrific job at the graduation ceremony. His profound ability to understate things is magnificent. He just mesmerized the students. We're very proud that he's an alumnus and pleased with his success. We've given about fifteen honorary doctorates to such people as Bishop Tutu and Dick Thornburg. Dean is the only alumnus to date to get one."

For Dean, it was an irony—but a delightful one—to receive an award like this from an institution that had nearly expelled him after his first year.

On his way to Shippensburg, Dean returned to Bedford to see friends and relatives. By phone, he had met Ned Frear, publisher of the *Bedford Gazette*. Years earlier, Ned had read something by Alan Dean Foster and surmised in print that Foster might be one of Dean's pseudonyms. Dean had called to correct him. Alan Dean Foster was a real person. From that time forward, they had kept in touch, and Ned had written regular columns to let the people of Dean's hometown know about his latest achievements. Ned was also a partner in the local bookstore, so he set up a book signing there that was attended by many people that Dean had known, including grade school teachers.

Dean reunited with Larry Johnson, and he and Gerda joined Larry and his wife at the famous Ed's Steak House—the restaurant that Dean had so yearned to enter as a kid. It made him laugh to see that although the food was quite good, the decor that he had imagined to be the ultimate in elegance back then was actually ordinary steakhouse decor. How much his life had changed!

He had another strange occurrence in Bedford. Dean's Aunt Virginia had arranged with the current owners of Dean's childhood home to allow him to go inside and see it. They drove Dean and Gerda over to that side of town. Dean thought it might be interesting to see the place, but he was surprised to find that he was having a stronger and more negative reaction the closer they got to the house.

"We pulled up in front," Dean remembers, "and I could not get out of the car. I got very shaky and I said, 'We've got to go.' I couldn't even *look* at the place. I was stunned at my reaction. I could not physically get out of the car. I asked Aunt Ginny to call the people and apologize. I just had to leave. I couldn't even speak. So we left."

He does not know whether something may have happened in the house that he still has not remembered, or whether he was merely reacting to all those desperate days of his youth and to his mother's suffering there. Later, when he wrote *Dark Rivers of the Heart*, featuring a man with repressed memories of an atrocity that he had witnessed at his home, Dean wondered if there was some connection.

In Shippensburg, commencement was scheduled in Seth Grove Stadium for Saturday, May 6, at eleven o'clock. Eight hundred and six seniors were receiving bachelor's degrees, along with one hundred graduate students receiving master's degrees. The afternoon before, Dean gave a talk on "The Trials and Tribulations of Young Writers Entering the Publishing Process," and that evening he was honored at a reception at the president's house.

Richard Forsythe was happy to see his former student again. They spent time in his Chambersburg home, catching up on their separate lives, but Richard worried that Dean was not putting any time into preparing. "I said, 'Dean when are you going to work on your speech?' He said he wasn't going to worry about it. And the morning when we were going to Shippensburg, I picked him up and saw that he had no papers with him, so I said, 'You must have left your notes in the hotel room.' He said, 'No, I didn't.'" Although Dean explained that he always spoke extemporaneously, Richard continued to worry that he was going into the ceremony without knowing what he would say.

After the graduates came in and were seated, Dean was introduced by President Ceddia. Quoting Dr. Harold Gleason, English department chair during Dean's undergraduate days, he described the honoree as "a consistently polite and moderate young man," commenting that this former student, equipped with a degree in English from the university, had gone on to have a career "of almost unparalleled productivity and success." By that time, Dean had already written fifty books, had been translated into seventeen languages, and had forty-five million copies of his novels in print throughout the world.

"It is his integrity of purpose," Gleason wrote in the official citation, "that distinguishes his novels from the avant-garde on the one hand and the sensational on the other . . . In tribute to his pre-eminence as a figure in contemporary American literature, his unflinching advocacy of freedom and openness in human relations, and his embodiment of the ideals of a liberal education, we confer the degree of Doctor of Letters, *honoris causa*, upon Dean Ray Koontz."

Even at that moment, Dean still had not composed his speech.

"I conceived it as I walked up to the podium," he admits. "I decided to tell a few anecdotes about my days at Shippensburg and drop in a few observations. Between the sharper truths about life in the working world, I kept them laughing."

As Dean looked out over the crowd of more than three thousand, all waiting patiently for what he might say, he told them he was supposed to boil down all the wisdom he had learned into ten minutes and it suddenly dawned on him that he might have some trouble filling up that much time. That got a laugh. He talked about his stint in Saxton, his year at Mechanicsburg, and a campus "sit-in" in which he had once participated as a student to protest the food in the cafeteria. One item of advice in a tongue-in-cheek list of hard-won truths that he wished to impart was this caution: "Never pick a fight with a man who has the words 'Born to Die' tattooed on his forehead." Then he got more serious.

"I told them the truth," says Dean. "I made it funny, but I structured it around advice for life."

He looked the crowd over and said, "Most speakers would come here to tell you what's happening in the world and how to meet it, but I'm here to tell you that most of what they say is a load of lies. You applaud them because they make you feel good. But I'm going to tell you what it's really like out there — advice that will do you some good. They may tell you the world needs and wants you young people with your fresh faces and your fresh ideas — that industry and the arts and education all want you to come as fast as you can to take over the reins of society. They want you to succeed. I'm here to tell you, this is not true. They don't want your fresh ideas. Everyone out there has his own ideas of how things should be and how everything should work, and the last thing he wants to do is listen to *you*. Your ideas will be reviled. You won't be welcomed. This is human nature. Everyone is afraid of people with new ideas because they've spent their lives selling their specialty—and if their own ideas become passé, they don't want to hear about it. If I've learned one lesson in life, it is that you can have all the ability in the world and it means absolutely nothing without perseverance."

He let this sink in and then concluded, "So when you leave here today, be a little despondent, but be a little courageous, because they may not want you, but they need you."

Some people were surprised by how blunt Dean had been, but he felt he owed the students the truth. Afterward, Richard Forsythe gave a party at his house and invited many people who had known Dean during his college days, including Fay Bitting.

On the drive back to California, Dean and Gerda stopped in Cedar Rapids, Iowa, to meet Ed and Carol Gorman. Dean wrote about this in a humorous Afterword to Ed's collection of stories, *Moonchasers*, reprinted later in *The Dean Koontz Companion*. Ed remembers being in a bookstore with Dean and looking over all the Ed McBain/Evan Hunter books still in print. "Dean remarked on how astonishing it was to see an author who was seventy years old and still had every single book in print. He really admired this accomplishment."

7

Berkley published *The Servants of Twilight*, originally a Leigh Nichols novel, in paperback under Dean's name. On the *Publishers Weekly*'s bestsellers list it went to number five, and then to number one, where it stayed for four weeks. It debuted at number one on *The New York Times* list, where it stayed for five weeks. Berkley planned to reissue all of the Nichols books under Dean's name. They also put new covers on Dean's older paperback novels, using the artist Don Brautigam, who worked closely with Dean to produce a look more representative of the work between the covers.

Dean also published a short story, "Trapped," in an anthology called *Stalkers*. Originally he had written it for *Redbook*, but they had put him through such agony over the editing of it that he ultimately pulled the piece and allowed his friends Ed Gorman and Marty Greenberg to use it in an anthology. In the wake of *Watchers*, *Redbook* had requested a two-part novella dealing with genetic engineering. Dean had written and submitted it. They had then decided to put it all in a single issue, but in that case, it needed to be cut. Dean had complied as far as he could, but he would not cut it as much as they wanted. They offered to do the cutting, and Dean declined.

The story is about a young widow who must protect her ten-year-old son from the rat-like creatures unleashed by a recombinant DNA research facility near their home. In light of Dean's use of rats as representative of dark and demented inner forces, this is clearly a story about his own mother's protection of him against his father's genetic legacy. They both feel trapped, but she fights to ensure that he will survive and move on.

That year, Dean and Gerda bought a house in Tustin and remodeled it, but before moving in, they put it on the market for resale when they decided that they needed a larger library and more office space for assistants.

[1]*The New York Times*, February 8, 1989.
[2]Dean R. Koontz, *Midnight* (New York: Putnam, 1989), p. 235.

TWENTY

Closed Chapter on an Open Book

1

DEDICATED TO SIX OF DEAN'S FORMER TEACHERS, *THE BAD PLACE* was published in January 1990, and became Dean's next number one bestseller. This was the year of the Persian Gulf Crisis, when United Nations forces liberated Kuwait from Iran's aggression. In the U.S., the shocking magnitude of the countrywide savings and loan debacle was realized, an economic recession pushed in, and President Bush violated his "read my lips" no-new-taxes campaign pledge by signing a five hundred billion tax package for the purpose of deficit reduction. As a backlash to the "greed is good" eighties mentality, celebrity entrepreneurs like Milken and Trump lost their clout, and the politically correct movement arose to support minority diversity. What seemed a positive step on behalf of oppressed people was to grow into a politicized weapon of power.

The Bad Place was one of Dean's darkest and most imaginative stories, with a villain reminiscent of Bruno Frey from *Whispers*. Dean explored the "stain of Eden" and crafted a biblical allegory even as he was telling a story of incest, monstrosity, and horror. Each character has a fatal flaw, yet the story ends on a note of hope, with the imminent birth of a child created in love. The lead characters, while portrayed as a modern-day Nick and Nora Charles from Dashiell Hammett's detective novel, *The Thin Man*, represent at a deeper level the archetypal Adam and Eve seeking Paradise.

Richard Forsythe, Dean's former professor from Shippensburg and now a close friend, thought that *The Bad Place* was his best book. "His imagination is at its peak here," he said. "Dean sets up some pretty difficult technical problems for himself in this book." He was most impressed with how Dean managed to present the thinking processes of a boy with Down's syndrome. He also noticed Dean's method of gradually shortening the segments as he jumped from one character to another, to subtly increase tension and make the book feel as if everything were happening at once.

Dean also pulls in the broader social and cultural aspects of Orange County as more than just a backdrop for the action. He includes such elements as minority cultures, the Santa Ana winds, the fruit-dotted landscape, and even posters of Disney characters to keep the southern California flavor. That it is set in California, a land considered by some a paradise, is important to the overall dark effect of the allegory.

The protagonists are Bobby and Julie Dakota, a high-tech detective team that serves primarily universities, corporations, and other institutions rather than individuals. Married to each other, they have obvious links to Dean and Gerda. Like Dean, Bobby has a sense of humor and is an optimist willing to give anyone the benefit of the doubt. He hates bugs, fears chaos, and loves swing music. (Dean's favorite music is from the era of Benny Goodman and Glenn Miller, and an early title for this novel was "One O'Clock Jump.") Bobby craves order and stability and finds himself attracted to Asian culture for its discipline, neatness, sense of tradition, structure, and control. He desperately needs Julie, feeling that without her, his sense of purpose would die. Julie is pessimistic (or, as she sees it, realistic), cautious, strong, protective, and ever aware of many people's potential for evil. She also loves swing music, and has dreams of a peaceful life. She differs from Gerda in that she is driven by a strong nihilistic streak, and has a brother, Thomas, who has Down's syndrome, a genetic condition that results in mental retardation. Julie and Bobby devote much of their off-duty time to this boy.

"I did a lot of reading about Down's syndrome," says Dean, "and we've been involved with charities for the disabled for quite some time, so I've been around people with Down's. They're absolutely loving and sweet-tempered—and *interesting*. Thomas has a great sense of humor. His role in this book is to be able to say things about life and about people that are true, but that might seem mean coming from another character. When I was writing from his point of view, it had this magical quality. Everything Thomas looked at—how he looked at it—made it new and different to me, and it got to be great fun to write those scenes. It was a difficult voice to sustain, because it wasn't just conveying his thoughts in misused grammar and syntax, but getting his tilted sensibility."

Julie and Bobby are joined in a common dream: They want a house by the sea and early retirement so they can enjoy their lives and care for Thomas. Often they will reverse roles, with the optimist becoming a cautionary voice—a technique that shows a fluidity between dualities common to most polarized characters in this novel. These two share an awareness of the brevity of life and the need to focus on what is significant. Love and fear, to them, are indivisible, because real love involves risk and vulnerability.

The Dakotas are called into an unusual case involving Frank Pollard, an amnesiac who arrives in their office with an exotic bug and a pocket full of gems. Subsequently we learn that he can teleport himself from place to place and is on the run from his demented giant of a brother, Candy, who wants to kill him for killing their psychotic mother. Candy and Frank also have sisters who are twins and who raise hordes of cats (which mimic them in their narcissism). As twins, they symbolize mirrors—this family's relationship to evil. All of them are products of a mother whose madness and bizarre sexuality had resulted in genetically defective children. Her own parents had been brother and sister and she had been a hermaphrodite who had impregnated herself. Having had children without benefit of intercourse, she believes their births and their missions are holy. She even fed Candy on blood from the palm of her hand (the stigmata defiled) and he consequently drinks the blood of his victims in an unholy ceremony of transformation into evil (an evil he views as righteousness). He reflects the sociopath in a novel that, in one scene, a character named Hal is reading, *The Last One Left*, by John D. MacDonald. (Hal reads MacDonald for the same reasons that Dean did, and *The Last One Left* is the same novel that first alerted Dean to the true nature of his father's aberrant traits.) The entire family is the essence of genetic and spiritual chaos; they are an evil mutation and their home is hell, The Bad Place.

Even the teleportation that Frank can achieve is an anarchic metaphor, because with each trip, his genetic structure becomes consistently disordered until he mutates into something unrecognizable. This mirrors the genetic chaos resulting from incest and the psychological madness of drugs, both of which influenced the births of the bizarre siblings.

Thomas, the boy of limited intelligence but purity of heart, is the exact opposite of the two-hundred-twenty-pound Candy, whose intelligence is equally limited through a genetic defect, but who embodies rampaging evil in the form of the unrelenting and unrelieved drive of male hormones. Candy embodies the motivations of the world's worst murderers in his zeal and self-righteous justifications. Candy and Thomas are psychically connected, enacting Dean's philosophy that the same kinds of traits can be manifested as either good or evil, depending on the character of the person who directs the energy. Thomas is aware of Candy, and to protect Julie, he telepathically explores this man whom he knows only as The Bad Thing. That draws Candy to him; Candy then kills him, making Thomas the Christ figure who sacrifices himself for Julie and Bobby. Dying, Thomas learns there is a light filled with love toward which he is going; he manages to communicate this revelation to Julie, to relieve her darkness. Dreams can be realized, she discovers, but it might be at a cost. The survivors' duty is to preserve, through memory, a person (Thomas) they love: "... they tended the flame of memory, so no one's death meant an immediate vanishment from the world; in some sense the deceased would live on after their passing, at least as long as those who loved them lived. Such memories were an essential weapon against the chaos of life and death . . . an endorsement of order and of meaning."[1]

Initially Dean had loved the character of Thomas so much that he had tried to keep him alive. Then the story began to fall apart. Dean agonized for two days and then went back to rewrite the problem scene. "The book is based on the Christian mythos. Thomas was Christ," he says. "He was a holy innocent in a corrupt world. Christ didn't live, and as soon as I started violating the inspiring mythology, *The Bad Place* stopped working."

The other Christ figure is Frank, who also sacrifices himself to stop the rampaging Candy. His middle name is Ezekiel, a biblical prophet who had experienced apocalyptic visions. He is represented in art as the one who will provide a new heart and spirit, as well as being a motif in the Last Judgment. Frank uses his own mutation to destroy Candy, chaos devouring chaos. The sick family imbibes its own poison, as exemplified in the man-eating cats, which devour people as food with no concerns outside themselves.

Throughout this novel, Dean constructs patterns of dichotomies such as vulnerability/safety, chaos/stability, the twins/the Dakotas, and innocence/corruption. He explores how easily one end of a polarity can change to the other, or at least be superficially similar enough to be vulnerable to corruption. Candy and Thomas both have psychic ability as the result of genetic defects, but in one it manifests as evil, in the other as innocence. Candy is the exaggeration of the worst human potential, while Thomas is the best. It shows Dean's two sides—the dream both realized and unrealized: There is some good in the bad (Frank among the Pollards) and there is some bad in the good (gaining paradise at Thomas's expense).

The Bad Place was a Literary Guild main selection—a deal that was settled before the manuscript was even finished. Putnam also published a limited edition of 250 copies, finely illustrated by Phil Parks. The novel stayed on the bestsellers list for fifteen weeks and ended up as the number twelve bestselling book for the year, with some 387,578 copies sold. It also went to number one in paperback, selling over two million copies during its initial stint on the list.

This novel was the first one that was made into a full-length audio version. Dean had allowed an audio abridgment of *Lightning*, and had found the cuts imposed on the material so intolerable that thereafter he licensed the Reader's Chair to do his next few books on tape.

"We met Dean at the ABA in 1990," says Delia White of the Reader's Chair. "We had published only one title at the time. He liked that we published unabridged and was instrumental to our obtaining the rights. I'm sure we wouldn't be where we are today if it weren't for his influence."

"Because I've virtually surrendered a piece of my life to each book," Dean said, "I can't bear to license an abridged audiotape." A full reading of *The Bad Place* required ten cassettes. The Reader's Chair did the same for *Cold Fire* and *Hideaway*.

Though *The Bad Place* received many strongly positive

reviews, some critics found Frank's demise and the explanation for Candy's evil repulsive, although most recognized the high degree of imagination that had gone into such a story. Almost no one commented on the biblical allegory. For the most part, the critics concentrated on the complex characters, pace, or the plot.

"This is white-knuckle, hair-on-the-back-of-the-neck-curling reading," said *The Los Angeles Book Review*, "as close to actual physical terror as the printed word can deliver." *Rave Reviews* noted "the cascading torrent of emotion" and "explosive climax." *Publishers Weekly* said, "Koontz soars beyond the limits of *Midnight*." *The New Orleans Times-Picayune* compared Dean's strange world to that of Flannery O'Connor and Walker Percy. In *Kirkus*, the reviewer called the novel "wildly eclectic . . . but not derivative: Koontz shrewdly refashions the borrowings and welds them to his own inventions." *The New York Times* recognized the painstaking work put into the powerful and credible characterization of Thomas, and Michael Collings in *Mystery Scene* said this novel is about us: "Its monsters are our monsters, writ large."

2

Dean delivered *The Bad Place* as the second book on a three-book contract, but Phyllis Grann wanted commitment from him for the future, so she offered to fold the third book into the next contract, which would be for four books, at $2.5 million per book. This meant that his advance for the next novel would be much higher than she had originally offered. She also paid $1.5 million for a collection of short stories, projected to be published by 1993.

Dean signed the contract, but it turned out to be his last with Putnam.

3

Just six days after he had typed "The End" on *The Bad Place*, Dean sold the rights to Warner Brothers for a theatrical film.

He was also to write the screenplay, and he delivered two drafts. The second draft created so much buzz that Don Johnson—who had been trying to find a way to work with Dean—hoped that it might be a vehicle for him and Melanie Griffith—to whom he was married at the time. Dean had long felt that Johnson was underestimated as an actor and was enthusiastic about working with him. For a brief period, the script was hot at Warner—until the CEO read it. "What genre is this in?" he asked. "It doesn't seem marketable. It's science fiction and suspense and romance and drama. I'm confused." Suddenly, in deference to the top guy, all the other executives became confused as well! They dumped Dean's script and set about developing the book into a straight, cheesy horror movie with a new writer. The product failed to reach film: Dean tried to buy back his script, even offering more money than he had been paid, but Warner would not sell.

In May, Paramount studio green-lighted the screenplay of *Midnight* that Dean had written for Mace Neufeld and Bob Rhemie. Several good directors were interested in it, but the producers chose one that Dean felt would make it into a slasher-type picture. "After a long phone call and a meeting with him," Dean says, "I was very distressed. I thought he didn't understand the story at all. The only things that interested him were gore and eroticism, and he wanted to replace original aspects of the story with material that was painfully derivative. So I withdrew from the project." *Midnight* was subsequently shelved.

The one movie that did get done was *The Face of Fear*. It was one of the four movies that Warner had sold to CBS television. Dean had written one script for this earlier for another company, which had been shelved, and now he had to work with someone else's adaptation. He was the co-executive producer with Grant Rosenberg, for the producer Lee Rich. "I've found everyone at Warner and CBS to be bright, flexible, and fun to work with," Dean said at the time. "They're not classic genre producers; they are much broader and more mainstream."

Farhad Mann was the director, and Dean liked what he saw of Farhad's work: "I liked the visuals in *Nick Knight*. It was a vampire movie and he did a lot of scenes from the vampire's point of view in flight. I don't know how he did these things on such a small budget. I also liked his work on *Max Headroom*. He created the whole unique look of it. Of the directors they were proposing for *The Face of Fear*, I thought he had a much better visual sense than anyone else. And he's honest."

"That was the first time I had met Dean," says Farhad. "I was hired through Warner Brothers. I'd always loved his writing, so that's the reason I chose that project. They liked my point of view and I was hired."

The film went into production in June, based on Dean's script, with a tight schedule of twenty-one days for completion. Dean was working on *Cold Fire*, but changes to the script were needed so quickly that he did not have time to meet his deadline for Putnam. He estimated that each week he devoted to the film, he was working one hundred hours per week. What he was able to send Phyllis Grann—a partial manuscript of four hundred pages—was received with great delight. From what she could tell, she said, it was the best novel he had written yet. That surprised him, considering how much attention he was giving to the filming.

"Dean was terrific to work with," says Farhad. "He's very at ease and cooperative. I was amazed. He was open to changes, fast in getting things done, and cinematic. He really understands filmmaking in terms of storytelling in a visual sense. The screenplay had been written by someone else and had a lot of problems, but within a couple of weeks, Dean just turned it around. It moved."

Farhad's vision was to create a very suspenseful and realistic film, but since they were shooting in Los Angeles and the story took place in Manhattan, he had to recreate the scenery with special optical shots. "I used eleven different locations to create that building. We painted and used lighting to make the colors and textures consistent."

The principal actors, Lee Horsley and Pam Dawber, had already been cast—and now Kevin Conroy, Bob Balaban, and William Sadler were added. Farhad managed to shoot the entire movie on schedule, which is a relatively short period for a television movie, and on a tight budget. "I had a terrific script and someone I could talk to every day, when things had to change quickly. And when you have a writer with imagination and passion, it takes you pretty far."

The most difficult aspects for him were having the actors rappel down the building. "We were in Los Angeles, so you couldn't aim the camera and show palm trees or buildings that people recognize. I needed three mat shots to make the scenes feel as if they were in New York, and Dean was enormously helpful. He fought for those shots. When the executives didn't want to release more money, he was ready to pay for them himself. He'd fight with the studio regarding certain things, and he really supported me as a director. That's unusual. If he likes you, he works with you. He doesn't let you be hanged. And he wants quality."

Pam Dawber, the actress playing Connie, agreed that working with Dean was a positive experience. "He seemed to have no ego at all with this movie," she said. "He didn't think his words were etched in stone. He just wanted this movie to work."

CBS aired *The Face of Fear* on September 30, 1990, against the second-year premiere of the popular television show *Twin Peaks*. *The Wall Street Journal* saw an advance showing and gave it a positive review, saying the killers were especially terrifying. The movie won the ratings battle for that night.

4

Shortly thereafter, one of the major television networks approached Grant Rosenberg—who was then at Paramount—about doing a summer anthology show with Dean. "I came up with a show to be called *Strange Highways*," says Dean. "The main character's name was Bobby Strange, and he traveled around with his dog in a pickup truck. He supported himself by playing music on a guitar, washing dishes, and doing odd jobs. Music was the only thing that sustained him. Every show opened with this voice-over that said that someone had killed his family. It was to be this very disturbing, mysterious background, with the impression that he was on the run. He says, 'Maybe because of my own experience with the darkness, wherever I go people come up to me with stories they've never been able to tell others, things they've seen, things that have happened to them.' They were all eerie stories and some would have sprung out of stories of mine."

Rosenberg and the executives at Paramount Television were happy with the concept and sure they would nail it down with no problem. Interest at the network waned, however, and Dean eventually used the show's title for his collection of short stories.

5

When Dean and Gerda sold their second home in Orange, they found a place in Newport Beach, which is one of Orange County's most spectacular coastal towns, south of Los Angeles and southwest of Anaheim. It surrounds the largest yacht harbor in the United States, in which are seven residential islands. Dotted with celebrity homes, Newport Beach is part business center and part resort. From their house, located not far from Fashion Island, Dean and Gerda could see out to Balboa Peninsula and the ocean beyond.

The Victorian-style house, sitting on a quiet cul de sac in a gated community, was in move-in condition, but they were used to making each and every home they lived in their own, so they spent nine months on a remodel. When it was finished, the previously darkish home was filled with light. White carpets lined the floors and the circular stair that dominated a large, skylighted hallway, and the walls were all painted a pale peach with glossy white trim. Sunlight streamed in through large windows in nearly every room of the three-story house. They filled it with antiques, Chinese porcelains, original art, and their collection of fifty thousand books. Dean and Gerda each had an office, and once again, Dean lined his with a copy of each of his books in all editions. He also hung original artwork of his covers on the walls and installed a massive, custom-made walnut desk with drawers designed to fit his specific needs. Although he had a view, he kept the blinds drawn to concentrate on his work. He describes this office in *Mr. Murder*.

6

Dean finally finished the manuscript for *Cold Fire*, based initially on an idea he had been pondering for some time. "For a period I was fascinated with Jung and the concept of synchronicity," he says. "I wanted to do a novel that *explained* synchronicity. But of course it is a mystery of existence that *can't* be explained! So I had to settle for using it as a major device in a way that shows that coincidence can be more than mere coincidence."

Dean had read a book, *Incredible Coincidence*, in which he had found a particularly fascinating case that involved a businessman and a patrolman in El Paso, Texas. The patrolman, Allen Falby, had crashed his motorcycle into the tailgate of a truck, rupturing an artery and nearly severing one of his legs. A businessman named Alfred Smith witnessed the accident and used his tie to bind Falby's leg and save his life.

Five years later, Falby was on highway night patrol when he received a call about a bad accident. He reached the wreck before the ambulance and found that the victim was bleeding badly from a severed artery in his leg. Falby applied a tourniquet and pulled him from the car. Then he recognized this man as the same person who had saved his own life.

"That story so impressed me," Dean remembers. "You wonder what's at work here. For years, I had thought about a story based on an ordinary person who finds himself caught in amazing incidents that have no explanation. I wanted to write a novel about somebody who was always, uncannily, in the right place at the right time, whose life just dripped synchronicity—and then try to make meaning of it. That ended up being *Cold Fire*, but it never was the novel I wanted to write. It actually turned into something else, but the idea came from the concept of synchronicity.

"If you were to build up a series of breathtaking incidents like this, I think you could write a riveting story, but you'd better have a payoff. You have to explain it with some power greater than man. You'll either have aliens, which I've done. Or God. But it's hard to write about God in modern fiction. You're dealing with the ineffable, and I could never quite figure out a story that would be satisfying in the end. It would have to be enormously spiritual, working at another level.

"I think, on an unconscious level, we're more in tune with the realities of existence than we are on a conscious level. Colin Wilson touches upon the thought—which I agree with—

that our culture narrows our vision. It allows us to see things in a certain way, but prevents us from seeing in other ways. We may have the capability to see three hundred sixty degrees, but we basically see life in a narrow wedge. If only we could look at the world with no prejudices, with our senses wide open to reception, we might see everything in a totally different way, but we are led to view the world within certain cultural constrictions.

"Our fear of death starts at an early age—that awful moment, somewhere between the ages of five and eight—and a tremendous amount of human potential is extinguished. We become fearful, but also intensely focused because we become aware of the ticking clock, aware of our mortality. We can't think about death constantly, of course, or we couldn't go forward. Everything would seem meaningless. These forces of the human condition narrow what we're capable of seeing. But I think on an unconscious level, we are *obsessed* with our mortality. We're always aware that there are other dimensions to life. If we could get in touch with the repressed part of our consciousness that is fundamentally attuned to the nature of creation and our place in it, we'd find greater potential within ourselves. I think on that deeper level we have an innate sense of right and wrong, and we have a connection to the infinite. As a writer, I enjoy the possibility of other dimensions."

Cold Fire was dedicated to Nick and Vicky Page, and Dick and Pat Karlan. It opens with poems from *The Book of Counted Sorrows* that prepare readers for the idea that nothing in life is what it seems. Sociological observations are a stronger part of the narrative in this story than in any previous novel, particularly the self-indulgence and selfishness of the early nineties culture. Dean comments on the state of irresponsible journalism and the emphasis on violence over stories of hope and courage. Such stories are shown to side with chaos, not with the human spirit that strives for purpose and coherence. He sees a world around him that *breeds* rather than fights monsters, in terms of false values and victim mentalities.

The scene set in the church in the desert is an allegory suggesting that people who seek meaning in social or political movements are doomed to frustration; only spiritual values and one-on-one commitments (love, friendship) will provide satisfaction, but society seems to be moving away from this solution to its problems. Life without meaning is unbearable — we are creatures who must have some sort of spiritual purpose. The other theme is that we often spend our lives struggling with the consequences of unresolved sorrow. A sense of purpose can aid us.

In an interview, Dean mentioned that the inspiration for this novel came from his love of books. "It's about what books mean to me," he said in *Fear* magazine. "I was talking to someone else who had a difficult childhood who also found that reading books was a way to escape. I wanted to write about the value of books."

The heroine, Holly Thorne, is a disillusioned journalist in Portland, Oregon, searching for meaning in her life. She hates being alone and wants to improve upon the world that God has made. She is distressed by the deteriorating sense of values in society at large, but hope is born when she encounters Jim Ironheart heroically saving a child. He rebuffs her even as he invites her closer, which intrigues her. She traces him to California through a series of extraordinary stories about him saving people, and insists that he tell her about himself. She is the most feisty of Koontz's female characters to date, determined and competent. Through her, Jim learns more about himself, and eventually realizes the truth about his inner conflicts. She is a Lois Lane to Jim's Superman, but with a decidedly more psychological twist.

Jim's parents had been victims of random violence and, as a young boy, he had been unable to help them — even though he had been experiencing some nascent psychic powers. Subsequently he had developed a savior complex. He views himself as channeling God's will when his powers allow him to predict imminent catastrophe. This was affirmed for him when, after a daring rescue in a Nevada desert, he collapses outside a church and the priest who finds him says that Jim exhibited the stigmata, which had returned the priest to his faith.

Holly follows Jim onto a plane which he is driven to board because he *knows* someone on it will need him. He doesn't know who he is about to save — or from what — but after take-off, he realizes that the plane is fated to crash and that most of the passengers will die. There is a certain child that he must save. He also shows Holly where to sit to have a chance at survival. Now she knows she is on to an extraordinary story, but she begins to be plagued by dreams of a pursuing monster. Jim knows this thing from his own dreams and calls it The Entity. He takes Holly to his childhood home north of Santa Barbara, where suddenly he recalls encountering The Friend—a being on an alien spaceship in the bottom of a mill pond. The alien shows itself now to Holly and Jim, and claims to be the one sending Jim on his miraculous missions, saving the lives of people destined to make great contributions to humanity.

Holly remains skeptical, despite The Friend's warnings to beware The Enemy—a second alien presence that is the embodiment of every movie monster ever to threaten a ten-year-old boy. Eventually she realizes that the entire scenario is based on a novel that Jim had read as a child, *The Black Windmill*, and that both The Friend and The Enemy are not aliens but aspects of his own consciousness. *He* is as dangerous as he is benevolent—both a dark and light miracle. The fantasy had given him a sense of purpose and the feeling of redemption when he had failed to save his parents. However, his rage and despair had added a dark edge, a way to punish himself. Subconsciously he had drawn Holly to himself because of her talent for forcing an issue. She had brought him to the truth—that psychologically he had projected outside himself nonhuman entities rather than fragmenting into multiple personalities. He had saved himself this way before his shadow side became powerful enough to annihilate him. Yet, despite dissolving this fantasy, Jim finds he can still save lives, so he and Holly set forth together with this destiny and their love as their shared sense of purpose.

To frame the tale, Dean uses several autobiographical elements. The town where Jim takes Holly has the flavor of Bedford, where Dean grew up. He buys his scary novels at the local drug store, as Dean did, and knows where the town bully lives. He also keeps his grandfather in a nursing home that is like the one that Dean had found for his father's remaining years. Ray was still living there even as Dean wrote the novel.

Cold Fire was a main selection of the Literary Guild and Doubleday Book Club. It hit number one on *The New York Times* bestsellers list in the same year that Robert Bly's men's movement was gaining ground and Deborah Tannen was teaching men and women that they just did not understand each other. *Cold Fire* remained a bestseller for over three months, and Putnam issued a limited edition of 800 copies, illustrated by Phil Parks. In paperback, it remained on the list for ten weeks.

Newsweek did an article on Dean and many more reviewers took notice, although some continued their repetitive comparisons to Stephen King. This book had the best reviews of any to date. The UPI said, "An extraordinary piece of fiction with unforgettable characters. It will be a classic." Clarence Peters, for *The Chicago Tribune*, said, "Koontz's characterizations are hardly surpassed by his ability to sustain the suspense and keep the most bizarre story plausible," although *The West Coast Review of Books* felt the ending came too quickly, that the reader needs a little more breathing space after so much fast-paced action. Dean's hope to be noticed for provoking a range of emotions was fulfilled in the *Arkansas Democrat*, with Susan Pierce's comment: "But it's in the description of emotional states—from love to despair—that Koontz consistently hits the bull's eye, evoking reactions of, 'Yes! I know exactly how that feels!'" She also noted that the novel emphasizes the conviction that life without purpose is the greatest horror of all.

7

After finishing *The Face of Fear* for CBS, Dean set to work developing a screenplay for *Cold Fire*. He showed it to Farhad Mann, with whom he wanted to work again. Farhad was delighted, both with the script and with Dean's appreciation. He suggested some changes and Dean incorporated them.

"I had written a draft," says Dean, "and he picked it apart. He's the only director I've ever seen who can pick a screenplay apart and give good input about linear storytelling and genuinely deep characterization. We worked together and got a screenplay that we both loved. Farhad wanted Holly to have a solid relationship before meeting Jim, such as being the mother of a child. Then when she encounters Jim, she has to leave her daughter in the hands of her mother—with the ultimate rescue being a highly dramatic sequence in which the daughter is at risk. It really did make the script more dynamic."

Thus, in the screenplay, some of the plot twists change. In addition to the new character—the daughter—there is a professor who explains the nature of poltergeist activity and sets Holly on the track of psychological possibilities. Jim also gets the opportunity to live out the scene of random violence from his childhood in a way different from in the book, and he discovers (as in the novel) that his power can be a tool of either death or life; it is up to him to decide.

Farhad and Dean pitched this screenplay to key producers and studios. Several studios were enthusiastic. Then, when the executives read the script and realized that the enemy was Jim himself, they balked. "We had two different studios say, 'We would buy the project if there really were aliens in the pond,'" says Dean. "'And it must turn out that the aliens really are guiding him and there really is a good alien and a bad alien.' In both cases, the studios were willing to put up big money. It would have been a fifty million dollar picture, at least, but Farhad and I didn't pursue those avenues because we knew that we'd be destroying the integrity of the piece. I'm committed to keeping it off the market until I can get it done right."

8

In July, Dean signed a contract with Dean Mullaney, publisher of Eclipse Books, to publish graphic adaptations of one of his works. Scripted by Ed Gorman and painted by Anthony Bilau, his novella, "Trapped," appeared as an eighty-page, full-color graphic novel in 1993. No more have followed because Dean has mixed feelings about the medium. "Few graphic novels are flat-out wonderful, and I don't want to do them unless I control the process and we can hit a homer every time."

9

In the last few months of his father's life, Dean again thought about having DNA tests done. Gerda urged him to do it, but when he watched his father's increasingly angry behavior, he finally realized why he had put it off so long: He did not wish to discover definitively that Ray Koontz *was* his father. At least, if he never knew the truth, he could imagine other, more comforting, possibilities. "The truth does not always set us free," he later wrote about this decision. "Sometimes fantasy can enhance our lives more than science, self-deception more than truth. In the exercise of imagination, we can achieve liberation that can never be attained when we are encumbered by the leaden weight of cold facts."[3]

Ray died on September 16, 1991. Dean had him cremated the same evening, and although there was a plot beside Florence reserved for Ray in Bedford, Dean elected not to disturb her rest. He put Ray's ashes in an urn and sealed it into a marble niche in a mausoleum in Fullerton, California.

Dean organized a memorial service, but no one came. "This is the most terrifying thing I can imagine," he says. "To have lived a whole life and no one cares that you were here. My father's life is a perfect reflection of the idea that when you always operate to personal advantage, you alienate yourself from everyone—from meaning, from hope. His situation in the end was pretty bleak. When we made a list of who we needed to tell that he had died, it was very short. Of those we did tell, there wasn't a one who would have come to the funeral. Not even if it had been in Bedford, I suspect."

Dean's subsequent books show his progression of working through some of the issues that still felt incomplete. He had already written *Hideaway*, with its underlying struggle between father and son. His next novel, *Dragon Tears*, would confront the sense of chaos that his father had always represented to him. He was not sure that he had even remembered everything about his life with his father—a thought provoked by his inability to go into his childhood home two years before—and some of the more deeply buried fears were now to surface as he created characters based on Ray who presented his heroes and heroines with difficult moral struggles.

"Honestly, it was a time of great relief for me because my father had died," Dean recalls. "This burden that he'd always been was finally removed from us. Gerda and I went out for drinks that evening, and I said, 'Isn't this terrible? It's almost like we're celebrating.' We stayed there from five until midnight just talking about our experiences with him. I could not think of a single moment in my entire life—not *one* two-minute stretch—where my father and I had any conversation or any shared experience that wasn't stressful, that was actually father to son, that was pleasant and worth remembering. I can't imagine anything sadder."

Dean was then plagued by a recurring dream.

"After my father died, I had this dream seven or eight times within the space of a few weeks, and then I never had it again. In the dream, I'm in the basement of the house as it was when I grew up. My grandfather had dug out the cellar and had plastered a couple of inches of concrete over the dirt, so the walls had this smooth, hand-formed feeling to them. There was a coal room, and the coal was delivered through a chute from outside. Nevertheless, you accessed the coal room from inside the cellar, itself. It was a fairly dark place, spidery. The dream was always in or around this space, and it was always related to the furnace. In some of the dreams, I'd be in the basement, and in some, I'd be coming down the basement steps. In one dream I was behind the furnace. I'd fallen asleep in the space back there. I woke and heard a noise and saw that the basement was full of the light from the open furnace. My father was at the furnace door, and when I came out from where I'd been sleeping, he was shocked to see me. He demanded to know what I was doing, whether I was spying on him. He pushed me back into the corner and threatened that he was going to kill me right there. It was frightening, and I woke up just gasping, unable to get my breath.

"Sometimes in the dream I would come down the cellar steps and see him at the furnace. He would turn around and see me at the base of the steps and come running across the basement to grab me and push me up against the wall. He would say, 'You're not even supposed to be home,' and then threaten to kill me. And it always centered around that furnace. I'm sure my father never burned a body in the furnace, but that is definitely the feeling of the dream, that something terrible happened in that basement and was being covered up, and somehow I found it. The feeling in the dream is that I've seen something I'm not supposed to have seen. That's what's really frightening.

"It's weird to me that, after he died, I should have this dream repeatedly, and then just have it go away. I don't really believe in repressed memories, but sometimes I think this dream was almost a memory, because it was excruciatingly vivid."

[1]Dean R. Koontz, *The Bad Place* (New York: Putnam, 1992), p. 379.

[2]*Fear*, September 1988.

[3]Dean Koontz, "Beautiful Death" in *Beautiful Death* (New York: Penguin Studio, 1996).

TWENTY-ONE

Entropy, Evil, and the Struggle for Transcendence

1

THE NEXT NUMBER ONE BESTSELLER, WHICH CAME OUT EARLY in 1992, was *Hideaway*. It was inspired by the evolving science of resuscitation medicine. A few years earlier, Dean had read about the reanimation of a child who had been dead for sixty-six minutes and was brought back to life without suffering brain damage. He soon forgot the article. Then one day in 1990, he went to search for story ideas to link together certain themes that intrigued him. He wanted to write about people confronted with genuine evil in an antireligious age that denied the existence of Evil with a capital E, that insisted on Freudian shades of gray. How would a modern couple cope and adapt to the sudden *possibility* of the uncanny and the spiritual? He went through everything in his file without finding a suitable story. "Suddenly the premise for *Hideaway* came to me fully developed," he says.

This experience showed him the value of reading widely and allowing the subconscious to process the material, because it had certainly delivered. He went to the University of California at Irvine and discovered a wealth of material on the subject. He also talked with writer and physicist Greg Benford, who was able to answer a lot of his questions about surviving very cold temperatures.

Hideaway is a highly significant novel on the theme of deadly intimacy between father and son, juxtaposed with the bond of devils and angels potentially linked by the same forces in the unknown. Dean uses a quote from Shakespeare, "O, what may man within him hide, Though Angel on the Outward side." Although he had once considered himself an atheist, Dean had come around to the belief that there is more to life than the perceived world; there is purpose and "mysteries perhaps unpierceable." Having little patience with either codified religions or New Age enlightenment, he believed that spiritual power lay within each individual, in a "long-term application of intellect to the vital questions of existence." His reading in modern physics and molecular biology—the proposal by some scientists in these disciplines that we might be living in a created universe—had recast his thinking.

Dean was writing *Hideaway* as he was struggling to free himself of his codependence with his father, who was by then eighty-one years old. He had managed to cut down his visits to Ray, but not to the extent suggested by his doctor. There is no doubt that his childhood sense of his father plays out in this novel, with his father's penchant for being a veritable devil. The only atonement possible is to redirect all energy that could potentially be evil— the result of being associated with his father—toward goodness. Dean also expresses his fear that that psychosis may skip a generation, as it does in the Nyebern family in the novel, and that not having children is better than trying to cope with and cover over the heinous acts of a possible genetic throwback.

Lindsay and Hatch Harrison have lost a four-year-old son to cancer, which took a terrible toll on their marriage. An accident on an icy road sends them into a river, drowning Hatch, but he is resuscitated after eighty minutes. He and Lindsay decide to repair their lives by adopting a child, and know they can expedite the process by adopting one with a handicap. They meet ten-year-old Regina, a feisty girl with a deformed hand and foot, who is nevertheless full of life. When Lindsay and Hatch adopt her, she gets caught up in a nightmare imposed on them by another resuscitation patient, Jeremy Nyebern.

Jeremy, who calls himself Vassago, after a prince of hell, is a sociopathic boy who had killed his mother and sister and had then committed suicide in an attempt to join his idol, a previously executed murderer who had written about satanic visions. Jeremy's own father, Jonas Nyebern, who was also Hatch's physician, had resuscitated the boy in the hope of discovering why he had murdered the rest of the family. He realizes that it was an inherited sociopathic illness from his own murderous father, which had skipped a generation.

Nyebern's desire to redeem his bloodline is similar to Dean's, although he goes about it in a different manner. He collects religious art that inspires in him some belief in atonement, and then donates each collection. He and Hatch have a conversation about evil that expresses Dean's own feelings about it at that point in his authorship: that psychosis may have a genetic cause, but that evil itself might be a very real force in the world—an energy wholly apart. Nyebern states that no expert has ever proposed a satisfactory explanation for monstrous sociopathic violence. "The only cogent answer," it seems to him (and Dean), "was that the human species was imperfect, stained, and carried within itself the seeds of its own destruction."[1] The Church calls it Satan; science calls it the mystery of genetics, but neither offers satisfactory solutions or preventives. Evil endures, as always.

"In this novel," says Dean, "evil can be traced to three sources: human behavior; the transmittal of sociopathic behavior through damaged genes, which is the most terrifying because it is the most arbitrary and relentless; and possibly to evil as a supernatural force. . . . Nothing in the book prevents the reader from embracing either the totally supernatural or the more logical interpretation of events. . . . The way you interpret it at first pass may tell you something about your own subconscious attitudes."[2]

Nyebern fails to understand how his impulses have transformed a tool that could be used for good into one that wreaks destruction. His reanimations bring back a devil (Jeremy) and an angel (Hatch).

Jeremy lives in Fantasy World, a defunct amusement park that had gone bankrupt the night he killed his best friend on a ride and then set fire to the Haunted House. His own secret hideaway is in service tunnels under the park, and his "church" is in the Funhouse, where he brings victims to kill in the process of creating a sculpture out of their bodies to present to Satan. He is fascinated solely with the dead, and where he lives bears similarities to Dante's ninth circle of hell, with Satan in the center. Resentful of being brought back to life, he wants to earn his way back to hell by committing monstrous acts. Since he and Hatch were resuscitated under similar circumstances, they can see through each other's eyes. Vassago sees Regina and Lindsay, and decides to add this mother and daughter to his creation—an echo of his own mother and sister. He grabs Regina, forcing Lindsay and Hatch to pursue him to the Funhouse. When Vassago captures Lindsay, Hatch attacks, surprised to hear himself saying he is Uriel, the

Archangel. He uses a crucifix to kill Vassago and restore moral balance in the world. Whether he is actually transformed via supernatural forces or whether this is merely the way Vassago perceived him is left to the reader to decide.

One of the settings in this novel is Zov's Bistro, a contemporary Mediterranean restaurant in Tustin where Dean and Gerda often have dinner. Dean claims he has never had a bad meal there, and has become friends with Zov and her husband, Gary. He dedicated *Dark Rivers of the Heart* to them.

In *Hideaway's* subplots, Dean took a shot at art critics by linking them to predatory insects and to the unfeeling sociopath. Some seem to have no concern for people's feelings, and one, Hornell, gets his due when he becomes Vassago's target. Dean also comments on the deleterious effects of the erosion of values in modern society. The killer, Vassago, is linked with nihilistic subcultures that have no love of life and lose themselves in drugs, dirt, music, and chaos.

Although he had based Vassago on real-life sociopaths, Dean worried that this character's behavior was too extreme to ring true to the reader. But in July, while he was still working on the book, a story broke in the papers about a man named Jeffrey Dahmer. Thirty-one-year-old Dahmer was arrested in Wisconsin for killing fifteen young men (with other counts pending), and then cooking and eating their flesh. He had dismembered some while they were still alive and had taken photos and videotapes of his "art." Body parts of all kinds lay around his apartment, including severed heads in the refrigerator.

Dean realized that nothing he could create in fiction could be half as extreme as human behavior in the real world, and he stopped worrying about his Vassago.

The continuing theme of toxic intimacy is explored in several relationships in this novel. The central association is that between Vassago and his father and grandfather, but there is also one between Hatch and his father. If anyone in this novel is Dean, it is Hatch. He likes to sing along with oldies and lives in a Mediterranean-style house. His father, like Dean's, had been quick-tempered, angry, verbally abusive, and controlling: "Secretly he cherished irritation and actively sought new sources of it."[3] The father had believed he was not destined to be happy, and anything—or nothing—could set him off. Hatch fears the potential for having the same temper, and he is even more terrified of losing control, so he strives to make himself mellow and tolerant. "Having been raised under the hateful and oppressive hand of his father, he had surrendered innocence at an early age in return for an intuitive grasp of aberrant psychology that had permitted him to survive."[4] Even so, his anger lies within, ready to erupt, and it gets resolved only when it emerges as righteous anger that attacks evil—as Dean does in his novels. Righteous anger taps what he inherited from his father and purifies it for better purposes. In that way, he is nothing like his father. He uses the same energy and obsessiveness, but channels it into a more creative process. Hatch shares with Vassago, as Dean shares with his father, a feeling of relentless pressure, but he makes it work for himself and for humanity, rather than in an abusive, self-defeating way. In the end, each person perceives the world in his or her own way and takes from it different lessons. The potential is present for good or ill, and the person's own character make all the difference.

Hideaway was the only novel in four months to knock *Scarlett*, a sequel to *Gone With the Wind*, from the top spot on the bestsellers list. It was a Literary Guild main selection and remained on the list for three months. It was also number one in paperback.

Phyllis Grann was the first to understand that *Hideaway* only appeared to be supernatural, but was not necessarily so. Few reviewers echoed her sentiments, and some viewed the supernatural twist as a miscalculation. *The Washington Post*'s critic said, "Though rife with familiar theological arguments, his novels have always conveyed the belief that innate goodness ultimately *must* triumph over evil because good and evil originate in the human heart. Indeed, long before most of his colleagues, Koontz realized that this bedrock concern of horror fiction could be addressed through non-supernatural scenarios." In *The San Francisco Chronicle*, Alix Madrigal pointed out that "Koontz asks us to believe in a vision of hell that he himself has discredited," and he disliked being pulled into Vassago's perspective. Yet most reviewers were more enthusiastic. David Forsmark in the *Flint Journal* said that the questions Koontz raises about life, death, good, and evil, are "worthy of C. S. Lewis," while *Kirkus* called the book a "grandly melodramatic morality play." That reviewer went on to say that "Koontz's novels crest bestseller lists not only for their heart-pounding horrors, but also for their celebrations of righteousness and redemption." The Associated Press called it "a chiller capable of leaving emotional bruises on the reader," while *Michigan State News* cited the author's "incredible gift for the art of language."

2

Pat Karlan sold the film rights for $600,000 to Tri-Star Pictures and Summers-Quaid Productions, who said they wanted to make it into a "classy suspense movie." They developed a script, changing writers twice. (Dean had no time to work on a script just then.) They signed Jeff Goldblum and Christine Lahti to star in it, and Brett Leonard to direct. Dean liked the final draft of the screenplay and had high hopes. The producer of the picture seemed to understand the book, including the complicated subtext. Then the good screenplay was replaced by one that Dean considered "inept and cheesy." To make matters worse, they changed the character of Regina from a handicapped adoptee to a promiscuous teenage girl who *willingly* goes with Vassago.

After sitting through forty minutes of the November 1994 screening at a Long Beach preview, Dean walked out in disgust. He found the whole thing offensive, so he threatened legal action with Tri-Star to get his name off the credits. The nature of the story was completely changed, and he did not want his own vision associated with that presented on the screen. What to him had been a story about a disabled girl using wit and courage in the face of adversity had been turned into an outright horror story. In a letter to the studio, he called it "astonishingly incoherent, filled with contradictions and moronic logic. . . . This script has a viewpoint that is the antithesis of everything my work stands for and is offensive when it is not simply boring." The only draft of the script he had read and approved had been thrown out. He offered to repay all the money he had been given for the rights in exchange for removing any trace of his association with the project. But he could only persuade the studio to *minimize* the use of his name. Tri-Star did not use his name in trailers or put it above the title in their ads.

Agreeing with Dean, the critics found it dull, imitative, and clichéd. *Daily Variety* said it "fell short of satisfying visceral entertainment."

Dean decided not to sell film rights again unless he wrote the screenplay, was named co-executive producer, and/or profoundly respected the talents of the producer and director.

3

Dean was becoming increasingly unhappy with both his publisher and his agent. He felt that *Hideaway* had not been given the promised support. The publisher had talked about doing forced distribution on this book to really push copies into the bookstores, but that had not occurred. When Dean complained to Claire Smith about what he felt was a glass ceiling being imposed on him, he remembers that she tried to mollify him rather than taking action. As often in the past, he felt that she sided with the publisher even when he was complaining about an egregious breach of promise. He believed that he could get much more money and support from another publisher, but his agent argued for the wisdom of staying put. He began to feel that he might need a new agent.

After Putnam backed off the promised promotion and ad plans for *Hideaway*, Dean had to look forward to *Dragon Tears* with the hope that there would be a more aggressive publication. But then he learned that the print run would be only slightly higher than the previous novel, with no more ad money, and he realized that nothing was going to change. Phyllis Grann would stick to her conservative formula, even though Dean felt it was a good time in his career to be bold. Sell-through was very high, largely on word of mouth, and it was the ideal moment to capitalize on that. Perhaps the cautious approach had worked for other writers, but Dean was impatient with this methodical pace.

He felt subsumed under a general policy rather than treated as an individual. He asked Grann to raise his advance and she did, but she still offered much less than he felt he would receive elsewhere. The money was not important in itself—but he knew from bitter experience that publishers would often push hard only those books on which they were genuinely at risk of losing money.

If they made fortunes without a hard push, they would never take the risk—and Putnam had made out exceptionally well on all of Dean's titles, with limited advertising and promotion. Writing is about communicating, and Dean—as do all authors—wanted to reach as many people as possible with his ideas.

Claire Smith tried to persuade Dean to accept what was offered, so he left her and called Robert Gottlieb of the William Morris Agency. He had met Gottlieb at the American Booksellers Association convention in Anaheim one year, and Gottlieb had expressed enthusiasm for Dean's work. They had chatted for a moment and then had gone their separate ways. Gottlieb was now prepared to fly to California to meet with him and Gerda to see if they were all in agreement.

Robert Gottlieb had gotten his start as an agent in the mail-room of the William Morris Agency, then had become an assistant in the Literary Department. He became an agent in 1982, and seven years later became one of the youngest agents to head that department. By 1992, he had become an executive vice president and was elected to the board of directors. On his client list are such high-profile authors as Tom Clancy and Evan Hunter/Ed McBain.

Gottlieb had read and admired Dean's novels for years. "Dean is a compelling author," he says. "He writes what I would call serious commercial fiction. He's a true novelist and craftsman, and he has honed that craft with an eye toward perfection throughout his professional career.

"My philosophy as an agent is to be a gateway of opportunity for my authors, which means that I need to be knowledgeable about all the different possible formats in which intellectual property rights can be exploited. Dean is in a unique position in that there is a universe of formats for his work. It's a question of organizing it, focusing it, and concentrating it in such a way that it will leverage all the other values of his business. It's my job to see to it that his business is always growing."

Gottlieb felt that much was wrong with the Putnam contracts Dean had signed, and he wanted them revised (with no commission to him) as part of any deal for new books. He also wanted Dean's advances to be nearly tripled. Ultimately Putnam agreed to ninety-five percent of the requested terms, but in light of what both Gottlieb and Dean believed were woefully inadequate past contracts, they decided that *all* matters had to be settled favorably in order to proceed.

Gottlieb let Sonny Mehta at the Knopf Publishing Group know that he could make a bid as well for a three-book package, so he did. Dean accepted it. Although there was a gentlemen's agreement that the terms would not be made public, the very next day's *Wall Street Journal* reported that Knopf had paid $18.9 million for three new novels and another $10 million for six backlist books to be published in paperback by Ballantine.

Phyllis Grann was disappointed. "We are sad to see Dean leave," she said at the time, "but happy to know he will be published by one of my best friends and a publisher I totally admire."[5] In *The Wall Street Journal*, she said that Putnam simply could not afford the deal.

Dean says, "I have always admired Phyllis enormously, even when I've disagreed with her. As she herself would be quick to say, 'It's business, nothing personal.' But the fact is that she had offered the same terms as Knopf—and our deal broke down over other issues, mainly terms of the contracts already in force there on twenty-five backlist titles."

Dean realized that he now had an agent who would fight for him and get him the best possible terms. "He has vision," Dean says. "He reads the novels and understands them. I can talk to him about them—and he has a business strategy for the next ten years! He knows that in modern publishing, you *must* succeed financially in order to have a chance to say what you want to say, as a writer, to the largest possible audience. Maybe it's sad that art cannot flourish without commerce—but that's the hard truth."

"I view myself as Dean's partner, as his agent, his manager, his friend," Gottlieb states, "and as someone who is his most ardent advocate in all situations."

4

In July 1992, New Jersey resident Linda Kuzminczuk was reading a novel by sisters Dawn Pauline Dunn and Susan Hartzell, called *The Crawling Dark* when she felt a sense of familiarity. She was certain she had read something like it before. It was about a town whose residents are all discovered dead and a sheriff and his deputy who assist two siblings who have returned there. That sounded to her like Dean Koontz's novel *Phantoms*, which she had read five years earlier. When she checked, she noticed that not only were the plots similar, but virtually whole passages were plagiarized. She typed up a letter to Putnam, who forwarded it to Dean. He took immediate legal action. The two women, who wrote together as Pauline Dunn, and their publisher, Zebra Books, had to withdraw not only that novel from the market, but their previous one as well. Called *Demonic Color* and also published by Zebra, it, too, exhibited similarities to *Phantoms*. The women forwarded their $2,500 advance to Dean's attorney to offset his substantial legal fees, and were required to place an ad in *Publishers Weekly* announcing their action.

"It seems to me if you were going to do this," Dean said at the time, "it would make a lot of sense to choose an obscure book by a dead author."[6] With over three million copies of *Phantoms* in print at that time in the United States alone, their chances of getting caught were fairly high.

Dean was grateful to Linda Kuzminczuk for looking out for his interests, and every year he sends her a signed copy of each of his new novels.

5

The next novel was Dean's fifth number one bestseller in a row. For the byline of this one, he dropped his middle initial, which he had used since he began to be published, for two reasons. First, authors had once used initials as a matter of course, but now it seemed old-fashioned to do so. Second, with his growing success, publishers used his name on two lines on the jacket, the better to make it large, and the "R." dangling on the end of the first line was simply ugly design. Besides, the "R." stood for "Ray," which was his father's name. It seemed appropriate to put that behind him. Subsequently, during Berkley's in-house Halloween party that year, Susan Allison and her coworkers dressed in costumes as usual, but also made a tombstone for the "R"—rest in peace.

Dedicated to Ed and Carol Gorman, friends in Iowa, *Dragon Tears* is an anti-Freudian novel about personal transformation through the power of the will. Dean had wanted to call it *Ticktock*, and had briefly thought of calling it *Split Second*, but finally settled for *Dragon Tears*, a symbol of bitterness which Dean explained in the poem he wrote for *The Book of Counted Sorrows* to open Part Three.

A major theme is that moral responsibility and commitment fend off entropy, while excuses for victimhood merely contribute to society's decline. Dean opened the novel with several poems from *The Book of Counted Sorrows* and one from country singer Garth Brooks. The central theme that radiates throughout the novel is an etching by Francisco de Goya, which represents the dissolution of self by greedy ego, and which is portrayed by a voracious character whose development is arrested in a narcissistic twelve-year-old mentality. "The work was menacing, abrasive to the nerves, conveying a sense of horror and despair, not least of all because it included the figure of a giant, demonic ghoul in the act of devouring a bloody and headless human body."[7]

Dean's endless experimenting with point of view is this time best studied in the part of the story told through the perspective of Woofer, a dog. Dean believed that this allowed for an interesting way to comment on the world, since a dog would have a very different angle. It was a challenge to create a narrative voice for the dog that would seem genuine and not anthropomorphic.

In the story, partners Harry Lyon and Connie Gulliver are cops. Harry loves order, while Connie never fails to note the signs of entropy all around. She was abused as a child and has no family, so she heads into risk with abandon. Her attitude reflects that of other social elements that Dean describes in which entropy is a factor.

According to this concept in physics, all living systems transform energy, and some of that energy gets lost in the process. The Second Law of Thermodynamics states that any system tends to run down over time and needs a new influx of energy to keep going. Entropy is a measure of how far from equilibrium a given system is, a calibration of the degree of disorder. The law states that the disorder of a system can never decrease, and when it reaches the state of maximum entropy, it cannot support growth. It falls apart. Not only were the principles of thermodynamics of fundamental importance to all branches of science, but Dean felt they served as accurate metaphors for human psychology. Without the energy influx of meaning and hope, entropy in the form of depression and other types of breakdowns could set in.

In the attic above a restaurant, Harry shoots a mass murderer after a frantic chase. Subsequently he encounters a kid, Bryan, who is fascinated with all the violence and blood. When Harry, in anger at the boy's insensitivity, shoves him, he makes himself a target for retaliation. The boy, Bryan, has special powers. Among other things, he can stop the flow of time at will—a phenomenon that he calls The Pause—and he uses this ability to torment people, particularly the homeless. He views himself as a god who must weed out society's worst elements, and he goes even further by constructing and energizing a golem to warn his victims of their imminent demise.

Harry and Connie experience The Pause—but unlike others, they are allowed to move because Bryan wants to have a game of chase. There ensues an almost magical pursuit through a stop-time world where every ordinary object is wondrous.

The dog Woofer leads them to the nursing home where Bryan's mother lives, and she tells them about his controlling grandmother and his subsequent violence. She also tells them where to find him—and there follows a fearful confrontation in the dragon's lair, Bryan's strange home.

The enemy of humanity is our psychological attraction to entropy, the book tells us. Commitments based on immaturity and greed are doomed to failure. By the end of the story, the will to do good and maintain one's integrity triumphs over spiritual disintegration.

Dragon Tears debuted at number one on January 24, 1993, and spent ten weeks on the list of *The New York Times*. It was number one in paperback in September.

Kirkus called this novel "an electrifying terrorfest" and a "vise-tight tale." *Publishers Weekly* said, "Koontz romps playfully and skillfully through this grownup enchantment . . . as irresistible as a sack of brownies." Paul Sutter, in an Ontario paper, said, "Like fine wine, he keeps improving with age. . . . Horror doesn't get more precise and potent." In *People* magazine's "Picks and Pans," *Dragon Tears* was called solid, credible, and "incredible."

6

Early in 1992, Dean and Gerda decided to go into partnership with Jose J. Perez on a company they called Perfection Custom Cabinetry (later Perfection Custom Wood Designs), with a showroom at 1570 Lewis Street in Anaheim. It opened that year on October 5, displaying full rooms and vignettes, including a unique modern kitchen, an Art Deco bedroom, and a Biedermeier office. Zov's Bistro catered the open house with exotic appetizers and desserts.

"We bring the architect's style of the home into the cabinetry, and into free-standing furniture to ornament and enhance that style," Dean told *Design Journal* during the press preview. "We look at an entire room and create cabinetry to reflect and reinforce the ambiance." Because of his and Gerda's great admiration for the talent of Jose Perez, they hoped to see the company become legendary among designers and architects.

Gerda assumed the role of president, although she had resisted the idea of doing this at all. Dean was secretary, while Jose was vice president, designer, and master craftsman. They had known one another for over ten years, dating from the first job Jose had done in the Koontz's Orange County home. He had built a fireplace and a series of bookcases. Subsequently he put custom libraries in each of their successive homes, installing beautifully detailed crown molding, wood paneling, cabinetry, and window seats. When Dean and Gerda had prepared to move to Newport Beach, they had gone through a number of otherwise fine homes in which they had noticed substandard woodworking. That had given them the idea that there was a market in high-end woodworking and design. They knew that Jose could manage that. They based the company on a philosophy expressed by Winston Churchill: "By striving for perfection in any task, you give purpose to your existence . . . and make the world that much less of a mean and sorry place."

Gerda ran the front office, set up all of the business systems, and contributed to the designs. She and Dean shared a preference for contemporary styling, and for Art Deco and Art Nouveau, but the company offered a wide variety of traditions, from rustic Southwest to Rococo. They had a professional brochure, designed and written by Dean, in which he stated, "We all seek a perfect world. However, reality defeats us because most things lay beyond our control. Perfection is glimpsed only in the petals of a flower, moonlight silvered surf, or a crimson sunset. . . . At Perfection Custom Cabinetry we believe that the pinnacle can be achieved."

Promising to meet every deadline, never make excuses, and to respect homeowners' property, he assured prospective buyers that whatever could be conceived could be made. For each full-color photo of a piece already made, he provided an evocative description and suggested further fantasies involving the "visual symphony" of the woodwork.

"It got to be a major operation," says Dean. "We identified a niche of high-end cabinetry and developed our own approach. Gerda and I bought a warehouse separate from the company, but the company used it. We started out with eight master cabinetmakers. Within a year and a half we had fifty-three employees, and it had grown into this absolute nightmare—because we still had been able to find only eight true masters. We had no problem getting the work, but we were having enormous problems getting it properly built. The problem was that the California economy had been in recession so long that most of the master cabinetmakers had moved to states where there was still a building boom—Nevada, Arizona, Texas. We would bring in guys who were apprentices and train them. Six months, eight months, down the road they would be far better cabinetmakers—and then they would quit and go to Nevada, where they could get even better money, *and* pay no income tax! We were already paying twenty percent above what anyone else here was paying for master cabinetmakers, so there was no way we could compete.

"We reached the point where we saw that we'd created this business, we'd identified a market, we were sitting on a million dollars in contracts and more were coming through the door every day, but the labor pool wasn't here. We were really running a cabinetmaking school! Every dollar of work we put out the door was costing us a dollar and thirty cents. The losses were getting ridiculous. If we could have had enough men as good as our core group, the thing would have been enormously profitable, but we finally had to shut the doors. We delivered the work we owed, wound the thing down, and closed it up."

Not only had this venture been financially unfeasible, but the time that Dean and Gerda ended up investing was enormous. "At its peak, it was taking thirty hours a week of my time and sixty of hers. It was unbelievable. And I came to have an absolute disgust for the insanity of the government regulations imposed on businesses. I was horrified to see how much of our average worker's wages went into state and federal taxes. Not as high a percentage as I paid—but too damn much!"

It had been an interesting experience, and Dean's own home showed the high degree of skill these craftsmen could achieve, but he was happy that he could return his attention to writing. So was Gerda. At least, both agreed, this hard-won knowledge of business and manufacturing would provide new material for fiction one day. Everything was material.

7

Joe Stefko, drummer for the rock group The Turtles, ran a small press, Charnel House, with Tracy Cocoman. They approached Dean to produce a limited edition of 750 copies of *Beastchild*, which Dean revised by removing grammatical errors from editing done on earlier versions. "We do everything by hand," says Joe. On the lettered version, he used a cover made from lizard skin because "we like to put some element of the story into the binding." Three years later, Dean would allow him do a limited edition of *Dark Rivers of the Heart*.

Dean had one more book for Putnam before he moved on to his new publisher. The next few years would see some interesting changes in his fiction.

[1]Dean R. Koontz, *Hideaway* (New York: G.P. Putnam's Sons, 1992), p. 295.
[2]Tyson Blue, "A Conversation with Dean Koontz," *Cemetery Dance* (Spring 1992), p. 23.
[3]*Hideaway*, p. 179.
[4]Ibid., p. 201.
[5]*Publishers Weekly* (August 10, 1992), p. 15.
[6]*Asbury Park Press*, July 2, 1992.
[7]Dean Koontz, *Dragon Tears* (New York: Putnam, 1993), p. 212.

TWENTY-TWO

Autobiography

1

THE LAST OF DEAN'S NOVELS FOR PUTNAM, *MR. MURDER*, WAS published in October 1993. The book had numerous autobiographical parallels, with a male protagonist as a suspense writer who was trying to shed a reputation with which the media had saddled him. "I was never pursued by an evil twin clone, but everything else in *Mr. Murder* was pretty much out of my own life," says Dean.

He dedicated the book to artists Phil Parks and Don Brautigam. He included several poems from *The Book of Counted Sorrows* and, because the novel is in part about the interaction of fiction and reality and the difficulty of separating truth from fantasy in the modern world, there is a line from a book by Laura Shane, the protagonist of *Lightning*. Indeed, lines from the lead character's books are also used as epigraphs, as if "Marty Stillwater" exists outside the novel as well as in it. The poem that Dean wrote as part of the story subsequently became the basis for a children's book, *Santa's Twin*, published three years later.

Once again, the psychopath that gives the suspense its momentum is driven by need—a craving that must be satisfied at all costs. He is an emotional vampire, a man/machine without a soul but with an appetite for other people's lives. He is society itself at its most superficial, media-driven level—he shows us how we might recreate ourselves as soulless beings through such things as media, politics, and junk food, and thereby have a hand in the destruction of our own humanity. We forge our own insatiable appetites and feed our addictions.

Dean presents the psychopathic perspective in the present tense as a way to capture the episodic, moment-by-moment nature of his experience. This character, Alfie, has no memory and no sense of purpose. He does not even know his name.

Despising his outsider status, he wants to kill those from whom he is different. For him, "Need fosters frustration, frustration grows into anger, anger leads to hatred, hatred generates violence—and violence sometimes soothes."[1] Oddly, he is a counterexample to the theory that Dean likes to cite, that madmen are always convinced of their sanity. Alfie does question his, but he is quite mad.

Marty Stillwater lives with his wife, Paige, and two daughters, Emily and Charlotte (named after the Bronte sisters), in Mission Viejo, a town not far from Newport Beach. Marty is a writer, and his wife is a child psychologist who has survived the girlhood trauma of discovering her parents' bodies after a murder-suicide. Like Gerda, she is resilient, resourceful, and independent.

Marty tries to use his writing to transform the worst scenarios into images of optimism and hope. "It was always his nature to find reasons to be upbeat even when common sense suggested pessimism was a more realistic reaction. He was never able to stew in the gloom for long."[2] He possesses an acute sense of mortality and spends his life trying to cope with it, understanding that the curse of the writer's imagination is to get himself sucked into dark possibilities—although when later alerted to imminent danger, he realizes that this "curse" can also be a blessing. He likes to put his characters into difficulties and challenge them to find a way out, as if reassuring himself through them that he can always emerge triumphant. Marty is his own toughest critic and revises each page of his books as many as twenty or thirty times. He dislikes publicity and self-promotion. "To him, the books were what mattered, not the person who wrote them."[3] Like Dean, Marty prefers staying home. His in-home office overflows with books of his in every foreign edition, original paintings from dust jackets, a couch meant for "plotting sessions" that he never uses, and a computer with an oversized monitor. He likes the novels of James M. Cain and Elmore Leonard, but tends to prefer reason, logic, and the triumph of the social order over vigilante solutions. Dean also takes the opportunity through Marty to take a poke at some of his critics.

Marty's dilemma begins when he finds himself slipping into an eerie state of altered consciousness. On the first occasion, as he is dictating notes for a novel, he experiences a fugue, later discovering that a long section of the tape recording features nothing but him repeating the two words "I need . . ." Marty doesn't realize that he is actually experiencing a mental linkage with a killer named Alfie. Alfie is a clone created by a clandestine fascist political organization called The Network, and he is used as an assassin who can never be traced back to his masters because he doesn't know who they are or even who he himself is. He is to be the first in the "Alpha" series of genetically engineered and mind-controlled killers to be used to both disrupt and control society. The Network intended to clone Alfie from the bone marrow of its founder's dead son. Accidentally, that tissue sample was switched with Marty's—and the killer is not merely his identical twin but is fundamentally *Marty* in all ways but one: the killer has no soul.

Tormented by the meaninglessness of his existence, Alfie breaks his conditioning and sets out to kill Marty and take his place, thus acquiring an instant family, a life, and purpose. There is nowhere Marty can go to escape this doppelganger, which symbolizes one's own internal toxins. Dean's concern over his genetic legacy is reaching its peak in this novel, as if his father's death allowed him to now face the real issues. He is definitely writing about himself and his determination to be rid of this potential for sociopathic madness. "Somehow, the wrongness was within him."[4]

"*Mr. Murder* was a key book about yearning for family and holding them together against destructive influences from an outside force," says Dean, "except that this is really an inside force. It's Marty's evil potential. So in a sense, I was working out the issues of my father."

In fact, Dean mentions that writing *Mr. Murder* was similar to writing *Watchers*: He felt confident that both books were working. Since they are parallel in their use of genetic and psychic links between good and evil, it is clear that Dean sees himself as a person infected with negative potential that he cannot escape, but which he *can* struggle against to preserve those things that make him human. "Not to be melodramatic and imply that I am different from anyone else in this regard. We all have dark potential, and we all resist it—or not."

Alfie invades Marty's home (another metaphor of not being

safe within one's own self) and Marty flees with his family to
his parents' cabin. He tries to enlist the aid of the police, but in
light of the *People* profile, they believe that this is a publicity
stunt. The Network uses their pawns in the media to hype the
story. Realizing the medical mix-up, they plan to kill Marty.
They also discover that Alfie, who was designed to be impotent,
has been raping women across the country, and they realize
that they may have created something that could endanger the
human race—if he is also fertile. Alfie has miraculous self-
healing abilities and is therefore nearly unstoppable. For his
superhuman metabolism to work, however, he must consume
fearful amounts of food. When Alfie has finally cornered Marty
and his family, Network agents intervene and shoot him repeatedly, until he must cannibalize himself in his effort to heal.
Then one agent (The Network's weak link and one of the most
amusing figures in a cast with numerous comic *and* scary characters), who is inspired by Star Trek novels to become a hero,
puts an end to the madness. He kills the other agent and helps
the family to escape and acquire new identities. They take the
names of Ann and John Galt, a wink at Ayn Rand's novel, *Atlas
Shrugged*, for its depiction of a collapsing civilization.

This Network agent, Clocker, is the mythological guardian,
inspired by a mythological universe. He is one of many such
figures in Dean's novels. "It's appealing to believe that there
are such people in life," says Dean. "We'd all like to think, as
we make our way day to day, that when crises arise, we have
champions in the world who will defend us as we need them.
Believing that such heroes live among us makes us feel a certain *rightness* about our society, makes us feel that there is a
hope of justice and judgment. But the unspoken reason it has
an appeal is because it implies that there's meaning and purpose to existence, that we're not just stumbling blindly through
a random universe. When you need help, help will be there, if
you know how to look for it, receive it, and accept it. That's the
appeal of the guardian angel. We want to believe we are
watched over, that we are not alone."

At the end of the novel, the Stillwater family is in perpetual
hiding. Marty leaves behind his murder mysteries and best-
selling career to publish under a new name the poem "Santa's
Twin"—the story he has been telling his two daughters, the

plot of which parallels what has been happening to him. Fiction and reality interweave again, one reinforcing and vitalizing the other. Several years later, Dean himself returned to this poem, finished it, and published it, not as the work of "Marty Stillwater" but as his own. Fiction and reality ever interweaving.

Within the framework of this novel, Dean discusses the process of writing, both in terms of suspense and poetry. He includes many of his own beliefs about writing as therapy, promoting the writer's instinct over that of any therapist. According to him, unless its intent is nihilistic, storytelling condenses life and gives it order. As Marty says, "You can't analyze the deeper effects storytelling has on us, can't figure out the why and how any more than King Arthur could understand how Merlin could do and know the things he did. . . . Life is so damned disorderly, things just happen, and there doesn't seem any point to so much of what we go through. Sometimes it seems the world's a madhouse. Storytelling condenses life, gives it order. Stories have beginnings, middles, ends. And when a story's over, it *meant* something, by God, maybe not something complex, maybe what it had to say was simple, even naïve, but there was meaning. And that gives us hope, it's a medicine."[5] With its structure, with its emotion, with its ability to engage the mind and the heart, fiction is hope. As it was for a small boy, Dean Koontz, who took shelter in his room with books, listening with one ear to his drunken father rage downstairs, escaping from reality into worlds on printed pages.

He also spends a lot of time developing the loving family as a womb of safety, even when the home itself is violated. Although Paige's family had been just the opposite, she was able to overcome her horror and become a devoted mother. Marty and Paige both find great satisfaction in their two daughters, and the girls feel sure that their parents will protect them. It is the family whose members are willing to put their lives on the line for one another that holds civilization together. Whether the threat is from outside or within, a family that pulls together in love—as Dean and Gerda do—can defeat it.

As usual, Dean develops patterns of images in which a single source can house the potential for either safety or danger— just as his own family had done when he was growing up. The home, personal identity, society, the writer's imagination, the family, the gift of stamina—even Santa Claus—are all charged positively and negatively. Freedom to choose and the determination to maintain integrity against the negative are the principal factors in preserving the good.

Mr. Murder debuted at number eight and remained on the bestsellers list for fourteen weeks, but broke Dean's record of successive number one bestsellers. Most critics praised this book for its action and characters. As with previous novels, it was a main selection for the Literary Guild and Doubleday Book Club, and an alternate for the Mystery Guild.

The New York Times gave it a lot of space for review, dismissing the similes and homilies, but admitting that such "distractions" counted little against "the resounding variations Mr. Koontz plays on this good story, here craftily retold. They allow him to counterpoint the new horrors among us with the old horrors always inside us." This novel earned a starred review from *Publishers Weekly*, which said, "Playing on every emotion and keeping the story racing along, Koontz masterfully escalates the tension. He closes the narrative with the most ingenious twist ending of his career." *The Washington Post* called it "superb," while *Kirkus* said, "Terrific visceral energy, wonderfully creepy. Koontz nails the reader to the page."

Savoy bought the film rights in a straight-purchase deal in 1996. They signed Dean as co-executive producer and gave him approval over the screenwriter and director. With a strong script by Stephen Tolkin, they then signed Bruce Willis for $20 million to play Marty Stillwater, and for the first time, it looked to Dean as if one of his novels was going to be made into a major motion picture of high quality. However, Savoy eventually lost so much money on its early slate of pictures that it pulled out of the film business, and Bruce Willis moved on. Ultimately ABC and producer Rob Lee brought in Tolkin to readapt *Mr. Murder* for a miniseries, hopefully to air in 1998.

2

That same month, Dean published a short essay in *TV Guide* called, "Why We Love Horror" (not his title). In it, he claims that "*all* of us delight in good suspense stories because the human condition itself is a long, scary movie." He goes on to discuss the role of television in providing horrific entertainment. He cites *The Outer Limits*, a show from the mid-sixties, as being the "scariest television series there ever was," because it was the first to hint that mundane reality might not be so safe. Current suspense movies, Dean says, fail to live up to the shows that he recalled from earlier years, and he discusses the many ways they cheat viewers with false suspense and poorly crafted stories. Where good story comes first, he states, the suspense is honest, and the filmmaker does not need to manipulate the viewer.

3

Dean's new contract with Random House included seven backlist books for paperback release from Ballantine. The first of these, *Winter Moon*, was based on his 1975 novel, *Invasion* (by Aaron Wolfe), and came out in 1994. The title is taken from a line in one of his poems from *The Book of Counted Sorrows*. Dean retained the science fiction premise, but wanted the themes and characterization to be closer in style to his more mature work. He also wanted to depict the concerns of someone living in the turbulent city of Los Angeles in modern times—and by story's end, turn pessimism into optimism, entropy into growth. This novel, too, became more of a story about the power of family than it had been before, and a denunciation of forces that contribute to the decline of society. Paranoia becomes sober realism.

In this "revision," by the time he got to the point where *Invasion's* first chapter starts, Dean had written eighty thousand words of *Winter Moon*. "As I got into it," he says, "there were things I didn't really like about the first one. I wanted this to be a *very* solid book; I didn't want to dump an old title off on readers just to make a buck. I decided I wanted to open it in Los Angeles, get rid of the Vietnam War angle from *Invasion*, and deal with more contemporary issues. Once I did that, there was no turning back. It just started to roll, and I couldn't stop it." He also updated the alien, changing it from a simple insectile entity into something amorphous and stranger, something more akin to malignant greed and chaos—which he considered a more terrifying image to readers, and a better parallel to the senseless violence of the city. "Everything becomes me" the alien says.[6] Dean gave the boy (still named Toby) a loyal golden retriever, and the only overlaps between novels are a section delineating the types of aliens in science fiction and Toby's role, although he ends up as more a hero than a puppet. Otherwise, Dean claims, he did not keep a single sentence from the original novel. Instead of the fifty thousand word *Invasion*, he now had a tale of one hundred thirty-five thousand words.

The protagonist, Jack McGarvey, is a cop in Los Angeles who gets shot by a famous film producer who is high on PCP. In such a nihilistic society, the media soon turn this arrogant man into a dark hero, while Jack is vilified. When Jack and his wife, Heather, inherit a ranch in Montana that promises to deliver them from the encroaching violence, they decide to move. They soon learn, however, that things are just as threatening in Montana. The man who had lived in the house before them had died of fright fighting off an alien species that sought to invade him. His diary records his observations. During a blizzard, Jack is forced to seek outside help, while Heather and Toby try to ward off the alien attack. They find its source in a caretaker's cottage, and although they manage to destroy it, they fear parts of it may have survived and be able to regenerate. Realizing that safety lies in their inner resources, they return to Los Angeles. "Home was not a perfect place. But it was the only home they had, and they could hope to make it better."[7] This is a metaphor of self, family, and humanity itself. Danger and safety are both present within, and efforts must be made to strengthen one over the other.

This novel hit number one in paperback on January 31, 1994, and stayed on the list ten weeks.

The Funhouse was also reissued that year, getting as high as number two.

4

Early in 1994, Dean and Gerda decided to purchase two and a half acres of land in a prestigious development known as

Pelican Hills. They wanted to build a new house rather than renovate yet another. Every house they had lived in to that point had needed work, and the renovations had taken months, with considerable aggravation for them. Better, they thought, to have one built completely to their specifications while they continued to live in comfort in their home in New-port Beach. They planned a large, three-level, Italian Mediter-ranean-style estate that would have a magnificent view of the Pacific Ocean, Catalina Island, Newport Harbor, and most of Orange County. It was projected by the media to become one of Newport Beach's largest residences.

"We spend so much time in our home," Dean explains, "and we needed more space. We don't travel, so our home is very important to us. That's what we want to spend our earnings on."

After developing and rejecting two architectural approaches, the Koontzes hired Leason Pomeroy, an internationally acclaimed architect based in Orange County, to design a Frank Lloyd Wright–inspired house that would be intimately related to the land rather than imposed on it. Dean hired Mike Martin, a contractor he trusted, to oversee the project, which was expected to take as long as five years, including design time.

He also had a business staff by now that included someone to answer phone calls and sort through fan mail, someone to design computer programs and track his publishing and other business interests, an executive secretary, and a fourth person to liaison with business associates and assist with research. Friends kidded him about his professed plans to cut back his work hours, and he and Gerda both realized that, despite their success, they seemed to be working harder than ever.

5

In March, Berkley published a trade paperback edition of *The Dean Koontz Companion*. It was edited by Martin Greenberg, Ed Gorman, and Bill Munster.

Marty Greenberg had first met Dean in 1981 when he had asked about including "Soft Come the Dragons" in his anthol-ogy, *Dragon Tales*. He had hundreds of anthologies to his credit, and eventually became partners with Ed Gorman on *Mystery*

Scene magazine. He also had edited companions to the work of other writers, including Tom Clancy and Tony Hillerman.

"What makes this *Companion* unique compared to other books like this that I've done is that it's seventy percent Dean's voice," Greenberg says. "He was very generous." Included is a long interview that Ed Gorman conducted, reprints of many of Dean's articles and essays, his first short story, several articles by other writers about his style of writing, one article about the movies made from his books to that time, and a comprehensive bibliography. Dean also gave them part of one of his newsletters for fans called "The Ten Questions Readers Most Often Ask."

Headline in England issued a hardcover edition.

6

In April, Dean issued a statement of copyright infringement against Mark Masztal and H&M Publishing. They had produced a sixty-page chapbook of poetry that Dean had written for his novels and had called *The Book of Counted Sorrows*, attributing it to "Anonymous." They claimed they had printed only a small quantity and had distributed them only as gifts, not for profit. They had also mentioned the fact that this book had been produced without Dean's permission. "My attorneys reached an agreement with him," he says, "to recover and turn over to us all copies printed." Included in Dean's notice of copyright infringement was a warning that he would take legal action and seek punitive damages against anyone selling this chapbook to collectors. "Like a trademark," he says, "a copyright can be lost for failure to enforce; therefore the author will have no choice but to vigorously and relentlessly pursue those who deal in even a single copy of the publication."

Dean also received a letter from a woman who informed him that she would be writing and marketing a sequel to *Watchers*, although she was changing the dogs from golden retrievers to chows. Then he heard from two film students who had written a screenplay of *Lightning* and were already in contact with producers. They felt they needed nothing but a letter of permission from him. It was the third unauthorized screenplay in four months. Dean was stunned that people appropriated his work for their own profit—and then were often miffed when he declined to let them do so. "Film schools appear to teach *nothing* about ethics or intellectual property rights!"

Late in 1994, he was battling with Roger Corman over yet another sequel to the film *Watchers*, a straight-to-video film called *Watchers III* from Concorde-New Horizons. Corman was in Milan, Italy, promoting the film with the Koontz name above the title, so Dean sued him for breach of contract, claiming that no such "proprietary credit" was permitted. Corman was using his name on the packaging in a way that suggested his endorsement and involvement—while Dean, in fact, *loathed* all three *Watchers* films that Corman had made. Corman sued Dean for libel, slander, emotional distress, and conspiracy to interfere with trade. With some help from federal judge Sonja Sotomayor, a settlement was reached which gave Dean much of what he wanted. Dean's name would still appear on the video box, but not in the large-size print that Corman had originally planned and not above the title. The sticker would read: "Based on the novel, *Watchers*, by Dean R. Koontz." Subsequently both parties dropped their suits. "I spent more money on legal fees to protect my rights," says Dean, "than I was paid for the film version in the first place—but I did so happily. I'll go to *any* length in a fight like that when I know I'm in the right. Principle really does matter more than money."

7

An offbeat project that Dean took on was an artist biography for Capital records to accompany the rock group Megadeth's "Youthanasia" CD. He had listened to the music and had thought it had more substance than other heavy metal; it had an interesting positive quality that surprised him. In speaking with Dave Mustane, the group's founder, Dean felt that he shared some common experiences with this man. He called his essay "Godzilla vs. Megadeth," and talked humorously about the band, their exploits, and their history. "What's important about Megadeth," he wrote, "is that their music is fun. It's rock 'n' roll, kids. It was always meant to be about fun. About freedom. About life and getting on with it."

He did something else that was unusual for him: He agreed to be taped for a profile to be aired on the sci-fi cable channel. It was part of the *Masters of Fantasy* series and was called "The Mind of Dean Koontz." On the program, aired August 20, 1994, he explained his cross-genre style and answered questions from fans about his childhood adversities, his dreams, and his desire to stay out of the celebrity spotlight.

8

Gerda decided to take a trip to Europe while Dean was hard at work on his next novel. Zov had invited her along. They spent a week in Paris, a week in Provence, and then took a day trip across the border into Italy—the homeland of Gerda's father, who was from Sicily. Gerda had always wished to travel more, but Dean's deadlines and reluctance to fly limited these opportunities.

During the entire twelve days that she was gone, Dean was nearly frantic with worry. "I was nuts!" he exclaims. "Friends invited me to dinner, but it wasn't the same. I was sure her plane was going to go down. I had her call me from the airport as soon as she landed, and then I felt good for a day, until I remembered that she would have to fly back. This is a burden to her, because she might have done more things on her own, but she knows I get into this state. I do feel badly about it. But we have only been apart twice in thirty years of marriage, and she is a part of me in ways mere words can never express."

The theme of loneliness is a constant throughout Dean's novels, from first to last. Although most of the protagonists are loners of one sort or another, they all seek connection and attempt to build some semblance of family. "I probably write best about loneliness because it's a genuine fear," Dean acknowledges. "You can't help but write out of your own fears. I define myself by my relationships with friends, but with Gerda most of all. I sit alone in a room by choice to work, but it would be intolerable for me not to have connections that matter deeply to me."

9

Late in 1994, Dean saw the publication of the first book on his new contract for Alfred A. Knopf Publishing Group, an imprint which had long been associated with literary tradition. Since 1960, they had been part of Random House, owned by the Newhouse media empire. They prided themselves on publishing major voices worldwide and enjoyed priority among reviewers and award competitions. Among their authors were many Nobel Prize winners.

Dean's editor was Knopf president, Sonny Mehta, who also oversaw the Vintage and Pantheon imprints at Random House. He had been hired in 1990, and his background and ideas caused quite a stir at the venerable house. Some critics feared that his love of commercial fiction might diminish Knopf's reputation. He was an Indian from New Delhi, educated at Cambridge, and known as a passionate reader and a marketing whiz. He was also known for his inscrutable moods. He edited some twenty authors a year and conducted the marketing programs for many others, among them Carl Hiaasen, Josephine Hart, and Bret Easton Ellis. He liked to say that publishing should be provocative, and he invariably came up with ideas that would get booksellers' attention. His number two person was Jane Friedman. Together they handled Dean's editing and promotion.

Considered a major contributor to Knopf's successful growth, Jane Friedman had joined Random House in 1968 in the publicity department. She was currently executive vice president at Knopf, publisher of Vintage, and president of Random House audio, which she had founded.

Dean had told Sonny Mehta that he was writing something very different from what he had done previously, and Mehta encouraged him to follow his instinct.

"You've made numerous changes in the past," Mehta told him, "and your readers have always gone with you."

Dean was pleased. He had expected the usual caution and concern over his career. "I'd never felt so free," he says. "Unconsciously, I had been reining myself in to minimize the arguments, and I only became aware of that when I considered some of the ideas that were bouncing around in my head—and suddenly realized why I had been postponing them."

After eleven months and three weeks of writing sixty hours a week, Dean turned in the manuscript of *Dark Rivers of the Heart*, his most ambitious book to date, both from a literary and political perspective. Mehta read it, made notes to help sharpen some scenes, and gave it back to Dean to polish. Dean felt he had received a very professional editing job. What Mehta said had been insightful, precise, and succinct. There were no struggles over endings, titles, or subject matter. It seemed to Dean that he had found a publishing home where he would be able to go in many directions.

In the book, Dean tackles a number of political issues: government use of high technology to spy on its citizens, victimology as a corruption of justice, and the chilling effects of asset-forfeiture laws. He sees bloated government budgets as inspiring zealots to extend their jurisdiction beyond its original boundaries, and he explores the growing trend of police agencies to become dangerous paramilitary organizations. Since there was no element of the fantastic in this book, he used numerous techniques to convey the *feeling* of the fantastic through style and mood. "I also tried to convey it through a tone that I might call 'hyper-real,' which involves using numerous pumped-up narrative techniques, and a density of character and plot, that bring the book as close as possible to going over the top without actually *letting* it go over the top."[8] He wanted to assault both the "lie of political solutions" and the "lie of Freudian theory."

Although he had sprinkled his political leanings throughout his books and had been called a libertarian by many critics, Dean was not interested in being so firmly categorized. A libertarian calls for a severely limited government, elimination of entitlements, and a totally free market. Only freedom, they say, enables people to live the most fully human lives. Dean had even included libertarian characters in some of his novels, and although he agreed with many libertarian positions, he disagreed with others. Despite what some critics claimed about his "libertarian" soapboxes, his political philosophy was, he felt, more complex.

"There are things I'm libertarian about," says Dean, "there are things I'm liberal about, and there are things I'm conservative about. In matters of religious faith, most libertarians are nonbelievers. Most of them don't believe there's any role for religion in public life, and I think that if we're going to have a meaningful public policy that has a moral base, there must be something that gives law a moral basis—and that something is, for me, the belief in God-given rights that no law can abridge. I'm also strong on civil rights and minority participation in *every* aspect of public and private life—while many libertarians are laissez faire on the issue. I hate being labeled and pigeon-holed, when issues like abortion or immigration are so complex."

In *Dark Rivers of the Heart*, and in an Introduction to Alan Bock's *Ambush at Ruby Ridge*, Dean took a stand on an issue of great importance to him: What happens when a powerful faction of the government becomes pathological? The FBI's violent raid on the Branch Davidians at Waco, Texas, had disturbed him, as had the ambush at Ruby Ridge on the Randy Weaver family in which Weaver's wife and son were unaccountably shot and killed. "They had different beliefs, but they weren't harming anyone," says Dean. "The government's argument was that they launched this violent assault [at Waco] to save the children—but they *killed* all the children. We saw paramilitary operations where we should have seen responsible *police* operations. Authority run amok."

Through the character of Roy Miro in *Dark Rivers* we see the consequences of having someone in power who believes that power is its own justification. Dean had collected numerous stories depicting what he considered to be governmental abuse of citizens, such as cases involving misuse of the asset-forfeiture laws and the antidrug statutes. "In the newspaper," he said in an interview, "I read about the government trying to gain control of everyone's computer for the purpose of illegal eavesdropping, by requiring the 'clipper chip.' This gives them the power to monitor us at all times without the niceties of court orders, search warrants, and the rules of law." He was especially concerned that innocent citizens could be stripped of their property and livelihood, and even their lives, by people acting on totalitarian principles. To his mind, when something like the asset-forfeiture law was applied not merely to drug lords, but in more than two hundred other types of criminal situations, its interpretation was too fluid to be safe in the hands of zealous law enforcers. Dean clearly explains what he means by this in his Afterword to the hardcover edition of *Dark Rivers of the Heart*.

This is the novel in which Dean also felt he was finally more directly approaching the subject of his father. Ray was now deceased, and Dean wanted to dig into the psychological ramifications of being the son of a sociopath. "That was the first time I dealt bluntly, head-on, with those issues," he says. "Spencer's father is far worse than mine was, so it's hyperbole, but I dealt with it in that fashion to highlight the issues. In various books, I've struggled to work out the consequences of a childhood gone wrong due to abuse. But I was on a more conscious level in *Dark Rivers*."

He dedicated the novel to his friends, Gary and Zov Karamardian, owners of the restaurant that he and Gerda frequented, and opened it with his own poetry, which expressed the idea that we may be moved by a force we cannot see — the force of destiny. The destiny of place, time, culture, and genetics. There are a number of characters whose personalities and actions mirror those of others, as well as numerous significant symbols that move the story along. Dean also worked with patterns in nature — most strongly apparent in the scene in the desert — to emphasize or reinforce thematic points.

Spencer Grant, forty-six, is a former police officer and part of the Multi Agency Task Force on Computer Crime. He bears a deep scar on his face from a childhood incident, which is a reminder of the psychological scars he bears from his father, Steven Ackblom, who murdered forty-two women (including Spencer's mother). Spencer fears that the same "dark rivers" course through his own heart via shared blood, and he shuns the possibility. He rescues an abused dog that he names Rocky (after the character in the eponymous movie) and these two parallel each other throughout the novel in their fear and courage. Both appear to be cowed by their pasts, yet when pushed to it, both confront what they must.

Subconsciously motivated by the repressed memory of a bloodstained door, Spencer enters a bar called The Red Door and meets a waitress who interests him.

"The first sentence sets up the whole book," says Dean. "'With the woman on his mind and a deep uneasiness in his heart, Spencer Grant drove through the glistening night, searching for the red door.' The woman could refer to the waitress, or to a woman he thinks he might have killed on a terrible long-ago night when he was under his father's spell, or it could be his mother. Setting up subtle references to key women in the story was intentional—but the red door as a deeply buried symbol in Spencer's psyche was not part of my conscious plan. I got to the end of Part One and only then realized I was going to have the words 'red door' again and that they would refer to the bloody palm prints. I remember my excitement. The image resonates on so many levels when you get to it the second time, and you know you've only just begun to understand the way the outer story and inner story of this character connect. When I wrote the first sentence, I didn't know that the red door would have further significance—or at least didn't know it on a *conscious* level.

"All of his life, Spencer has been trying to find his way back through the red door, back across that threshold he crossed on that terrible night in his youth. When he goes into this bar, pushes open this red door and finds this waitress, Valerie, he's found the way out of the nightmare of his life. I think the more you polish and enrich the text on a surface level, the more engaged you become on a subconscious level and the more things you do you're not even aware of—until later.

"My original intention was to write a variation on the old movie *Laura*, in which a cop investigates the murder of a woman, and in talking to people about her and seeing her photograph, he falls in love with her. You've got this fascinating situation where he's falling in love with someone he could never know—because she's dead—and then it turns out she's not dead after all! *Dark Rivers* is a variation on that. Spencer meets Valerie once and then she's gone from his life—but it's the first real human connection he's had in so long that he's compelled to follow through to find her, to give himself to the possibility of hope."

When the waitress disappears under mysterious circumstances that involve armed federal agents, Spencer traces her to Las Vegas and discovers that her real name is Ellie Summerton. Like him, she has been traveling under a pseudonym. (Grant had taken his own false name from two actors who

often played men of courage and strong principles.) He pursues her to offer his help, but nearly drowns in a flooded river
(a metaphor of being nearly overcome by the "dark river"
inside him). A rat—his frightening inner self—gets close to
him, but drowns before it can bite him. This incident foreshadows the rats that live in torture chambers under the barn
where Spencer's father had committed his atrocities. "Rats
represent a lot of things in this book," Dean explains. "They
are an externalization of the twisted side of human nature.
They symbolize the things that Spencer is afraid exist in his
own mind. They live mostly below our level of awareness—in
wells and shadows—and when we encounter them, we are
repelled by them, but they're always there, quietly operating."

Ellie, a nurturing female who parallels his mother, rescues
him. He admits to her that he is Michael Ackblom and she
reveals that she was married to a computer genius who was the
son of a corrupt politician. The politician has had his own son
and Ellie's parents killed, but she escaped and he has sent out
government forces in pursuit. To track her down, he uses the
very computer network—"Mama"—that his son had invented to
serve as a formidable anticrime resource. Each time federal
forces learn of her whereabouts and nearly capture her, she
leaves behind cockroaches stuck on pins to remind her father-in-
law of what he is and to warn him that she will nail *him* if she can.

The man in charge of finding and eliminating Ellie is Roy
Miro, who loves Pooh characters, yet heads a secret government agency which is supported by redirected government
funding under the control of the Justice Department. "His
name, Miro," Dean notes, "means that he mirrors many
aspects of our society, especially that we pretend to admire
compassion but actually reward ruthlessness." On the side,
Roy "euthanizes" people whom he believes lead lives that
cause them pain. He views this activity as a holy calling—a
service to his victims and a step toward improving society by
weeding out the sick, the disabled, and the despairing. In that
respect, he also mirrors Spencer's father, who thought that
pain was the most intense expression of life and who viewed
his killings as part of his art. Both subsume human life to an
aesthetic ideal. (Ackblom even thinks he could be a successful
politician in today's world.)

Roy also abuses the asset-forfeiture law by using it to strip from a man who had crossed him nearly everything of value — his home, his bank account, his good name. "Morality was relative, and nothing done in the service of correct ideals could be a crime,"[9] according to Roy.

The principal difference between Roy and Spencer is the way they approach moral issues: "Roy never agonizes," says Dean. "He *knows* what's right. He feels himself to be superior and understands what's best for everyone. Spencer thinks through the ramifications of everything he does. A moral person is someone who has to think about his actions, about his impact on other people. My fear of large institutions is that so many people, when they become part of that big organization or great cause, surrender their judgment and accept as received wisdom a pat series of answers. They stop thinking. To buy into a set of political answers is to lose your humanity. You become increasingly capable of doing terrible things and feeling morally justified. Roy is the organizational individual who never questions his motivations, who believes that good intentions matter more than what horrors might result from them."

During Roy's pursuit of Spencer, he encounters a woman, Eve Jammer, who kills people strictly for money. They are two of a kind and they pursue a bizarre relationship of mutual admiration for each other's methods and motives. "Eve is the ultimate narcissist," says Dean. "She comes close to solipsism — which is the opposite of Ellie, who lives for other people." When Dean was writing this, he realized how unusual it was to have two such mentally unbalanced people bond, and he delighted in seeing where this "romance" would go. He called this subplot "psychos in love."

When Roy realizes that Spencer is with Ellie, he discovers Spencer's connection to Ackblom. He then uses his credentials to free Ackblom from prison and bring him to where he suspects Spencer is going — his former family home outside Vail, Colorado.

There Spencer confronts his childhood nightmares. As a boy, he was roused from sleep by a distant cry. Drawn to the barn where his father's art studio was housed, Spencer had discovered his father in the act of murder. He had also seen his father's handiwork: corpses of women in various stages of decomposition, plastered into various poses in a wall "sculpture." As an adult, he still half believes that he may have had a hand in killing the last victim. The red door is his passage into his own subconscious. The two red doors—the one at the bar and the one in the barn—are the roads inward, one to evil, the other to good.

As memories surface and illuminate for Spencer what "the red door" really is, Roy shows up with Spencer's father. Steven Ackblom shoots Roy to get him out of the way, and then taunts Spencer with the suggestion that he, too, is capable of such atrocities because he has his father's dark blood. Rocky attacks Ackblom, triggering Spencer's own burst of courage. Spencer then resists "genetic destiny" with his realization that he had tried to *save* the dying woman—that he has his mother's blood, too, and thus has the potential to be good. He kills his father and purges his soul.

"I've been writing books about fate and destiny, and in this book that theme is very strong," Dean acknowledges. "The text is saturated with water and blood imagery, and the title is *Dark Rivers of the Heart*, which refers to destiny. In the book, there are three aspects to destiny. First, destiny is our blood, our family. Second, destiny is in the stars, our own course set within us when we were born, because life has a spiritual purpose. Third, destiny is a result of how we choose to exercise our free will, for we can reject the power of blood (genetics) if we are strong enough to be what we *want* to be. All three of those are reflected in the book."

Spencer and Ellie escape, adopt new identities, and, assisted by a guardian group of citizens opposed to totalitarianism and corruption (who had also helped the victim of the asset-forfeiture law), they marry and start a family. The unborn child is a symbol of hope for Spencer's psychological legacy.

The resistance group in this novel serves as the mythical guardian. Its members are citizens who have lost their rights due to legal abuses. They insist that information is protection—"knowledge should be the first and foremost weapon in any resistance."[10]

Yet even as the novel ends on Dean's typical optimistic

note, he indicates that all is not well. Roy has survived and, with Eve, is planning his political triumph via manipulation and presidential assassination. Then Eve and Roy can freely carry out their "mercy killings" without the hindrance of accountability.

"I believe very strongly that good always triumphs, but usually in the long run," says Dean, "not always in the short run. There are short-term advantages to being able to do wicked things. Life is an endless moral contest, a struggle against opposing forces. And neither side triumphs every time. Roy and Eve go on . . . as evil always does."

Before the paperback of this novel was issued, subsequent changes made the Afterword dated, so Dean deleted it. "There had been a change of Congress right after the hardcover was published. The first thing they passed was a rule change requiring that any law that Congress passed had to apply to all members of Congress, past, present, and future. Prior to that, they exempted themselves from the laws they imposed on the rest of us! Then there was a court decision on the asset-forfeiture laws that changed it—not enough, but somewhat. The Afterword no longer applied. The issues dealt with in the book are dynamic, always changing, and I didn't want to have to update the Afterword every year. So I removed it and allowed the story to speak for itself."

Dean had long feared his own heritage from an abusive, schizotypal father. Now that his father was dead, he felt free to explore the deep pockets of his fears to try to purge himself of the anger and the need to compulsively examine himself for any sign of his father's traits. He is like Spencer, who believes he must revisit his childhood trauma to heal. Even if he was destined to follow certain psychological patterns—which he refused to accept—he knew that he could triumph over those received from his father by embracing those from his mother. The novel affirms that he is an agent with free will and initiative rather than ruled by something in his blood against which he may have no defense. Genetics is not destiny, or if it is, then hopefully it can be modified by kindness, mercy, honesty, and virtue. "Otherwise," says Spencer, "I can't tolerate the person I will become, the things I will do, or the end that will be mine."[11] He has changed identities in an effort to rid himself of his

father's curse, which reminds us of Dean's belief that his real
father might in fact be someone else. The fantasies provide
needed separation. His hope is that our lives are free of the
chains of fate, except for the one destiny that is freedom.

"I identify with Spencer," Dean admits. "I hate the idea of
even unintentionally hurting someone, and Spencer is like this.
He kills someone and it's justifiable, yet it gnaws at him and he
overanalyzes it. I'm always looking for that sign of my father,
who was quick to take offense at anything from anybody. My
behavior comes from never wanting to be like that."

Steven Ackblom, as a parallel to Roy Miro, symbolizes a
government that has forgotten its paternal position and has
become pathological in its desire to control rather than serve
and enable citizens. There is sometimes a fine line between federal agent and thug. The fears of the citizens of this country,
Dean believes, should be the same as those that Spencer harbors: The source of what we believe to be our protection may
well be dangerous. The misshapen rats that live beneath the
barn where Ackblom took his women represent government
agencies that operate in a clandestine manner, abnormal in their
moral development. Roy is the epitome of this breed. He is a
rat, but like the rat in the river that had threatened Spencer,
was stopped short before he could carry out his aggression.
Dean writes, "As individuals, as families, as neighbors, as members of one community, people of all races and political views
are usually decent, kind, compassionate. But in large corporations or governments, when great power accumulates in their
hands, some become monsters even with good intentions."[12]

On that fateful night in his youth, as Spencer approached
the barn, a white owl flew at him out of the night, startling
him. Briefly he mistook it for a guardian angel—his mother.
But perhaps it was indeed just that. This is similar to the phone
call that Dean received just before the nearly deadly encounter
with his own father. Interestingly, both Spencer's father and
Dean's were wielding knives. Spencer had felt guilty all his life
because he could not save his mother from his father, just as
Dean wished he could have rescued his own mother from his
father's cruelty. "I see my mother as having been killed by a
lifetime of stress," Dean says. "She died young. There was
nothing I could do about it. When I was a kid, I felt very

frustrated. It seemed as if there should have been something I could do, but I had no power."

Rocky, Ellie, and Spencer all mirror one another in their triumph over past abuse and their ability to show courage where needed. They refuse to be battered down, no matter how great the forces against them. Destiny drew them together to heal.

"This novel took a long time to write and I was exhausted," Dean recalls. "But I also had an exhilarated feeling. It was written out of deep concern over things I saw going wrong in society. The writing was cathartic. Seeing the government increasingly assuming the role of a parent and seeming to become dysfunctional and crazy—this was too much a reflection of what my father was like when I was a kid. In this book, I pulled those elements together. Much of what our government does has a profound impact on each of us, and when it's out of control . . . well, that's like living in a house with a psychotic parent."

10

Dark Rivers got as high as number seven on *The New York Times* bestsellers list and stayed on the list for almost three months. First printing was set at 650,000. In paperback, it went as high as number two.

Kirkus said this novel had "unrelenting excitement, truly memorable characters and ample food for thought." According to *Locus*, this was "the best book he has ever written." *Boston Magazine* noted the mix of optimism and pessimism regarding the "dark rivers" in everyone's heart, and *The New York Times*, which cut back on the space they had allotted to his last novel, called it a "believable high-tech thriller." *Entertainment Weekly* compared Koontz to King and thought there was more substance in *Dark Rivers*. A few reviewers noted the similarities to George Orwell's *1984*, with the rats and the "Big Brother" atmosphere; some thought it paranoid or exaggerated, but *Cosmopolitan* called it "timely." *The Denver Post* considered the writing "as usual . . . flawless: clean, clear exposition, colorful description, precise narration, and realistic dialogue."

Even Dean's agent, Robert Gottlieb, was impressed enough to make a comment: "Every so often in a creative person's life, there comes a defining moment when he moves up to another plateau. I see that in *Dark Rivers*. It's a watershed novel."[13]

Although Dean still did not wish to do promotional tours, he felt that Mehta and Friedman had been so supportive of his new direction that he owed them some cooperation. He agreed to field questions from radio talk show hosts, newspapers, and magazines, and even went on television—eventually giving a hundred interviews. He did more book signings than usual, but still did not agree to anything that required getting on an airplane.

The Washington State Bar News requested permission to reprint the section that Dean had written about the victim of the asset-forfeiture law. He granted it in the hope that more lawyers would come to understand the dangers of such statutes.

When Dean later wrote a Foreword to Alan W. Bock's *Ambush at Ruby Ridge*, he was quick to say that he did not have much in common with Randy Weaver, the separatist who lost his wife and son when the FBI opened fire on his cabin. Even so, a difference of beliefs—even if those beliefs are distasteful—can never justify shooting someone. He felt that the government dealt with the Weaver situation neither sanely nor democratically. He observes the entrapment, trickery, and inappropriate use of force as a sign of increasing government repression. If we, as citizens, fail to hold the government accountable—and we can only do that if we are informed about the potential for oppression—then we are the victims only of ourselves. Dean then mentions that his research for *Dark Rivers* involved information about assaults against citizens similar to the Weavers and the Branch Davidians at Waco, Texas. "The number of such incidents seems to argue that the Department of Justice, as currently constituted, is either blind to the need for visible justice for *all* citizens . . . or is so preoccupied with avoiding the political fallout that comes with admission of mistakes that it risks creating the widespread impression of bias and conspiracy."[14] His own feeling about politicians, which he has expressed from his very first novels, is that they are not so much conspirators as incompetent people in pursuit of petty self-advantage. No matter which end of the spectrum they support, they all have essentially the same motives.

Film rights were sold to CBS, and Lawrence Cohen was hired to write a screenplay for a miniseries. The project took a long time to develop, and after an executive change at CBS, it was dropped from the network's schedule.

With the sale that year of a sixteen-book package to Indonesia, Dean was now being translated into thirty-four languages.

11

The next revision for Ballantine was *Icebound*, published in 1995, based on Dean's David Axton novel, *Prison of Ice*. Dean updated it and deepened the characterizations, but left the plot essentially intact. First printing was set at two million copies, and it went directly to the number one spot for mass market paperbacks.

"He's managed his career well," said Claire Ferraro, editor-in-chief at Ballantine. "He always had his eye on the long haul, because he realized that if he were successful some day, those backlist titles would be worth a great deal more." About his extensive revisions, Ferraro said, "Dean feels strongly a commitment to his readers and wants to make sure they enjoy his earlier books to the same degree they do his later books."

In April, Berkley reissued his revised *The Key to Midnight* in paperback under his own name and sold over two million copies. It remained a bestseller for two months.

[1]Dean Koontz, *Mr. Murder* (New York: Putnam, 1993), p. 29.
[2]Ibid., p. 109.
[3]Ibid., p. 40.
[4]Ibid., p. 14.
[5]Ibid., p. 251–53.
[6]Dean Koontz, *Winter Moon* (New York: Ballantine, 1994), p. 326.
[7]Ibid., p. 472.
[8]Michael Collings, "Dean Koontz," *Mystery Scene* (no. 45, 1994).
[9]Dean Koontz, *Dark Rivers of the Heart* (New York: Alfred A. Knopf, 1995), p. 114.
[10]Ibid., p. 482.
[11]Ibid., p. 247.
[12]Ibid., p. 87.
[13]*Orange Coast* (November, 1994), p. 45.
[14]Dean Koontz, Foreword, *Ambush at Ruby Ridge* by Alan W. Bock (New York: Berkley, 1996), xi–xii.

TWENTY-THREE

Intensity

1

IN MAY OF 1995, *STRANGE HIGHWAYS* BECAME THE FIRST BOOK under the Brandon Tartikoff imprint, published in hardcover by Warner Books. It was Dean's collection of fourteen stories that had originally been part of a contract for Putnam. When Dean had moved on to Knopf, he had negotiated with Warner to revert the film rights to *Oddkins* by moving the collection from Putnam over to Warner. The collection included a number of previously published short stories, including "Kittens," a revised version of the novel *Chase*, and a new novel, itself titled *Strange Highways*.

First printing was set at 500,000 copies and the collection was featured by the Literary Guild and the Doubleday Book Club. Its first week out, it landed on the number eleven spot on *The New York Times* list and stayed on the list for seven weeks, unusual for a collection of stories, which generally fare less well than novels.

The title novel, *Strange Highways*, was set in Pennsylvania with numerous autobiographical associations. It is about life choices, of what might have been had another choice been made. The two brothers in the story form a surface metaphor of Dean's own dual potentials: what he could become, under his father's influence, and what he actually did to resist that by continually affirming goodness through his writing.

Joey Shannon returns home to the fictional town of Asherville after his only remaining parent, his father, has died. He has not been there in twenty years, having made nothing of his life and wanting to avoid a place filled with painful memories. As he enters his childhood home, he remembers much pain. His descriptions indicate that this is in fact the house where Dean grew up. "The house is similar, yes," Dean admits. "And the town has the feel of Bedford—though a

Bedford combined with some of these coal-mining towns in the Scranton area."

Joey's brother, PJ, had slept in the basement of this house, near the furnace (recall Dean's dream of the furnace immediately after his father's death). "Why I put PJ in the basement," says Dean, "I don't know. It just seemed that he ought to be there, removed from the rest of the family. It was a few years after my father's death and that dream of the furnace, so it's strange. If I believed in repressed memory, I'd say there's a repressed memory here."

PJ had been a star athlete, confident and skillful in every way—and a psychotic killer. One day, while home from college (at Shippensburg), Joey had accidentally discovered his brother's secret life. He had been forced to decide whether to turn his beloved older brother in to the cops and destroy his entire family, or "forget" what he knew. He chose the latter and consequently led a wasted, impotent life while his brother went on to fame and glory as a roving writer—what Joey himself had aspired to be. Upon Joey's return, he finds himself back at that crossroads, given another chance to reconsider the worst decision—and most cowardly act—of his life.

Leaving town after his father's funeral, Joey comes to a crossroads and sees before him Coal Valley Road, which has long been closed, in fact, bulldozed away because it led to a town that long ago had collapsed into a dangerous and unquenchable underground mine fire. Turning onto this impossible road, he discovers a young woman stranded by her car. Her name is Celeste and she is the angel through whom he can make new choices that could redeem him and change everything. Twenty years earlier, she had been one of PJ's victims. Joey finds himself back in time—on that fateful night of his youth. Celeste will become PJ's victim again unless Joey rewrites history. They return to her town, Coal Valley.

"The town is based on Centralia, Pennsylvania," Dean explains. "There are a couple of people still hanging on there although they were supposed to have been physically removed by the government years ago. Centralia was undermined by mine fires. Buildings and streets collapsed into the burnt-out shafts; they had the vent pipes with the sulfurous fires coming out of them—yet people were still living there. For a long time, the government tried to abandon them, and ultimately most of them were relocated at public expense. The town was condemned, and I always thought it would make an interesting background. I don't know how many people around the country realize this place existed, but it's so obvious for a story of the supernatural; the symbolism is almost too perfect."

There are twelve residents left in the doomed town, and Joey realizes that PJ wants to kill them all in symbolic style in a deconsecrated church. He wants to make himself into a dark god. Joey wants to stop PJ, but realizes that whenever his belief flags, the past he had actually lived reasserts itself, and PJ grows stronger. Celeste keeps urging him to believe in a higher power, which is difficult for him, but when he finally takes the leap, he manages to turn the tide and defeat his brother. His entire future changes. He marries Celeste and learns that he will become a published writer and the author of *Strange Highways*—fulfilling the dream he sacrificed when, on the first pass through his life, he made that one dreadfully wrong choice to "forget" his brother's criminality.

The deconsecrated church was Joey's life—he had emptied it of all meaning and had to reconsecrate it before he could do anything worthwhile. He accepted God's presence and gained the strength he needed to set things right. There are many images of transubstantiation sprinkled throughout, from the Catholic ceremony to what Joey does with his own psyche. Transubstantiation turns wine into the blood of Christ and offers redemption to believers. Joey shares the blood of a murderer and must transform himself in order to redeem the blood and reject his brother's taint. He does this through faith and defiance.

"The concept of Transubstantiation is fascinating," says Dean, "and I hadn't realized how much I've always used it. Catholicism is a very fleshy religion: the blood and the suffering. Protestantism is substantially dry. It's a religion of distance. In its Catholic expression, religion is organic. It gets right into the muck of existence. Blood is such a central image, and then there's the virgin's tears. All Catholic families I know are generally emotional. The tears flow. When religion steps into these realms, when it's not afraid to talk about the blood and the suffering, there's a meaning to suffering. In Communion, this *is* the body and blood of Christ laid upon your tongue. It brings an intimacy to the experience that's eerie and wonderful."

When Joey rescues Celeste in the rain, he passes through a baptism, a cleansing. He moves from pessimism to optimism, from passivity to active commitment. The two sides of a self—the capacity for good or evil—flow into and out of each other. Joey needs not only resistance to evil, but love from and for Celeste in order to succeed. After that, with belief, all things are possible.

Allowing PJ to get away with murder in the past had dissolved Joey's integrity. He could not become a novelist, because novelists get to the truth of things and he had turned away. Even so, as Dean did in response to his father, Joey had researched the psychotic mind extensively and had learned enough to arm himself for this extraordinary encounter, this magical second chance.

His brother was as steeped in symbolism as Joey, but had inverted it for his own purposes. When Joey had first discovered PJ's foul deeds, PJ had offered him thirty dollars (thirty pieces of silver) to stay quiet. The basement and the furnace parallel the sinkholes and fires of the mining town. PJ feels at home there because it is a dying town, like his dying soul, and it reeks of hell. He had set everything up through religious symbols in order to empower himself with their defilement. Joey had changed that and turned them back to good.

The story, for Dean, has some redemptive value.

"There are certain moments I give to characters that express lessons from my own life. I've learned, for instance, that what we most regret are sins of passivity. With my mother, I could have been more directly expressive. I could have told her more directly how much I loved and respected her. Of course, I grew up in a house where you didn't talk about your feelings. But I wish, especially just before she died, that I'd been better at expressing what I felt. You do redeem yourself by writing, by letting the characters be better people than you were. Which is why I try to make the characters so compassionate. More attuned to each other. I'm saying, *that is how I should have been when so often I was not.*"

In a review of this collection, English professor Michael Collings wrote that "one of the trademarks of Koontz's fiction is his ability to explore contrarieties and to leave them identified, if not always fully resolved ... The title piece is an eerie search for individual meaning that couples an overtly supernatural plot with an intense psychological trauma of guilt and betrayal."[1]

To promote this book in its paperback form, Dean threw a party for as many booksellers as Warner was willing to fly out to Newport Beach, and held it on board a hundred-twenty-foot luxury yacht. He invited his magician friend, sleight-of-hand artist Barry Price, to perform tricks and he devised contests to keep people entertained. For one contest, he offered to use the name of the winner in his next novel. Barbara Christman won, and she showed up in *Sole Survivor*.

2

In interviews promoting the publication of *Dark Rivers of the Heart* at the end of 1994, Dean had expressed a certain degree of confidence that he had faced down those issues about his father still hovering from childhood. The novel had seemed to him cathartic. "I remember finishing *Dark Rivers* and saying, 'Now *that's* behind me — the issue of how you get through terrible trauma and overcome it and don't let it taint you — but then look at *Intensity*. The same concerns are expressed through a female character and it's *not* behind her. If there's any book where those issues are in the foreground, it's *Intensity*. How weird that they're such a major piece of *Dark Rivers* and I'm thinking that I've put them behind me — yet in the very next book, they're the centerpiece. In fact, I think I dealt with them better in this book than ever. More directly, more honestly, more powerfully."

Dean dedicated *Intensity* to his mother, who had been his guardian as a child and to whom he owed his belief in human resilience. In his opening poem, he emphasized love, hope, faith, and courage as key factors in resisting the darkness. He had needed about six months of seventy-hour weeks to write this novel, and he had worked hard on patterns of archetypal images and metaphors — among them knights and dragons.

In the opening sentence, the "dragon," Edgler Foreman

Vess, a muscular "homicidal adventurer" who seeks power and control, is bathed in red, and there are many images of fire as Dean describes the sunset. "He seems to be ablaze," says Dean, "which foreshadows what will happen to him. And you see that he is strangely attuned to the natural world. He's as much animal as human, and his perception of the world is different from that of an ordinary person. There are many blood images—the sun is red as it sinks; the grass turns red."

Subliminally Vess then is associated with the lead character as she and her friend come into a shimmering red light. The shadows flicker "shark-swift" across the windshield of their car, which suggests the presence of a predator. Dean continues to use setting, forces of nature, and objects all around to set mood and pace, subtly tying one paragraph to another so that one image leads readers continually toward the next in a progression. When Dean wants a heightened sense in a certain setting, he focuses on concrete details, such as what Chyna first sees on opening a nightstand drawer in a room where murder has been committed: "In the mortal fall of light, she discovered a pair of reading glasses with yellow reflections in the half-moon lenses, a paperback men's adventure novel, a box of Kleenex, a tube of lip balm, but no weapon."[2]

"There's something about that set of words," says Dean, "that is more real than having her see Kleenex and lip balm, or just see a book. It feels hyper-real." He also describes objects with words that convey motion and feeling.

As the scene moves away from Vess, Chyna Shepherd enters. She is a twenty-six-year-old grad student, a "multi-channel worrier," who is interested in criminal psychology, in part because she is burdened by past abuse from her cruel mother. She goes home for the weekend with a friend, Laura Templeton, who has been targeted that night by Vess. Chyna hides as he goes through the house and destroys the family, one by one. Her first instinct is to protect herself, as she has done all through her life, by hiding under the bed. "Until this experience," says Dean, "Chyna is a case of arrested development. Part of her is still a child because there are a lot of things she's afraid of. She's built a decent life, but she's still in a survival mode. I think that's me in some ways. I've often said I don't think that I'd have become successful if I hadn't had the bad example of my father, the determination to be unlike him, and the street savvy that told me how to take care of myself. Without that same combination of motives and qualities, Chyna would not survive the night she endures in *Intensity*."

Chyna finally comes out and realizes that Laura is just barely alive. When Vess carries Laura outside to his motor home, Chyna gets in to rescue her friend. Laura dies and Chyna discovers yet another body inside. The place is an abattoir on wheels. She then learns that Vess has imprisoned a young girl in his home, and if Chyna fails to make a personal commitment to save this girl—Ariel—then the girl will die. Until this point, she believed that survival meant not taking chances. Now she begins to realize that physical survival means nothing if it comes at the discovery of her own emotional frigidity and spritual poverty. Her heroism gradually grows out of her humanity. Chyna hides herself in the motor home until they arrive at Vess's house. Vess is aware of her presence and decides to let her live so he can study her.

He keeps four highly trained Doberman pinschers to guard his property, but he lets Chyna enter his house, then traps her. Tied up and afraid, she nevertheless confronts him. As she tries to understand his weird worldview based on what she has learned of psychological theory, he plays mental games with her, and finally insists that he is a singularity—none of her theories fit his case. Madness, he insists, is not always about some set cause and effect. He was not abused as a child. He loves killing for its own sake.

Vess gets empowered from playing word games with his name: From the letters, he makes as many words as he can that have striking associations, such as "God fears me." Dean had seen the name, Edgler, in a newspaper and it had seemed ugly to him. "That's why it stuck in my head," he explains. "And I just thought that Vess was a good villain's name. The sibilants are like the hiss of a snake." Vess also derives power from concentrating fully on physical sensation—pleasure or pain—to produce a state of synesthesia, in which the senses blend together, so that he might feel an odor or see a sound. It is a state of consciousness often described by saints in deep meditation, but Vess shows that it can as easily become a tool of the deranged mind. To convey Vess's point of view effectively, the author crafted metaphors and similes with a synesthesiac quality, a daring device that definitely conveys the strangeness of Vess's mind.

Vess views himself as a Nietzschean superman, as suggested by his command word, Nietzsche, for his guard dogs. He interprets this to mean that he is "beyond good and evil" and thus has no accountability save to himself; he lives like a god, with no remorse, no limits, total need. What feels right *is* right. His type, he says, wind up in politics. His point of view is written in present tense to emphasize his immersion in the sensations of the moment—having no past and no future—and his total narcissism isolates him inside his own world view. He is reptilian, a Palmetto bug, and the spider is his totem.

Dean had based him in part on a real life serial killer, Edmund Kemper III, whose crimes had shocked the nation. As a child, Kemper prayed that everyone in the world but him would die. He killed pets and mutilated dolls. At the age of fifteen, he shot and killed his grandparents just to see what it would be like. He was arrested and institutionalized, but with his mother's help, he was freed at age twenty-one. He tried to convince three psychiatrists to recommend that his juvenile record be sealed so that he could pursue his interest in law enforcement. When he could not achieve this, he befriended police officers in Santa Cruz. At six feet nine inches tall and two hundred eighty pounds, he was an intimidating figure with an IQ of 136 and seemingly gentle ways. He idolized John Wayne. However, he claimed to suffer from "zapples" that sent him into a state of murderous rage. In the early seventies, Kemper began to pick up girls, murder and mutilate them, and have sex with their corpses. He exulted that he was winning over death. "I was the hunter and they were the hunted," he later told a psychiatrist.[4] He also carved flesh from the legs of two victims to eat, thereby making them part of him and possessing them forever. He then killed his mother, whom he hated, and a friend of hers that he had invited over. Not long afterward, he turned himself in to face eight counts of murder. He asked to be executed, but was given life imprisonment instead. After the trial, psychiatrist Herbert McGrew said, "Kemper is a marvelous example of the fact that psychiatrists don't know everything."[5]

Vess leaves to go to his job, and Chyna frees herself and finds the imprisoned girl, Ariel. They escape together in the motor home, but encounter a sheriff—who turns out to be Vess. Just when it seems there is truly no escape, Chyna uses a cigarette lighter to ignite spilled gasoline and engulf Vess in flames. She is the knight delivering the maiden from the fire-breathing dragon.

Since Ariel's parents are dead, Chyna gets custody. She realizes that life is about taking risks on behalf of others and making connections. In the final words of the novel: "It is the purpose for which we exist. This reckless caring." She ditches psychology for fiction, believing there is more about human nature in the pages of novels. Out of the letters of her name, she forms the word "peace."

"This book is an argument against the cynicism of modern times," says Dean. "We're told that people are essentially self-centered and that there are no heroes. I don't believe that. I think there are heroes everywhere."

One of the key themes in the back story of this tale is the negative impact of Freudian theory on our culture. There is a hint of this when Chyna comes into Laura's room after Vess has been there, and sees a picture of Freud looking down upon the mayhem. His theory seems as impotent in that moment as Chyna, who has studied him in school. He cannot illuminate Vess's behavior any more than she can stop it.

"In essence, Freud says we're not responsible for what we do," Dean says, "we're formed by parents and society and culture. I came across a statement of Nabokov's to the effect that the two great evils of the century are Freudianism and Marxism. Too true. I think Freudianism has saturated our culture and corrupted our law. [The first] two juries could not decide what to do with the Menendez brothers, for instance, because they bought into the Freudian idea that we are what we are solely because of what others have done to us. By this logic, the Menendez brothers are victims. So is Kemper. By this logic they deserve pity and rehabilitation. But they *can't* be rehabilitated. No one has *ever* been able to rehabilitate a genuine sociopath. They are lost forever. Evil *does* exist. And because of Freud's victimology theories, they are turned loose.

"The other effect of Freudian theory on society is that it

encourages people to feel that they are not responsible for their actions. It's the idea that there's no real good and evil. That expands in people's minds and leads to cynicism about standards of conduct. I think these are terrible influences on society. It leads to a huge decline of civility, to popular entertainment that panders without having any moral function, and to a loss of people's ability to tell the difference."

While that attitude seems pessimistic, Dean actually intends for it to be the starting point for readers to recognize that they are not victims of their pasts and not irrevocably shaped by the forces of childhood. "One of the reasons I wrote *Intensity*," Dean says, "is to say you don't have to be what others make you. I was always determined to get out of my situation. I was not dragged down by it. If you allow yourself to be dragged down, then the person who abused you has won." Chyna, a victim of abuse, can rise above it and take responsibility for transforming from a self-protective coward to a self-sacrificing heroine. "Chyna isn't going to turn out according to Freud's expectations," says Dean. "She's going to make herself into a happy, productive, and *heroic* person. Freud's view of the human mind is too simplistic. He sees us as machines, easily programmed, but not easily *re*-programmed." The toxic bond between mother and daughter need not infect Chyna's life choices or her sense of self. She can make life what she wants it to be rather than believing that "sooner or later in every dream there's a boogeyman."[6]

The character of Vess reveals that Dean's understanding of evil has evolved. Even in *Dark Rivers of the Heart*, the psychiatrist in charge of Steven Ackblom says to Roy Miro, ". . . there *is* evil in the world. Evil that exists without cause, without rationalizations. Evil that doesn't arise from trauma or abuse or deprivation."[7] She points out that Ackblom is sane and knows the difference between right and wrong. As a prime example of the sociopathic mind, he chooses without compulsion to do monstrous things, fully knowing they are monstrous. The psychiatrist's condemnation of Freud and Jung, and her disillusionment with psychiatry's need and ability to explain such human behavior, echoes Dean's attitude.

"I wince when I look back on *Whispers*, in which every character is explained," he says. "Up through *Whispers*, that was the way I developed bad guys. Even in *Watchers*, The Outsider is a created creature that didn't ask to be born, so you can build a natural sympathy for it.

"But my understanding of evil has evolved in the sense that I've come to believe that evil is not wholly a product of society and culture and parental malfeasance. We all have a capacity for evil, but some of us have an absolute *love* of doing the wrong thing. Therefore, I've come around to the attitude that evil is a real force in the world. Having to support my father those fourteen years, going through hell with him when I was a child, then being up close to him again as an adult—that helped finally to push me to an anti-Freudian position.

"There is absolutely no known case of anybody rehabilitating a true sociopath. Whatever is wrong with those people may be genetic. Someday we'll recognize certain genetic damage that's the same in every sociopathic personality. Then some people would say, well, that's not evil if it's a medical condition. Yes and no. It's an *incurable* medical condition—at least at this stage—and it results in tremendous human pain and suffering for the victims of these people. So on a practical level, what is the difference between that and true evil? To me, there are identifiably evil acts, and society needs to separate those from crimes of passion or circumstance and *never* excuse them.

"Vess believes that violence is glamorous, fun, and he is darkly compelling, because evil does have its appeal. So Chyna has to be tremendously interesting as a character, has to have triumphed against terrible odds. I wanted her to be Vess's equivalent. I don't want the reader to finish the book with more of an interest in Vess than in Chyna. That often happens in books like this: They celebrate the dark side, as does Vess himself. I am not that kind of writer.

"We have built a world in which we pretend that we don't believe in evil. We claim that all human motivation is in tones of gray, no pure black and white. Yet in movies and books we are fascinated with vile characters with no redeeming qualities, like Hannibal Lecter [from *Silence of the Lambs*] and his ilk. We are fascinated because we know on a visceral level that these depictions of pure evil are true—and that our sophisticated pretensions to a belief in the Freudian gray are just that—pretensions. In our hearts, we *know* that evil walks the world."

Another of *Intensity*'s background themes is the idea of the uncanny. Twice, majestic elk appear in unlikely places just when Chyna is most desperate. This seems a mystical event to her, as if they symbolize a higher power that is assuring her she will survive. She interprets the strange appearance of these animals to mean that she is not alone, and each time she regains both her physical strength and her will. The fact that she *does* survive against all odds suggests that the elk do indeed represent a higher power, but the issue remains—as with all symbols of the uncanny—ambiguous. The reader decides.

Dean wrote a Preface to this novel for *Intensity*'s Franklin Mint edition in which he discussed how he was driven to write it by outrage and by the need to understand the changing roles of evil and heroism in "a society increasingly willing to accommodate the former out of misplaced compassion, while viewing the latter with skepticism." He claims to have envisioned Chyna full-blown as a character who disproves, through her heroism, all theories that insist on the helplessness of the abused. She thus becomes his own alter-ego, the person who acts out what he seeks to believe: that no one need be held back by the difficulties of childhood and, conversely, that evil has no simple causal explanations.

He confirmed this in an interview with Robert Morrish: "I am very much like Chyna in *Intensity*—or would like to think I am. I identified so strongly with her and with her journey from an abusive childhood to a life of decency and hope, that I could literally feel her terror and exhilaration and despair as she was struggling through that story."[8]

3

Intensity's cover design featured a bright chartreuse and orange geometric pattern that created an almost optical illusion of movement. It was eye-catching and different from anything done previously for Dean's books. Artist Chip Kidd designed it after reading the book and realizing that the cover art had to be bold. He used "two colors of equal value that vibrate and fight against each other."

Because he liked the aggressive way that Knopf was

packaging him, Dean agreed again to do promotional work. It
was an exhausting schedule that included four Fridays of radio
tours, each one involving six hours of interviews with disc
jockeys and talk-show hosts from all over the country during
prime-time driving hours—135 interviews altogether. He also
did book signings, newspaper interviews, and television
shows. Knopf used television spots, newspaper ads, a blitz of
copies to booksellers, and floor displays in bookstores to promote the novel. The strategies worked as, in its first crucial
weeks, *Intensity* outsold *Dark Rivers* four to one.

The first printing was set at 525,000. *Intensity* debuted at
number nine on the *Times* bestsellers list and went to number
one the second week. It stayed there for three weeks and
remained on the list for thirteen.

Publishers Weekly said the story raced fast enough to give
readers whiplash and that it might be "the most viscerally
exciting thriller of the year." *Kirkus* agreed, calling the novel "a
suspense masterpiece that leaves its competitors in the dust."
Some critics thought it had gratuitous violence, while Mark
Harris thought it unbelievably effective and said in *Entertainment Weekly*, "*Intensity* scared me stupid." Peter Millar in the
London Times said it was a novel about catharsis and the power
to do good as well as evil: "There are sound undercurrents in
Koontz's work, [and] they run very deep." *The New York Times*
cited the "tumbling, hallucinogenic prose," and said, "Serious
writers might do well to examine his technique."

4

Film rights were sold to Mandalay Television Entertainment in
association with Tri-Star Television for a four-hour miniseries
to premier on the Fox network. John C. McGinley was cast as
Vess and Molly Parker as Chyna. Stephen Tolkin wrote the
script and Yves Simoneau was chosen as director. It was
intended to come out simultaneously with Dean's next novel,
but delays forced it to air later in the year, during the first
week of August. There were numerous changes to the story.
For example, white wolves were substituted for the elk; a
woman encountered Chyna during her pursuit of Vess and

alerted police; a police officer got involved; and the ending involved a fire inside Vess's house. However, Dean felt that the essence of the story remained. Having experienced so many disappointments, he was delighted with this film. "For the first time, filmmakers succeed in capturing the essence of what I do—the thematic cross-currents and especially the emotional content. They realized I'm not a horror writer."

5

The Eyes of Darkness was reissued by Berkley in paperback that year, debuting at number seven on *The New York Times* list, and climbing up one more rung, to stay on the list for seven weeks. Dean had changed some of the Cold War references, but kept the story essentially the same.

6

In November 1996, HarperCollins issued Dean's illustrated book, *Santa's Twin*. Dean's editor there was John Silbersack.

Dean had finished the poem he had started in *Mr. Murder*, in which Marty Stillwater told his daughters about Santa's infamous brother, Bob. It seems Bob is messing up Christmas, so two girls, Emily and Charlotte, go to the North Pole to rescue Santa and restore order. Despite its overt thrust as a Christmas story, it still reveals Dean's concerns with the toxic bond of family—how the same source can produce both good and evil, and how one brother's badness can threaten to topple the other's goodness. In the end, innocence and love provide the conduit for good to triumph. The prankster, Bob, changes his tune when he realizes how much what he has done would hurt his sweet mother.

"Phil Parks [the illustrator] just knocked himself out and did some of the best work he's ever done," says Dean. "When he puts a pen to paper, wow! My agent wanted to take it to someone who has a reputation for thinking in especially creative ways about odd properties like this, so he took it to John Silbersack."

With a limited release of 130,000 copies, this book sold out long before Christmas. Phil Parks added the humorous twist of placing snowmen strategically in each illustration, in a "Where's Waldo?" format. Sometimes they were obvious, sometimes hidden. He also placed a picture of Dean in the bedroom of the little girls. It was his thirteenth illustrated book with Dean, and since his work was being done on spec, Dean bought all of the original art in advance. That way, Phil was able to concentrate on the art without worrying about paying the bills.

"It was a lot different than illustrating a novel," says Phil, "because you had to figure how many lines of verse to each page and try to pull a piece of action from each scene. I use a cinematic approach. I go over the story and then try to reel it out in my head like a film. The struggle is to bring that out on paper, getting the composition and the placement of the characters right. I had to keep it moving. If there wasn't much action for several pages, I had to change the perspective to keep it visually interesting."

Nearly simultaneous with *Santa's Twin* was a lengthy Foreword that Dean wrote for a book of David Robinson's cemetery photographs, titled *Beautiful Death*. In it, he writes about his mother's grave, the difficult years, and his suspicion that he is not the true son of Ray Koontz. Many people back in Bedford were surprised by some of Dean's revelations—particularly his speculation about Uncle Ray. Nancy Eckard was certain that her father-in-law had been overseas and could not have been Dean's father. Dean continued to believe in the possibility.

[1]*Mystery Scene* (no. 49, 1994).
[2]Dean Koontz, *Intensity* (New York: Alfred A. Knopf, 1996), p. 36.
[4]Margaret Cheney, *Why: The Serial Killer in America* (Saratoga, CA: R&E Publishers, 1992), xi.
[5]Ibid., p. 159.
[6]*Intensity*, p. 5.
[7]Dean Koontz, *Dark Rivers of the Heart* (New York: Alfred A. Knopf, 1995), p. 459.
[8]*Cemetery Dance*, Summer 1997.

TWENTY-FOUR

Mysterious Skies

1

WHILE WAITING FOR *SOLE SURVIVOR* TO BE PUBLISHED, DEAN sent a proposal to Knopf for his next project. It was to be a three-book series that featured a repeating central character in very unusual circumstances. Sonny Mehta and Jane Freidman both expressed enthusiasm, not only about *Sole Survivor*, but also about Dean's new idea. Knopf put together an impressive offer.

Even so, Dean had concerns other than money. Writing careers are supported not just by advances and royalties, but by a vision within the publishing house that includes increased print runs and advertising budgets, strategic publicity, and a ready supply of books for quick turnaround on orders. He wanted to be certain that these considerations were part of the overall plan. He still had four paperback books left on his contract with Ballantine and, thus far, his novels with them had not seemed to be supported in the marketplace as well as Berkley had supported previous titles.

In the meantime, other publishers were aware that *Sole Survivor* was the third of Dean's books for Knopf and that no further deal had yet been announced. When Knopf's option expired, several publishers made overtures to Robert Gottlieb. Dean listened to the various ideas on how his career could be enhanced and waited for Random House to assure him that something similar could happen with his Knopf/Ballantine deal. The more he heard, however, the more he realized the impact of publishing philosophies on his career. Random House seemed caught in a downbeat mood, viewing the unprecedented number of book returns throughout the industry that year as a sign of darker economic times ahead. They had even begun the practice of discounting books in place rather than pay the expense of having them returned, which annoyed authors. This attitude seemed to hang over every conversation, clashing with Dean's desire to pursue growth and enhancement.

In addition, he felt there was no clear understanding at Knopf/Ballantine of the nature of his work or of the audience to which it appealed. He knew from experience, for instance, that half of his audience was female, but his publisher persisted in the belief that he sold largely to men.

As he pondered his situation, he decided to make a dramatic change in his personal life. He shaved his mustache and got hair implants. "I admit to vanity!" People who knew him well hardly recognized him and those who had known him in his younger days thought he looked the way he had in college. "After years of being recognized," he says, "I've regained my anonymity, at least for now." (In a newsletter to fans, he joked that the mustache removal had been performed by a crack team from the U.S. Army Corps of Engineers with lasers, explosives, and sandblasting equipment.)

The change proved to be fun and to revitalize his views of his future. He had come a long way and he intended to go further yet.

At the age of fifty-one, Dean had already seen six of his novels becomes number one bestsellers in hardcover and eleven in paperback. Worldwide, his book sales totaled over 175 million copies, with additional sales per year of 17 million. He had been translated into thirty-eight languages. Since 1977, when his career had become relatively stable, Putnam had published thirteen of his novels, Knopf three—and sixteen of his backlist titles had been reissued with great success, some revised and some not. It seemed time to take another leap.

On Friday, December 6, 1996, Dean decided to sell his three-book series to Bantam Books of the Bantam Doubleday Dell Publishing Group, owned by Bertelsmann AG. He became Bantam's largest-selling name in fiction, and they were willing to pay him the highest advance he had ever received. Indeed, other publishers competing with Bantam had also made offers that would have been his personal best—including Putnam, who wanted him back.

Dean had responded strongly to Bantam publisher, Irwyn Applebaum, however, and it was his belief in Applebaum's intelligence and savvy that settled him on this house, rather than any others. Bantam issued a press release quoting Dean as saying, "I have not embarked on this change for financial reasons. I have been proud to be published by Knopf and Ballantine, and I value the time I spent with everyone there, and the work they did on behalf of my books."[1] He explained that, just as in his writing, he relied on intuition as a guide in his career, and this move felt right to him. "My gut feeling was that it was time for a change."

Publisher and president Irwyn Applebaum, delighted by this coup, told his sales force that he had just concluded a very good deal with a successful author, but he would not reveal Dean's identity until the sales conference in Florida a few days later. The salespeople gasped in disbelief that Dean Koontz had left Knopf, but the gasp was immediately followed by resounding enthusiasm. Applebaum got a standing ovation.

It was not Dean's first book with Bantam. Back in 1972, he had written *The Flesh in the Furnace*, and in 1973, *Demon Seed* for Bantam. But that was virtually another writer in another age. Now, as one of the bestselling writers in the world, he was coming in with an idea for a series, the sort of project he had never done before.

His move caused a lot of speculation in the publishing world. When Dean denied that his reasons were financially motivated, *Publishers Weekly*'s Judy Quinn suggested that perhaps he had backed off from his professed literary aspirations. In fact, just the opposite was the case. He had liked working with everyone at Knopf, admired them, but had felt not entirely sure that his more ambitious recent work was wanted there. He was inspired again by Bantam's intense response to the literary *possibilities* of his proposed series.

Dean left the media to devise their own theories, and began to concentrate on his new directions.

2

Sole Survivor was due out on February 6, 1997. Dean had written the entire novel based on the sense of the uncanny that he had used for his short story "Twilight of the Dawn." Having begun years previously to layer his suspense with literary devices, he had braided several different themes together, loosely at first, and then had pulled them tightly together into a complex denouement. Each theme had its own pattern of motifs such that almost every reference and image—even seemingly insignificant ones—functioned on multiple thematic levels.

For an interview that was to appear online on the Barnes & Noble website, Dean said that the inspiration for the novel came from his extensive reading in quantum physics, chaos theory, and molecular biology. "During the past ten years," he remarked, "quite a few nonfiction books have been written about the surprising intersection of science and faith in our time—and the debates it has sparked in the scientific community, but I'm not aware of a novel that has used this as a springboard for a story."

The question that interested him was, if science learned something that could prove that there is life after death—how would someone react to this proof? Dean created several characters who respond in different ways. The lead character, Joe Carpenter, has the most difficulty, since he is suffering the most. He is unable to accept the existence of God unless he also gets some explanation for human pain and suffering. For Dean, while God may have a dark side, the most profound morality nevertheless is rooted in the spiritual, so each person must come to grips with the reality of suffering without losing hope. Thus, he willingly tackles the unpopular subject of God's impact on human endeavors, seldom a subject in modern fiction, and one that risks offending some readers. He pairs faith's sense of mystery and dread with a catalogue of suspense techniques to enhance tension and add drama.

Although we want to believe in ultimate goodness and therefore have hope, we see around us chaos and destruction, and we become anxious. The constant clash of these emotions breeds inevitable tension. It becomes difficult to entrust our lives to a benign creator. We want clarity. We rarely get it. We therefore step with uncertainty toward a spiritual dimension.

In *Sole Survivor*, Joe Carpenter must reconcile his bitterness and anger about the cruelty of existence with growing evidence that life has a larger purpose and meaning, a spiritual dimension. He has lost his wife, Michelle, and his two daughters, Chrissie and Nina, in the crash of a 747 so horrendous that most of the three hundred thirty passengers could not be identified. A year later, he still cannot come to grips with this tragedy. He is merely "waiting for the morning when he would fail to wake."[2] He has already quit his job as a crime reporter for the *L.A. Post* and lost touch with all of his friends. He feels only numbness and impotence. He cannot bring himself to believe in a God or an afterlife, so he remains psychologically safe in a universe of indifferent mechanical laws. As he sits watching the ocean—a source of both life and death—he notices only the exanimate creatures that wash ashore.

Getting Joe's perspective was one of the most difficult Dean had ever tried. "When I started *Sole Survivor*," he says, "I was foolish enough to think that writing about Joe would be easy because his terrible loss would instantly make him a sympathetic figure to the reader. But as I began to write, I realized that if I didn't handle Joe with extreme care, he would be so bleak that no one would want to read about him. For research, I talked to many people who had lost children. What I learned from them made it easier to write about Joe—though in the process I heard stories that broke my heart. Once I got through that scene in the first chapter where Joe remembers his family's funeral, I began to get a handle on it, but it was difficult to sustain the right tone with him throughout the book." Dean wanted to capture the hard, abrasive quality of intense despair without slipping into the theatrical bleakness of noir fiction. "In most modern fiction, despair is portrayed so romantically that it becomes appealing. The hero becomes a brooding James Dean–like figure. That's bad fiction. It's hokum sentimentality. I didn't want Joe to come off that way."

In an early scene on a public beach, Joe encounters a young boy who exemplifies exactly that romantic nihilism that sentimentalizes alienation and despair. Joe is baffled and ultimately angered by him. His own deep anguish becomes more real to us when the author places this boy before us by way of comparison.

Joe suddenly discovers that he is under surveillance, but he cannot fathom who might be watching him, or why. That same day, he encounters a black woman taking photos of the graves of his deceased family, and she flees when the men who were watching him suddenly show up at the cemetery and go after her. Joe learns that her name is Rose Tucker and that she claims to be the sole survivor of the fatal crash, which seems to him utterly impossible. He contacts others who lost loved ones in the crash and discovers that this woman has visited each of them with photos of the graves. She claims to possess knowledge that will change everyone forever, and she seems, indeed, to have been on the fatal Flight 353. Even more alarming, soon after she leaves, each of the persons to whom she has revealed this knowledge commits suicide—and flamboyantly. When Joe witnesses three of these suicides in one terrifying five-minute period, he knows for certain that the true story of the crash of that airliner is far different from the *official* story. And he knows, too, that here is something that will sooner or later shatter his bleak but strangely comfortable assumptions about the meaninglessness of life.

Joe contacts Barbara Christman, the former National Transportation Safety Board official who was in charge of the crash scene investigation, and she confirms that there was much more to the catastrophe than a mere mechanical failure. The cockpit recorder revealed that one of the pilots had suffered a psychotic episode and had intentionally taken the plane into a nosedive, a piece of information that was later covered up with threats and murder. Together Joe and Barbara visit a farm near the crash scene and Joe learns that Rose had gone there directly after the crash with a little girl. Joe immediately believes this child was his daughter, Nina.

He sets out to find Rose, knowing now that agents of the government and something called Teknologik Corporation— where Rose had worked as a geneticist—are trying to silence her and conceal the truth about the crash. Joe locates Rose through her friends, and she tells him that she did indeed have a child with her that night, but the girl is in hiding, for she holds within her the evolutionary hope and spiritual fate of humankind. There are people who would rather destroy her than allow her to bring enlightenment to the world.

Joe learns that scientists at Teknologik, including Rose, were involved in genetically engineering children with paranormal abilities. Some of them were destructive and some dysfunctional, but one was a healer who could bestow on anyone she touched a vision of the true spiritual nature of life, an intimate awareness of God and an afterlife. Rose had taken her out of the high-security labs for her protection. Now the researchers are using the powers of the most malignant child they have created to locate and destroy both Rose and this miraculous girl.

Although Joe realizes this child is not his daughter, a powerful urge within him, related to his deceased wife's life-enhancing qualities, propels him to defy the darkness and rescue the girl. Her powers offer the hope for actualizing human potential for virtual godhood. Joe himself continues to reject her offers to heal his own soul, but finally she breaks through his defenses and changes him for the better.

As an author, Dean always uses imagery for deeper purposes than description alone. The narrative is suspended in webs of thematically linked metaphors and similes. In *Sole Survivor*, light—and consequently shadow—is the primary motif for the figures of speech that enhance the novel's themes. These begin on the first page, when the grief-crippled Joe looks out a window and sees ". . . the ragged black shapes of evergreens and eucalyptus. To the west was a fat moon glimpsed through the trees, a silvery promise beyond the bleak urban woods."[3] The moon is the promise of hope through faith, and the urban woods are the human condition. In this figure of speech, Joe's journey from despair to transcendence is subtly foreshadowed.

Later, as a change in weather drives Joe and Barbara out of the meadow where the plane crashed and into the woods, we read, "Down through the vaulted conifers came fluttering white wings of storm light, and again, and still more, as if the cracking sky were casting out a radiant multitude."[4] This occurs just when Joe is at the depth of his despair, having seen the very spot where his family perished—but also when he is beginning to have the hope that one of his daughters has somehow survived. He is in a storm of emotion, and the lightning is the knowledge he has acquired. The reference to fallen angels reminds us that knowledge is both a blessing and a curse—and therefore it foreshadows what will happen to Joe. While achieving transcendence, he must also accept what has happened to his family—all of this exists within one image of storm light. Within the novel there are hundreds of light images, such as fire, with an equally complex purpose.

Dean is also aware of the impressions created by names, and he often relies on archetypal figures. Joe Carpenter is Joseph the carpenter, the father of Christ, who was also a carpenter—and in the story he becomes the protector of Nina, who is a Christ-like figure. Rose Tucker alludes to the Virgin Mary: She helped to create the holy child without benefit of sexual intercourse. She also gives the child her first name, calling her Mary. Mercy Ealing, a farmer's wife, is a central character at one of the most pivotal points of the novel, and Barbara Christman, ironically, is the real name of a woman who had won a contest wherein Koontz offered to use her name in his next novel. It fits, however, since she suffers for the truth and risks the ultimate sacrifice of her life to get significant information to Joe. Even Nina, which means "grace" in Hebrew, plays off the number nine, a mystical symbol of truth and completion.

There are numerous allusions to God, heaven, and sacred figures from mythology. Throughout the novel, Koontz plants hints of spiritual possibilities by building descriptive metaphors from such names as Stonehenge, Grendel, the moon goddess Diana, and the biblical Shadrach, Lazarus, Joshua, and Mark. On the wall at the Ealing ranch is a religious calendar featuring Andrew, Christ, and Simon Peter. Cats and dogs—significant symbols in most world mythologies—are sprinkled here and there as subliminal reminders.

When Joe regains his desire to live, and with it a sensitivity to the spiritual realms beyond mundane reality, he meets people who foreshadow what he will soon learn about life and faith. Believing that the Ealings may know about Rose Tucker, he visits their Colorado horse ranch. Mercy Ealing, whose successive miscarriages prevent her from having children, accepts her fate and finds other ways to create. As she discusses what she knows about the night of the crash, she rolls cookie dough into a ball, an image of God forming a planet. (Humorously, she even says if she knew all the answers, she would *be* God and she would not want that job for anything.) Despite death and disappointment, she accepts the fate God gives her, believing that a better world awaits them. She is a model of faith for

Jim, who needs this interlude to regroup and prepare for a higher state of consciousness.

The titles of the four sections form a spiritual progression. "Lost Forever" captures the physical reality of Joe's dead family and the spiritual possibility for Joe, if he fails to transcend his pain. "Searching Behavior" points out the many levels on which the novel is structured: Joe searches for meaning and hope; grieving parents (including Joe) go through a phase called "searching behavior," in which they believe they see their child alive; the spiritual organization, Infiniface, is searching for Rose, as are the people who operate the lab from which she escaped. The third section is "Zero Point," which is defined as the instant a child dies, because for the parents all future events are dated from that point. It serves as a metaphor of Joe's initial spiritual condition. Finally, "Pale Fire" is the burning flame of hope within the heart of individual characters.

The paradoxical unity of seemingly opposing forces that constitute a complex concept of God occurs in a variety of images that repeat the same theme: good and evil may arise from the same source. Trying to repress, deny, or stamp out evil denies that it is part and parcel with the whole. God's shadow is associated with death, destruction, chaos, and madness. As such, it possesses great vitality, and mirrors our own inner world, a duality of reason and irrationality, logic and paradox, order and chaos, finite and infinite. Neither pole is reducible to the other, separable, or derivative. These contrary energies operate together and provide the tension of life, along with its consequent anxiety. God's shadow brings unspeakable suffering into human existence, yet we must accept it or risk an overidealized relationship to higher forces. Dean uses aspects of nature, color, setting, and weather to remind us how closely associated are the manifestations of light and dark. An oleander bush, for example, is described as beautiful, but it is also highly poisonous.

The juxtaposition in many descriptions of the mundane and the mythical, the ordinary and extraordinary, indicates a desire to impress readers with the close association of our day-to-day life with the sacred dimensions. Dean subtly suggests that the supernatural intrudes on the natural world, for example, in his description of a meadow as a monastery, or a stream of almost mystical light coming through a high window in the men's lavatory.

Sole Survivor also features guardian figures, as in other Koontz novels, and they have an even greater mythological quality this time. He develops an organization of intelligent people, Infiniface, who are profoundly interested in the interface between scientific discoveries and spirituality—one of his own passions—and who provide safe passage for Joe and Rose. They stand in awe of Rose, who they believe has broken important ground in the *scientific* search for spiritual answers. Like Dean, they believe that the ultimate purpose of human intelligence is to seek knowledge, understand the workings of the universe, and become God's equals.

Rose herself is a guardian to the child first given a number for a name, later called Nina. The genetically engineered boy, whom we know only by his lab number, is a child without a guardian, treated only as a military "asset," and he becomes fiercely destructive. His goal one day is to destroy everyone. He is evil incarnate. However, Nina gains a protector in Rose and is thus able to reach her full glorious potential.

Rose is just one of the nurturing females in the novel. There is also Barbara Christman, Mercy Ealing, Joe's mother-in-law, and the child herself. All extend protection and offer guidance. When Joe moves toward them, he experiences inner peace. As his fate merges with Nina's, Joe becomes more resilient and more amenable to the complexities of the human condition.

In some of Koontz's earlier writing, the human experience is more clearly separated into good and evil, light and dark, and the myth he observes is that which urges us to defeat darkness and move toward the light. As he matures as a writer, however, while he still cautions that evil is a real force in the world, he recognizes that the soul is too complex to divide into neat categories. In *Sole Survivor*, with Joe's experience of the impact of doubt and faith, anger and healing, the author offers a dramatic means whereby readers may consider their own inner chaos and the idea that within the ultimate mystery of the universe some benign deity may reside that offers possibilities.

When Tim Hely Hutchinson of Headline in London read the manuscript, he immediately faxed Dean a note in which he expressed his enthusiasm: "The central vision is broader, deeper, and brighter than ever."

3

Knopf's initial printing was 400,000 copies, with an immediate demand for four more printings of 10,000 apiece. In its first week, *Sole Survivor* debuted at number one on *The Wall Street Journal's* list, number two for hardcover fiction in *USA Today* and *The Washington Post*, behind Patricia Cornwell's *Hornet's Nest*, number three for *The L.A. Times* and *Publishers Weekly*, and in fourth position on *The New York Times Book Review* list. The next week, it went to number one on both the *Times* and *Publishers Weekly* list, and remained there for yet another week until John Grisham's *The Partner* supplanted it. It stayed on the list for ten weeks. Knopf reported that early sales were better than they had been for *Intensity*. Dean did a round of bookstore signings in California and agreed to another grueling schedule of drive-time radio shows, even as he finished up the revision of *Demon Seed* for Berkley—all this while he continued working on his first novel for Bantam.

To Dean's surprise—since he had felt sure a novel with such a spiritual theme would fare badly among critics—he received outstanding reviews. *Kirkus* called *Sole Survivor* "masterfully styled, serious entertainment," and indicated that these were Dean's "great years." Similarly, *The London Times* was impressed with the spirituality: "This is a book to keep you awake reading long into the night, but for once not afraid to turn out the light." *The Atlanta Constitution* rated the novel as "among Koontz's best . . . taut plotting, stark terror, and sweet redemption." *Booklist*, too, said that Koontz "has never done it better," although *Publishers Weekly* wished for the return of the quicker pace of *Intensity*. In *The New York Times*, Charles Salzberg thought the descriptions were unnecessarily flowery, but said it was nevertheless an exciting story. In the *Hamilton Ontario Spectator*, the reviewer called it a "well written piece of literature that exploits our despair over the human condition, but repays the reader with a profound sense of hope." Among other descriptions were "taut," "riveting," "richly imagined and vital," "daring," and "impossible to put down." The author was even compared to John Milton in theme and technique, and many critics noted his increasingly literary style and his surprising avoidance of cliché.

4

In March, *Ticktock* was published in the United States. It had already been released in hardcover nine months earlier in England, to critical acclaim, and Ballantine was publishing it as a paperback original, one of the seven novels they had bought as part of the Random House contract. It jumped to number four on *Publishers Weekly* list and number seven on *The New York Times*, rising as high as number two during its two-month stint.

Dedicated to Gerda, "with the promise of a Scootie of our own," the novel ostensibly begins as a horror story, then rolls into a screwball comedy that exhibits more clearly than any novel to date Dean's absurdist sense of humor. In an Afterword, Dean explains that the screwball comedy has strict requirements: a smart male who is confused by the other eccentric characters; an appealing but flighty female who is not as dumb as she seems; the female lead's strange family; dialogue that puts characters at cross-purposes; chaotic plot twists; and "if possible, there ought to be a dog."[5]

He had begun writing *Ticktock* after *Dark Rivers of the Heart* in order to get some relief from the darkness of that previous story, but had found the book lacking in some way he could not define, so he had written *Intensity* instead. When he returned to *Ticktock*, he was ready for it.

He decided to make his male protagonist a member of a minority group. "There are so many people out there who never get written about," he explains. "There are writers who never tackle interesting viewpoints, like Thomas in *The Bad Place* or Woofer in *Dragon Tears*. I don't think I've ever seen a Vietnamese-American as a lead character in popular contemporary fiction." Dean had found most of the Vietnamese-Americans that he had met to be charming, industrious, and intelligent. They often thanked him for his positive portrayal of them in his books. He appreciated the fact that many of them had endured enormous pressures to adapt to a new homeland, which generated tensions in the home. Dean felt he had learned enough about his contact with this culture to write from the perspective of an Americanized young man who resists becoming a prisoner of his ethnic identity.

Tommy Phan, a Vietnamese-American journalist and crime novelist, wants to free himself from the expectations of his family. He struggles with guilt, but needs his own identity. His very traditional mother dismisses his desire for personal freedom and wants to bring him back into the fold. One day, Tommy finds a rag doll on his porch and he takes it inside. It proves to be no ordinary doll, as he soon discovers, when it takes on a destructive life of its own and leads him on a wild chase through his house. The doll grows larger and appears to be indestructible, so Tommy flees the house. This brings him into contact with a waitress named Deliverance Payne—Del—who exudes mystery, courage, wit, and resilience. Del takes Tommy home, where she introduces him to her unusual Labrador retriever, Scootie. The ever-transforming rag doll—now the size of a man—locates them, and the chase is on, with much destruction in its wake. Stealing a Ferrari, Del takes Tommy to meet her mother, a woman who never sleeps, who answers to any of five names, and who somehow manages to listen to live Big Band performances on what she calls a "transtemporal radio."

The demon-doll is still after them, so they flee again. Tommy discovers that his mother is somehow implicated. He and Del go to her, and she takes them to an eccentric friend, her hairdresser, who had devised the doll as a way to scare Tommy back into the arms of his family. The demon just got a little out of hand! When all is finally resolved and the demon is dispatched, Del asks Tommy to marry her. He agrees, and she lets him in on her secret: She is a "star child," the result of a union between her mother and an intelligent and gifted alien race. Tommy's mother accepts her, with some reservations, and the stage may be set for more adventures.

Although Dean did not believe he would write a book quite like this again, early readers of the manuscript urged him to consider a sequel or even a series. He was gratified by the enthusiastic response—over two thousand fan letters within the first month of publication—and decided to give that some thought.

Ticktock takes a new and different path into the theme of

family. Although Tommy initially resists his family's proprietary embrace, he finds that he needs them. Solidarity diminishes the threat, but only with balance: Family members need
to respect tradition as embodied in Tommy's mother and
brothers, but remain open to individual possibilities, such as
those that Del represents. Tommy also discovers that while
family life may appear to be chaotic or pose a threat to individuality, within the chaos can be a source of wholeness and healing. Standing too much on one's own without the resources of
others can make one vulnerable. Assimilation into another culture has its own demands on the soul.

The issue of family versus the individual runs parallel to the
theme of rationality versus folklore. Both are dimensions of reality, while each by itself is incomplete. Tommy cannot accept
himself until he embraces all aspects of who he is. Spurning his
racial identity, he seeks to be an idealized American—not unlike
the detective hero of the novels he writes—but this is a person
he can never be. The tools that are distinctly American—guns,
fists, rationality—fail Tommy in his struggle with the demon
doll. He must resort to the magic and folklore of his people.

The primary theme is that of creating one's own destiny.
Dean includes two poems from *The Book of Counted Sorrows* to
emphasize this idea—that freedom is key to human identity.
Action, not reaction, is the source of solutions.

Dean personally edited the audiotape abridgement of this
book for Random House. He had already written an abridged
script for *Icebound* and had realized that, for some books, cuts
in the right places could be achieved to retain the integrity of
the story for a different format. But he wanted to be the one to
make that judgment. "It's an interesting thing to do," he
remarks. "It made me look at my work in a totally different
way, as theater rather than as a novel. It made me think about
how I approach things, but I don't think I'd do it a third time."

5

Dean liked Mandalay's production of *Intensity* so much that he
sold *Sole Survivor* to them for the same treatment, without marketing it elsewhere.

In the autumn of 1997, Miramax/Dimension released their feature film of *Phantoms*, directed by Joe Chappelle, with a script written by Dean. Starring Peter O'Toole as Timothy Flyte, it also featured Joanna Going, Rose McGowan, Liev Schrieber, and Ben Affleck.

Peter O'Toole was pleased with the part. Even before accepting the role, he had called Dean to express his enthusiasm, saying his thirteen-year-old son has asked him when he was going to appear in a movie that someone his own age would want to see. "I think I've got one now," he laughed. He predicated his deal on the promise, by Miramax, that not one word of Dean's script would be changed in his scenes.

"It's amazing to have a film shot from a script that I wrote and feel works," Dean says. "And to have such a fine actor in it."

6

While immersed in the promotion for *Sole Survivor*, Dean revised his 1973 science fiction novel, *Demon Seed*. His intention was to update the computer technology, but he had changed the story significantly before he was done. Reading the novel he had written more than two decades earlier, he cringed: "I was so appalled when I reread it. The thing was written so fast. All the elements were there, but now I have the skills to realize the concept in a way that I couldn't previously." In the intervening years, technology had caught up with science fiction and he was able to change the settings from the far future to the present day.

Demon Seed is still about a computer wanting to remake itself into a sensate being by impregnating a woman, but her character has shifted and deepened, and the computer's sociopathic nature is now more manifest. The computer, Proteus, embodies a proprietary male attitude of domination and control, even as it claims to have no violent intentions, and insists it would never treat its beloved as mere property. It is male because it is the brainchild of a man—Susan Harris's husband—who had also tried to control her.

Susan's trouble with males goes back to her childhood, where out of fear for her life she had submitted sexually to her father. In order to purge herself as an adult, she has invented a virtual reality program called "Therapy" in which she has programmed various scenarios, including the one she feared most but that never came to pass — her murder at her father's hands.

Proteus talks about Susan in ways reminiscent of nineties-style cybersex, and his descriptions of his motives soon reveal how self-deceived he is. "I loved the computer's voice," Dean says. "He was so scary yet so pathetic." Proteus's fantasies about Susan are so clearly linked to what her father had done to her that it seems as if she has created him from within her own fears. She has given the home computer that controls the house her father's name, and it is through this computer that Proteus has managed to gain entrance. His planned imprisonment and rape (through a very imaginative surrogate) and her virtual reality sessions coincide almost too well.

Susan has programmed her virtual image therapy to run as almost a psychological Russian roulette. It arbitrarily draws her, one scenario at a time, into envisioning and feeling what her father might have done — which Dean has described as being the real terror of a sociopath: the random and unpredictable assault. In fact, Susan's self-created and self-initiated therapy seems to function as Dean's novels have done for him: Afraid as a child that his father might kill him and his mother, he creates increasingly dangerous interactions between his villains and his heroes, as if vicariously to experience — in the virtual reality frame of fiction — the struggle, the fear, and the eventual triumph.

Susan endures violence and the threat of violence, but in this version of the novel, she is her own rescuer rather than being rescued by outside agents. She allows herself to go into her deepest fear, survives it, and by gaining strength from it, is able to overcome her tormentor. "Now I've experienced the worst my father could ever have done to me," she explains. "He's killed me in VR, and he can't do anything worse than that, so I'll never be afraid of him again."[6] In the end, she wins by virtue of her own inner strength.

Dean was pleased with the way the novel turned out. "It's given me the idea that some of the books I thought I'd never revise might be revisable. What carries the story is the narrative voice of the computer and ironic tone. The way to revisit some of my earliest books, I think, is to recast them in unusual points of view."

7

For a book edited by Richard Chizmar, called *Screamplays*, Dean wrote a Foreword entitled "Great Art and Muppet Hatred." The contents of the book are screenplays once written by some of today's horror novelists. In the essay, Dean talks about his own experiences writing in this format, and how different it is from writing a novel. He also tells of his misdaventure with a "genius" film director and his evolving caution toward Hollywood.

8

Dean's next project would be to finish his first novel in the series he would deliver to Bantam. *Fear Nothing* and the two books to follow it would feature the same characters, Christopher Snow and his dog. As with all of this author's novels, these three would concern the triumph of individuals over difficult odds, transforming the injustices of life into blessings. Friends, as community and extended family, would play a large role, and through tales of suspense, the virtues of persistence and commitment would be affirmed.

[1]"Dean Koontz's Move," *The New York Times* (December 10, 1996).
[2]Dean Koontz, *Sole Survivor* (New York: Alfred A. Knopf, 1997), p. 3.
[3]Ibid., p. 3.
[4]Ibid., p. 168.
[5]Dean Koontz, *Ticktock* (New York: Ballantine, 1997), p. 310.
[6]Dean Koontz, *Demon Seed*, revised (New York: Berkley, 1997), p. 290.

TWENTY-FIVE

Shadow and Light

Art is essentially serious and beneficial, a game played
against chaos and death, against entropy.
—John Gardner

IN A BIOGRAPHY SUCH AS THIS, IN WHICH PSYCHOLOGICAL PAT-
terns are grounded in the work—and vice versa—it needs to
be stated that discussing the inner world of the writer is not
about reducing that person's work to basic psychological elements. It means merely that there are interesting parallels to be
found between life and fiction when an imagination is as rich
as that of Dean Koontz. The patterns are there, but the way
the biographer interprets them is often highly personal. Patterns that stand out to one person may do so every bit as much
because of who that person is as because of who the subject is.

Dean spent his childhood in a home where tension and
uncertainty reigned. The chaos alarmed him. Only his
mother's attention and good humor reassured him. When he
was four, he found a warm, stable place, where reading and
family gave him the feeling of acceptance, warmth, and security. It was a magical place that became part of his memories,
side by side with the chaos. Both the safety of stability and the
frightening unpredictability of disorder were absorbed by him
through sustained exposure, and it seems that he has spent his
life recreating this safe place, but has done it, paradoxically, by
also recreating chaos.

In part, his father's moods frightened him—but also gave
him the motivation to explore his own mind and talent. Ray's
dysfunctional modeling, and perhaps his genetic legacy, seems
to have provided Dean with access to his own diverse mental
threads, so that what was madness in one became creativity in
the other. Studies on creativity and schizophrenia have shown
an interesting link: Both display the richness and versatility of
the human mind, and both involve an imaginative world where
metaphor gains supremacy—they *add* something to the way
the world is, to make it more tolerable. The essential difference

is that the creative person can direct his mental processes to become productive, while the mentally ill person tends to become disoriented and potentially destructive.

Dean's writing is filled with images of chaos—aliens, madness, drugs, hybrids, mindless violence, entropy, renegade organizations, and deranged deities—so that he could use his best skills to impose order and transform them. He has repeatedly tested his inner power to purify corruption and turn chaos into stability by writing increasingly ambitious books and by diving ever more deeply into his complex layers. He also has kept his professional life in flux by taking on not only the uncertainties of freelance writing, but numerous projects simultaneously. He puts himself under constant pressure to live with and defeat the chaos by challenging himself to keep it all organized and deliver it according to a plan—with ever the threat that he might not manage. Control has been firm, but still has an underlying fragility that drives him to seek greater mastery. Yet he has managed to retain the stability needed to ensure that the chaos remains an instrument of creativity. And for that, he draws on the strength of his mother and of those people who sought to help him on his way.

In her book *The Transcendent Child*, psychologist Lilian Rubin describes the sort of person who can survive the difficulties of such a family. Dean's life shows many parallels to her examples: He was the child who distanced himself from aspects of his family and insisted that he would be different. He would not be victimized. He was able to leave it behind and to gravitate to people who acted as guardians or surrogate parents—teachers, friends, business associates, and his wife, Gerda. From them, he learned about the possibilities of another type of life, and from feelings of marginality, he developed a vision for himself that helped him confront his fears and seek mastery over them. He learned to be vigilant toward challenges to his vision and to reinvent himself in whatever way was necessary to achieve what he set out to do.

Thus, those inner parts of himself that potentially conflict have been held together in a dynamic tension that fuels his drive and motivates his continuous production of stories. Parallel to the content of his novels, the actual writing of them has been essential to reconciling his body memories. Although he has feared his father's influence, he has sensed that as long as he affirms the ability to turn his destiny in the way he desires, control and sanity will triumph. Over and over he asserts his own will. He avoids situations that might give some unknown agent control over his life, and wherever possible, keeps sign-posts of stability always at hand—a solid marriage, an orga-nized office, reliable personnel, a steady supply of ideas, an ambitious reading program. This kind of anchoring allows him to venture ever further into the dark realms of his imagination.

Where such unrelenting challenge might defeat someone else, it works for him, in part because he generalizes these same conflicts to society at large. Ever alert to how social agencies that are set up to protect us are also in a position to inflict harm, Dean has used his books to develop in readers a broad social conscience. In the same way that he armed him-self with knowledge about his father's abnormal condition, he urges people to defend themselves against the inherent dan-gers of encroaching social and political institutions that have lost their moral code. In this way, he is a writer who finds ways to ensure not only his own health and safety, but that of others around him.

His numerous transforming encounters with "guardians" along the way have helped him to focus his vision and maintain his belief in the essential goodness of humankind. To him, they are like people giving water to the long-distance runner who must constantly strive to break his own record. Through dif-ferent guises of chaos and insanity, he persists with the mes-sage that such forces must not be allowed to reign, and he ensures that his characters form bonds that provide purpose and peace. A family remade out of kindred souls is his primary symbol of refuge and redemption. A new birth within such a family symbolizes a fresh start and the hope for a better life.

Yet the end point for Dean is not mere victory over chaos, or even self-protection. It is more ambitious than that. He must redeem the madness—purify it of its destructive elements and imbue it with purpose. Via his own humanity, he seeks to make the devil into God. He wants to transubstantiate dark forces into something positive, to make the space of manhood that his father had vilified into something secure and even sacred. Rather than move toward the feminine where it feels safe, he brings the feminine into the masculine by making his female characters strong, resilient, and credible. That way, he develops a sense of manhood without having to associate it with the tainted masculinity of his father. He also creates a world of equals wherein anyone, male or female, can—and should—look to their own resources to make life on this planet a better place for everyone.

If he were to leave one thing behind, it would be a positive message: to defy all forces that make people victims and affirm those that inspire initiative and responsibility. "I want to say to the reader," Koontz states, "'Take my hand. We're going to go through this terrible place, and things will happen that are too horrifying to think about, but it's going to be all right at the other end. There's going to be meaning and a purpose to this. Trust me.'"

BIBLIOGRAPHY OF
GENERAL RESOURCES

Apter, Michael. *The Dangerous Edge: The Psychology of Excitement*. New York: The Free Press, 1992.

Arieti, Silvano. *Creativity: The Magic Synthesis*. New York: Basic Books, 1976.

Arieti, Silvano. *Understanding and Helping the Schizophrenic*. London: Karnac, 1979.

Backlar, Patricia. *The Family Face of Schizophrenia*. New York: Jeremy P. Tarcher, 1994.

Belmont, Lillian, and Frank A. Marolla. "Birth Order, Family Size, and Intelligence." *Science* 182 (1973): 1096–1101.

Berheim, Kayla F., and Richard Lewine. *Schizophrenia: Symptoms, Causes, Treatments*. New York: Norton, 1979.

Black, Claudia. *It Will Never Happen to Me: Children of Alcoholics*. New York: Ballantine, 1981.

Blevins, William. *Your Family, Your Self*. Oakland, CA: New Harbinger Publications, 1993.

Bock, Alan W. *Ambush at Ruby Ridge*. New York: Berkley, 1996.

Briggs, John. *Fire in the Crucible: The Self-Creation of Creativity and Genius*. Los Angeles, CA: Jeremy P. Tarcher, 1990.

Cheney, Margaret. *Why: The Serial Killer in America*. Saratoga, CA: R&E Publishers, 1992.

Clute, John, and Peter Nicholls. *The Encyclopedia of Science Fiction*. New York: St. Martin's Press, 1995.

Combs, Allan, and Mark Holland. *Synchronicity*. New York: Paragon House, 1990.

Costello, Matthew J. *How to Write Science Fiction*. New York: Paragon House, 1992.

Csikszentmihalyi, Mihaly. *Creativity*. New York: Harper-Collins, 1996.

——*Flow: The Psychology of Optimal Experience*. New York: Harper & Row, 1990.

Dalby, Gordon. *Father and Son*. Nashville, TN: Thomas Nelson, 1992.

Delbanco, Andrew. *The Death of Satan: How Americans Have Lost the Sense of Evil.* New York: Farrar, Straus, and Giroux, 1995.

Diagnostic and Statistical Manual of Mental Disorders: DSM-IV. 4th ed. Washington, DC: American Psychiatric Press, 1994.

Diamond, Stephen. *Anger, Madness, and the Daimonic: The Psychological Genesis of Violence, Evil, and Creativity.* Albany, NY: State University of New York Press, 1996.

Edelstein, Andrew, and Kevin McDonough. *The Seventies: From Hot Pants to Hot Tubs.* New York: Dutton, 1990.

Evans, Fred. *Psychology and Nihilism.* Albany, NY: State University of New York Press, 1993.

Fiedler, Leslie. *Love and Death in the American Novel,* rev. ed., New York: Stein and Day 1966.

Forest, Gary. *Alcoholism, Narcissism and Pathology.* Northvale, NJ: Jason Aronson, 1983.

Frank, Arthur W. *The Wounded Storyteller.* Chicago, IL: University of Chicago Press, 1995.

Frear, Ned. *Bedford County: A Brief History.* Bedford, PA: Frear Publications, 1985.

Friel, John, and Linda Friel. *Adult Children: The Secrets of Dysfunctional Families.* Deerfield Beach, FL: Health Communications, 1988.

Gallagher, Winifred. *I.D.: How Heredity and Experience Make You Who You Are.* New York: Random House, 1996.

Gardner, John. *On Moral Fiction.* New York: Basic Books, 1978.

Gelvin, Michael. *The Quest for the Fine.* London: Rowman & Littlefield, 1996.

Gitlin, Todd. *The Sixties: Years of Hope, Days of Rage.* New York: Bantam, 1987.

Goleman, Daniel. *Emotional Intelligence.* New York: Bantam, 1995.

Gordon, Lois, and Alan Gordon. *The Columbia Chronicles of American Life, 1910–1992.* New York: Columbia University Press, 1995.

Gorman, Ed., ed. *The Fine Art of Murder.* New York: Carroll & Graf, 1993.

Grahame, Kenneth. *The Wind in the Willows.* London: Puffin Books, 1908.

Greenberg, Martin, Ed Gorman, and Bill Munster. *The Dean Koontz Companion*. New York: Berkley, 1994.

Halberstam, David. *The Fifties*. New York: Villard, 1993.

Hare, Robert. *Without Conscience: The Disturbing World of the Psychopaths Among Us*. New York: Pocket, 1995.

Harris, Bud. *The Father Quest*. Alexander, NC: Alexander Books, 1996.

Hawkins, Harriett. *Classics and Trash: Traditions and Taboos in High Literature and Popular Modern Genres*. Toronto, Canada: University of Toronto Press, 1990.

James, Edward. *Science Fiction in the Twentieth Century*. Oxford, England: Oxford University Press, 1994.

Jute, Andrew. *Writing a Thriller*. London: A&C Black, 1994.

Key, Wilson Bryan. *Subliminal Seduction*. New York: Signet, 1972.

Koontz, Dean. See complete Koontz chronologies.

Kotker, Joan G. *Dean Koontz: A Critical Companion*. Westport, CN: Greenwood, 1996.

Lane, Brian. *Chronicle of Twentieth Century Murder, Vols. I and II*. New York: Berkley, 1995.

Lesser, Wendy. *Pictures at an Execution: An Inquiry into the Subject of Murder*. Cambridge, MA: Harvard University Press, 1993.

Lester, David, ed. *Serial Killers*. Philadelphia, PA: The Charles Press, 1995.

Levoy, Gregg. *This Business of Writing*. Cincinnati, OH: Writer's Digest Books, 1992.

Lifton, Robert J. *The Protean Self: Human Resilience in an Age of Fragmentation*. New York: Basic Books, 1993.

Malardi, Bill, and Bill Bowers. *The Double: Bill Symposium*, Akron, Ohio: D:B Press, 1969.

Mandell, Judy. *Book Editors Talk to Writers*. New York: Wiley, 1995.

McKennon, Joe. *A Pictorial History of the American Carnival*, Vol. III, Sarasota, FL: Carnival Publishers, 1981.

Miller, Alice. *The Drama of the Gifted Child*. New York: Basic Books, 1981.

Mills, C. Wright. *The Power Elite*. Oxford, England: Oxford University Press, 1956.

Munster, Bill, ed. *Sudden Fear*. Mercer Island, WA: Starmont, 1988.

Napier, Augustus Y., with Carl A. Whitaker. *The Family Crucible*. New York: Perennial, 1978.

Noll, Richard. *The Encyclopedia of Schizophrenia and the Psychotic Disorders*. New York: Facts on File, 1992.

O'Brien, Geoffrey. *Dream Time: Chapters From the Sixties*. New York: Penguin, 1988.

O'Kane, Francoise. *Sacred Chaos: Reflections on God's Shadow and the Dark Self*. Toronto, Canada: Inner City Books, 1994.

Person, Ethel. *By Force of Fantasy*. New York: Basic Books, 1996.

Pert, Candace. "Emotions in Body, Not Just in Brain," *Brain/Mind Bulletin*, 11(4) (1986): 1.

Philips, Michael, ed. *Philosophy and Science Fiction*. Buffalo, NY: Prometheus, 1984.

Ramsland, Katherine M. *The Art of Learning*. Albany, NY: State University of New York Press, 1992.

Randles, Jenny, and Peter Hough. *Encyclopedia of the Unexplained*. New York: Barnes & Noble Books, 1995.

Ressler, Robert K., Ann Burgess, and Jim Douglas, eds. *Sexual Homicide: Patterns and Motives*. New York: Free Press, 1988.

Rodari, Gianni *The Grammar of Fantasy*, translated by Jack Zipes. New York: Teachers and Writers Collaborative, 1973, 1996.

Rossi, Ernest L. *The Psychobiology of Mind-Body Healing*. New York: Norton, 1993.

Roth, Martin. *The Writer's Complete Crime Reference Book*. Cincinnati, OH: Writer's Digest Books, 1990.

Rubin, Lillian. *The Transcendent Child*. New York: Basic Books, 1996.

Samenow, Stanton E. *Inside the Criminal Mind*. New York: Times Books, 1984.

Scarf, Maggie. *Intimate Worlds: Life Inside the Family*. New York: Random House, 1995.

Schama, Simon. *Landscape and Memory*. New York: Alfred A. Knopf, 1995.

Simon, Robert. *Bad Men Do What Good Men Dream*. Washington, DC: American Psychiatric Press, 1996.

Skal, David. *The Monster Show: A Cultural History of Horror*. New York: Penguin, 1993.

Sulloway, Frank J. *Born to Rebel: Birth Order, Family Dynamics and Creative Lives*. New York: Pantheon, 1996.

Sykes, Charles J. *A Nation of Victims: The Decay of the American Character*. New York: St. Martin's Press, 1992.

Todorov, Tzvetan. *The Fantastic: A Structural Approach to a Literary Genre*. Ithaca, NY: Cornell University Press, 1975.

Vaughan, Alan. *Incredible Coincidence: The Baffling World of Synchronicity*. New York: Ballantine, 1979.

Washburn, Katharine, and John Thornton, eds. *Dumbing Down: Essays on the Strip-Mining of American Culture*. New York: Norton, 1996.

Watson, Lyall. *Dark Nature: A Natural History of Evil*. New York: HarperCollins, 1995.

Wells, H. G. *The Island of Doctor Moreau*. Bantam (1896), 1994.

Woodruff, Paul B., and Harry A. Wilmer, eds. *Facing Evil*. La Salle, IL: Open Court, 1988.

CHRONOLOGY OF ARTICLES

1969

"What Do Editors Mean When They Say, 'Sorry, but the motivation is missing.'?" *Writer's Digest*, March.

"Diligently Corrupting Young Minds." *Science Fiction Review*, June.

1971

"A Veritable Cornucopia," *Tomorrow and ... Seven.*

1972

"Always an Open Door for the Paperback 'Category' Novel." *Writer's Digest*, January.

1976

Author's Introduction to *Night Chills*, Atheneum.

1984

"When Should You Put Yourself in an Agent's Hands?" *The Basics of Writing and Selling Fiction*, Writer's Digest Press.

1985

"Situation Critical." *Writer's Yearbook '85*, Writer's Digest Press.

1987

"Tater Baron." Foreword to *The Nightrunners*, by Joe Lansdale, Dark Harvest Press.

"The Coming Blaylockian Age." Foreword to *Two Views of a Cave Painting*, by Jim Blaylock, Axolotl Press.

"Keeping the Reader on the Edge of His Seat." *How to Write Tales of Horror, Fantasy, and Science Fiction*, edited by J. N. Williamson, Writer's Digest Press.

"Why Novels of Fear Must Do More than Frighten." *How To Write Tales of Horror, Fantasy, and Science Fiction*, edited by J. N. Williamson, Writer's Digest Press.

1988

"The Truth About Christmas." Chapbook by Charles de Lint.

"A Genre in Crisis." *Night Visions 4*, Dark Harvest Press. Revised for *Proteus*, Shippensburg University, 1989.

1989

"The Man Who Knows All About Hippodurkees." Foreword to *The Stress of Her Regard* by Tim Powers, Charnel House.

"Ghost Stories." Afterword for *Post Mortem*, edited by Dave Silva and Paul Olson, St. Martin's Press.

1990

Guest Editorial. *Afraid*, June.

1992

"Oh, To Be in Cedar Rapids When the Hog Blood Flows." Afterword to *Prisoners*, by Ed Gorman, Forge.

"Rex Stout and Nero Wolfe." Introduction to *Where There's a Will* (reissue), Bantam.

1993

"Why We Love Horror." *TV Guide*, October.

"Mr. Bizarro." Foreword to *Blood Test*, by Jonathan Kellerman, Dark Harvest.

1994

"My First Short Story." *The Dean Koontz Companion*, edited by Martin Greenberg, Ed Gorman, and Bill Munster, Berkley.

"Koontz, Would You Just Shut Up Already?" *The Dean Koontz Companion*, edited by Martin Greenberg, Ed Gorman, and Bill Munster, Berkley.

"You'll Either Love It or Hate It—Or Just be Indifferent to It." *The Dean Koontz Companion*, edited by Martin Greenberg, Ed Gorman, and Bill Munster, Berkley.

"How To." *The Dean Koontz Companion*, edited by Martin Greenberg, Ed Gorman, and Bill Munster, Berkley.

"Koontzramble." *The Dean Koontz Companion*, edited by Martin Greenberg, Ed Gorman, and Bill Munster, Berkley.

Afterword to *The Funhouse* (reissue), Berkley.

Afterword to *Dark Rivers of the Heart* (hardcover only), Alfred A. Knopf.

"Godzilla vs. Megadeth." Rock biography for "Youthanasia" CD, by Megadeth.

1995

"Illusion, Truth, and the Whole Damn Thing." Introduction to *David Copperfield's Tales of the Impossible*, edited by David Copperfield and Janet Berliner, HarperCollins.

"A Note To The Reader," *Icebound*, Ballantine.

Afterword to *The Key to Midnight* (reissue), Berkley.

1996

Afterword to *The Eyes of Darkness* (reissue), Berkley.

Foreword to *Ambush at Ruby Ridge*, by Alan W. Bock, Berkley.

Preface to *Intensity*, Franklin Mint Edition.

"Beautiful Death." *Beautiful Death: Art of the Cemetery*, by David Robinson, Penguin Studio.

1997

"A Note to the Reader." *Ticktock*, Ballantine.

Introduction to *Hell House* (reissue), by Richard Christian Matheson, Buccanneer Books.

"The Fox in the Chicken Suit," Introduction to *Fiends*, by Richard Laymon, Headline Books.

"Great Art and Muppet Hatred." *Screamplays*, edited by Richard Chizmar, Ballantine.

CHRONOLOGY OF SHORT FICTION

1965

"The Kittens," "Of Childhood," and "This Fence," *The Reflector*, Winter 1965-66 issue

1966

"It," "Sam: the Adventurous, Exciting Well-traveled Man," "Something About This City," and "Hey, Good Christian," *The Reflector*, May.

"The Standard Unusual," "Once," "Mold in the Jungle," "A Miracle is Anything," "Flesh," "The Rats Run," "Some Disputed Barricade," "For a Breath I Tarry," "Holes," "Cloistered Walls," and "I've Met One," *The Reflector*, Fall.

"The Kittens," *Readers and Writers*, May/June

1967

"Where No One Fell," *The Reflector*, Spring

"Soft Come the Dragons," *The Magazine of Fantasy and Science Fiction*, August

"Love 2005," *Mr.*, November

"To Behold the Sun," *The Magazine of Fantasy and Science Fiction*, December

1968

"A Darkness in My Soul," *Fantastic Stories*, January

"The Psychedelic Children," *The Magazine of Fantasy and Science Fiction*, July

"The Twelfth Bed," *The Magazine of Fantasy and Science Fiction*, August

"Dreambird," *Worlds of If*, September

1969

"In the Shield," *Worlds of If*, January

"Temple of Sorrow," *Amazing Stories*, January

"The Face in His Belly," Perihelion, Parts 1 and 2, Spring and Summer

"Killerbot," *Galaxy*, May (also called "A Season For Freedom")
"Where the Beast Runs," *Worlds of If*, July
"A Dragon in the Land," *Venture Science Fiction*, August
"Muse," *The Magazine of Fantasy and Science Fiction*, September

1970

"A Third Hand," *The Magazine of Fantasy and Science Fiction*, January
"The Good Ship Lookoutworld," *Fantastic Stories*, February
"The Mystery of His Flesh," *The Magazine of Fantasy and Science Fiction*, July
"Beastchild," *Venture Science Fiction*, August
"The Crimson Witch," *Fantastic Stories*, October
"Shambolain," *Worlds of If*, November-December
"Unseen Warriors," *Worlds of Tomorrow*, Winter
"Nightmare Gang," *Infinity One*, edited by Robert Hoskins, Lancer

1971

"Bruno," *The Magazine of Fantasy and Science Fiction*, April

1972

"The Terrible Weapon," *Trend*, January/February
"Cosmic Sin," *The Magazine of Fantasy and Science Fiction*, February
"Altarboy," *Infinity Three*, edited by Robert Hoskins, Lancer
"Ollie's Hands" *Infinity Four*, edited by Robert Hoskins, Lancer (revised for *Horror Show* in 1987)
"A Mouse in the Walls of the Global Village," *Again, Dangerous Visions*, edited by Harlan Ellison, Doubleday

1973

"Grayworld," *Infinity Five*, edited by Robert Hoskins, Lancer
"The Sinless Child," *Flame Tree Planet*, edited by Roger Elwood, Concordia
"Terra Phobia," *Androids, Time Machines and Blue Giraffes*, edited by Roger Elwood and Vic Ghidalia, Follett

"The Undercity," *Future City*, edited by Roger Elwood, Trident Press

"Wake Up to Thunder," *Children of Infinity*, edited by Roger Elwood, Franklin Watts

1974

"Night of the Storm," *Continuum I*, edited by Roger Elwood, Putnam

"We Three," *Final Stage*, edited by Roger Elwood and Barry Malzberg, Charterhouse

1986

"Down in the Darkness," *The Horror Show*, Summer

"Weird World," *The Horror Show*, Summer

"Snatcher," *Night Cry*, Fall

"The Black Pumpkin," *The Twilight Zone*, December

1987

"The Interrogation," *The Horror Show*, Summer

"Hardshell, *Night Visions 4*, Dark Harvest

"Miss Attila the Hun," *Night Visions 4*, Dark Harvest

"Twilight of the Dawn," *Night Visions 4*, Dark Harvest

1988

"Graveyard Highway," *Tropical Chills*, edited by Tim Sullivan, Avon

1989

"Trapped," *Stalkers*, edited by Ed Gorman and Martin H. Greenberg, Dark Harvest

1992

"Trapped," graphic novella adapted by Ed Gorman, Eclipse

CHRONOLOGY OF BOOKS

1968

Star Quest, Ace Double
1969
The Fall of the Dream Machine, Ace Double
Fear That Man, Ace Double

1970

Anti-Man, Paperback Library
Beastchild, Lancer (revised and published in hardcover, Charnel House, 1992)
Dark of the Woods, Ace Double
The Dark Symphony, Lancer
Hell's Gate, Lancer
Soft Come the Dragons, Ace Double
The Pig Society (with Gerda Koontz), Aware Press
The Underground Lifestyles Handbook (with Gerda Koontz), Aware Press
Bounce Girl (with Gerda Koontz), Cameo (Aware) (reprinted as *Aphrodisiac Girl*, Oval Press, 1973)
Hung (pseudonym withheld at author's request), Cameo (Aware)

1971

The Crimson Witch, Curtis
Demon Child, "Deanna Dwyer," Lancer
Legacy of Terror, "Deanna Dwyer," Lancer

1972

Chase, "K. R. Dwyer," Random House (hardcover)

Children of the Storm, "Deanna Dwyer," Lancer
The Dark of Summer, "Deanna Dwyer," Lancer
Dance with the Devil, "Deanna Dwyer," Lancer
A Darkness in My Soul, Daw
The Flesh in the Furnace, Bantam
Starblood, Lancer
Time Thieves, "Leigh Nichols," Ace (Dobson: London, hardcover, 1972)
Warlock, Lancer
Writing Popular Fiction, Writer's Digest Books (hardcover)

1973

Aphrodisiac Girl (reprint of *Bounce Girl*), Oval Press
Blood Risk, "Brian Coffey," Bobbs-Merrill (hardcover)
Demon Seed, Bantam (revised and reissued, Berkley, 1997)
Hanging On, M. Evans & Company (hardcover)
The Haunted Earth, Lancer
Shattered, "K. R. Dwyer," Random House (hardcover) (reissued, Berkley, 1985)
A Werewolf Among Us, Ballantine

1974

After the Last Race, Atheneum (hardcover)
Strike Deep, "Anthony North," Dial Press (hardcover)
Surrounded, "Brian Coffey," Bobbs-Merrill (hardcover)

1975

Dragonfly, "K. R. Dwyer," Random House (hardcover)
Invasion, "Aaron Wolfe," Laser (revised and reissued as *Winter Moon*, Ballantine, 1994)
The Long Sleep, "John Hill," Popular Library
Nightmare Journey, Berkley
The Wall of Masks, "Brian Coffey," Bobbs-Merrill (hardcover)

1976

Night Chills, Atheneum (hardcover)

Prison of Ice, "David Axton," Lippincott (hardcover) (revised and reissued as *Icebound* by Ballantine, 1995)

1977

The Face of Fear, "Brian Coffey," Bobbs-Merrill (hardcover)
The Vision, G.P. Putnam's Sons (hardcover) (reissued, Berkley, 1986)

1979

The Key to Midnight "Leigh Nichols," Pocket Books (Piatkis, London, hardcover, 1979; first U.S. hardcover edition, Dark Harvest, 1989) (revised 1995, Berkley)

1980

The Funhouse, "Owen West," Jove (Headline, London, hardcover, 1992) (reissued, Berkley, 1994)
The Voice of the Night, "Brian Coffey," Doubleday (hardcover) (reissued, Berkley, 1991)
Whispers, G.P. Putnam's Sons (hardcover)

1981

The Eyes of Darkness, "Leigh Nichols," Pocket Books (Piatkus, London, hardcover, 1981; first U.S. hardcover edition, Dark Harvest, 1989) (revised and reissued, Berkley, 1996)
The Mask, "Owen West," Jove (Headline, London, hardcover, 1989) (reissued, Berkley, 1988)
How to Write Best-selling Fiction, Writer's Digest Books (hardcover)

1982

The House of Thunder, "Leigh Nichols," Pocket Books (Piatkus, London, hardcover, 1982; First U.S. hardcover edition, Dark Harvest, 1988) (reissued, Berkley, 1992)

1983

Phantoms, G.P. Putnam's Sons (hardcover)

1984

Darkfall, Berkley (*Darkness Comes*, W.H. Allen, London, hardcover, 1984)

Twilight, "Leigh Nichols," Pocket Books (Piatkus, London, hardcover, 1985; First U.S. hardcover, Dark Harvest, 1988) (rereleased as *The Servants of Twilight*, Berkley, 1990)

1985

The Door to December, "Richard Paige," Signet (by "Leigh Nichols," Inner Circle, London, hardcover, 1988) (revised and reissued, New American Library, 1994)

Twilight Eyes, The Land of Enchantment (hardcover) (W.H. Allen, London, hardcover, 1987) (revised with a sequel and reissued, Berkley, 1987)

Shattered, "K. R. Dwyer," Berkley (reissue of Random House 1973 edition)

1986

Strangers, G.P. Putnam's Sons (hardcover)

The Vision, Berkley (reissue of G.P. Putnam's Sons 1977 edition)

1987

Shadowfires, "Leigh Nichols," Avon (Collins, London, hardcover, 1987; First U.S. hardcover edition, Dark Harvest, 1990) (reissued, Berkley, 1993)

Watchers, G.P. Putnam's Sons (hardcover)

Twilight Eyes, Berkley (revision, with a sequel, of Land of Enchantment 1985 edition)

1988

Lightning, G.P. Putnam's Sons (hardcover)
Oddkins: A Fable for All Ages, Warner (hardcover)
The Mask, Berkley (reissue of Jove 1981 edition)

1989

Midnight, G.P. Putnam's Sons (hardcover)

1990

The Bad Place, G.P. Putnam's Sons (hardcover)
The Servants of Twilight, Berkley (reissue of *Twilight*, Pocket Books 1984 edition)

1991

Cold Fire, G.P. Putnam's Sons (hardcover)
The Voice of the Night, Berkley (reissue of Doubleday 1980 edition)

1992

Hideaway, G.P. Putnam's Sons (hardcover)
Beastchild, Charnel House (hardcover revision of Lancer 1970 edition)
The House of Thunder, Berkley (reissue of Pocket Books 1982 edition)

1993

Dragon Tears, G.P. Putnam's Sons (hardcover)
Mr. Murder, G.P. Putnam's Sons (hardcover)
Shadowfires, Berkley (reissue of Avon 1987 edition)

1994

Dark Rivers of the Heart, Alfred A. Knopf (hardcover)
Winter Moon, Ballantine (comprehensive revision of

Invasion, Laser 1975 edition) (hardcover, Headline: London, 1994)

   The Funhouse, Berkley (reissue of Jove 1980 edition)

   The Door to December, "Richard Paige," Signet NAL (revision of Signet 1985 edition)

1995

   Strange Highways, Warner (hardcover)

   Icebound, Ballantine (revision of *Prison of Ice*, Lippincott, 1976)

   The Key to Midnight, Berkley (revision of Pocket Books 1979 edition)

1996

   Intensity, Alfred A. Knopf (hardcover) (Headline: London, hardcover, 1995)

   Santa's Twin, HarperCollins (hardcover)

   The Eyes of Darkness, Berkley (revision of Pocket Books 1981 edition)

1997

   Sole Survivor, Alfred A. Knopf (hardcover)

   Ticktock, Ballantine (Headline: London, hardcover, 1996)

   Demon Seed, Berkley (revision of Bantam 1973 edition)

1998

   Fear Nothing, Bantam (hardcover)

GENERAL CHRONOLOGY

1945

Dean was born in Everett, Pennsylvania on July 9 to Florence and Ray Koontz. His family moved that year from Everett to Bedford, Pennsylvania.

1949

Dean stayed with Louise and Bird Kinzey, where he first got pleasure from books.

1953

Dean wrote short stories and sold them to relatives.

1956

Dean won twenty-five dollars and a wristwatch in an essay contest about being an American.

1957

Dean developed an interest in bizarre disappearances.

1962

Dean met Gerda Ann Cerra, and had his first date with her at a high school dance.

1963

Dean graduated from Bedford High School and went to Shippensburg State Teachers College to major in English. While there, he converted to Catholicism.

1965

Dean won a prize for "The Kittens" from an *Atlantic Monthly* writing contest, and won honorable mention for an essay in the same contest.

Dean became short story editor for *The Reflector*, Winter 65–66 issue.

Published in that issue:
"The Kittens"
"Of Childhood"
"This Fence"

1966

Dean finished his college degree in English at Shippensburg Teachers College; his official graduation was the following spring.

Gerda and Dean got married on October 15 and honeymooned in Williamsburg, Virginia.

Dean worked as a teacher/counselor in the Appalachian Poverty Program in the Tussey Mountain School District in Saxton, Pennsylvania.

In *The Reflector* May issue he published:
"It"
"Sam: the Adventurous, Exciting, Well-traveled Man"
"Something About This City"
"Hey, Good Christian"
In the Fall issue, he published:
"The Standard Unusual"
"Once"
"Mold in the Jungle"
"A Miracle is Anything"
"Flesh"
"The Rats Run"
"Some Disputed Barricade"
"For a Breath I Tarry"
"Holes"
"Cloistered Walls"
"I've Met One"
Also published that year:
"The Kittens," *Readers and Writers*

1967

Dean taught English at Mechanicsburg, Pennsylvania.
Published that year:
"Where No One Fell," *The Reflector*
"Soft Come the Dragons," *The Magazine of Fantasy and Science Fiction*, August (This was Dean's first professional sale.)
"Love 2005," *Mr.*, November
"To Behold the Sun," *The Magazine of Fantasy and Science Fiction*, December

1968

Published that year:
Star Quest, Ace (first published novel)
"A Darkness in My Soul," *Fantastic Stories*, January
"The Psychedelic Children," *The Magazine of Fantasy and Science Fiction*, July
"The Twelfth Bed," *The Magazine of Fantasy and Science Fiction*, August
"Dreambird," *Worlds of If*, September

1969

Gerda offered to support Dean for five years, and he quit teaching to be a full-time writer.
Florence, Dean's mother, died in February at age fifty-three, when he was twenty-four. Before she died, she told him she had to tell him something about his father.
Published that year:
The Fall of the Dream Machine, Ace
Fear That Man, Ace
"In the Shield," *Worlds of If*, January
"Temple of Sorrow," *Amazing Stories*, January
"The Face in His Belly," *Perihelion*, Spring/Summer
"Killerbot," *Galaxy*, May
"Where the Beast Runs," *Worlds of If*, July
"A Dragon in the Land," *Venture*, August
"Muse," *The Magazine of Fantasy and Science Fiction*, September

"What Do Editors Mean When They Say 'Sorry, but the Motivation is Missing'?" *Writer's Digest*, March

"Diligently Corrupting Young Minds," *Science Fiction Review*, June

1970

Dean hired the Scott Meredith Agency to represent him. Published that year:

Anti-Man, Paperback Library

Beastchild, Lancer (This book was a finalist on the ballot for a Hugo Award, short novel category.)

Dark of the Woods, Ace

The Dark Symphony, Lancer

Hell's Gate, Lancer

Soft Come the Dragons, Ace

The Pig Society, Aware Press

The Underground Lifestyles Handbook, Aware Press

Bounce Girl, Cameo (Aware)

Hung, Cameo (Aware) (Dean's first use of a pseudonym.)

"A Third Hand," *The Magazine of Fantasy and Science Fiction*, January

"The Good Ship Lookoutworld," *Fantastic Stories*, February

"The Mystery of His Flesh," *The Magazine of Fantasy and Science Fiction*, July

"Beastchild," *Venture Science Fiction*, August

"The Crimson Witch," *Fantastic Stories*, October

"Shambolain," *Worlds of If*, November-December

"Unseen Warriors," *Worlds of Tomorrow*, Winter

"Nightmare Gang," *Infinity One*, edited by Robert Hoskins, Lancer

1971

Published that year:

The Crimson Witch, Curtis

Demon Child, "Deanna Dwyer," Lancer

Legacy of Terror, "Deanna Dwyer," Lancer

"Bruno," *The Magazine of Fantasy and Science Fiction*, April

"A Veritable Cornucopia," *Tomorrow and . . . Seven*

1972

Dean started to read John D. MacDonald.
Henry Morrison became Dean's agent.
Published that year:
Chase, "K. R. Dwyer," Random House (This was Dean's first hardcover.)
Children of the Storm, "Deanna Dwyer," Lancer
The Dark of Summer, "Deanna Dwyer," Lancer
Dance with the Devil, "Deanna Dwyer," Lancer
A Darkness in My Soul, Daw
The Flesh in the Furnace, Bantam
Starblood, Lancer
Time Thieves, "Leigh Nichols," Ace
Warlock, Lancer
Writing Popular Fiction, Writer's Digest Books
"The Terrible Weapon," *Trend*, January/February
"Cosmic Sin," *The Magazine of Fantasy and Science Fiction*, February
"Altarboy," Infinity Three, edited by Robert Hoskins, Lancer
"Ollie's Hands," *Infinity Four*, edited by Robert Hoskins, Lancer
"A Mouse in the Walls of the Global Village," *Again, Dangerous Visions*, edited by Harlan Ellison, Doubleday
"Always an Open Door for the Paperback 'Category' Novel," *Writer's Digest*, January

1973

Published that year:
Aphrodisiac Girl, reprint of *Bounce Girl* (Oval Press)
Blood Risk, Brian Coffey, Bobbs-Merrill
Demon Seed, Bantam
Hanging On, M. Evans and Company
The Haunted Earth, Lancer
Shattered, "K. R. Dwyer," Random House
A Werewolf Among Us, Ballantine
"Grayworld," *Infinity Five*, edited by Robert Hoskins, Lancer
"The Sinless Child," *Flame Tree Planet*, edited by Roger Elwood, Concordia

"Terra Phobia," *Androids, Time Machines and Blue Giraffes*, edited by Roger Elwood and Vic Ghidalia, Follett

"The Undercity," *Future City*, edited by Roger Elwood, Trident Press

"Wake Up to Thunder," *Children of Infinity*, edited by Roger Elwood, Franklin Watts

Gerda published that year:

A Darker Heritage, Lancer

1974

Gerda quit her job to work for Dean.

Published that year:

After the Last Race, Atheneum

Strike Deep, "Anthony North," Dial Press

Surrounded, "Brian Coffey," Bobbs-Merrill

"Night of the Storm," *Continuum I*, edited by Roger Elwood, Putnam

"We Three," *Final Stage*, edited by Roger Elwood and Barry Malzberg, Charterhouse

1975

Gerda and Dean moved to Las Vegas, Nevada.

Claire Smith became Dean's new agent.

Published that year:

Dragonfly, "K. R. Dwyer," Random House

Invasion, "Aaron Wolfe," Laser (Collectors thought this was written by Stephen King.)

The Long Sleep, "John Hill," Popular Library

Nightmare Journey, Berkley

The Wall of Masks, "Brian Coffey," Bobbs-Merrill

1976

Gerda and Dean moved to Orange, California.

Published that year:

Night Chills, Atheneum (This was Dean's first work emphasizing a cross-genre approach.)

Prison of Ice, "David Axton," Lippincott

1977

Ray Koontz, Dean's father, arrived in California with only a suitcase.

The first film based on one of Dean's works, *Demon Seed*, opened April 1.

Published that year:

The Face of Fear, "Brian Coffey," Bobbs-Merrill

The Vision, Putnam

1979

Published that year:

The Key to Midnight, "Leigh Nichols," Pocket Books (This was Dean's first paperback bestseller.)

1980

Published that year:

The Funhouse, "Owen West," Jove (This was Dean's second paperback bestseller.)

The Voice of the Night, "Brian Coffey," Doubleday

Whispers, G.P. Putnam's Sons (This was a key novel—one of Dean's first attempts at a story with a large canvas and a complex psychology; it was his first paperback bestseller under his own name.)

1981

Published that year:

The Eyes of Darkness, "Leigh Nichols," Pocket Books

The Mask, "Owen West," Jove

How to Write Best-selling Fiction, Writer's Digest Books

1982

Published that year:

The House of Thunder, "Leigh Nichols," Pocket Books

1983

Published that year:
Phantoms, G.P. Putnam's Sons

1984

Published that year:
Darkfall, Berkley (Originally meant as a third Owen West novel, it was put under the Berkley imprint.)
Twilight, "Leigh Nichols," Pocket Books
"When Should You Put Yourself in an Agent's Hands?" *The Basics of Writing and Selling Fiction*, Writer's Digest Press.

1985

Published that year:
The Door to December, "Richard Paige," New American Library
Twilight Eyes, The Land of Enchantment
Shattered, "K. R. Dwyer," Berkley (reissue of Random House 1973 edition)
"Situation Critical," *Writer's Yearbook '85*, Writer's Digest Press

1986

Published that year:
Strangers, G.P. Putnam's Sons (This finalist for the World Fantasy Award was also Dean's first hardcover bestseller.)
"Down in the Darkness," *The Horror Show*, Summer
"Weird World," *The Horror Show*, Summer
"Snatcher," *Night Cry*, Fall
"The Black Pumpkin," *Twilight Zone*, December

1987

Ray tried to kill Dean with a knife; he was evaluated at a hospital and placed in a retirement home.
Dean became first president of Horror Writers of America.

Published that year:
Shadowfires, "Leigh Nichols," Avon
Watchers, G.P. Putnam's Sons
Twilight Eyes, Berkley (revision of Land of Enchantment 1985 edition)
"The Interrogation," *The Horror Show*, Summer
"Hardshell," *Night Visions 4*, Dark Harvest
"Miss Attila the Hun," *Night Visions 4*, Dark Harvest
"Twilight of the Dawn," *Night Visions 4*, Dark Harvest
"Keeping the Reader on the Edge of His Seat," *How to Write Tales of Horror, Fantasy, and Science Fiction*
"Why Novels of Fear Must Do More than Frighten," *How to Write Tales of Horror, Fantasy, and Science Fiction*

1988

Ray got another knife and tried to kill Dean, who took it from him and nearly was shot by police. He had to go to court to keep his father in psychiatric care until he could find a place for him.

Roger Corman's film version of *Watchers* was released.

A contract for five backlist books to Berkley fell through.

The first book about Dean, *Sudden Fear*, edited by Bill Munster, was published.

Published that year:
Lightning, G.P. Putnam's Sons
Oddkins, A Fable for All Ages, Warner
The Mask, Berkley (reissue of Jove 1981 edition)
"Graveyard Highway," *Tropical Chills*, edited by Tim Sullivan, Avon
"A Genre in Crisis," *Night Visions 4*, Dark Harvest

1989

A scheduled trip to England fell through; Dean was too ill from stress to go.

Dean was given an honorary doctorate degree from Shippensburg University. On that trip, he went to see his former home, but couldn't get out of the car.

A new deal was made with Berkley for a six-book package.

Published that year:

Midnight, G.P. Putnam's Sons (This was Dean's first number one *New York Times* bestseller.)

"Trapped," *Stalkers*, edited by Ed Gorman and Martin H. Greenberg, Dark Harvest

"Ghost Stories," *Post Mortem*, St. Martin's

1990

A television movie of *Face of Fear* was made by Warner Brothers to be aired on CBS, with Dean as co-executive producer, and using his teleplay.

Watchers II by was produced by Roger Corman.

Cinepix produced a direct-to-video film version of *Whispers*.

Published that year:

The Bad Place, G.P. Putnam's Sons (This book became a number one bestseller.)

The Servants of Twilight, Berkley (reissue of *Twilight*, Pocket Books 1984 edition)

1991

Ray Koontz died from degenerative alcoholic syndrome.

Gerda and Dean moved to Newport Beach, California.

Published that year:

Cold Fire, G.P. Putnam's Sons (This book became a number one bestseller.)

The Voice of the Night, Berkley (reissue of Doubleday 1980 edition)

1992

Dawn Dunn and Susan Hartzell were caught plagiarizing *Phantoms* in a 1991 book, *The Crawling Dark*, and the 1990 *Demonic Color* (Zebra); they were forced to put a half-page ad in *Publishers Weekly* and give their advance to Dean.

Robert Gottlieb of the William Morris Agency became Dean's new agent.

Knopf offered $18.9 million for three books and Dean switched to Knopf; Ballantine bought seven backlist titles for reissue.

Trimark Pictures released a film version of *The Servants of Twilight*.

Published that year:
Hideaway, G.P. Putnam's Sons (This book became a number one bestseller.)
Beastchild, Charnel House (hardcover revision of Lancer 1970 edition)
The House of Thunder, Berkley (reissue of Pocket Books 1982 edition)
"Trapped," graphic novella adapted by Ed Gorman, Eclipse

1993

Published that year:
Dragon Tears, G.P. Putnam's Sons (This book became a number one bestseller.)
Mr. Murder, G.P. Putnam's Sons
Shadowfires, Berkley (reissue of Avon 1987 edition)
"Why We Love Horror," *TV Guide*, October

1994

Gerda and Dean purchased two and a half acres at Pelican Hill to build a dream house.
Dean reached a settlement with Mark Masztal and H&M Publishing for issuing *The Book of Counted Sorrows*.
A legal battle ensued with Roger Corman over the film *Watchers III*.
Martin Greenberg, Ed Gorman, and Bill Munster published *The Dean Koontz Companion*.
Published that year:
Dark Rivers of the Heart, Alfred A. Knopf
Winter Moon, Ballantine (revision of *Invasion*, Laser 1975 edition)
The Funhouse, Berkley (reissue of Jove 1980 edition)
The Door to December, "Richard Paige," New American Library/Signet (revision of 1985 edition)
"Godzilla vs. Megadeth" for the "Youthanasia" CD
"My First Short Story," *The Dean Koontz Companion*, Berkley
"Koontz, Would You Just Shut Up Already?" *The Dean Koontz Companion*, Berkley
"You'll Either Love It or Hate It—Or Just be Indifferent to It," *The Dean Koontz Companion*, Berkley

"How To," *The Dean Koontz Companion*, Berkley

1995

Tri-Star released a film version of *Hideaway*; Dean fought to get his name taken off the ads.
Published that year:
Strange Highways, Warner
Icebound, Ballantine (revision of *Prison of Ice*, Lippincott, 1976)
The Key to Midnight, Berkley (revision of Pocket Books 1979 edition)
"Illusion, Truth and the Whole Damn Thing," *David Copperfield's Tales of the Impossible*, HarperCollins

1996

Published that year:
Intensity, Alfred A. Knopf. (This book spent three weeks as the number one bestseller.)
Santa's Twin (illustrated by Phil Parks), HarperCollins
The Eyes of Darkness, Berkley (revision of Pocket Books 1981 edition)
"Beautiful Death," *Beautiful Death: Art of the Cemetery*, by David Robinson, Penguin Studio

1997

Miramax released its film version of *Phantoms*.
Intensity was adapted for a miniseries on Fox network.
Published that year:
Sole Survivor, Alfred A. Knopf
Ticktock, Ballantine
Demon Seed, Berkley (revision of Bantam 1973 edition)
"Great Art and Muppet Hatred," *Screamplays*, Ballantine

1998

Published that year:
Fear Nothing, Bantam (hardcover)

INDEX